Fabricating Authenticity in Soviet Hungary

The Afterlife of the First Hungarian Soviet Republic in the Age of State Socialism

Péter Apor

ANTHEM PRESS
LONDON · NEW YORK · DELHI

Anthem Press
An imprint of Wimbledon Publishing Company
www.anthempress.com

This edition first published in UK and USA 2015
by ANTHEM PRESS
75–76 Blackfriars Road, London SE1 8HA, UK
or PO Box 9779, London SW19 7ZG, UK
and
244 Madison Ave #116, New York, NY 10016, USA

First published in hardback by Anthem Press in 2014

Copyright © Péter Apor 2015

The author asserts the moral right to be identified as the author of this work.

All rights reserved. Without limiting the rights under copyright reserved above,
no part of this publication may be reproduced, stored or introduced into
a retrieval system, or transmitted, in any form or by any means
(electronic, mechanical, photocopying, recording or otherwise),
without the prior written permission of both the copyright
owner and the above publisher of this book.

British Library Cataloguing-in-Publication Data
A catalogue record for this book is available from the British Library.

Library of Congress Cataloging-in-Publication Data
The Library of Congress has cataloged the hardcover edition as follows:
Apor, Péter.
Fabricating authenticity in Soviet Hungary : the afterlife of the First Hungarian Soviet Republic
in the age of state socialism / Péter Apor.
pages cm
"Also available as an ebook"–Title page verso. Includes bibliographical references and index.
ISBN 978-0-85728-110-4 (hardback : alkaline paper) –
ISBN 0-85728-110-0 (hardback : alkaline paper)
1. Hungary–History–Revolution, 1918–1919–Influence. 2. Hungary–Politics and government–1918–1945. 3. Hungary–Politics and government–1945–1989. 4. Memory–Political aspects–Hungary–History–20th century. 5. Collective memory–Hungary–History–20th century. 6. Political culture–Hungary–History–20th century. 7. Authenticity (Philosophy)–Political aspects–Hungary–History–20th century. 8. Communism–Hungary–History–20th century. 9. Dictatorship–Social aspects–Hungary–History–20th century. 10. Hungary– Social conditions–20th century. I. Title.
DB955.A68 2013
943.905–dc23
2013043360

ISBN-13: 978 1 78308 419 7 (Pbk)
ISBN-10: 1 78308 419 7 (Pbk)

Cover image by Béla Uitz: *Vörös katonák, előre!* (Red soldiers, forward!) 1919.

This title is also available as an ebook.

Fabricating Authenticity in Soviet Hungary

CONTENTS

Acknowledgements		vii
List of Illustrations		ix
List of Abbreviations		xi
Introduction		1
Chapter 1	Prefiguration: The First Hungarian Soviet Republic and the Rákosi Dictatorship before 1956	27
Chapter 2	Resurrection: The Emergence of 1919 and the Counterrevolution after 1956	61
Chapter 3	Lives: 1919 in the Postwar Trials of War Criminals	101
Chapter 4	Funeral: The Birth of the Pantheon of the Labour Movement in Budapest	125
Chapter 5	Narration: History, Fiction and Proof in the Representation of the First Hungarian Soviet Republic, 1959–65	165
Epilogue	The Agitators and the Armoured Train	199
Index		209

ACKNOWLEDGEMENTS

Writing history is an essentially collaborative activity shaped by intellectual interaction and community, even though individual works are usually attached to individual authors. As such, this book is the outcome of much proliferating discussion, criticism and debate. I would like to name a few of my partners in these conversations, to whom I owe much gratitude. István Rév, Bo Stråth and Gábor Gyáni read more than one version of the entire manuscript and never refused to help, improving the text with their suggestions and criticism. I am particularly grateful to Lusia Passerini, Andrea Pető and István Papp for their forthright and useful comments concerning the entire text. The help of Claudio Fogu and James Mark were indispensible in finalizing Chapters 2 and 4.

The work of the historian is rarely successful without the contributions of archives and archivists. Hereby, I would like to thank for their selfless help the staff in the Borsod-Abaúj-Zemplén County Archives, the Budapest City Archives, the Hungarian National Archives, the Hungarian Radio Archives, the Open Society Archives and the Archives of Political History and Trade Unions. I would like to thank especially archivist István Simon and director Katalin Zalai. I would also like to thank Pasts, Inc., Center for Historical Studies, Central European University and the Institute of History, Humanities Research Center, Hungarian Academy of Sciences for their support in the production of this book.

And finally, special gratitude goes to my most persistent reader and honest critic, my wife: this book is shared, as with many other things, in life.

I would like to dedicate this book to the memory of Reinhart Koselleck, for the gift of fatigueless curiosity and appreciative wisdom, which he was never reluctant to share with a then young researcher.

LIST OF ILLUSTRATIONS

Figure 1	'Előre munkások!' (Forward workers!), *Pártmunkás*, 30 March 1949, cover page.	47
Figure 2	'Rákosi Mátyás a Vörös Hadsereg élén' (Mátyás Rákosi heading the Red Army). Endre Kovács, Gyula Simon, Béla Bellér, *Történelem* IV (Budapest, Tankönyvkiadó, 1950), 27.	48
Figure 3	The 30th anniversary of the First Hungarian Soviet Republic. Historical Photographic Records of the Hungarian National Museum 477. ME/II/A, Box: Political Life: Anniversaries 1949–56. Registry no.: Hungarian Labour History Museum 78.854.	51
Figure 4	'Six members of the guard were hanged by their feet and beaten half to death following a firefight in Republic Square'. White Books, vol. 1, 14.	68
Figure 5	'Corpses of the murdered in front of the party headquarters'. White Books, vol. 1, 21.	68
Figure 6	'A female staff member of the party committee is kicked, beaten with a rifle butt and has her hands twisted'. White Books, vol. 1, 13.	69
Figure 7	'A victim whose corpse was "bestially" dismembered'. White Books, vol. 1, 17.	70
Figure 8	'In 1919… and in 1956'. White Books, vol. 5, 170–71.	98
Figure 9	'1919 and 1956'. White Books, vol. 5, 172.	99
Figure 10	The road leading to the mausoleum. Author's drawing based on the map in the *Guidebook to Fiumei úti sírkert (Kerepesi temető)* (Budapest: Budapesti Temetkezési Vállalat, 2007), 12.	144
Figure 11	The heroes' plot. Courtesy of the author.	144
Figure 12	The sepulchre of the Jacobins. Courtesy of the author.	145
Figure 13	The sepulchre of the martyrs of the Hungarian Soviet Republic. Courtesy of the author.	146
Figure 14	The walkway to the mausoleum. Courtesy of the author.	148

Figure 15	'More than 2 billion forints have been accumulated for the memorial of the great dead of the labour movement'. *Népszava*, 20 March 1958, 3.	149
Figure 16	'To Arms! To Arms!' OKISZ Commemorative Exhibition for the Soviet Republic. Historical Photographic Records of the Hungarian National Museum 48. ME/II/B, Culture: Exhibitions 1957–62. Registry no. 59.233.	151
Figure 17	OKISZ Commemorative Exhibition for the Soviet Republic. Historical Photographic Records of the Hungarian National Museum 48. ME/II/B, Culture: Exhibitions 1957–62. Registry no. 59.235.	152
Figure 18	'1919–1959'. *Népszabadság*, 21 March 1959, cover page.	153
Figure 19	'A néphatalom hű őrzője' (The true guardian of people's power). *Szabad Föld*, 22 March 1959, cover page.	154
Figure 20	Colonel László Lukács's tomb. Courtesy of the author.	163
Figure 21	'The Establishment of Organizations'. Historical Photographic Records of the Hungarian National Museum 48. ME/II/B, Culture: Exhibitions 1957–62. Registry no. 59.525.	187
Figure 22	The exhibition of the railworkers' union for the 40th anniversary of the First Hungarian Soviet Republic. Historical Photographic Records of the Hungarian National Museum 48. ME/II/B, Culture: Exhibitions 1957–62. Registry no. 59.524.	187

LIST OF ABBREVIATIONS

BAZ ML	Borsod-Abaúj-Zemplén Megyei Levéltár Mezőcsáti Fióklevéltára (Archives of Borsod-Abaúj-Zemplén County, Mezőcsát Branch)
BFL	Budapest Főváros Levéltára (Archives of the Capital Budapest)
FN	*Felvidéki Népszava* (People's voice in Northern Hungary)
MOL M-BB	Magyar Országos Levéltár Budapesti Pártbizottság iratai (BFL XXXV.1.a.3.) (Hungarian National Archives, Records of the Budapest Party Committee)
MOL M-BP	Magyar Országos Levéltár Budapesti Ideiglenes Intéző Bizottság iratai (BFL XXXV.1.a.1.) (Hungarian National Archives, Records of the Budapest Temporary Executive Committee)
MOL M-KS	Magyar Dolgozók Pártja és Magyar Szocialista Munkáspárt iratai, Központi szervek (Hungarian National Archives, Records of the Hungarian Workers' Party and the Hungarian Socialist Workers' Party, Central Organs)
MSZMP	A Magyar Szocialista Munkáspárt ideiglenes vezető testületeinek jegyzőkönyvei (Minutes of the Temporary Central Organs of the HSWP). 11 November 1956 – 26 June 1957. Series editor Sándor Balogh. Vols 1–5 (Budapest: Intera Rt, 1993–98).
NSZ	*Népszabadság* (People's freedom)
OSA	Nyílt Társadalom Archívum (Open Society Archives)
PIL	Politikatörténeti és Szakszervezeti Levéltár (Archives of Political History and Trade Unions)
SZM	*Szabad Magyarország* (Free Hungary)
SZN	*Szabad Nép* (Free people)
WB	*Ellenforradalmi erők a magyar októberi eseményekben* (Counterrevolutionary forces in the October events in Hungary), aka 'Fehér Könyvek' (White Books), vols 1–5. (Budapest: Kiadja a Magyar Népköztársaság Minisztertanácsa Tájékoztatási Hivatala, 1956–58).

INTRODUCTION

1

What makes abstract historical interpretations authentic? This theoretical question troubled Communist Party leaders and propaganda historians in Hungary during the years that followed the restoration of dictatorship after the suppression of the anti-Stalinist uprising in October–November 1956. János Kádár's government, which had been established only by the military might of the Soviet Union, attempted to obtain legitimacy on the basis of a curious historical argument. Meanwhile, the new Communist leadership justified the suppression of democratic and independent aspirations by claiming to protect Hungarians against the peril of counterrevolution. It built the image of October 1956 on its alleged historical connection with 1919 and the White Terror that followed the fall of Béla Kun's short-lived Soviet Republic. Since it was vital for Kádár and his fellow party leaders to reify the imaginary historical continuity between the 'first' and 'second' editions of the White Terror, it became crucial to construct a credible representation of the First Hungarian Soviet Republic that suited the comprehensive revision of modern Hungarian history.

The subject of this work, therefore, is the crooked history of the revisions of the First Hungarian Soviet Republic between the years of its 30th and 40th anniversaries, 1949 and 1959. This particular historical event grew from a relatively isolated detail of the self-history of the Hungarian Communist movement into the most highly praised national celebration. These ten years, however, did not mark only the rapid accumulation of historical knowledge, but rather the radical break and reformation of Communist power in Hungary that was demanded by the challenges of the Hungarian Revolution in October 1956. The transformation of the historical appraisal of the first Hungarian commune was inseparable from the role 1919 played in the Communist revision of 1956.[1]

The First Hungarian Soviet Republic is barely present in contemporary historical thinking.[2] Except for a few obscure groups within the radical leftist subculture, the

---

1 On the afterlife of 1956 in Hungarian society and politics, see István Rév, *Retroactive Justice: Prehistory of Post-Communism* (Stanford: Stanford University Press, 2005); Heino Nyyssönen, *The Presence of the Past in Politics: '1956' after 1956 in Hungary* (Jyväskylä: SoPhi Academic Press, 1999); Beverly James, *Imagining Post-Communism: Visual Narratives of Hungary's 1956 Revolution* (College Station: Texas A&M University Press, 2005); András Mink, 'The Revisions of the 1956 Hungarian Revolution', in *Past in the Making: Historical Revisionism in Central Europe after 1989*, ed. Michal Kopeček (Budapest/New York: CEU Press, 2008), 169–78; Zoltán Ripp, '1956 emlékezete és az MSZMP', in *Évköny X. Magyarország a jelenkorban*, ed. János M. Rainer and Éva Standeisky (Budapest: 1956-os Intézet, 2002), 233–50.
2 The history of the First Hungarian Soviet Republic appears an ephemeral episode; a futile but bloody dictatorship that was supported incomprehensibly by leftist groups, but not the peasantry

historical legacy of 1919 is left largely unexamined. While there is lively interest in the history of postwar Sovietization and in the subsequent Hungarian Stalinism, as well as in the anti-Stalinist 1956 revolution, from the perspective of today, the history of the First Hungarian Soviet Republic seems to end rather abruptly, making no intelligible impact on either the socialist dictatorship of the second half of the twentieth century or on contemporary Hungarian society and politics. It is rather apt that the only post-Communist monograph devoted specifically to Béla Kun's regime in Hungarian is written by an outsider: high-ranking Israeli diplomat Eytan Bentsur, who spent two years in Budapest as the undersecretary of the Embassy of Israel in 1966–67. Bentsur's father himself was born to a Hungarian-speaking Jewish family in Transylvania, Romania and emigrated to Palestine during the 1930s. For Bentsur the history of the Hungarian commune was linked directly to Béla Kun as a person. He was interested in how a Magyarized Transylvanian petit bourgeois Jewish intellectual like Kun had become a radical leftist activist and then a Bolshevik dictator.[3] For most Hungarians, however, since the disintegration after 1989–90 of the Communist framing of history, these short and unsuccessful revolutionary experiments seem largely incomprehensible. It is true that there have been some attempts to rethink the history of 1919 from the perspective of the new, nation-centred historical narrative that was thought to appropriately replace the former Communist one.[4] It is also true that there have been some recent attempts to interpret the post-WWI Communist rule as part of the pan-European wave of paramilitary violence. Although the fresh transnational framing may provide some interesting new insights into the history of those turbulent years, it has no stake in reinterpreting the complexities of the Soviet Republic. In fact, it focuses rather on the roots and sociopolitical context of the White Terror, making the Hungarian commune into a kind of prehistory, which seems necessary for the proper understanding of the right-wing ideological violence.[5]

---

and the working class. Tibor Hajdú, 'A Tanácsköztársaság helye a magyar történelemben', *Múltunk* 39 (1–2) (1994): 3–16. Currently, there is hardly any serious research concerning the Soviet Republic or the history of 1918–19. A few studies and comprehensive books on the history of the twentieth century attempt to provide new meaning to 1919 by recontextualizing the event: Lajos Varga, 'A forradalom konszolidációjának esélyei 1918–1919-ben', *Múltunk* 55 (3) (2010): 4–24; Pál Pritz, 'Kun Béla után – Horthy Miklós előtt. Magyarország és az antant 1919 nyarán', *Múltunk* 55 (3) (2010): 25–45; Mária Ormos, 'Agyműtét, 1919. Magyar kérdőjelek a 20. század elején', *Múltunk* 55 (3) (2010): 46–71; Tamás Krausz and Judit Vértes, eds, *1919: A Magyarországi Tanácsköztársaság és a kelet-európai forradalmak* (Budapest: l'Harmattan, 2010). Boldizsár Vörös examines the politics of history of the Soviet Republic: *'A múltat végképp eltörölni'?* (Budapest: MTA TTI, 2004).

3 Eytan Bentsur, *Láng Európa szívében: Kun Béla hatalmának 133 napja* (Budapest: KuKK, 2010). The Hungarian edition is based on the 2004 Hebrew edition.

4 This is what the only recent volume by a Hungarian historian on the events of 1918–19 tries to do: Konrád Salamon, *Nemzeti önpusztítás 1918–1920* (Budapest: Korona, 2001).

5 Remarkably, extensive research in this field has been done by a Hungarian-born historian based in the United States: Béla Bodó, 'Paramilitary Violence in Hungary after the First World War', *East European Quarterly* 38 (Summer 2004): 129–72; 'Militia Violence and State Power in Hungary, 1919–1922', *Hungarian Studies Review* 33 (1–2) (2006): 121–56. Péter Konok offers exciting new perspectives: 'Az erőszak kérdései 1919–1920-ban. Vörösterror–fehérterror', *Múltunk* 55 (3) (2010): 72–91.

Such approaches, as a rule, have not succeeded in changing the marginal position of the events of 1919 in broader historical thinking. At best, or rather worst, the Soviet Republic made sense for a militant nationalist reading of history, which 'rediscovered' Communist terror and hoped to establish evidence of a concerted assault on allegedly authentic Hungarian national culture. For such ideological statements, the predominantly Jewish background of most of the leaders of the Hungarian commune has become the most important fact of the events.

The striking presence of persons with Jewish ancestry among revolutionary elites was an important fact, indeed, although for different reasons than those presumed in right-wing mythology. Such persons were influential (although not exclusively) in leftist, progressive and radical movements in pre- and post-1914 Europe. For many of the rapidly assimilating members of Jewish families in Central and East-Central Europe, particularly in Germany, Austria, Hungary and Poland, revolutionary commitments meant an opportunity to transcend national and religious identities in exchange for transnational ones. For the German revolutionary Rosa Luxemburg, who came from a Jewish family in Poland, it was a promise to integrate and reconcile the double commitment to Polish national freedom and universal emancipation, including, of course, Jewish groups. It is also true, however, that many who were retrospectively considered Jewish in radical right-wing thinking came from already assimilated families, like Kun himself or the world-famous philosopher György Lukács, for whom revolutionary radicalism was rather a revolt against his wealthy capitalist family background than against any particular Jewish cultural legacies. The First Hungarian Soviet Republic, which was proclaimed on 21 March 1919, was hence part of a pan-European wave of post-WWI revolutions. Leftist radicalism grew stronger in several Central and Eastern European countries, particularly Russia, Germany, Austria and Hungary, where social tensions and the disastrous outcome of the war were correspondent to the growing disappointment with respective governments and monarchies. Communist parties were formed in the course of 1917–18, some of whom managed to establish their own governments, such as in Russia (November 1917), Berlin (January 1919), Munich (April 1919) and Hungary (March 1919).[6]

The impact of Lenin and the Russian Bolshevik Revolution was crucial. On the one hand, for many Communists and radical leftists the revolution proved that it was possible to overthrow capitalism by political will. On the other, Lenin established himself for many years as an important figure of the international labour movement and had a particularly good relationship with radicals in Germany. Lenin and Soviet Russia also directly impacted the Hungarian radicals. Several former social-democrat activists from Hungary, who were captured by the Russians in the eastern front during WWI, were introduced to Bolshevik ideas in POW camps, became radicalized and fought as internationalists for the Red Army. Béla Kun, the commissar of foreign affairs in the Hungarian Soviet government, and Tibor Szamuely, the leader of the Hungarian Red Terror troops, were founding members of the Hungarian branch of the Communist (Bolshevik) Party of

---

6 A good account: Iván T. Berend, *Decades of Crisis: Central and Eastern Europe before World War II* (Berkeley: University of California Press, 1998).

Russia and boasted of being members of Lenin's personal bodyguard. They returned to Hungary in the autumn of 1918 to establish the Communist Party of Hungary in November. The Bolshevik-educated former prisoners of war were joined by a domestic group of young radicals who called themselves revolutionary socialists, which commonly referred to the radical social democrats in Central and Eastern Europe who were deeply disappointed with their parties' policies of negotiation. The most emblematic person of this group was Ottó Korvin, former bank clerk, who became chief of the Communist police during the Soviet Republic.

When the Communist Party of Hungary was formed, the revolution had already taken place in the country. Since 1867, after the appeasement of the Viennese emperor and Hungarian elites, the Austrian Empire had consisted of two parts, Austria and the Kingdom of Hungary, and the state had accordingly been called the Austro-Hungarian Monarchy. By the early twentieth century, the autonomous Hungarian government had to face several serious problems: the growing social radicalism reflecting the huge inequalities between the elites and, mostly, provincial poor; growing political discontent because of the exclusion of the industrial working classes from political participation; and national conflicts as Slovak, Romanian, Croatian and Serbian ethnic minorities demanded more collective political rights. Following the assassination of Crown Prince Franz Ferdinand in Sarajevo, the event that escalated WWI, the Hungarian government was very reluctant to launch military action. The matter, however, was decided by the Viennese central imperial government, which convinced Hungarian politicians of the need to go to war, and the country entered the battle against the Entente, fighting on the Italian, Serbian and Russian fronts alongside Imperial Germany.

As defeat loomed for Austria–Hungary, troops began to dissolve, domestic discontent grew and separatist tendencies became dominant. Pacifist political opposition in Hungary was led by Count Mihály Károlyi, who pursued a republican and pro-Western politics. He was supported both by the influential social democrats and the smaller group of liberals. When the king refused to appoint him as prime minister, in October protesting crowds of workers and soldiers demonstrated in Budapest, and by the end of the month the protests had expanded to major urban centres throughout the country. The protesters occupied important public buildings and centres of communication in the capital, and soon forced the king to accept Károlyi as the head of the government. The new government proclaimed the independent republic on 16 November 1918. The republican government, however, had to tackle enormous difficulties: the supply of food and public services declined, social discontent and political radicalism grew, while the new regime was unable to counterbalance the troops of neighbouring states rapidly occupying territories of prewar Hungary. The Entente itself was not very supportive of Károlyi: for them a quick and sustainable postwar ordering of the region was more of a priority, and they saw their regional allies – Romania, Czechoslovakia and Yugoslavia – as the potential guarantee for such plans. The republican government decided to face the challenge: radical rightists and Communists were arrested and Károlyi began to reorganize the army. His idea was to reshape the government exclusively from social democrats, whom he considered as more capable of securing the international support of Austria and Soviet Russia, which he saw as potential allies for a renitent (opposing territorial claims supported by the Entente) but still republican Hungary. The social democrats, however, were afraid of governing without the Communists, probably fearing their subversive potential, and agreed to form a common government. The principles of the new regime, however, were defined by the Communists, who insisted on a Soviet republic form of government, and proclaimed the new regime on 21 March 1919.

The government of the Soviet Republic thus consisted of the Hungarian Communists and a group of social democrats. The left-wing social democrats (such as Jenő Landler and Vilmos Bőhm, commanders of the Hungarian Red Army), supported the idea of the dictatorship, whereas the right-wing socialists (such as trade union leaders Zsigmond Kunfi, Gyula Peidl and Károly Peyer), did so only half-heartedly. In spite of this the two workers' parties were formally unified on 21 March. The commune soon followed the Russian example: it nationalized industries and housing, began to form state farms and took hostages from the alleged 'class enemies'. At the beginning, the Communist regime was supported by the urban industrial working classes and many of the progressive intellectuals. However, propertied peasants – the majority population of the provincial territories, now at the disposal of the Soviet Republic – were hostile from the very beginning, as were the urban middle-classes and members of the traditional gentry. The Communist experiment also frightened the Western powers as well as Hungary's neighbours. The Hungarian Red Army was at war from April until its last days in July 1919. Aurél Stromfeld, a former officer of the General Staff of the Austro-Hungarian Army during WWI, who became the chief of the General Staff of the Red Army, was able to launch a successful campaign against enemy troops (the so-called 'northern campaign'), after Communist leaders had succeeded in mobilizing the Budapest workers to join the army in May. Nonetheless, the Communist leadership could not secure sufficient social support and failed in its diplomacy to obtain recognition from the great powers. Following the withdrawal of troops from the north, it rapidly lost the support of those who fought for the Soviet Republic hoping it could defend national interests and territories. In June and July, desperate peasants rebelled in the provinces and likewise disappointed nationalists in the capital. The Communist terror troops reacted with harsh brutality, executing hundreds in revenge. Lacking a social base and professional military expertise, the Red Army lost all of its battles and began to dissolve.[7] As a consequence, the Soviet Republic resigned on 31 July and after a short transitional period a counterrevolutionary regime came into existence led by Admiral Miklós Horthy.

Horthy was supported by radical right wingers, the gentry and the traditional middle classes, and the peasantry believed he would restore their property rights. The West also

---

[7] Literature that refers to the basic framing of modern Hungarian history in notes 6–11 and 13 has been selected to suggest English language works, which may orientate the reader best concerning these periods: Rudolf L. Tőkés, *Béla Kun and The Hungarian Soviet Republic* (New York/Washington/London: Praeger, 1967); György Borsányi, *The Life of A Communist Revolutionary: Béla Kun* (Boulder, NJ: Social Science Monographs, 1993); György Péteri, *The Effects of World War I: War Communism in Hungary* (New York: Social Science Monographs, 1984); Iván Völgyes, *The Hungarian Soviet Republic, 1919: An Evaluation and a Bibliography* (Stanford: Hoover Institution Press, 1970); Ivan Völgyes, ed., *Hungary in Revolution, 1918–19: Nine Essays* (Lincoln: University of Nebraska Press, 1971).

considered him to have the potential to restore order in spite of his endorsement of the brutal atrocities that White Terror troops inflicted on Jews, Communists and leftists in 1919–20.[8] Although Horthy and his followers considered the Versailles peace treaty, which detached two thirds of the prewar territories from Hungary, only as a temporary measure that might give the country the necessary time to prepare for revision, the new elite decided to ratify it. With these diplomatic solutions having pacified society, Horthy became regent of the country for the next twenty-five years.[9] The radical right wing and Christian conservative middle classes, which had feared that the prewar leftist progressive programs would lead to catastrophe and the collapse of national values, considered the Soviet Republic only as an event that evidenced their former anxieties. They saw it as a Jewish Communist conspiracy against Hungarian national integrity and blamed the Jews and Károlyi for the debasing of the old kingdom. In spite of the consolidation and moderate modernization in the 1920s, an antiliberal, antidemocratic, anti-Semitic, revisionist, nationalist, conservative culture dominated Hungarian politics throughout the entire interwar period.[10] As a consequence, Hungary gradually joined the German–Italian alliance during the 1930s. In this process, Prime Minister Gyula Gömbös (1932–36), an advocate of Mussolini's ideas on the organization of society, played a crucial role. Although other prime ministers, namely István Bethlen (1921–31), Pál Teleki (1920–21, 1939–41) and Miklós Kállay (1942–44), tried to preserve diplomatic connections to non-Axis powers, the country went into war against the USSR on the side of Germany, motivated mostly by the hopes of the leadership to secure more territories back from a grateful German government. Hungary also sent her Jews, mostly from the countryside, to concentration camps. However, as defeat in the war became evident, Horthy and his government tried to cut its ties with the Third Reich, resulting in the occupation of the country by the Wehrmacht on 19 March 1944. In October of the same year the regent and his close followers attempted to sign an armistice, however the German army prevented the coup. Hitler appointed Ferenc Szálasi, leader of the Hungarian fascist Arrow Cross Party, to be prime minister, leading to the brutal persecution and killing of Jews and antifascists in Budapest. However, he did not rule the country for long, since the Red Army had expelled the Germans by mid-April 1945. Stalin began to create a zone of Soviet-friendly, although not necessarily Communist, states in East-Central Europe immediately after the war, from Poland to Bulgaria. As tensions began to grow between the antifascist powers in 1947, the Soviet leadership, which grew concerned about the possible loss of its security zone, increasingly encouraged its regional Communist parties to consolidate their positions in government and to exert their dominance in politics.

---

8 Béla Bodó, 'Iván Héjjas: The Life of a Counterrevolutionary', *East Central Europe* 37 (2010): 247–79; 'Hungarian Aristocracy and the White Terror', *Journal of Contemporary History* 45 (Winter 2010): 703–24; *Pál Prónay: Paramilitary Violence and Anti-Semitism in Hungary, 1919–1921* (Pittsburgh: University of Pittsburgh Press, 2011); 'The White Terror in Hungary, 1919–1921: The Social Worlds of Paramilitary Groups', *Austrian History Yearbook* 42 (2011): 133–63.

9 Thomas Sakmyster, *Hungary's Admiral On Horseback: Miklós Horthy, 1918–1944* (Boulder: East European Monographs, 1994).

10 Ignác Romsics, *István Bethlen: A Great Conservative Statesman of Hungary, 1874–1946* (Boulder: Social Science Monographs, 1995).

The split between the antifascist powers ended up in the division of Europe by 1949. In Hungary, after a short democratic period, the Communist Party took over in 1948. Its first secretary was Mátyás Rákosi, a well-known figure of the international Communist movement who had been also a commissar in 1919. He returned from the Soviet Union together with other exiled Hungarian Communists, including Imre Nagy, later prime minister during the revolution in 1956. Other Communists remained in the country and organized the party illegally during the war. Their leading personalities were – among others – János Kádár, who became general secretary after 1956, and László Rajk, a well-known victim of the purges in 1949.[11]

2

Considering the general disinterest in the history of the First Hungarian Soviet Republic it is hardly believable today that 1919 – a date normally used as shorthand for the experience of the first Communist dictatorship – was a crucial historical experience that shaped Hungarian political culture throughout the twentieth century. The interwar political system which emerged out of the turmoil of 1919 claimed itself to be a 'counterrevolutionary' regime defending society from the alleged menace of a second Bolshevik revolution: its elites repeatedly instrumentalized the fears of a return to 1919 among the elite and middle classes. The memory of 1919 was also controversial for the political Left. Various groups within the émigrés and domestic Left regularly blamed each other for the failure of the revolution. Bitter fights over the appropriate interpretation of the failures of 1919 divided the illegal or exiled Hungarian Communists into various factions; for those residing in the USSR during the 1930s the correct interpretation of this failure often became a matter of life and death, as during the Stalinist purges Hungarian Communists sought to avoid persecution by accusing each other of having betrayed the cause of the revolution. Following 1945, the re-emerging Communist Party had to fight these negative associations of revolution tied to popular memories of 1919 when it tried to establish itself a national and democratic political force.[12]

The memory of 1919, however, became ubiquitous in the Hungarian society of the 1960s and 1970s. In 1969 a gigantic monument commemorating the first Communist state was erected in György Dózsa Boulevard in Budapest, where mass rallies of the regime would take place on 1 May and on other outstanding occasions. Margaret Island (Margitsziget), a favourite walking site of Budapest's inhabitants, was inseparable from the story of its opening for the proletarian children in 1919 – the island previously had been a private property of Archduke Joseph Habsburg (József főherceg). The children's pioneer camps around Lake Balaton and the summer holidays in the resort in general evoked the state-funded camps of proletarian children in 1919. Most Hungarians knew the story of the glorious battles of the Red Army around Miskolc and Kassa-Košice. Armoured trains, the glorified weapons of the army, stood at railway stations in various

---

11 Ignác Romsics, *Hungary in the 20th Century* (Budapest: Osiris, 1999).
12 Martin Mevius, *Agents of Moscow: The Hungarian Communist Party and the Origins of Socialist Patriotism 1941–1953* (Oxford: Oxford University Press, 2005), 69–86.

cities like Miskolc or Püspökladány. The author of this work himself was once a Red guard on 21 March in a school celebration. It is often presumed, based on memories like these, that the Soviet Republic was celebrated in the same manner during the whole period of Communist rule. 'An elevating, glorious one hundred and thirty-three days – we learnt this in school for forty years', as a journalist in one of Hungary's leading newspapers put it in 1990.[13] And as another claimed, popular memory was reluctant to preserve the Soviet Republic in spite of 'remembering the free entrance to Margaret Island, the proletarian children's summer holiday at Lake Balaton, or even "the patriotic battle of Kassa and Miskolc"'.[14]

During the first half of the 1960s, monuments dedicated to the Soviet Republic mushroomed in the country. On 29 April 1961, the Central Committee of the Hungarian Socialist Workers' Party approved the request of the village of Bélapátfalva to erect a monument to the fallen soldiers of the Hungarian Red Army. The local council wanted to commemorate one of the sites of the northern campaign and was committed to mobilizing voluntary work to prepare the foundations and stone works for the construction.[15] On 26 June 1962, the secretariat of the party accepted plans for the monument in the town of Nagykanizsa, to be co-financed by the ministry and the local authorities.[16] In June–July 1965, the Central Committee discussed the proposal for erecting a statue of Béla Kun's (a bust, to be placed in an suitable architectural environment in the capital).[17] The plans for the monument and the spatial reorganization were finished that year, though the party decided to postpone its unveiling until the 50th anniversary in 1969.[18]

The strategies of the Communist authorities to rewrite national history in light of their own political interests formed part of the age-old story of using and abusing representations of the past in order to claim legitimacy in the present. Although one can find many instances where rulers, lords or communities have based their claims for rights upon documents, evidence or interpretations of the past, the politics of history has become an integral part of exercising power for modern states. Modern political thought was inherently connected to a philosophy of history based on the secular teleology of straightforward progress and the general laws of human development. Modern states and political classes, therefore, incorporated their self-identities in a temporal logic as either outcomes or harbingers of universal history.[19] Nations, as forms of modern political consciousness, planted their identities in the unbroken continuity of past, present

---

13 György Pilhál, 'Ha' (If), *Magyar Hírlap*, 21 March 1990, 3.
14 László N. Sándor, 'Nincs ünnep Magyarországon' (There is no celebration in Hungary), *Magyar Hírlap*, 21 March 1991, 21.
15 MOL M-KS 288/7/106.
16 MOL M-KS 288/7/136.
17 MOL M-KS 288/41/42, 288/41/45.
18 MOL M-KS 288/41/47.
19 Reinhart Koselleck, 'Zeitschichten', in *Zeitschichten: Studien zur Historik* (Frankfurt: Suhrkamp, 2000), 1–20; Odo Marquard, 'Universalgeschichte und Multiversalgeschichte', in *Apologie des Zufälligen* (Stuttgart: Reclam, 1986), 56. A good comprehensive volume on Enlightenment historical writing is Olga Penke, *Filozofikus világtörténetek és történetfilozófiák* (Budapest: Balassi, 2000), 98–107.

and future.[20] The politics and rituals of history, consequently, became inevitable facets of modern civic activity. History and politics, or historians and politicians, in turn emerged as two closely interrelated fields during the nineteenth century. Scholarly and political elites frequently overlapped, and achievements in historical research and prose could be converted into political influence.[21] Representations of history produced political rights and vice versa.[22]

The politics of history became one of the most important components of modern symbolic politics. Although a politics of symbols was used in premodern societies to build authority, hierarchies and domination, after the French Revolution it transformed into a means of participation in politics. Revolutionaries, whose desire was to establish the ideal state of society and politics on the principles of the 'general will', sought for means to reveal it and make it manifest. Symbols and rituals were believed to be a means of making the people aware of their position and of expounding the voice of the nation. These practices, however, shaped a profoundly new political culture, which eventually generated new modes of exercising power.[23] Historical festivals that established the ideal state of time and space and rendered the transparent political body tangible were indispensable in this new type of symbolic politics.[24]

Public, collective and institutionalized forms of historical representation obtained particular importance in postwar Europe. Most of the European states instituted a series of legal processes against war criminals, local collaborators and Nazi perpetrators, including members of wartime governments, military units and municipal administrations. In addition to the intention to name perpetrators, these trials often looked for broader historical explanations for fascism, the war catastrophe and the successes of Nazism.[25] In the early postwar years various antifascist myths developed in Europe: the myths of resistance in Italy or France, the myths of neutrality in Sweden or Switzerland and the myth of Austria as Hitler's first victim.[26] Europeans wanted to forget the recent past; they

---

20 Benedict Anderson, *Imagined Communities: Reflections on the Origin and Spread of Nationalism* (London: Verso, 2006), 187–206.
21 Walter Laqueur and George L. Mosse, eds, *Historians in Politics* (London/Beverly Hills: Sage, 1974); Gérard Noiriel, *A történelem 'válságáról'* (Budapest: Napvilág, 2001), 241–6, 274–7; original French edition: *Sur la 'crise' de l'histoire* (Paris: Belin, 1996).
22 David I. Kertzer, *Ritual, Politics, and Power* (New Haven/London: Yale University Press, 1988), 13; Simonetta Falasca-Zamponi, *Fascist Spectacle: The Aesthetics of Power in Mussolini's Italy* (Berkeley/Los Angeles/London: University of California Press, 1997), 89–118; James von Geldern, *Bolshevik Festivals, 1917–1920* (Berkeley/Los Angeles: University of California Press, 1993); Orlando Figes and Boris Kolonitskii, *Interpreting the Russian Revolution: The Language and Symbols of 1917* (New Haven/London: Yale University Press, 1999).
23 Lynn Hunt, *Politics, Culture, and Class in the French Revolution* (Berkeley/Los Angeles: University of California Press, 1984).
24 Mona Ozouf, *Festivals and the French Revolution* (Cambridge, MA/London: Harvard University Press, 1988).
25 The catastrophe of the war can be understood here and elsewhere to encompass military defeat, Nazi occupation, the Hungarian Holocaust and the physical destruction of infrastructure.
26 Richard Ned Lebow, Wulf Kansteiner and Claudio Fogu, eds, *The Politics of Memory in Postwar Europe* (Durham, NC/London: Duke University Press, 2006); István Deák, Jan T. Gross and Tony Judt, eds, *The Politics of Retribution: World War II and Its Aftermath* (Princeton: Princeton

were longing for a new beginning and began to perceive the war as a radical break with the preceding period. Europeans began to see prewar societies and politics as something to be profoundly changed, as a past full of dead ends and wrong tracks.[27] Although the general framing of historical narratives blamed the Germans or the fascists, it also allowed the construction of a multiplicity of antifascist identities including leftist, liberal and Christian ones. The antifascist consensus became the solid foundation of rebuilding democracies in Western Europe. This consensus, in fact, was confirmed by all subsequent revisions of recent history. Interpretations of the recent past saturated the visions of the future of Europe in the forthcoming decades. These debates were firmly linked to the controversies generated by the colonial past, the emerging awareness of the Shoah as the major catastrophe of Western civilization, and the radical criticism of the 1968 generation of their parents' and grandparents' possible involvement in the sins of the past.[28]

The emerging Communist dictatorships in Eastern Europe were no different in terms of how historical debates defined political visions and identities. Nonetheless, there was a crucial difference between the two sides of the Iron Curtain. In Western Europe even strongly politicized historical debates were occurring in a relatively open public sphere, where it was in principle possible to make interpretations based on the available evidence and to remain in public disagreement on various matters. In Eastern Europe, on the contrary, Communist authorities were striving to close down the opportunities of free and open debate, and tried to control access to historical evidence and to dominate the production of narratives about the past. Through school curricula, academic history, historical movies, museums and festivals, the Communist parties of Eastern Europe tried to create an authoritative voice in representations of the past, which they hoped would justify their rule. Typically, such representations were framed as various nationalizing and often nationalist mythologies, which integrated freedom fights and revolts into a progressive set of consecutive events culminating in the logical victory of the Communist parties. During the Stalinist 1950s, such representations mostly took the shape of nationalist narratives highlighting the anti-German legacy of East-Central European political history, particularly in Poland, Czechoslovakia and Hungary, or the legacy of freedom fights against the Ottomans in Southeastern Europe, Romania and

---

University Press, 2000); Henry Rousso, *The Vichy Syndrome: History and Memory in France since 1944* (Cambridge, MA: Harvard University Press, 1991); Pieter Lagrou, *The Legacy of Nazi Occupation: Patriotic Memory and National Recovery in Western Europe, 1945–1965* (Cambridge: Cambridge University Press, 2000).

27 Tony Judt, 'The Past is Another Country: Myth and Memory in Postwar Europe', *Daedalus* 121 (4) (1992): 83–97.

28 Alf Lüdtke, 'Coming to Terms with the Past: Illusions of Remembering, Ways of Forgetting Nazism in West Germany', *Journal of Modern History* 65 (Summer 1993): 542–72; Bernhard Giesen, 'National Identity as Trauma: The German Case', in *Myth and Memory in the Construction of Community: Historical Patterns in Europe and Beyond*, ed. Bo Stråth (Brussels: PIE – Peter Lang, 2000), 240–47; Charles S. Maier, *The Unmasterable Past: History, Holocaust, and German National Identity* (Cambridge, MA/London: Harvard University Press, 1988).

Bulgaria.[29] The core of these narrative framings had been developed during the 1930s, when official Communist politics was used to construct broad popular antifascist fronts and national unity. As nationalist ideology proved to be dangerous during the crisis of Stalinism in 1953–56, when popular unrest turned nationalist arguments against the Communist parties themselves, the authorities began to refine the frames of historical representation. The new type of narratives remained also nation-centred, but instead of openly building on nationalist sentiments, they tried to focus on the class content of domestic revolutionary traditions and attempted to globalize them by linking such legacies to the emerging anti-imperialist political culture of the decolonizing 1960s.[30]

In spite of these differences, a particular Manichean framing of history remained in use throughout the entire Communist period. This master narrative was established during the postwar years and was firmly linked to the general antifascist myth of the Communists. According to the mainstream Communist interpretation, which had been developed during the 1930s in close connection to the Comintern leader Dimitrov's trial in Leipzig by the Nazis, fascism was the extreme form of capitalist dictatorship, born as a desperate attempt of capitalists to save capitalism and balance the growing power of Communism. Consequently, Communism was seen as the main target and the only genuine opponent of fascism. This interpretation, in the end, turned all history into a rigid antagonism of fascism and Communism. If fascism was basically capitalism and, thus, social reaction, and Communism was the vanguard of social progress, then all historical movements, forces, persons and events could be, and in fact had to be, categorized as either of them. Although the Communist brand of the antifascist myth was most spectacular in the German Democratic Republic (GDR), which was described as the stately embodiment of German antifascist progressivism, each of the Eastern European satellite elites developed their own national version.[31]

---

29 Maciej Górny, 'Past in the Future: National Tradition and Czechoslovak Marxist Historiography', *European Review of History* 10 (1) (2003): 103–14; Maciej Górny, 'Marxist History of Historiography in Poland, Czechoslovakia and East Germany (late 1940s – late 1960s)', in *The Sovietization of Eastern Europe: New Perspectives on the Postwar Period*, Balázs Apor, Péter Apor and Arfon Rees, eds (Washington, DC: New Academia Press, 2008), 249–63; Izabella Main, 'Memory and History in the Cityscapes in Poland: The Search for Meaning', in *Inquiries into Past and Present*, ed. D. Gard, I. Main, M. Oliver, J. Wood (Vienna: Institut für die Wissenschaften vom Menschen, 2005), 5. Lucian Boia, *History and Myth in Romanian Consciousness* (Budapest: CEU Press, 2001), 215–16; Cristina Petrescu, 'Historiography of Nation Building in Communist Romania', in *Historische Nationsforschung im geteilten Europa 1945–1989*, ed. Pavel Kolař and Miloš Řeznik (Cologne: SH-Verlag, 2012), 158–65.
30 Michal Kopeček, 'Historical Studies of Nation-Building and the Concept of Socialist Patriotism in East Central Europe 1956–1970', in *Historische Nationsforschung*, 121–36.
31 Alan L. Nothnagle, *Building the East German Myth: Historical Mythology and Youth Propaganda in the German Democratic Republic, 1945–1989* (Ann Arbor: University of Michigan Press, 1999), 93–131; Ingo Loose, 'The Anti-Fascist Myth of the German Democratic Republic and Its Decline after 1989', in *Past in the Making: Historical Revisionism in Central Europe after 1989*, ed. Michal Kopeček (Budapest: CEU Press, 2008), 59–63; Annamaria Orla-Bukowska, 'New Threads on an Old Loom: National Memory and Social Identity in Postwar and Post-Communist Poland', in *The Politics of Memory in Postwar Europe*, 178–96.

The history of the revisions of the First Hungarian Soviet Republic is a contribution to the understanding of Communist power in the perspective of symbolic politics. Communist Party states declared a radical break with the past and wanted to introduce new beginnings. The Communist dictatorship in Hungary began the reorganization of historical institutions in 1948. Many established university professors lost their positions or were forced to retire. Before reshaping traditional academic institutions, the party established its own historical institute, the Hungarian Institute for Labour History, in 1948. The leadership of the Historical Society was replaced in March 1949. The new president, Erzsébet Andics, became one of the main Stalinist hardliners and dominated the discipline until 1956. The Academy of Sciences retained the membership of only 102 of its 260 members. In 1950, special departments of Marxism–Leninism were formed at all universities and 175 new textbooks were published, most of which were translations of Soviet works.[32] The Communist leadership used its freshly obtained dominance in the institutional network to revise national history and to orchestrate monumental historical festivals making these claims manifest.

In spite of the confident manifestations of radical new beginnings, Communists based their politics and representations of history on earlier canons and genres. The Hungarian Communist leadership had to reflect on the immense tradition of the politics of history, festivals and commemorations. Hungarian society had developed a rich tradition of historicized political culture and an extraordinary sensitivity to historical culture, at least since the suppression of its revolution in 1849. In Hungary, political rights and authority are regularly justified on the basis of solving or taking sides in pending issues and controversies of the nation's past. Political culture and credibility were affected to a great extent by the position one occupied in disputes between Catholics and Protestants, pro-Habsburg and pro-independence groups, or progressives and traditionalists.[33] Central among these themes was the interpretation and representation of 1848–49. The revolution of 15 March 1848 was the founding event of modern Hungarian identity; it even influenced the national symbols: the tricolour flag, the national anthem and the national coat-of-arms. Legislation during those two years, particularly the laws sanctioned by the Austrian emperor on 11 April 1848, founded the modern state system,

---

32 Ignác Romsics, *Clio bűvöletében: Magyar történetírás a 19–20. században* (Budapest: Osiris, 2011), 356–77; Tibor Huszár, *A hatalom rejtett dimenziói* (Budapest: Akadémiai, 1995), esp. 38–44, 50–56, 85–93, 294–5; Romsics, *Hungary in the 20th Century*, 360; Ferenc Glatz, 'Hajnal István történetírása', introduction to István Hajnal, *Technika, művelődés* (Budapest: MTA TTI, 1993), xviii. On the Academy of Science see also János Pótó, 'Harmadik nekifutásra', *Történelmi Szemle* 36 (Spring–Summer 1994): 79–110; and György Péteri, 'Születésnapi ajándék Sztálinnak', *Századvég* 1 (1989): 18–35. On the replacement of the scientific elite see Judit Bíró and Mária Székelyi, 'A tudomány újjáépítése, 1945–1950', *Szociológiai Szemle* (Autumn–Winter 1996): 81–104. The following book is also useful, although it was written from a late socialist perspective: Andor Ladányi, *Felsőoktatási politika 1949–1958* (Budapest: Kossuth, 1986), 18–163.

33 András Gerő, *Imagined History: Chapters from Nineteenth- and Twentieth-Century Hungarian Symbolic Politics* (Boulder: East European Monographs, 2006); Árpád von Klimó, *Nation, Konfession, Geschichte: Zur nationalen Geschichtskultur Ungarns im europäischen Kontext (1860–1948)* (Munich: Oldenbourg, 2003); Gábor Gyáni, 'Történetírás: a nemzeti emlékezet tudománya?', in *Emlékezés, emlékezet és a történelem elbeszélése* (Budapest: Napvilág, 2000), 95–127.

legal equality, government responsibility to the elected parliament and citizenship rights including voting and education. The declaration of April 1849 in turn established the idea of an independent, republican, secular state in Hungarian society. Political culture was largely shaped by interpretations of 1848–49, as the event provided arguments both for the idea of a responsible constitutional and elitist state and for more radical visions of a progressive republican democratic society. The memory of 1848–49 remained alive in Hungarian society: its symbols and culture evaded popular folklore. Political reform programs regularly evoked the ideas of the period, both in 1918 and in 1946 when both postwar republics used 1848–49 as the model for their own visions of creating a modern Hungary.[34] By the 100th anniversary of 1848, visions of the future were dominated by the Communist party. It orchestrated a spectacular set of celebrations on 15 March 1948 for the anniversary of the 1848 revolution and the anti-Habsburg war of independence. The aim of these performances was to establish the Communist party as the heir of the national liberation and democratic movement, thus turning the tiny elite of leftist radicals into the true vanguard of national spirit.[35]

Communist-fostered historical culture in East Central Europe drew on earlier traditions of state-centred narratives, which focused on the political implications of all types of histories. The history of class struggles and revolutionary movements was, in many ways, an alternative political history that replaced previous upper classes and elites with lower classes, peasants and workers as the main agents of defining the course of state development and politics. Sometimes this was not even the case: Communist historiographies partially kept the canon of great historical figures, particularly leaders of national fights for independence, and added to it with peasant rebels of the Middle Ages and antifascist martyrs of the recent past. Communist historical culture perpetuated the cult of great men and the focus on state and nation: the means of framing contemporary historical narratives in classic nineteenth-century narratives.[36] The regular failure of revolutions in East-Central Europe and the collapse of national states during the war, such as the Hungarian Bolshevik regime in 1919 itself, were embedded in a typical narrative tradition of regional historical cultures. The failure of nineteenth-century national and nation state projects contributed to the genesis of a particular tragic sense of the past in East-Central and Southeastern Europe, which dwelled on past glory and

---

34 András Gerő, *Imagined History*.
35 Mevius, *Agents of Moscow*, 111–262; József Litkei, 'Borrowed Cloth' (MA thesis, Central European University, Budapest, 1999), 54–61; András Gerő, *Az államosított forradalom* (Budapest: Új Mandátum, 1998), 9–19; György Gyarmati, *Március hatalma: A hatalom márciusa* (Budapest: Paginarum, 1998), 96–114; Balázs Apor, 'Hatalom és történelem', *Budapesti Jelenlét* 26–7 (2–3) (2000): 59–70; Róbert Szabó, 'Politikai propaganda és történelmi ünnep', *Történelmi Szemle* 40 (Autumn–Winter 1998): 215–27; Róbert Szabó, 'Pártok, politikai propaganda, történelmi ünnepek Magyarországon 1945–1948', *Sic itur ad astra* (2–4) (1993): 261–72; Alice Freifeld, 'The Cult of March 15: Sustaining the Hungarian Myth of Revolution, 1849–1998', in *Staging the Past: The Politics of Commemoration in Habsburg Central Europe, 1848 to the Present*, ed. Maria Bucur and Nancy M. Wingfield (West Lafayette: Purdue University Press, 2001), 255–85.
36 Hayden White, *Metahistory: The Historical Imagination in Nineteenth-Century Europe* (Baltimore: Johns Hopkins University Press, 1973), esp. 169–75.

contemporary decline, futile heroism and the martyrdom of small nations for the sake of humanity or civilization.[37]

Nonetheless, using the memory of 1919 as a justification for Communist rule was no easy task. In fact, the memory of the First Hungarian Soviet Republic had a special, twisted history. It was integrated into a narrative, which, in many ways, had different functions than to simply provide historical antecedents and identity for the Communist Party. Contrary to what might be assumed, the Communist takeover of 1949 did not mean the automatic elevation of 1919 into the core of national historical memory; in the context of building Hungary on a Stalinist model it had problematic associations – chief among them its leader Béla Kun's demise during the Stalinist purges. The Soviet Republic did not play any significant role in the construction of the historical process that was crystallized around the connection of 1848 (the democratic revolution) to 1948 (the foundation of the people's democracy during the immediate postwar period). Although the 30th and 35th anniversary of its proclamation were commemorated, respectively, in 1949 and 1954, these celebrations rather remained inner festivities of the Communist Party in contrast to its subsequent national scope. Although in retrospect the number of commemorative articles appearing in the official press seems to be high, in the contemporary context they are brief notes lost in the overall journalistic output of the time. As the first chapter of this book demonstrates, before 1956 the Soviet Republic was considered only the prefiguration or prelude of the postwar Communist regime, rather than its origin.

The mode of looking for analogies in the past, rather than for temporal sequences was typical of Stalinist historical representations. In spite of prompting historical origins, the purpose of evoking scenes from the past in this period was not only to demonstrate that the Communist states were the successors of such traditions. The historical representations of the 1950s in the Communist-dominated political cultures in Eastern Europe typically did not merely create an account of historical development leading to the establishment of Communism. On the contrary, they depicted the past as a series of episodes that had predicted and were preludes to the eventual post-WWII fulfilment of the earlier unrealized, half-developed and immature desires and expectations. This montage-like representation was essentially a cinematic technique and, hence, film quickly became a favourite medium of contemporary Communist historical propaganda. In Hungary, a masterpiece of this genre was *A Magyar Néphadsereg Napja* (The day of the Hungarian People's Army; 1951), which was composed of historical scenes of Hungarian soldiers.[38] Produced specifically for an audience of soldiers, the film put 29 September 1951, the day that became the official festivity day of the Communist army, into a broader historical context. That day was the 103rd anniversary of the first victory of the Hungarian army during the revolution of 1848. The directors first of all capitalized on this connection to

---

37 Monika Baár, *Historians and Nationalism: East-Central Europe in the Nineteenth Century* (Oxford: Oxford University Press, 2010), 224–55; Balázs Trencsényi, *The Politics of 'National Character': A Study in Interwar East European Thought* (Abingdon/New York: Routledge, 2012), 22–3, 75, 90–92.
38 *A Magyar Néphadsereg Napja*, Hadtörténelmi Levéltár, mozgófilm tár (Archives for Military History), 105.

construct a historical succession. The film opens with a soldier of the new Communist army in the foreground, and in the background, somewhat blurred, stands a soldier of the army in 1848. Following the scene of the battle, depicted by contemporary paintings, the film continues with a proclamation of the First Hungarian Soviet Republic, illustrated by old documentaries. These pictures are followed by footage of Soviet artillery firing during the siege of Budapest in 1944. The Soviet victory is interpreted as a turning point in Hungarian history: the short representation of the recent past finishes with a picture of a monument dedicated to the liberating Soviet army, meanwhile the narrator explains that this event provided the Hungarian nation with the opportunity to realize the aspirations of its past. The following scenes clarify his meaning: while the narrator talks about the party and its first secretary constructing socialism, the film depicts the reconstruction of the railway (symbolized by a pioneer railway boy), the building of factories and housing estates, a harvest, and children in a playground or at the funfair.

From this perspective the immense respect paid to the first proletarian system seems rather a new development. Narrative representation of the history of the Soviet Republic went in very different directions before and after the revolution in 1956 within the two slightly dissimilar Communist regimes. Although the institutional system did not change significantly after 1956, several crucial figures of the previous regime were fired. For instance, the director of the Institute for Party History, who had played a crucial role in the construction of the history of the Soviet Republic in the 1950s, was criticized and subsequently replaced.[39] Whereas between 1957 and 1962 24 monographs and collective volumes were issued on various aspects of the dictatorship of the proletariat in 1919, in the slightly longer period between 1949 and 1956 only eight volumes appeared within this field. Nevertheless, virtually none of them could be regarded as a methodical historical narrative based on laborious archival research. Two of the publications were simply printed versions of public lectures by party leaders, one of them was an illustrated album, four books were devoted only to particular details of the first Communist regime, while the last contained studies grounded mainly on personal memories of the authors. In comparison to the pre-1956 years, a genuine scholarly boom occurred around the Soviet Republic after 1956. Apart from the twenty-four professional publications, a few memoirs and novels concerning the history of 1919 were republished. These works were printed previously in exile, and some of them never in Hungary. Volumes of archival documents were published, which inevitably signifies an increasing professional interest in a certain segment of the past. Eleven compilations consisting of original records were issued. Research on local history was also reinvigorated, and studies concerning various minor or major details of the dictatorship of the proletariat flooded the professional journals. By 1964 Communist historiography was already capable of summarizing the results of this research and collecting a bibliography to foster further scholarship.[40] The Communists interpreted this fact as a sign of improvement in the regime, claiming

---

39 Ladányi, *Felsőoktatási politika*, 164–217.
40 András Siklós, *Az 1918–1919. évi magyarországi forradalmak* (The revolutions in Hungary in the years 1918–1919; Budapest: Tankönyvkiadó, 1964). All my bibliographical details come from this volume, 177–90.

that after de-Stalinization and the removal of the nefarious personality cult previous obstructions that stood in the way of the truth were averted.

The history of 1919 became one of the central elements of Communist historical culture only after October 1956. On 23 October 1956, the public protest in support of Polish reforms initiated by party secretary Gomułka turned into a demonstration against the Hungarian Communist leadership. Hungarian society, which since 1949 had experienced brutal oppression, economic shortages and privation under the Stalinist Rákosi regime, erupted with overwhelming force against domestic Stalinists. Protesters demanded that Imre Nagy, who led a course of reforms for a more liberal economy and open cultural life in 1953 before his expulsion from the party, be appointed prime minister. The frightened and puzzled Stalinists, who were shocked by the level of popular unrest, accepted the demands. Nagy tried to pacify the country by promising economic reforms, more liberal politics and amnesty for political prisoners, however he was unable to contain the growing radicalism. Armed groups were formed in Budapest and fought the attacking Soviet troops, national committees and workers' councils were established and soon took over virtually all local administrations, while a few Communist Party members and security police officers were even killed. Non-Communist parties went public and finally Nagy himself allowed his government to become pluralist. Political democracy was in the making by the end of October 1956; the political and social milieu was broad and colourful. A leading force was the group of young reform-minded party intellectuals who gathered around Nagy and fostered the idea of a democratic socialism. They were soon joined by another intellectual group critical of Stalinism, the populists, who promoted the development of agricultural provincial societies, improving the economic and cultural standards of the rural population and their chances for political participation. Former members of postwar democratic political parties also became active, focusing on the issue of national independence and political pluralism. Industrial workers organized workers' councils, whereas in the countryside the local population established national committees, the organs of autonomous administration.[11] These various groups, interests and ideas were connected by their shared anti-Stalinism and anticapitalism. The unifying idea of 1956 was some sort of independent, noncapitalist Hungary. The Soviet leadership, fearing that the Communists might lose power totally, decided to intervene, however. János Kádár, who had been a militant activist and minister of interior during the postwar transformation but later jailed by Rákosi, and who partially supported a reform course and de-Stalinization in Hungary, was taken by the Soviets in early November to Moscow, where he was convinced to lead the restoration of Communist power and the Red Army troops that would secure it. Kádár established his government on 4 November, forcing Nagy and his followers to flee. Repressions were brutal and several hundred were executed, including Nagy himself.[12]

---

41 Éva Standeisky, 'Eszmék az 1956-os forradalomban', in *1956 az újabb történeti irodalomban*, ed. Gábor Gyáni and János M. Rainer (Budapest: 1956-os Intézet, 2007), 169–202; Standeisky, *Népuralom 1956-ban* (Budapest: 1956-os Intézet, 2010), 365–94.

42 György Litván, ed., *The Hungarian Revolution of 1956: Reform, Revolt and Repression 1953–1963* (London/New York: Longman, 1996).

Despite the restoration of party rule, 1956 became a sharp dividing line in the history of state socialism in Hungary, perhaps sharper than in Poland and surely sharper than in Czechoslovakia. Stalinism fell virtually overnight in October 1956 as the leadership of Rákosi and Gerő collapsed. Although Kádár's leadership had to use the old Stalinist cadres, they were convinced that Stalinism had no future for Hungarian socialism. This was shared by the contemporary Soviet leadership as well, which under Khrushchev also ran a course of de-Stalinization and was interested in establishing a loyal, pacified Hungary and calming tensions between society and the party elite. Following a few years of suppression, Kádár managed to make peace with most of society by the early 1960s. The compromise was based on two principles: the taboo on 1956 and unconditional loyalty to the USSR on the one hand, and the promotion of socialist consumerism and breaking with Rákosist politics on the other. Rákosi and Gerő, the key party leaders before 1956, were ousted from the party and exiled to the USSR. The duplicity of relative flexibility and harsh limitations shaped late socialism in Hungary and generated what seemed to most contemporaries to be a special Hungarian form of state socialism.[43]

The crucial component of the Kádárist myth of political legitimacy was the argument that the revolt in 1956 had been a 'counterrevolution' that had wanted to overthrow the popular democracy, to restore capitalist exploitation in Hungary, to lead the country to colonial dependence on Western imperialism and to return to counterrevolutionary White Terror against all democratic and antifascist forces, particularly the Communists. The interpretations of the First Hungarian Soviet Republic became the crucial and decisive factor in transforming the anti-Stalinist insurrection in October 1956 into a genuine counterrevolution in Communist terms. For Communists the most shocking occurrence of 1956 was the siege of the Budapest party headquarters in Republic Square (Köztársaság tér), where the insurgents mercilessly massacred the captured defenders. The Communists realized that these radicals had been present from the very beginning of the rebellion and had in fact organized the movement, and after the occupation of the party headquarters the radicals openly called for the restoration of capitalist dictatorship and the extermination of the defenders of the Communist regime.[44] The experience of the First Hungarian Soviet Republic's demise seemed to confirm the suspicion that the massacre in Republic Square was a sign of counterrevolution. Commandos who called themselves counterrevolutionaries, and who aimed at the restoration of the pre-1914 social and political system, persecuted, tortured and executed Communists, leftists and Jews. For party leaders the two events were strikingly similar. From the Communist perspective the revolution in 1956 was none other than the second edition of the White Terror in 1919, and October 1956 experienced the second coming of the counterrevolutionaries of 1919.

---

43 János M. Rainer, *Bevezetés a kádárizmusba* (Budapest: 1956-os Intézet, 2011), 95–184.

44 The standard book on this subject is Ervin Hollós and Vera Lajtai, *Köztársaság tér 1956* (Budapest: Kossuth, 1974). A standard Communist interpretation of 1956 is János Berecz, *Ellenforradalom tollal es fegyverrel. 1956* (Budapest: Kossuth, 1969), although this book provides a somewhat different perspective and presents the revolution of 1956 as the manoeuvre of Western imperialism. The English translation is *1956 Counter-Revolution in Hungary: Words and Weapons* (Budapest: Akadémiai, 1986).

At least to the extent that it could provide legitimacy for Communist rule, this historical construction aimed at the destruction of the party's adversaries: the participants and heirs of the revolution. The purpose of this particular narrative was to destroy the self-esteem and identity of the revolutionaries by proving that in reality they were not fighting for freedom, democracy, national pride or social justice, but only for the restoration of capitalist or fascist oppression and for the sake of killing Communists and other decent people. Through this interpretation it was pronounced that the revolution was not the legacy of social democrats, liberals or national democrats, but exclusively that of the White Terror. The first known case of such manipulation of historical events was, most probably, the ancient Egyptian author Manetho, who inverted the statements of the Old Testament in order to prove that the Jews were not an ancient people with venerable institutions, but simply a herd of lepers who copied the institutions of Egypt. The practice of Communist historians thereby adjusted itself to the long tradition of a peculiar historical genre: counterhistory. This mode of constructing histories has only one definite aim: to deprive the target group of its self-identity.[45]

In many ways, the Communist revision of 1956 looks to be a form of historical 'revisionism': the denial of past events. Communist propaganda historians seemed to deny the progressive and democratic intent of the revolt in the same way that 'revisionists' of the Holocaust today claim that there was no extermination of Jews in death camps at all. As Kádárist police historians tried to erase the identity of participants in the events of 1956, so do Holocaust deniers attempt to deprive a community of its memory and to destroy the identity of Holocaust survivors: of Jews, Roma and all the other groups who were the victims of the Nazi's murderous practices.[46]

3

Nonetheless, there is a crucial difference between Holocaust deniers and Communist attempts to describe the events of October 1956. The publications of 'revisionists' are not based on any mode of factual rewriting: they are, in fact, obvious lies. Typically, they simply try to deny the existence of evidence: since there are no witnesses who experienced the gas chambers from the inside (as all of them died), evidence is doubtful. They claim that the final solution meant only the expulsion of Jews from the east, that death happened in 'natural' ways in the camps, that the genocide was only the

---

45 Amos Funkenstein, 'History, Counterhistory, and Narrative', in *Probing the Limits of Representation*, ed. Saul Friedlander (Cambridge, MA/London: Harvard University Press, 1992), 66–81.

46 Pierre Vidal-Naquet, *Assassins of Memory* (New York: Columbia University Press, 1992). See also the following printout: Pierre Vidal-Naquet and Limor Yagil, *Holocaust Denial in France* (Tel Aviv: University of Tel Aviv, 1996). The Bar Ilan University published a bibliography of the literature that denies the Holocaust and also of its analyses: Rivkah Knoller, *Denial of the Holocaust* (Ramat Gan: Bar Ilan University, 1992). A recent and profound work on the topic is Deborah Lipstadt, *Denying the Holocaust* (New York: Penguin, 1993). On the American case, see also: Michael Shermer and Alex Grobman, *Denying History: Who Says the Holocaust Never Happened and Why Do They Say It?* (Berkeley/Los Angeles/London: University of California Press, 2000); John C. Zimmerman, *Holocaust Denial: Demographics, Testimonies and Ideologies* (Lanham/New York/Oxford: University Press of America, 2000).

invention of Allied propaganda and that the remnants of gas chambers were in reality something else. These narratives have lost all connection with reality: '"Revisionism" represents no historical school, no type of historical discourse, but instead the pure and simple suppression of the historical object under study.'[47] In contrast, Communist interpreters of history put tremendous effort into connecting their representations to the actual remnants of the past.[48] These narratives were born during the attempt to put the traces left behind by history in order. Whereas deniers of the Nazi genocide aspire to erase the existence of physical sources and, therefore, build their interpretations over the deep hollowness of nonexistence, Communist historians were overwhelmed by records of atrocities and remnants of corpses, by living persons and rediscovered documents.

All over Eastern Europe, from East Germany to Yugoslavia, Communist parties and their intellectual infrastructures made enormous efforts to discover and to make publicly available the traces of the past that would actualize their interpretations of history. A series of postwar trials were used to connect concrete individuals and biographies to the narrative of the struggle of anti-Communist fascism and antifascist Communism. Several wartime sites of executions and mass murders were carefully reconstructed. The stories of Leningrad as the city of heroes that resisted the 'German fascists' to the last drop of blood, and of the incredible suffering the 'fascists' caused 'Soviet people', were partly made tangible and credible in the Piskaryovskoye Cemetery, which contained mass graves of those who died due to starvation, bombings and fighting during the siege, and where many Leningrad families, indeed, had relatives to mourn.[49] Jasenovac, the former concentration camp of the Croatian fascist movement, where no original traces had been left, was used as a memorial site in socialist Yugoslavia and was completed by a museum in 1968.[50] These museums, located on the actual sites of mass executions, exhibit in abundant detail the violence and torture that were inflicted upon the inmates. In the GDR, the former concentration camps in Buchenwald and Sachsenhausen

---

47 Pierre Vidal-Naquet, 'The Shoah's Challenge to History', in *The Jews: History, Memory, and the Present* (New York: Columbia University Press, 1996), 146.
48 During the 1950s and 1960s Communist historical practice was usually described as arbitrary construction based upon the transformation, invention and forging of facts according to the ever changing political aims of the party. Raymond L. Garthoff, 'The Stalinist Revision of History: The Case of Brest-Litovsk', *World Politics* 5 (October 1952): 66–85; Bertram D. Wolfe, 'Operation Rewrite: The Agony of Soviet Historians', *Foreign Affairs* 31 (Winter 1952/1953): 39–57; Alexander Dallin, 'Recent Soviet Historiography', *Problems of Communism* 5 (November–December, 1956): 24–30. This particular vision of Communist history writing was born in the Cold War analyses of Stalinist practices, however the interpretive framework sustained itself until 1989. See Vladimir Petrov, 'The Nazi–Soviet Pact: A Missing Page in Soviet Historiography', *Problems of Communism* 17 (January–February 1968): 42–50; George M. Enteen, 'Problems of CPSU Historiography', *Problems of Communism* 38 (September–October, 1989): 72–80.
49 Nina Tumarkin, *The Living and the Dead* (New York: Basic Books, 1994), 118–19.
50 Vjeran Pavlaković, '(Re)constructing the Past: Museums in Post-Communist Croatia' (unpublished manuscript), 11–12.

were restored and transformed into museums in the 1950s.[51] Even if the East German Communist Party had difficulties with the surviving barracks (as these housed not only the Communist prisoners of the Nazis, but after 1945 also prisoners of the Soviets and, therefore, were carefully demolished), the official narrative was built in close connection to other material evidence, particularly the mass graves that were preserved inside the camp. The new caretakers of the memorial site constructed a pathway, along which ran various graves that represented individual stations in the narrative of Communist antifascist resistance, clarified by the reliefs that were carefully added to these sites.[52]

Several new history museums in the region played crucial roles in fixing in the minds of visitors those documents and objects of the past that were considered crucial to the Communist historical narratives. The 1950 opening of the Museum für Deutsche Geschichte in Berlin had been preceded by careful institutional and ideological preparations monitored by the East German Communist Party.[53] The staff of the museum initiated a large-scale collection campaign and issued a general call to the population to search their own property for documents, letters, leaflets, photos, old membership cards, etc. that could demonstrate the struggle of the working class. The point of the designers was to allow the people contribute to the creation of their own museum, which, by looking at the objects they themselves had collected, would render museum visits into an effective authentication of the theoretical historical narratives that they read in textbooks.[54] In Bulgaria and Romania, where museums of history were non-existent before the war, new monumental institutions were set up in the early 1970s that offered spectacular exhibitions about the emerging 'socialist nations'. These museums, according to contemporary mainstream Soviet museology, were flooded with original documents and objects.[55] Authorities in the satellite countries also made efforts to produce new ritual calendars, which were hoped to attach the abstract historical narratives to tangible experiences through mass festivals. Poland was a striking example: the Communist authorities there tried to replace 3 May (the day of the 1793 Polish Constitution) with a new festival, the Day of Books, and 11 November (the day of independence in 1918) with 7 November (the Bolshevik Revolution in 1917).[56]

The value of historical narratives lies exactly in the fact that issues of power and dominance have been long connected to the creation of authentic accounts about the past.

---

51 James E. Young, *The Texture of Memory: Holocaust Memorials and Meaning* (New Haven/London: Yale University Press, 1993), 72–9; Mary Fulbrook, *German National Identity after the Holocaust* (Cambridge: Polity Press, 1999), 28–35.
52 Herfried Münkler, *Die Deutschen und ihre Mythen* (Berlin: Rowohlt, 2009), 431–5.
53 Stefan Ebenfeld, *Geschichte nach Plan? Die Instrumentalisierung der Geschichtswissenschaft in der DDR am Beispiel des Museums für Deutsche Geschichte in Berlin (1950 bis 1955)* (Marburg: Tectum-Verlag, 2001), 61–89, 110–40.
54 H. Glenn Penny III, 'The Museum für Deutsche Geschichte and German National Identity', *Central European History* 28 (3) (1995), 353.
55 Maria Bucur, *Heroes and Victims: Remembering War in Twentieth-Century Romania* (Bloomington: Indiana University Press, 2009), 171.
56 Izabella Main, *Political Rituals and Symbols in Poland, 1944–2002: A Research Report* (Leipzig: Leipziger Universitätsverlag, 2003), 13–35; Izabella Main, 'Nemzetek Krisztusa: A lengyel nemzeti ünnepek állami és egyházi manipulációja 1944 és 1966 között', *Regio* 12 (Autumn 2001): 69–88.

Truthful reconstructions of past happenings create rights, establish property and justify rule. Rights to land or property can be established by detecting the origins of ownership since early civilization. Processes to authentically verify past ownership featured in medieval legal practice, which created a sophisticated system of authentic oral and written evidence for this purpose. Facts of dynastic or legally appropriate ways of succession justify rulership. Dynastic histories, in which the credibility of claims was based on presumably authentic documents, were instrumental in establishing rights to thrones. The core of medieval jurisprudence in concert with history developed elaborate methodologies in this context. The idea of authentic historical origins appeared to shape claims for territorial rights and state control in modern European conflicts. States rivalling over certain territories (e.g., Romania and Hungary over Transylvania or Germany and Denmark over Schleswig-Holstein) elaborated complex historical arguments to support their control over the contested areas. These arguments never remained abstract: archaeological excavations and extensive archival research were generally funded to provide authentic evidence.

Nonetheless, the relationship to the past is far from being a predetermined process that merely reflects or projects preconceived ideological positions onto historical representations. This is true even for such an extreme case as the attempts of Hungarian Communists. The conception of modern Hungarian history was shaped through the construction of memorials, commemorative festivals and other types of representation, like historical films and documentary images. These were both affected by and had an impact on professional historical constructions, sometimes triggering contingent and unexpected consequences, even for official historians and party leaders. To comprehend this process in an appropriate way, one has to follow the intricate system of relationships that exist between the various representations of the First Hungarian Soviet Republic.[57] The history of representations is to be understood in the context of their multifarious mutual impacts. It is influenced by previous ideological-cultural constructions, but also affects, shapes and modifies subsequent ones. (Historical) representations have their own histories. The meanings of objects on display, architecture, images, memorial buildings, living persons, dead bodies or scholarly interpretations are impossible to detach from their own history. They are inseparable from those conventional social practices that shape the modes of reception and the ordinary cultural uses of the means of representation that historically are attached to them. It is simply impossible to load the objects of representation and exhibition with any type of voluntaristically chosen meanings: their histories influence and shape subsequent interpretations and prevent the rooting of others. This book strives to describe the web that connects creative imagination and the objects of representation, as well as historical traditions mobilized by the modalities and means of representation.[58]

---

57 Antoine de Baecque suggests the term 'non-quantitative serial history' for a method of studying vast collections of various forms of representations to draw lessons regarding their cultural, political and social implications: 'The Allegorical Image of France, 1750–1800: A Political Crisis of Representation', *Representations* 47 (Summer 1994): 114–17.

58 An important and telling example is provided by Michael Fehr in his account on the Ernst-Osthaus Museum in Hagen, Germany. His struggles to revitalize the museum were embedded in the constant creative adaptation to the various layers of historical legacy the institution

Thus, the second chapter investigates the emerging historical connection between the 'counterrevolutions' of 1919 and 1956 and its relationship with the effort to understand physical violence. It examines the attempts of the party historians to authenticate their historical abstraction through various historical, mostly visual, records: photography, exhibitions or personal presence in the courtroom. During this venture Communist historians established a thoroughgoing continuity of the counterrevolution from its alleged genesis in 1919–20, tried to prove its constant existence by evoking the Arrow Cross terror in 1944 and linked these historical events to the revolt in 1956. In this way, Kádár's propaganda historians renewed the thesis of the continuity of the counterrevolution between 1919 and 1944, which they would try to render credible and 'factual' by evoking the historical records of the postwar trials of former war criminals. The third chapter, thus, is a flashback to point out this important aspect of the genesis of the analysed historical continuity. These legal procedures staged real persons whose actual lives demonstrated the continuity of counterrevolution from 1919 until 1944, the German occupation and the takeover of the Hungarian fascist movement. The fourth chapter provides an analysis of the most monumental commemorative construction of the Communist era, that of the Pantheon of the Labour Movement. The memorial itself constructed a peculiar representation of history, similar to the medieval notion of the mystical body that played a crucial role in the self-construction of the party. Thereby the comprehension of historical continuity was crystallized around the bodies of the dead. The Pantheon, which was inaugurated on 21 March 1959, on the 40th anniversary of the Soviet Republic, revealed an overall, thus far hidden, connection among the tombs of the cemetery for the Communist observers. The party leaders recognized the existence of the continuity of the struggle between revolution and counterrevolution throughout modern Hungarian history, between the end of the eighteenth century and the middle of the twentieth. Hence, 1959 meant the culmination of this peculiar process of reinterpreting contemporary history. The final chapter closes the investigation with a profound examination of the characteristics of Communist historiography in order to establish its generic tradition as well as its foundation upon and relationship with real records. Historical writings in general – proper scholarship, fiction and documentary fiction – produced between 1959 and roughly 1965 remained deeply embedded in the tradition that had already been shaped by the 40th anniversary.

Subsequent transformation began after 1966, the 10th anniversary of the counterrevolution, boosted by the 50th anniversary of the Soviet Republic in 1969 and

---

revealed: 'A Museum and Its Memory: The Art of Recovering History', in *Museums and Memory*, ed. Susan A. Crane (Stanford: Stanford University Press, 2000), 35–59. Representation is not simply a reflection, claims Stephen Greenblatt, it is itself a social relationship linked to understandings, status hierarchies, resistances and conflicts: *Marvelous Possessions: The Wonder of the New World* (Oxford: Clarendon Press, 1991), 6. The 'sociology of associations' is Bruno Latour's concept for an understanding of human activities in the context of various objects, not as a reflection or projection of a definitive background structure, but as a network of mutual impacts, modifications and contingencies. He has provided a comprehensive summary of this method of description in *Reassembling the Social: An Introduction to Actor-Network-Theory* (Oxford: Oxford University Press, 2005).

culminating in the birth of the Revolutionary Youth Days (*Forradalmi Ifjúsági Napok*). The crucial aspect of these changes was related to the virtual disappearance of the memory of 1956 from Hungarian society in general and the party's disinterest in maintaining its visibility in public discourse. The Soviet Republic thus functioned as a replacement for the discourse on the counterrevolution and a means for 1956 to slip from the collective memory. Its story, however, remains outside the scope of this study, which seeks only to understand the history of the elevation of the Soviet Republic that occurred between 1949 and 1959.

Arguably, it was one of the most important aims of the Hungarian Communist leadership's politics of history to establish a network of interrelated objects, texts, persons and events in order to amalgamate the various representations of the Soviet Republic into a system of cross-references, interconnectedness and self-reflection. Party historians and propagandists aimed at creating a world out of the interpretations of 1919 with its own internal logic; they longed for a virtual reality where the representations would convince the audience of the hyperreality of the construction. Hungarian Communists thereby apparently tried to appropriate the capacity of the modern media of spectacles for building simulacra, the hyperreality of representations that establishes itself as reality. Modern ways of exercising power rest on the fascination obtained from spectacle. The organization of festivals, rituals, exhibitions and visual media appearances represent the ability of the source of power for action and of being present, thus having omnipotence and omniscience. Hence, spectacle demonstrates *potentia* and visibly attributes it to a well-defined source of power. These practices render power tangible and being present, whereas their audiences are subjected to representation. These techniques of representation, which most probably derive from the various practices of transmitting the image, depicting the body and narrating the history of the absolute monarch in Europe (although they have permeated modern consumer societies as well), were typically and effectively applied by modern dictatorships such as in Italy, Germany or the USSR.[59]

Nonetheless, the simulacrum of the Soviet Republic, the virtual reality of the continuous 1919–56, was regularly damaged, its credibility recurrently undermined. It was tricky to plausibly narrate the history of the dictatorship of the proletariat as the prefiguration of the Rákosi regime virtually without any names (especially Béla Kun, executed in the Stalinist USSR), dates, places or details. One would hardly be convinced that the participants of the 1956 revolution were the direct successors of the White Terrorists in 1919 simply by insisting on an abstract narrative mode of erasing the chronological divide between the two events. It was extremely difficult to manifest the continuity of revolutionary heroes and martyrs in the absence of actual physical bodies. The representation of history that the party leaders and propaganda historians wanted to put forward was full of blanks, contradictions and silences. This was a history where temporal continuities were established as bridging twenty years of chronological gaps, where workers were fighting against the workers' state and revolutionaries were executed by Communists, and where an attempt was made to erase certain events and people from

---

[59] Louis Marin, *The Portrait of the King* (Minneapolis: University of Minnesota Press, 1988); Falasca-Zamponi, *Fascist Spectacle*, 119–47; Von Geldern, *Bolshevik Festivals*, 175–207.

the account. In spite of the great abundance of historical evidence and mobilized details, this was an abstract, barely tangible, broken and puzzling narrative.

There is enough evidence to suggest that for the broader public the history of the First Hungarian Soviet Republic remained largely incredible and unattractive, even if it is almost impossible to learn anything about the social response to this chapter of official historical culture in the late 1950s and 1960s. Despite this, the party leadership stressed the importance of 1919 in balancing the nationalist potential of the memory of 1848 in the late 1950s.[60] State authorities and security services remained disinterested in how the population received the history of 1919, but they were obsessed with the reaction to the official interpretation of 1956.[61] The Communist Youth Federation (KISZ) began to produce reports on the experiences of historical anniversaries since the introduction of the Revolutionary Youth Days in 1967, a Spring festival of revolutionary celebrations that connected 15 March 1848, 21 March 1919 and 4 April 1945 (the official day of liberation from fascist yoke) into one virtual chronology. The Ministry of Interior started to produce daily reports at the end of the 1960s and it was mostly interested in containing the allegedly subversive potential of 15 March. The Research Centre for Public Communication, which created invaluable source material for historians about public perceptions on various issues in late socialism, was established in 1969. Nonetheless, these *ex post facto* documents provide interesting insights into the public perception of the official interpretation of 1919. One of the explicit aims of creating the set of Spring festivities was to balance the weight of 15 March, which the authorities often equated with nationalist and possibly anti-Communist sentiment, by emphasizing the importance of 21 March, an supposedly 'proper' socialist patriotic revolution.[62] In spite of the efforts, 21 March failed to set youthful souls on fire. Romantic revolutionary performances, the spontaneous participation of youngsters and the eruption of patriotic sentiments continued to occur on 15 March during the 1970s up until 1989, a fact that continuously worried the authorities.[63] In contrast, according to the 1974 public survey on patriotism and internationalism, fifty-four per cent of the interviewees had no idea what the commemorations of 21 March actually stood for.[64]

What is in the historical record that is able to shake the cautiously and skilfully mastered art of representation? What triggers the confusion if an apparently consistent narrative emplotment is confronted by the inconsistency of additional missing or contradictory details? Why does it prove ineffectual to prefigure ideological-cultural representations and allocate historical evidence to them? It seems that it is impossible to address the problems of the authenticity and credibility of historical representations without utilizing

---

60 Melinda Kalmár, *Ennivaló és hozomány. A kora kádárizmus ideológiája* (Budapest: Magvető, 1998), 156.
61 János Kenedi, *Kis állambiztonsági olvasókönyv. Október 23. – március 15. – június 16. a Kádár-korszakban*, vol. 1 (Budapest: Magvető, 1996).
62 PIL 289/4/209.
63 Kenedi, *Kis állambiztonsági olvasókönyv*, vol. 2, 7–182.
64 Zsuzsanna Wirth, 'A magyar egy kiváló ember, jól dolgozik, dicsőséges', *Origo*, 3 May 2013. Online: http://www.origo.hu/itthon/20130502-kozvelemeny-kutatas-a-hazafisagrol-a-kadarkorszakban-a-hetvenes-evekben.html (accessed 10 May 2013).

such old-fashioned conceptual tools as proof, evidence and factuality.[65] As in histories of science, it seems necessary to describe the process of historical investigations and accounts by paying adequate attention to the practices that connect historian and interpreter in a tangible and authentic way to the past, and to go beyond the detection of the political implications and relationships and culturally shaped meanings.[66] This book is a contribution to the cultural study of the epistemological relationship between authentic historical representation and evidence, and provides a close scrutiny of a particular case when ill-founded concepts on these matters led to the failure of attempts to construct credible narratives.

---

65 This is a program of study suggested by Carlo Ginzburg and others: Ginzburg, *History, Rhetoric and Proof* (Hanover/London: Brandeis/Historical Society of Israel, 1999); Suzanne Marchand and Elizabeth Lunbeck, eds, *Proof and Persuasion: Essays on Authority, Objectivity and Evidence* (Princeton/Brepolis: Shelby Cullom Davis Center for Historical Studies, 1996). The philosophical clarifications for the value of truth and the virtues of truthfulness have been recently provided by Bernard Williams in *Truth and Truthfulness: An Essay in Genealogy* (Princeton/Oxford: Princeton University Press, 2002).

66 Margaret C. Jacob, 'Science Studies after Social Construction: The Turn toward the Comparative and the Global', in *Beyond the Cultural Turn: New Directions in the Study of Society and Culture*, ed. Victoria E. Bonnell and Lynn Hunt (Berkeley: University of California Press, 1999), 95–120.

Chapter 1

PREFIGURATION: THE FIRST HUNGARIAN SOVIET REPUBLIC AND THE RÁKOSI DICTATORSHIP BEFORE 1956

On 21 March 1949, the Hungarian Federation of Freedom Fighters – a Communist partisan organization which allegedly consisted of wartime anti-Nazi resistance fighters, but which was mostly a fiction to convince Hungarians of the existence of an indigenous Communist resistance movement – organized a bicycle and motorbike race around blocks of flats in Budapest. The competition was part of a set of ceremonies commemorating the proclamation of the First Hungarian Soviet Republic on 21 March 1919. The director of the Institute for Party History, László Réti, justified its appropriateness as follows: 'We have to take care of, and improve the spirit of, fighting for freedom, a spirit the representatives of which construct with one hand, while with the other hand – if they must – they defend, even with weapons, their own constructions. The best illustrations for fostering this spirit of freedom fight are provided by the heroes who were fighting for the Soviet Republic.'[1] Of all the commemorative events of the 30th anniversary, this bicycle race was probably the most curious.

Postwar Hungarian Communists wanted to construct the history of 1919 as an instance of a 'usable past' and establish the First Hungarian Soviet Republic as the *praefiguratio* of their own regime. In this way they could benefit from previous Soviet exercises in historical typology, which identified episodes in the past as models for contemporary political action. Nonetheless, the 30th anniversary of the Hungarian Bolshevik regime in 1919 was not only an occasion for creating a historical interpretation adequate for the objectives of Sovietization. The ceremonies did not merely aim at making their conception of history authentic, but also at inducing a particular politicized relationship to historical time. Political rituals are effective means of transmitting those ideological messages previously formulated by political actors.[2] Yet the ceremonies the Hungarian Communists carefully designed to disseminate their political agenda failed to fulfil these goals. Their failure calls attention to the fact that the relationship between cautiously executed political rituals and the credibility of ideological messages is far from unambiguous. The case of the 30th anniversary of First Hungarian Soviet Republic provides an opportunity to examine how historical festivals function and what are the criteria of successful political rituals.

---

1 SZN, 21 March 1949, 3.
2 David I. Kertzer, *Ritual, Politics, and Power* (New Haven/London: Yale University Press, 1988), 13.

1

Between the end of the war and the Communist takeover Hungarian society barely encountered the memory of the dictatorship of the proletariat at all. Its anniversaries were not celebrated, its leading figures were not commemorated and no historical study was embarked upon. The First Hungarian Soviet Republic as a tradition was abandoned by the new democratic coalition of peasant-populist and left-wing parties, whereas the radical left wing that constituted part of this postwar coalition government also distanced itself from the political goals of the dictatorship of the proletariat, as well as from the promoters of its resurrection. The anniversary articles in *Népszava* (Voice of the people), the daily newspaper of the Social Democratic Party, considered only the example of the workers' unity as worth pursuing.[3] The social democrats, whose political outlook was the most radically leftist of the postwar period, were the only political group to ever consider the First Hungarian Soviet Republic as worth inserting into the series of progressive events in Hungarian history. Their 1946 brochure on major historical events, aimed at the broad masses, contained a radical interpretation of 1919 that justified even the Red Terror as necessary for defending the 'workers' revolution'.[4]

The Communist daily, *Szabad Nép* (Free people), on the contrary, warned against appealing to the traditions of the previous Soviet regime, even if it admitted that there were some merits to it and that there was a discernible democratic legacy from 1919.[5] The theoretical reasoning for this statement was provided by the chief Communist ideologue József Révai, who pronounced that whereas in 1919 a dictatorship of the proletariat against the bourgeois republic was justified by the revolutionary situation of the era, it would be an error in the postwar present, since the new popular front–led democratic republic no longer provided shelter for 'bourgeois reaction', but was rather based upon a democratic alliance between workers and peasants.[6] Consequently, whereas the democratic republic of October 1918 became a theme of party education, the Soviet Republic of 1919 was referred to only in a vague political-historical context and was not discussed separately.[7] On 17 January 1946

---

3 *Népszava*, 21 March 1945, 21 March 1946.
4 Ferenc Agárdi, 'Az 1919. évi munkásforradalom' (The workers' revolution of 1919), in *Századok és tanulságok* (Centuries and their lessons), ed. Géza Hegedűs (Budapest, 1946), 343–8.
5 SZN, 21 March 1946, 21 March 1947.
6 József Révai, 'Miért harcol a kommunista párt a független, szabad, demokratikus Magyarországért?' (Why does the Communist Party fight for the independent, free, democratic Hungary?), Hungarian Communist Party seminar leaflet no. 1 (Budapest: Szikra, 1945).
7 László Réti, *Pártunk harca a fasizmus és a reakció ellen* (The struggle of our party against fascism and reaction) (Budapest: Szikra, 1945); Erzsébet Andics, *A Magyar Kommunista Párt negyedszázados harca a fasizmus és a reakció ellen. Előadás a kezdőtanfolyamok részére. Vezérfonal* (The twenty-five year struggle of the Hungarian Communist Party against fascism and reaction) (Budapest: Szikra, 1946). Mátyás Rákosi and Erzsébet Andics addressed the period in their lectures at the central party seminar: Rákosi, *A magyar munkásmozgalom és a Kommunista Párt története 1914-től 1935-ig* (The history of the Hungarian labour movement and the Communist Party from 1914 to 1935) (Lecture at the Central Party School, 22 May 1946); Andics, *Az 1918-as magyar polgári demokratikus forradalom* (The 1918 Hungarian bourgeois democratic revolution) (Lecture at the Central Party School, 30 June 1945). See also András Siklós, *Az 1918–1919. évi magyarországi forradalmak* (The revolutions in Hungary in 1918–1919) (Budapest: Tankönyvkiadó, 1964), 173–5.

the party secretariat decided to discourage leading Communist historian Erzsébet Andics from writing a brochure on the history of the dictatorship of the proletariat for publishing house Anonymus.[8] The 1948 edition of Aladár Mód's *400 Years of Struggle for the Independent Hungary*, which was considered the most authoritative interpretation of modern Hungarian history from the point of view of the Communist party, contained no chapters on the 1919 radical Communist republic. Mód devoted only three sentences to 1919 in a general section on Hungarian progressive politics and the labour movement, criticizing the Communist Party for carelessly adopting the Social Democratic agricultural program that, he argued, had alienated the peasantry from the revolutionary cause and eventually resulted in the failure of the Communist regime.[9]

In some ways, for Hungarian party leaders, it would have been easier not to talk about 1919. Due to the fact that the memory of the dictatorship of the proletariat was unattractive for large segments of the Hungarian society, Communists tried to integrate their party into the history of the nation by describing their takeover in 1949 as the fulfilment of the democratic revolution and war for independence in 1848–49. Besides, the history of the first dictatorship of the proletariat in Hungary had remained a problematic and ambivalent legacy since the 1920s. Different factions of illegal and émigré party organizations fiercely debated the reasons for its downfall and its choice of tactics, particularly in the field of agricultural policy, and the party was still divided in the meanings they attached to its failure. Moreover, since many of the leaders had perished in the USSR during the Stalinist purges, many party members avoided these unpleasant recollections.[10] Although the Communist Party developed a spectacular cult of martyrdom – trying to 'nationalize' Communist victims of the White Terror in 1919, of the Horthy regime and of WWII – it emphasized the importance of wartime sacrifice as a model of the antifascist struggle.[11]

Nevertheless, in 1949, on the 30th anniversary of the proclamation of the First Hungarian Soviet Republic, the history work group of the Hungarian Workers' Party published a paper on the history of the dictatorship of the proletariat. The introductory paragraph stated that, 'The bourgeois and social-democratic historiography – in the service of capitalism – abused the glorious memory of the first takeover of the Hungarian working class for a quarter of a century. [...] It is time to present the history of the Hungarian commune in its true light according to its real historical significance.'[12] This was the beginning of a transformation in the memory of 1919: remembering the First Hungarian Soviet Republic was becoming an important concern for the new Stalinist Rákosi regime. The party began to consider it a firm duty to reassess the memory of the Hungarian commune after a long period of abuse during what Communist leaders called 'the Horthy regency'. On 19 January 1949, its secretariat accepted a proposal to

---

8 PIL 274/4/110.

9 Aladár Mód, *400 év küzdelem az önálló Magyarországért* (400 years' struggle for an independent Hungary) (Budapest: Szikra, 1948), 196.

10 György Borsányi, 'Gondolatok a Kommunisták Magyarországi Pártja történetéről (1918–1944)', *Múltunk* 40 (1) (1995): 3–37.

11 Martin Mevius, *Agents of Moscow: The Hungarian Communist Party and the Origins of Socialist Patriotism 1941–1953* (Oxford: Oxford University Press, 2005), 192–4.

12 László Réti, *A Magyar Tanácsköztársaság* (The First Hungarian Soviet Republic) (Budapest: Szikra, 1949), 3.

erect a sepulchre commemorating the martyrs of 1919.[13] The party leadership began preparations for a celebration of the 30th anniversary of the First Hungarian Soviet Republic on 2 February 1949 at a meeting of the secretariat. The political guidelines they composed suggested the promotion of ceremonies that espoused the legacy of 1919 for the 1949 Hungarian state: 'The Hungarian People's Democracy guided by the Hungarian Workers' Party is the successor to the traditions of the Hungarian Soviet Republic, follows its struggles and realizes its objectives.'[14] The document accepted by the Secretariat evoked the memory of 1919 to define the meaning of the 'people's democracy', the postwar regimes of Eastern Europe dominated by Communist parties.

From an ideological point of view, for the Eastern European Communist parties, including that of Hungary, the major issue of the postwar transformation was the definition of the concept of 'people's democracy'. Communists usually understood people's democracies as transitory state formations on the long road towards the final goal of socialism. However, the exact duration of this transition remained unclear until the beginning of the Cold War. Party leaders and ideologists debated whether it had to be interpreted as a protosocialist state of workers and peasants pursuing the tasks of democratic transformation (a means of slow and peaceful development towards socialism), or simply a not-yet socialist transitory phase (the form of various 'national roads' to socialism). However, the politics of East-Central European Communist parties were fundamentally transformed after their meeting in Poland on 22 September 1947, when they decided to found Cominform. This new organization, which emerged in the context of an allegedly increasing American threat to the USSR and the Soviet objective to construct a politically sympathetic bloc in East-Central Europe, was basically a means of Soviet control in East-Central European Communist politics. During the meeting, the Soviet leadership urged its allies to increase their dominance over home politics and to step up their attempts to gain power. Whereas the Polish and the Yugoslav Communists could represent themselves as models, others were criticized for believing that participation in coalition governments automatically meant 'people's democracy' and a peaceful road to socialism. People's democracies, according to Stalin himself, were means to exterminate the bourgeoisie; hence these functioned as genuine dictatorships of the proletariat.[15] The term 'dictatorship of the proletariat' referred to the transitory state formation leading from capitalism to socialism in classical Marxist language; a period

---

13 MDP Central Organs, Secretariat, MOL M-KS 276-54/26, 3, 20.
14 MDP Central Organs, Secretariat, MOL M-KS 276-54/28, 13–14.
15 Report on the 22 September 1947 meeting of the Cominform, Hungarian Communist Party, Politburo (3 October 1947), PIL 274/3/112, 5–36; Vladislav M. Zubok and Constantine Pleshakov, *Inside the Kremlin's Cold War: From Stalin to Khrushchev* (Cambridge, MA/London: Harvard University Press, 1996), 125–37; Joseph Rothschild, *Return to Diversity: A Political History of East Central Europe since World War II* (New York: Oxford University Press, 1989), 125–32; Richard J. Crampton, *Eastern Europe in the Twentieth Century* (London: Routledge, 1994), 255–60; George Schöpflin, *Politics in Eastern Europe, 1945–1992* (Oxford: Blackwell, 1993), 57–74. On Hungary, see: Ignác Romsics, *Hungary in the 20th Century* (Budapest: Corvina, 1999), 235–7; Lajos Izsák, *Polgári pártok és programjaik Magyarországon 1944–1956* (Pécs: Baranya Megyei Könyvtár, 1994), 115–16.

when the working class had to oppress its bourgeois class enemies in order to secure the victory of revolution for the sake of the entire society.

József Révai, who delivered a report on the Hungarian Communist Party at the Cominform meeting, was uncertain about the future political development of Hungary: he worried whether she would become a bourgeois or a people's democracy. Zhdanov himself, who was member of Stalin's closest team as chief Soviet ideologist shaping cultural policy during the 1950s, reported Révai's misgivings about the future of Hungary to Stalin on 24 September. Furthermore, a Soviet Ministry of Foreign Affairs report criticized the Hungarian Communist Party for nationalist deviations, sectarianism and its perceived underestimation of the power of class enemies in a report of December 1947.[16] In order to refute these criticisms, it was crucial for the Hungarian party leaders to demonstrate their faithfulness to the Soviet principles.[17] In a meeting of party cadres in January 1948, János Kádár, secretary of the Budapest Party Committee and deputy to the general secretary, claimed that Hungary was following the road to socialism as a trustworthy 'people's democracy'. Yet, the Hungarian Communists were repeatedly criticized by Soviet party leaders for deviating towards 'petit bourgeois' ideologies, myths of 'democratic socialism' and the 'Third Way', and for not taking seriously the leading role of workers and the fight against right-wing Social Democrats in April as well as in June, when the Soviet party leaders reviewed the draft program declaration of the new unified workers' party in Hungary.[18] In June 1948, following the removal from power of those peasant party politicians who opposed Communist dominance, the Hungarian Communist Party absorbed the independent Social Democratic Party, and hence took virtually all political and administrative power into its hands. Reflecting Soviet expectations, the newly unified congress of the Communist and Social Democratic parties accepted a declaration that clearly stated that the people's democracy was equivalent to the power of the working class.[19] Nevertheless, the difficulties of the Hungarian Communist leadership did not fade away as Cominform condemned the politics of the Yugoslav Communist Party as a nationalist deviation on 29 June 1948. Mátyás Rákosi was to give a speech

---

16 'Zhdanov's note to Stalin about Révai's report (24 September 1947)', in *Moszkvának jelentjük… Titkos dokumentumok 1944–1948*, ed. Lajos Izsák and Miklós Kun (Budapest: Századvég, 1994), 229–30; 'Information report on the Hungarian Communist Party to Stalin (9 December 1947)', in *Moszkvának jelentjük*, 241–8.
17 In this regard, the chapter can be read as a case study on the Sovietization of East-Central European historiographies. See, for instance, the collective volume: Balázs Apor, Péter Apor and Arfon Rees, eds, *The Sovietization of Eastern Europe: New Perspectives on the Postwar Period* (Washington, DC: New Academia Press, 2008), esp. 235–83.
18 'Baranov's letter to Suslov about the name of the planned unified workers' party in Hungary (3 April 1948)', in *Moszkvának jelentjük*, 255–6; 'Comments on the program declaration of the Hungarian Workers' Party (1 June 1948)', in *Moszkvának jelentjük*, 267–70.
19 The ideological discussion on the concept of the people's democracy, although it provided an apology for late Kádárism, is summed up accurately by Bálint Szabó, *Az 'ötvenes évek'. Elmélet és politika a szocialista építés első időszakában Magyarországon 1948–1957* (Budapest: Kossuth, 1986), 10–12. On Kádár's role, see Tibor Huszár, *Kádár János politikai életrajza. 1912–1956*, vol. 1 (Budapest: Szabad Tér-Kossuth, 2003), 123–5.

about this resolution to the Hungarian party leadership the next day, emphasizing the inevitability of war with capitalist elements during the transition to socialism. Other party leaders called attention to the importance of the indivisible unity of the international Communist movement, a development which was to lead to a more general criticism of ideas about 'national roads to Communism'.[20] The Polish Workers' Party had already denied the existence of a particular 'Polish way' by September that year, and was soon followed by the Hungarian general secretary, who claimed that there was no 'Hungarian way' in November. However, when in mid-December the congresses of both the Polish and Bulgarian Communist parties declared that the people's democracy was equivalent to the dictatorship of the proletariat – assertions apparently confirmed by Stalin himself – the Hungarian Communists began to lose their sense of security. The second in command, chief economic politician Ernő Gerő, who took part in the Polish congress, sent a letter to his comrades immediately after the party meeting, demanding that they follow the Polish example. Gerő argued that the idea of the people's democracy was a particular type of the dictatorship of the proletariat, which, although it was not Soviet in form, would come into existence with the support of the already existing Soviet system. Though there were debates concerning the precise ideological formulation, the Hungarian party leadership agreed to follow Stalin's definition.[21] The new concept was introduced into Hungarian political discourse through Mátyás Rákosi's editorial published in the party's daily on 16 January 1949.[22] On 5 and 6 March, the meeting of the Central Leadership (the Central Committee) argued for improvement of the dictatorship in order to bring the structure of the state and political order closer to the Soviet type. On this occasion, Révai emphasized the importance of Stalin's instructions in recognizing that the dictatorship of the proletariat is not a stage in the construction of socialism to be skipped over.[23]

Paradoxically, 1919, an event largely forgotten by Hungarian society and mostly hitherto dismissed by the Communist leadership, came to provide the best opportunity to prove that the emerging Communist regime in Hungary was a genuine dictatorship of the proletariat. Although the party's daily openly declared the First Hungarian Soviet Republic a dictatorship of the proletariat first in 1948, the 30th anniversary of the first Hungarian Communist state was in fact the first real opportunity for Hungarian Communists to testify that their own system equalled the criteria set by the Soviets for the postwar Eastern European regimes.[24] The comparison of the two periods made it possible to argue on the basis of empirical evidence that the Hungarian people's democracy in fact functioned as a dictatorship of the proletariat.

---

20 Rákosi's report on the resolution of the Cominform (30 June 1948), MDP Central Organs, Central Leadership, MOL M-KS 276/52/2, 2–20.
21 Szabó, *Az 'ötvenes évek'*, 21–32.
22 Mátyás Rákosi, 'A népi demokrácia néhány problémájáról' (On a few problems of the people's democracy), SZN, 16 January 1949.
23 József Révai, 'Népi demokráciánk fejlődéséről és a proletárdiktatúra kérdéséről' (On the development of our people's democracy and the question of the dictatorship of the proletariat), *Pártmunkás* 5 (March 1949): 15; Szabó, *Az 'ötvenes évek'*, 34.
24 'A magyar kommün emlékére', SZN, 21 March, 1948.

Remembering the First Hungarian Soviet Republic was necessary in the sense that 'we pursue the same fight we began then and our people's democracy basically has the same function that the Hungarian Soviet Republic had: that of the dictatorship of the proletariat constructing socialism'.[25] Official historiography was primarily intended to demonstrate that the First Hungarian Soviet Republic had been the first follower of the Russian socialist revolution. The luxuriously illustrated publication released for the 30th anniversary, for example, begins with Mátyás Rákosi's large portrait that depicts the general secretary as people's commissar of the first proletarian state. His picture is accompanied by those of the leaders of the Russian Bolsheviks: Lenin and Stalin, respectively. The first chapter of the book is titled 'Lenin and Stalin show the way'. The album contains an article by a leading Hungarian Communist historian, who cites Lenin while claiming that Hungary stands the closest to the Soviet Union. Apart from Rákosi, the publication evokes Tibor Szamuely, the leader of the Hungarian Red Terror, and refers to his exploits as a revolutionary hero who flew from Budapest to Moscow to meet Lenin and establish close personal connections with the two Soviet republics.[26]

The First Hungarian Soviet Republic, evoked to demonstrate the actual socialist character of the new Communist regime, became a means of shedding light on concepts such as 'people's democracy' and the 'dictatorship of the proletariat'. Communist historians and ideologists looked for those features of the First Hungarian Soviet Republic that equated to those of the newer Communist regime. Hungarian Communists, while Sovietizing national history, represented the first Hungarian Soviet regime as the *praefiguratio* of a postwar Communist state. According to this conception, while the 1919 dictatorship of the proletariat demonstrated aspects of Communism, these had only appeared in underdeveloped forms. Thus, the First Hungarian Soviet Republic, 'in its brief existence acted according to the function and vocation of the dictatorship of the proletariat. It created what our people's democracy, which also has the function of the dictatorship of the proletariat, creates in incommensurable domestic and international conditions, by the direction of the incommensurably more developed and mature Communist party, and by the leadership of incommensurably more experienced Communists.'[27] László Réti, director of the Institute for Party History represented the Soviet Republic, then argues:

> The Soviet Republic, which was the Third Hungarian Republic, held the Russian Soviet state up as its model. Our people's democracy, which is the Fourth Hungarian Republic, thanks not only its existence to the Soviet Union: the secure basis and support of its independence and peace is the great Soviet Union and its wise leader, Stalin.
>
> The Red Army of the Soviet Republic fought with weapons against the imperialism of the Entente. The army of our people's democracy guards in arms our independence and freedom and it is the guarantee of our peaceful work of construction.
>
> The Soviet Republic appropriated the land, the factories and the banks. Our people's democracy proceeds surely towards the entire liquidation of exploitation and the creation

---

25 SZN, 22 March 1949.
26 *A Magyar Tanácsköztársaság 1919* (Budapest: Szikra, 1949).
27 Réti, *A Magyar Tanácsköztársaság*, 27.

of the socialist society by the realization of land reform and the development of the farmers' cooperative movement, and by the nationalization of the banks and factories.

The Soviet Republic took care to raise the level of welfare of the workers. Our people's democracy regularly raises the standard of living of the workers and guarantees their cultural improvement by rebuilding the ruined country, by the creation of good currency, by the execution of the three years plan of country building and by the realization of the new five-year plan for the national economy.[28]

In 1949, for these Hungarian Communist interpreters of the past, a form of hierarchical historical representation that sought analogies in the past in order to provide orientation for the present was available in the already established genres of contemporary Soviet history. The mode of representing the past by the means of historical archetypes (*typoi*) was a dominant form of archaic Communist historiography until the mid-1950s.[29] In the first years following the Russian Revolution the depiction of the past occurred outside the historical profession to a significant degree. The principal reasons for this were both the lack of human and material resources available for research and scholarship, and, at the same time, state support for historical festivals and celebrations that replaced historians' interpretations and developed into a powerful new form of representing the past. The structure of these historical dramas based on popular culture was not shaped by the continuous narrative flow of historical time, but by sequences of independent episodes addressing apparently similar themes. Performances showed selected scenes of the revolutionary past.[30]

Parallel to this, the role of historical science – controlled ever more tightly by the party – changed as well. The leadership of the party expected historical writing to provide direct support for political tasks: historical interpretation was thus restricted to the explication of certain ideal social formations that were constructed according to political considerations.[31] From the middle of the 1930s, the politics of the party turned towards the amplification of patriotic emotions, and historical research focused on a few patriotic topics like the early Russian state formations or the reign of Ivan the Terrible and Peter the Great. These subjects attracted the interest of scientific organizations and policymakers, as in them the imperfect – yet characteristic – attempts of the centralized Russian state organization were recognized. These past phenomena were considered the historical archetypes of the Stalinist Soviet centralized state. Historical writing emphasized the reign of Ivan the Terrible as the period which saw the expansion of the Russian empire, the penetration into the Baltics, the creation of the secret police and

---

28 Ibid., 25.
29 Bernd Uhlenbruch, 'The Annexation of History: Eisenstein and the Ivan Grozny Cult of the 1940s', in *The Culture of the Stalin Period*, ed. Hans Günther (London: MacMillan, 1990), 266–87; John Barber, *Soviet Historians in Crisis, 1928–1932* (New York: Holmes and Meier Publishers, 1981), vii.
30 James von Geldern, *Bolshevik Festivals, 1917–1920* (Berkeley/Los Angeles/London: University of California Press, 1993), 112–13, 162–3.
31 On the first five decades of Soviet historiography the standard work today is still Konstantin F. Shteppa, *Russian Historians and the Soviet State* (New Brunswick: Rutgers University Press, 1962).

the resolute elimination of rivals. Peter the Great was represented as an organizer of the state who improved industry, the army and fleet, and generated a modern bureaucracy.[32] Events and figures of the past became the *typoi* of the anti-German struggle and its leader, Stalin. The general secretary himself established this connection in a radio speech on 7 November 1941: 'May you be inspired in this war by the courageous figures of our great ancestors.'[33] The Soviet leader then went on to refer to Nevsky (who won the battle against the Teutonic Order of Knights), Donskoy (who beat the Tatars), Suvorov (the famous general of Catherine the Great) and Kutuzov (Napoleon's victorious adversary).

The demand to construe historical prefigurations determined the shape of narrative representation. Historical representation of this type was interested in identifying and enumerating specific features that rendered historical interpretation as a sort of analysis of individual signs. Thus, it did not connect the events of the past according to causality, but compared them based upon their recurrent characteristics.[34] It was as if Communist historians acted according to the logic of sixteenth-century scientists, who had contemplated the order of the world and discovered that things were connected by a system of correspondences, revealed by various signs. Knowledge, thus, is formed by looking for signs and detecting correspondences.[35] Communists represented the past not as a straightforward road leading to the present, but as a series of distinct and conclusive episodes. The course of Hungarian history was interpreted a constantly recurring fight for freedom and independence from German imperial aspirations, which culminated in the revolution of 1848. In official historiography, Mód's *400 Years of Struggle* became an important presence in public discourse on the past. Mód connected sixteenth-century anti-Habsburg Protestantism, the participation of seventeenth-century Transylvanian protestant princes and armies in the wars of religion, the early eighteenth-century anti-Habsburg revolt of Prince Ferenc Rákóczi and the war of independence in 1848–49 into one continuous thread that allegedly determined the course of Hungarian history. In Mód's reasoning, this history was characterized by a constant tension between the popular classes, who remained the resolute forces of national independence and democratic transformation, and the ruling classes, who were always ready to compromise for their own particular class interests and abandon the national and popular cause. Nonetheless, with the rise of Communists, according to Mód, the goals of democratic transformation and national independence were inherently bound together and were eventually fulfilled

---

32 David Brandenberger, *National Bolshevism: Stalinist Mass Culture and the Formation of Modern Russian National Identity, 1931–1956* (Cambridge, MA/London: Harvard University Press, 2002), 29–58; Maureen Perry, *The Cult of Ivan the Terrible in Stalin's Russia* (London/New York: Palgrave, 2001), 85–105; Nicholas V. Riasanovsky, *The Image of Peter the Great in Russian History and Thought* (New York/Oxford: Oxford University Press, 1985), 255–90.
33 Nina Tumarkin, *The Living and the Dead* (New York: Basic Books, 1994), 63. See also Matthew P. Gallagher, *The Soviet History of World War II: Myths, Memories, and Realities* (Westport: Greenwood Press, 1976), 52–7.
34 See Rudolf Bultmann, 'Ursprung und Sinn der Typologie als hermeneutischer Methode', *Theologische Literaturzeitung* 4–5 (1950): 206–12.
35 Michel Foucault, *The Order of Things: An Archaeology of the Human Sciences* (New York: Vintage Books, 1994), 17–34.

in 1945, thanks to the advance of the Soviet Red Army that finally crushed the forces of the German reactionary classes.[36]

This particular historical conception emerged during the 1930s as part of Soviet attempts to form an international sociopolitical coalition against fascist dictatorships and provide popular backing for leftist politics. In this new ideological outlook, national interests and identity were presented as under threat from fascist expansionist and colonialist aspirations, whereas, in turn, the Communist parties were presented as the vanguard of nationally motivated defensive and patriotic movements. Communist intellectuals and ideologists began to rewrite national mythologies to construct progressive myths composed of series of prefigurations of nationalist independence struggles that in most instances culminated in the glory of the respective Communist party concerned. These mythical propaganda histories remained powerful throughout World War II and up until the Communist takeovers, and during the 1950s acquired the new name of socialist patriotism, which was made up of nationalist historical mythology and populist class principles.[37]

In practice, these historical constructions consisted of a series of national victories or tragic downfalls. Czechoslovak Marxist historiography considered national history as a collection of progressive traditions. It highlighted the events of the Hussite and nineteenth-century pan-Slavic movements as prefigurations of the Gottwald regime. Jan Hus was reshaped as a political leader of a social radical party and Jan Žižka as the popular leader of social radical masses.[38] Bulgarian Communists reshaped national heroes Hristo Botev and Vasil Levski, who had fought against the Ottomans, as direct precedents of postwar Communist politics and as the prefigurations of partisan struggle, centralized political leadership and postwar retribution. The Russian–Turkish war, which had ended Ottoman rule in Bulgaria, was represented as the prelude to post-WWII liberation: as Bulgarian Communist propaganda argued, the Russians helped the Bulgarians in 1877–78 as they did in 1945, while the Germans opposed genuine independence in the nineteenth-century just as they suppressed Bulgarians during the war.[39] In East Germany, the traditions of the native labour movement were emphasized and were completed by a certain populist reading of national history, in which peasant uprisings like that of Thomas Münzer in the sixteenth century occupied a central position as prefigurations of the democratic people's Germany. Historical representations in the GDR typically constructed the confrontation between Münzer and Martin Luther as the prefiguration of the 1919 conflict between radical Communist and opportunist Social Democrat positions. East German historical culture also rediscovered the Battle of Teutoburg, when the ancient Germanic tribes defeated the Roman legions, and praised it

---

36 Mód, *400 év küzdelem az önálló Magyarországért*; Mevius, *Agents of Moscow*, 111–262; József Litkei, 'Borrowed Cloth' (MA Thesis, Central European University, Budapest, 1999), 54–61.
37 Martin Mevius, 'Reappraising Communism and Nationalism', *Nationalities Papers* 37 (July 2009): 377–400.
38 Maciej Górny, 'Past in the Future: National Tradition and Czechoslovak Marxist Historiography', *European Review of History* 10 (1) (2003): 103–14; Bradley F. Abrams, *The Struggle for the Soul of the Nation: Czech Culture and the Rise of Communism* (Lanham/Boulder/New York/Toronto/Oxford: Rowman & Littlefield, 2004), 89, 97–101.
39 Yannis Sygkelos, 'The National Discourse of the Bulgarian Communist Party on National Anniversaries and Commemorations (1944–1948)', *Nationalities Papers* 37 (July 2009): 425–42.

as a forecast of the realization of the German nation's true spirit: the tireless fight against oppression. In a similar manner, the 1952 reassessment of Prussian generals Scharnhorst and Gneisenau was an attempt to create historical analogies for the newly established East German People's Army. The search for historical analogies was rooted in the wartime period also in the German case. Stalinist propaganda and German Communists in exile used the example of the Napoleonic wars as the model of Russian–German brotherhood-in-arms in 1943. In turn, the tribesmen of Teutoburg, Münzer's peasant fighters, German soldiers in the anti-Napoleon alliance and the revolutionary rebels of 1848 were all represented as the prefigurations of the East German People's Army.[40]

Polish historians had greater difficulty in transforming Communist Party history into a national one. Stalinist historiography in Poland could establish no progressive national tradition except for the various Polish uprisings in the eighteenth and nineteenth centuries which, nevertheless, implied strong anti-Russian sentiments. The anniversary of the first Polish Constitution of 1793 (3 May), which should have functioned as the prefiguration of the postwar people's Poland, was celebrated by the Communist authorities only in 1945–46 since it recurrently evoked hostility against the Russians, who were accused of being complicit in the destruction of the Polish state in the eighteenth century. Polish Communists tried to rely on the analogy of the Battle of Grunwald (Tannenberg) in 1410 – the victory of Russian armies against Teutonic Knights – and claimed that, in fact, the battle had been fought by Poles and Russians as brothers-in-arms against the Germans, exactly as in 1944.[41] To a certain extent Romanian Stalinist historiography showed similar features before 1958, when Slavic influence and Russian–Romanian relations were emphasized and national heroes were suppressed – with the except of Bălcescu, who became the mythical prefiguration of Romanian revolution.[42]

The Soviet model of writing history was transferred to the political cultures of the satellite countries first of all by university education. History education was dominated by translations of Soviet material: first of all, Stalin's *A Short Course in the History of the CPSU*, but also by brochures and textbooks that had originally been prepared for party colleges in the USSR.[43] The ultimate authority in Soviet history education, Aleksei Vladmirovich Efimov's textbook on modern history, was published in Hungarian

---

40 Maciej Górny, 'Nation-Building in Marxist Historical Narratives in East-Central Europe in the 1950s', in *Historische Nationsforschung im geteilten Europa 1945–1989*, ed. Pavel Kolař and Miloš Řeznik (Cologne: SH Verlag, 2012), 141; Mary Fulbrook, *German National Identity after the Holocaust* (Cambridge: Polity, 1999), 87; Herfried Münkler, *Die Deutschen und ihre Mythen* (Berlin: Rowohlt, 2009), 441–3, 450, 452.
41 Górny, 'Nation-Building', 140–46; Górny, 'Marxist History of Historiography in Poland, Czechoslovakia and East Germany (late 1940s – late 1960s)', in *The Sovietization of Eastern Europe*, 260–3; Zdzisław Mach, 'Continuity and Change in Political Ritual', in *Revitalizing European Rituals*, ed. Jeremy Boissevain (London/New York: Routledge, 1992), 59–60; Izabella Main, 'Nemzetek Krisztusa: a lengyel nemzeti ünnepek állami és egyházi manipulációja 1944 és 1966 között', *Regio* 12 (Autumn 2001): 69–88; Jan C. Behrends, 'Nation and Empire: Dilemmas of Legitimacy during Stalinism in Poland (1941–1956)', *Nationalities Papers* 37 (July 2009): 448.
42 Lucian Boia, *History and Myth in Romanian Consciousness* (Budapest: CEU Press, 2001), 215–16.
43 J. V. Sztálin, *A Szovjetunió Kommunista (Bolsevik) Pártjának története (Rövid tanfolyam)* (Budapest: Szikra, 1949).

in 1949.[44] It was preceded by a textbook on the history of socialism and social struggles by German Communist historian Max Beer, who spent the years 1927–28 working in Soviet academia in Moscow. His book was first published in Hungarian in 1945.[45] Although professional history was not necessarily thoroughly impacted, these textbooks and leaflets were instrumental in shaping the political uses and public representations of history, since party activists and Communist leaders were trained reading them.

The canons of Stalinist Soviet historical representation were mediated by those historians and party activists who had lived in the USSR during the interwar period and contributed to the shaping of this particular tradition. In Hungary, Erzsébet Andics (president of the Historical Association since 1949, who had taught in the Lenin School of the Comintern together with Georgi Dimitrov and Wilhelm Pieck and in the Krasnodar antifascist school during the war), Dezső Nemes (a supervisor of historical publications on behalf of the party) and Erzsébet Fazekas (wife to second in hierarchy party leader Ernő Gerő) were crucial figures of the transfer. The most instrumental, however, was József Révai, who was key to the shaping of progressive national historical myths in terms of national unity, national independence and patriotic propaganda.[46] He had in fact started to reframe Communist historical templates in the 1930s, constructing a peasant-populist version of national independence movements based on the dialectic of master and serfs. Révai's main argument was that national independence always rested on the success of exploited classes fighting for progressive goals, whereas the ruling aristocratic class ordinarily betrayed the national cause due to their perception of social progress as threatening. Aladár Mód made Révai's concept manifest in *400 Years of Struggle*, which was first published in 1943. This radical populist version of historical conflicts dominated the Hungarian Communist politics of history after the end of the war through both the period of coalition government and Stalinist rule. Patriotic sentiments and the appropriation of national history were the chief concerns of Communist cultural propaganda, as Révai testified in his address delivered at the Second Congress of the Hungarian Workers' Party on 26 February 1951.[47]

Communist propaganda historians tried to interpret the history of the First Hungarian Soviet Republic as a chapter in the national struggle for freedom by highlighting the support of the urban working classes and poor agricultural workers, the Republic's ability to successfully wage a defensive war, and the readiness of the ruling classes to ally with foreign governments. The campaigns of the Red Army were interpreted as a patriotic war of independence against imperialist powers and neighbouring expansionist countries. The activity of former Hungarian political and social elites against the 1919 commune was condemned as an antipatriotic betrayal, presented as it was an attempt to lead the soldiers of foreign armies onto Hungarian soil. By contrast, the Hungarian workers' army

---

44 Aleksei Vladmirovich Efimov, *Az újkor története* (Budapest: Szikra, 1949).
45 Max Beer, *A szocializmus és a társadalmi harcok története* (Budapest: Népszava, 1945).
46 Árpád von Klimó, 'The Sovietization of Hungarian Historiography: Failures and Modification in the Early 1950s', in *The Sovietization of Eastern Europe*, 240–5; Ignác Romsics, *Clio bűvöletében: Magyar történetírás a 19–20. században* (Budapest: Osiris, 2011), 357–8, 376.
47 József Révai, 'Az MDP II. kongreszusán mondott beszéd' (Speech delivered at the 2nd congress of the HWP), in *Kulturális forradalmunk kérdései* (Issues in our cultural revolution) (Budapest: Szikra, 1952), 35–40; József Révai, *48 útján* (Following 48) (Budapest: Szikra, 1948).

was compared to the revolutionary troops of 1848 and referred to as their successors.[48] The history of the Soviet Republic was arranged into an easily recognizable narrative structure that was determined by ideological frameworks; it regularly began with a description of the influence of the Russian Revolution in 1917 and the defeat in the war. According to the texts, Hungarian hardships were compounded by the deprivation of workers' rights, the despotism of the public administration and general privation. All this was to revolutionize the masses: peace demonstrations were held, and workers were increasingly capable of organizing themselves, even into workers' councils (soviets). The authors of these historical interpretations, chiefly Rákosi and Réti, generally stated that although the Social Democrats had held the revolution back, the masses themselves had nevertheless attained their goal. Their narrative proceeded as follows: a 'bourgeois revolutionary government' – as they had it – was formed, led by Count Mihály Károlyi; the workers, however, wanted a socialist government and continued demonstrating for one; the 'Social Democrat bourgeois regime' therefore arrested the Communist leaders; this measure did not, however, prevent an increase in popular support for the Communists. It became impossible to govern the country and thus the once reluctant Social Democrats were forced into conceding that a dictatorship of the proletariat should be proclaimed. The fall of the regime 133 days later was not only attributed to the numerical superiority of the enemy; the destructive role of the Social Democrats – many of them negotiated with the Entente the possibility of a democratic republic, then formed the first government following the resignation of the Communist commissars – in ensuring the collapse of the socialist regime was never forgotten.[49]

Histories of the First Hungarian Soviet Republic usually framed their object of study not as a phenomenon in itself but always as a 'preliminary chapter' whose story anticipated the appearance of something real that would only emerge in the future. Mátyás Rákosi, for example, stated that 'The First Hungarian Soviet Republic forms one of the most important chapters in the nation's history. […] In spite of its defeat it was a preparation for, a precursor to and a dress rehearsal for the current victories of our people.'[50] That is to say, the present was not caused by the past. The Soviet Republic of 1919 was not connected to the Rákosi regime by continuity, it was not presented as the cause or antecedent of the party state as it emerged in 1948. This was particularly the case in school textbooks, which by nature had to organize their material into distinct episodes or units: all of them concluded their accounts on the dictatorship of the proletariat with a description of its defeat and used a framework to narrate European history that gave no sense of continuity between 1919 and 1949. The chapters that followed the history of the proletarian state discussed the 'counterrevolutionary epoch' and WWII. The textbook

---

48 Aladár Mód, *400 év küzdelem az önálló Magyarországért* (Budapest: Szikra, 1951), 404–15.
49 Mátyás Rákosi, *A Kommunisták Magyarországi Pártjának megalakulása és harca a proletárforradalom győzelméért. A Magyar Tanácsköztársaság* (The foundation of the Party of Communists in Hungary and its struggle for the victory of the revolution of the proletariat. The First Hungarian Soviet Republic) (Budapest: Szikra, 1948); Réti, *A Magyar Tanácsköztársaság* and *A Tanácsköztársaság 30. évfordulója* (The 30th anniversary of the First Hungarian Soviet Republic) (Budapest: Budapest Irodalmi Intézet, 1949).
50 Rákosi, *A Kommunisták Magyarországi Pártjának*, 60.

issued to secondary schools isolated the history of 1919 from its aftermath in Hungary by inserting between them a section on European history during the interwar period.[51]

2

The ceremonies of the 30th anniversary lasted for two days. The first day, 20 March, was dedicated to cultural events. At ten o'clock in the morning Árpád Szakasits, president of the republic, inaugurated the memorial exhibition of the First Hungarian Soviet Republic; subsequently, at noon, a 'memorial table' dedicated to Jenő Landler (commander-in-chief of the Hungarian Red Army) was unveiled at the ceremonial renaming of a street. The primary aim of these two events was to familiarize their audience with the historical past, to make the knowledge obtained of the past public. In his inaugural speech, Szakasits emphasized the effort that the organizers had put into gathering the documents and mementos of the Soviet Republic; the Communist Party of Hungary then urged, 'Let hundreds of thousands of people visit this exhibition!'[52] A report in a contemporary newsreel on the exhibition highlights exactly this aspect: the film shows visitors walking by boards fixed to the wall, which display posters, newspapers and documents; the visitors are directly encountering an abundance of original historical records.[53] The exhibition was completed by a cinema showing original documentaries on the First Hungarian Soviet Republic.[54] The audience at the inauguration of the memorial table, then, could learn about Jenő Landler, 'the brave, self-denying leader of the Hungarian working class', who 'played a great role in the victories of the Hungarian Red Army and in the reorganization of the Communist movement after the defeat of the Soviet Republic'.[55] In contrast, on the following day political ceremonies took place in which the leaders of the community were expected to express their own relationship to the republic. In the morning, the parliament, the highest representative organ of the nation, pronounced definitively that it considered the First Hungarian Soviet Republic one of the most important occurrences of national history. 'The representatives of the parties organized themselves into the People's Front and presented themselves in great numbers at the Monday meeting of parliament. The majority of the representatives took their seats in dark clothes and ceremonial mood.' After the commemorative words, 'The representatives of the parties of the People's Front took to their feet and celebrated the Soviet Republic and its proletarian heroes with a long applause.'[56]

These ceremonies drew clear boundaries between two kinds of commemorative acts. Whereas the program of the first day was able to establish knowledge of the past, the

---

51 Gusztáv Heckenast, Béla Karácsony, Klára Feuer and László Zsigmond, *Történelem VIII* (for primary schools) (Budapest: Tankönyvkiadó, 1948) (a revised second edition was published in 1950), 190–91; and Endre Kovács, Gyula Simon and Béla Bellér, *Történelem IV* (for secondary schools) (Budapest: Tankönyvkiadó, 1950), 23–5, 62.
52 SZN, 20 March 1949, 3.
53 Newsreel 1949/55 in Magyar Nemzeti Filmarchívum (Hungarian National Film Archives), UMFI Records.
54 László Réti, 'Készüljünk márc. 21 megünneplésére' (Let's prepare to celebrate 21 March), *Pártmunkás* 5 (March 1949): 15.
55 SZN, 22 March 1949.
56 SZN, 22 March 1949.

events of the second day manifested the will of the present to remember. The exhibition on 20 March and the inauguration of the memorial table were rituals that described, with the help of the representation of 'objective knowledge', the Soviet Republic as an object of scholarly investigation which, therefore, belonged to the past and ceased to be an issue influencing political discussion – that is to say, an issue of the present. The exhibition hall displayed documents and photographs (i.e., facts) in rigidly arranged order, whereas the inauguration of the memorial table was an act of presenting the past to the public after obtaining knowledge about it. Consequently, the boundary between the two days of events indicated also the boundary between past and present. The past was clearly separated from the present, and the history of the First Hungarian Soviet Republic was represented as belonging to an irretrievable past. This did not mean, however, that the connection between past and present was diminished. The president of the republic pointed out in his opening speech that 'what began 30 years ago continues in complete glory now'.[57] Nonetheless, through the separation of the Soviet Republic as past, and as the will to remember of the present, the fact that their relationship was restored or created by the will of the present could be more readily emphasized. The representations of the past occurred on the less significant day – the eve of the anniversary – whereas at the height of the celebrations on the 21 March, the leaders demonstrated their intent to commemorate history. Thereby the real importance of the events and deeds of the past came from the present.

Although the meeting of the parliament in the morning of 21 March was the first political ritual that paid respect to the past, the ceremonial speech created only a vague connection between history and the community of remembrance. Imre Nagy's address pointed to the heroism of the struggles for the working class and for progress, and underlined the self-sacrificing nature of a battle which was often conducted against a numerically superior enemy, though he did not explicate the direct relevance of this struggle for the communities of remembrance.[58] The ceremony in the morning was followed by a ritual that honoured the martyrs of the Soviet Republic. The minister of interior, János Kádár, inaugurated the sepulchre for the heroes of the dictatorship of the proletariat. The ceremony was orchestrated as a solemn burial, in which posterity paid homage to those who had come before. The ceremonial meeting of the parliament, which declared the first commune a glorious and self-sacrificial struggle, provided the context for the burial rite by clarifying the idea that its successors could finally recognize the true significance of the past. In the funeral ceremony, which places the dead in their appropriate context, and closes the social and cultural process of death by marking an unambiguous border of living and dead, the so-called 'fighters' of the First Hungarian Soviet Republic were not only declared heroes, but also framed as 'dead souls' who eventually occupied their well-deserved places among the ancestors. 'A multitude of red flags were waving in the wind of the early spring over the graves, their mute dwellers testifying to their firm belief and faithfulness to the cause of the liberation of the

---

57 SZN, 20 March 1949.
58 SZN, 22 March 1949. On Nagy's speech see János M. Rainer, *Nagy Imre. Politikai életrajz. 1953–1958*, vol. 1 (Budapest: 1956-os Intézet, 1996), 376.

workers, when the red flags of revolution sank to the mud and the cruel White Terror, the murderous counterrevolution, was riding roughshod over Hungary.'[59]

Communists did not want to demonstrate that their regime originated from the First Hungarian Soviet Republic. On the contrary, they sought to manifest the glory of their present. On the one hand, the previous leaders of the Soviet Republic of 1919 who were honoured in 1949 filled no significant – if any – positions in the Rákosi regime. They were presented rather as, albeit respected, relics of a past era. On the other hand, leading figures of the Hungarian Workers' Party, who formed the younger second rank of Communists at the time, in reality played minor roles during the revolution of 1919. Nevertheless, they were honoured very highly in 1949. The fact that these persons represented the Rákosi regime rather than the proletarian regime of 1919 rendered it apparent that the ceremony did not glorify the past but the present. This intention was reinforced by the fact that on the honours list a prominent Communist economist, Jenő Varga, who was commissar of economy in the first Hungarian Soviet government, was replaced by Ernő Gerő, who was responsible for issues of economy in the Hungarian Workers' Party after 1945.[60]

According to Communists' self-perception, the Communist system after 1945 came into existence independently of the first proletarian state of 1919. The foundation of the second Communist regime was claimed to be a result of their own struggles either as antifascist resistance fighters or as clever and resolute revolutionary politicians during the democratic period between 1945 and 1948. The main cause of the foundation of the people's democracy of Hungary, however, was considered to be the victory of the USSR in the war: 'Lenin's prophecy was fulfilled in 1945, when we started to successfully realize the great initiative of 1919: the construction of socialism in our country.'[61] In their self-perception, Communists made a new start in 1945, even if the initiative had predecessors. This was the only connection between the two epochs of 1919 and 1945. As László Réti put it in 1949, 'This demonstrates the close relation between 21 March 1919 and 4 April 1945. In 1919 the Hungarian proletariat made a start on the journey that leads towards our liberation, the liquidation of class society and exploitation, and towards socialism. In 1945, the glorious Red Army of the Soviet Union liberated our country and made it possible for us to recommence our travels on this road and, this time, to arrive at its end.'[62]

The purpose of historical representation during classical Communism (roughly until the mid-1950s) was not to render particular interpretations of the past authentic, but rather to establish a particular form of temporal relationship. The problems that in 1945 lay before the victorious Communists with regards to their origins was very similar to the dilemmas faced by early Christianity: how to distance the new faith from its predecessors without denying important connections. For Christian theological thinking, the inclusion into scripture of the Old Testament, which documented the Jewish tradition before the birth of Jesus, was justified by the fact that it provided a prefiguration and precedent for the one central and truly meaningful story, that of redemption. Events and prophecies

---

59 SZN, 22 March 1949.
60 MOL M-KS 276/54/34.
61 Réti, *A Magyar Tanácsköztársaság*, 27.
62 Réti, *A Magyar Tanácsköztársaság*, 27.

included in the Old Testament foreshadowed – at a lower level and in an imperfect form – the fulfilment of the divine plan that the story of Jesus Christ embodied.[63] The forty years of wandering of the Jews in the desert foreshadowed the challenges that awaited early Christian communities.[64] For Christians, the true message of the Bible is the New Testament, the real significance of which becomes visible through the *praefiguratio* that appear in the Old Testament: the stories of the Jews are important only because these foreshadowed and prepared for – *preparatio evangelica* – the fundamental plan of God to redeem humankind.[65] According to the tradition of biblical exegesis, the New Testament is the key for the Old Testament, or, in other words, the New Testament is hidden in and reveals itself through the Old Testament.[66] The essential element of typological comparison is not the synchronic correspondence of distinct elements. The connection of *typos* and *antitypos* is temporal: it is based upon the juxtaposition of beginning and end that leads to hierarchical relation, which in turn depicts historical prefigurations.[67] The *praefiguratio* as a historiographical figure generates a picture of the past that has a peculiar impact on the present: this mode of depiction represents the state of the present perfect, desirable and final.

For Communists – who considered their takeover the fulfilment of history – the demonstration of the continuity of Communism, in order to assert their victory as the outcome of the historical process, was not as important as the identification of prefigurations of their system in the past in order to induce pro-regime political activism.[68] Victorious Communism – approximately 1949–56 in East-Central Europe – lived in a constant fever of presentist activism and, hence, exercised power with the continuous assignment of tasks and the mobilization of the population to solve them.[69] The power of the centralized system was based on sustained intervention. The party intended to be present in every sphere of life, presenting itself as an institution that understood all problems, could uncover all solutions and ensure the duty of every citizen to reach those goals. Communist parties implemented these techniques of mobilization through the 'campaign': a form of mobilization that implied close direction and observance by the

---

63 See Amos Funkenstein, 'Collective Memory and Historical Consciousness', *History and Memory* 2 (Summer, 1989): 14. On the historical consciousness in the Bible, see also Karl Löwith, *Meaning in History* (Chicago: University of Chicago Press, 1949), 182–90.
64 Early Church fathers interpreted the story of Jonah in a similar way as the *praefiguratio* of the sufferings of the Messiah. In this sense, the three days that the prophet of the Old Testament spent in the stomach of the whale foreshadowed the three days of the wandering of Christ in Hell between the Crucifixion and Resurrection: Michael André Bernstein, *Foregone Conclusions: Against Apocalyptic History* (Berkeley/Los Angeles/London: University of California Press, 1994), 3.
65 Rudolf Bultmann, *History and Eschatology* (Edinburgh: Edinburgh University Press, 1975). On this problem, see also Carlo Ginzburg, 'Distance and Perspective: Two Metaphors', in *Wooden Eyes: Nine Reflections on Distance* (New York: Verso, 2001), 143–8.
66 Northop Frye, *The Great Code: The Bible and Literature* (London: Harcourt, 1982).
67 Gerhard von Rad, 'Typological Interpretation of the Old Testament', in *Essays in Old Testament Hermeneutics*, ed. Claus Westermann (Richmond: SCM, 1963), 17–39.
68 Bultmann, *History and Eschatology*, 38–73.
69 'Presentism' is François Hartog's concept: *Régimes d'historicité: Présentisme et expériences du temps* (Paris: Seuil, 2003).

centralized power.⁷⁰ The planned economy itself fulfilled this function: the 'mobilization economy' was considered a struggle against backwardness and the enemy. The construction of socialism was presented as a long military campaign.⁷¹ Communist parties launched 'productivity competitions' to increase industrial as well as agricultural production. The Communist Party also capitalized on the ardent longing for activity of women who had had limited opportunity to engage in public life before the war. Women were sent out onto the streets in order to fight inflation and the black market, to demonstrate for prisoners of war or to mobilize for children's summer camps.⁷² In this way society was forced to live in a permanent activity which was focused on and directed towards the present.

In this sociopolitical order, 'culture and cultural work has to be conceived as a major field and task of battle', as a young Communist functionary of the Ministry for People's Education put it on 27 January 1950, at the National Meeting for People's Education. Culture was seen neither a means of leisure nor self-training, but a weapon for the party in the struggle for Communism: 'For us neither the dance movement, nor the choir movement, nor the theatre movement, nor the puppet theatres are goals in themselves, for us all these movements – including all the means of cultural work from lectures to the elimination of analphabetism [through the education of previously disadvantaged adults to obtain reading and writing skills] – are weapons in our struggle for realizing and supporting the politics of our party.'⁷³ Literature was regarded a special field of agitation and propaganda; its goal was to teach ideological tenets and political decisions, to illustrate achievements and to mobilize for tasks.⁷⁴ The Second Congress of the Hungarian Workers' Party articulated these tasks as follows: 'It is a must that our authors and historians evoke the glorious fights of these great heroes of the Hungarian people in the form of popular historical novels, short stories and historical treatises, in order to teach the new generation how to live, work and fight for the freedom of the Hungarian people!'⁷⁵

Arriving from this perspective, the doyen of Hungarian Marxist historiography, Erik Molnár, defined the purpose of the new Hungarian historical research as follows: 'Finally, it has to be kept constantly in view that when we rewrite Hungarian history according to the aforementioned principles, our task is not only finally to reconstruct the Hungarian past faithfully, but also, and primarily, to support, by the means of historiography, the Hungarian present to prepare the Hungarian future, namely to construct socialism.'⁷⁶ On 6 June of the next year the scholar addressed the Hungarian congress of historians

---

70 István Rév, 'Uncertainty as a Technique of the Exercise of Power' (unpublished manuscript, 1989), 10.
71 János Kornai, *The Communist System* (Princeton: Princeton University Press, 1992), 59.
72 Andrea Pető, *Women in Hungarian Politics, 1945–1951* (Boulder: East European Monographs, 2003), 37–9, 47–50.
73 Géza Losonczy's address at the National Meeting for People's Education, 27 January 1950. György Kövér, *Losonczy Géza, 1917–1957* (Budapest: 1956-os Intézet, 1998), 189–90.
74 János M. Rainer, *Az író helye. Viták a magyar irodalmi sajtóban 1953–1956* (Budapest: Magvető, 1990), 14–15.
75 *Magyar Nemzet*, 29 February 1952, 5.
76 Erik Molnár, 'A magyar történetírás a felszabadulás óta; eredményei, hiányosságai és legsürgősebb feladatai' (Hungarian historiography since the liberation: Its shortages, achievements and most pressing tasks), *Társadalmi Szemle* 8 (January 1952): 55.

and spoke about the essence of science in socialism: 'It is a weapon in the struggle against enemies within and without and a force of education that teaches our people about true patriotism, proletarian internationalism and the correct application of the lessons of the past. Hungarian Marxist historiography is an important ideological means of forming the socialist future.'[77] The same point was made in the introduction to the first publication by a group of young historians: 'The aim of all of their scholarly work is to contribute to the construction of socialism in our country.'[78]

The political instructions document issued by the secretariat of the party for the 30th anniversary valued the importance of the revolutionary tradition as follows: 'Learning from the mistakes made in the past, the Hungarian Workers' Party secures its leading position [...]. Based on the unity of the working-class principles, it laid the foundations of a solid alliance of workers and peasants by distributing the land of the big estates for the working peasantry and finishing off the old ruling classes and the agents of Western imperialism.'[79] Thus, 'the revolutionary experience of 1919 has played an exceptionally important role in the immense achievements of today'.[80] Evoking this past fulfilled a special function during the 1950s. The past was interesting only if it could directly aid the present. History was conceived of as a guide to contemporary issues – that is to say, history was treated in the sense of the classical proverb: *historia magistra vitae* (history as the teacher of life).[81]

These slogans were bound to concrete experiences, as the then minister of the interior, János Kádár, proclaimed in the ceremony of mourning devoted to the executed leaders of the First Hungarian Soviet Republic in the Kerepesi Cemetery: 'We have to remain faithful to the working people, to the working class as they were. We have to be courageous and act without hesitation as they did. We have to be unrelenting towards the enemies of the working class in the way the bourgeoisie was towards them.'[82] Imperatives of action were also articulated at the inauguration of the memorial tablet of Jenő Landler, commander-in-chief of the Red Army in 1919: 'We honour Jenő Landler's bellicose

---

77 SZN, 7 June 1953, 3.
78 Endre Gaál, *A szegedi munkásság harca a Tanácsköztársaságért, 1917–1919* (The fight of the workers of Szeged for the Soviet Republic, 1917–1919) (Budapest: Szikra, 1956), 7. The conceived purpose of historical scholarship was well defined during the Molnár debate in 1950. Erik Molnár was a distinguished Communist historian who composed an innovative interpretation of medieval Hungarian history based on the Marxist principles of historical laws of the productive forces. His work was strongly criticized by party officers as it did not serve the current struggles of the party. Litkei, 'Borrowed Cloth', 52–5. See also SZN, 7 November 1951 and 6 June 1953.
79 MDP Central Organs, Secretariat, MOL M-KS 276/54/28.
80 SZN, 22 March 1949.
81 History, according to the great ancient orator Cicero could be capitalized on as a collection of examples that might instruct the speaker as well as the audience. Although Christian religious philosophy imagined history as a linear process, it maintained the relevance of considering the past as exemplary. Church authors like Isidor of Seville, Bede the Venerable or Melanchthon accepted the potential of both biblical and heathen histories to be instructive for believers. In the eighteenth century one can still encounter formulations like this. For instance, Frederick the Great believed, too, that history was a school for rulers. Reinhart Koselleck, *Futures Past* (Cambridge, MA/London: Harvard University Press, 1985), esp. 3–27, 96–104, 202–12, 267–88.
82 SZN, 22 March 1949, 2.

revolutionary memory in the best way by further strengthening our party, increasing the power and readiness for struggle of the people.'[83]

This form of remembrance was reflected in the slogans issued for the 30th anniversary. A few of them referred back to history and connected it to current tasks:

> In the glorious spirit of the Soviet Republic, led by the working class, we construct the socialist Hungary!
> Following the revolutionary traditions of the glorious Hungarian Red Army, we strengthen our people's army which is there to guard the power of the workers and the independence of our nation!
> We have learnt from 1919: traitors, agents of the enemy, have no place in the party of the working class! We protect the worker–peasant alliance as our greatest precious treasure!

Others emphasized the agenda of the present without even a vague reference to the Soviet Republic:

> Forward for the victory of socialism under Lenin's and Stalin's flag![84]

The political instructions in the proposal for the 30th anniversary capitalized on the occasion to enumerate the tasks the party and the people's democracy were facing, after stating that the regime followed the way of the First Hungarian Soviet Republic:

> The people's democracy is proceeding surely on the way to constructing socialism by healing the wounds caused by the war and fascism, by mercilessly oppressing the enemies of the people, by raising the productivity of work to a level unreachable in capitalism, by a gradual realization of the social production in the agriculture that is a precondition of constructing socialism, by unifying the whole working people in the New Front of Independence for peaceful construction and for bellicose defence of the homeland.

As a final conclusion, however, it was stated: 'The guarantee of further advances on the way to socialism is our party, which has become stronger and united following the latest revision of membership and, headed by Mátyás Rákosi, the hero commissar of the First Soviet Republic, leads the Hungarian working people under Lenin's and Stalin's flag.'[85]

This general call materialized in initiatives such as that advertised on the cover page of *Pártmunkás* (Party worker), a weekly for Communist activists, published on 30 March 1949. On the front page is a poster-like image of a metalworker with hammer and red flag, with a factory and marching proletarians in the background (Fig. 1). The illustration contains a call: 'Forward workers! A message from Diósgyőr'. Diósgyőr was one of the largest steel factories in modern Hungary with a sizable workforce and strong radical

---

83 SZN, 22 March 1949, 4.
84 MOL M-KS 276/54/34.
85 MOL M-KS 276/54/28.

Figure 1. 'Előre munkások!' (Forward workers!), *Pártmunkás*, 30 March 1949, cover page.

leftist commitments. The inscription on the image provides further instructions as to how to read its message: 'In 1919 and today!' Diósgyőr had been the scene of one of the greatest victories of the Hungarian Red Army in 1919, a fact mentioned in all histories of the Soviet Republic. The support of Diósgyőr's workers for the Red troops became a legendary element in these narratives. This context makes the intended message of the front page illustration clear: support the Communist cause with the same enthusiasm and self-sacrifice as in 1919. Nonetheless, the picture makes no explicit reference to the past: it depicts no events, prominent characters, figures or objects of 1919.[86]

The same conclusion could be drawn from *The Trial of Rákosi*, published in 1950. The book contains extensive material on Rákosi's second trial in 1935, when he was accused of committing horrible crimes as a commissar of the Soviet Republic. Although the representation of the trial provides an opportunity to evoke the first dictatorship of the proletariat in Hungary, the volume centres on Rákosi's activity both as a commissar and a revolutionary hero in court. It cites in length Rákosi's speeches and puts the trial into the context of the international campaign for his release. The purpose of the publication is not to remember the Soviet state, but to make the secretary general into a hero.

---

86 *Pártmunkás* 5 (March 1949), cover page. The plants of Diósgyőr are currently bankrupt and largely abandoned. The factory, instead of glorifying industrial modernity, nowadays is the symbol of poverty and economic collapse. Unemployment is high, while workers, instead of being the hard core of leftist progressive politics, voted predominantly for right-wing radicalism in the last national elections of 2010.

Figure 2. 'Rákosi Mátyás a Vörös Hadsereg élén' (Mátyás Rákosi heading the Red Army). Endre Kovács, Gyula Simon, Béla Bellér, *Történelem* IV (Budapest, Tankönyvkiadó, 1950), 27.

This glorification, however, is not conceived as an end in itself. Instead, the foreword claims that: 'The Institute for the History of the Workers' Movement publishes this book in the conviction that it will strengthen and inspire many hundreds of thousands of people to work and struggle, and the shining example of comrade Rákosi will encourage readers to more fully accomplish their tasks and promote the construction of socialist Hungary.'[87] In the subsequent years, contemporary leaders would gain respect by describing their historical commitment to Communist goals. Attention was called to the fact that Rákosi had devoted himself to the cause of revolution from his youth, and accounts of his military campaigns against the bourgeois armies were a favoured topic in newspapers of the time. The fact that he had been condemned by the interwar regime for illegal activities was interpreted as an attempt by the government to eliminate a prominent supporter of the Soviet Republic.[88]

An image in the secondary school textbook *Történelem IV* effectively demonstrates the way in which the party encouraged the reading of history (Fig. 2). The picture is entitled 'Mátyás Rákosi heading the Red Army'. The photo actually depicts the would-be general secretary in the foreground walking by the side of a marching Red Army unit. The

---

87 *A Rákosi-per* (Budapest: Szikra, 1950), 11. The cult of the Communist leaders could be interpreted as a means to mobilize the population. On Rákosi's cult: Balázs Apor, 'National Traditions and the Leader Cult in Communist Hungary in the early Cold War Years', *Twentieth Century Communism* 1 (2009): 50–71. Similar patterns could be detected in the Lenin cult during the 1920s. The figure of Lenin was evoked to help inspire children to learn more or workers to labour more productively. See Nina Tumarkin, *Lenin Lives!* (Cambridge, MA/London: Harvard University Press, 1983).
88 SZN, 21 March, 1951.

wording, however, implies that Rákosi had been the leader of the Red Army. Hereby, a tension is created between the representation of the image and the caption. One interpretation could be that the Communist Party was simply falsifying history in order to foster the cult of its leader. Nonetheless, a second reading is possible. On the one hand, the representation does not explicitly state that Rákosi had been the commander-in-chief of the army. On the other, it represents an actual event: the general secretary heading up the Red Army troops as a commissar. The tension between the photo and the caption here rather refers to a *probability* of events: Rákosi could have been the leader of the army due to his substantial personal qualities. The image calls attention to the present: by pointing out the outstanding abilities of the current leader, it emphasizes the significance of the current state of affairs. The primary value of evoking history is not the construction of authentic representations of the past, but rather the establishment of a set of temporal relationships that could contribute to the mobilization of present-day construction.

3

The commemorations of the 30th anniversary reached their zenith at the final event, the ceremonial meeting of the party activists of Greater Budapest. The personal presence of Mátyás Rákosi at this one event alone was a clear indication of its importance. Meanwhile, as the relationship with the past was becoming more obvious, the delay to declare unambiguously the exact nature of this connection further increased the tension of expectation:

> The benches of the Sportcsarnok had already been filled at around half past four, half an hour before the beginning of the ceremonial meeting of the party workers organized by the Party Committee of Greater Budapest of the HWP. Everybody knows each other, everybody knows the songs: the crowd sings constantly until five o'clock. The huge hall is decorated with images of comrades Lenin, Stalin, Rákosi, Landler, Szamuely, Togliatti, Mao Tse-tung and Thorez and is filled with the sounds of the marches of the Hungarian Soviet Republic.[89]

This tension came to its peak soon enough:

> At five o'clock comrades Rákosi and Szakasits, the Central Committee, the Communist members of the government, the fighters of the Soviet Republic, and the leaders of the Party Committee of Greater Budapest enter the hall. Comrade György Marosán, deputy of the general secretary, opens the ceremonial meeting, which greets with rhythmic applause Comrade Rákosi and then the members of the Politburo and the leaders of the Soviet Republic, with György Nyisztor, people's commissar of agriculture of the Soviet Republic, who is sitting next to comrade Rákosi.[90]

---

89 SZN, 22 March 1949, 3.
90 Ibid.

The first speaker was Marosán, originally a member of the Social Democrat Party, but ardent supporter of the Communist cause, who took one step towards a definition of the relationship: 'We do not only celebrate the First Hungarian Soviet Republic, but also consider it as guidance and example.'[91] At the same time, although this formulation was becoming more and more standard, he nevertheless refrained from explaining why the present could turn towards the past for instruction.

The duty to provide the long, protracted answer to the question of the exact connection between past and present fell to László Rudas, well-known member of the old party and important ideologue of the movement. The ceremonial meeting of party workers clarified that only the Communist Party could cross the border between past and present. As one speaker poetically posed it, 'What was the First Hungarian Soviet Republic if not the first act of what we are doing today?'[92] Apart from the rhetorical effect, this conveyed an important message: the grounds for turning towards the past were provided by the deeds of the present. The old Communist fighter stood above the audience, surrounded by his fellow travellers Marosán and Szakasits. Nonetheless, their presence was overshadowed by the much bigger portraits of Communist Party leader Rákosi and the commander of the Red Terror groups in 1919, Tibor Szamuely, which were hung behind the speakers. Behind them, the fighters of the First Hungarian Soviet Republic, György Lukács, Ferenc Münnich, György Nyisztor and Béla Szántó, all headed by Mátyás Rákosi, were sitting facing the audience. The visual arrangement of the ceremonial meeting juxtaposed the past and present fighters of the Communist cause, and meant that Rudas's message was reinforced by the party (Fig. 3).[93] In this regard the meeting of party workers was the ritual counterpart of the inauguration of the sepulchre a few hours before. Whereas in the Kerepesi Cemetery the past – the First Hungarian Soviet Republic – was buried, in the Hall of Sports the dictatorship of the proletariat was resurrected and brought into the present by the will of the Hungarian Workers' Party. It was not the past which left its heritage to the present, but the present had the right and the capacity to evoke the past if necessary. During this last ritual – frequently loaded with heightened emotions – the hierarchical relationship of past and present and the primacy of the present was intended to become a tangible experience for the audience. Presenting the image of the first republic as the prefiguration of the second was supposed to boost enthusiasm for activism in the present, and provide an identity for party workers through which – in the context of these ceremonies – they could virtually live through the events themselves.

Nonetheless, it was extraordinarily difficult to turn the history of the First Hungarian Soviet Republic into a comprehensible experience. Following the emergence of the Stalinist line, which had crystallized during bitter internal fights within the movement

---

91 Ibid.
92 Ibid.
93 Newsreel 1949/55 in Magyar Nemzeti Filmarchívum (Hungarian National Film Archives), UMFI Records. Historical Photographic Records of the Hungarian National Museum 477. ME/II/A, Box: Political Life: Anniversaries 1949–1956. Registry no.: Hungarian Labour Movement Museum 86.53, 86.55, 86.56, 69.1056, 69.1057, 78.854.

Figure 3. The 30th anniversary of the First Hungarian Soviet Republic. Historical Photographic Records of the Hungarian National Museum 477. ME/II/A, Box: Political Life: Anniversaries 1949–56. Registry no.: Hungarian Labour History Museum 78.854.

in the 1930s, Hungarian party leaders regarded Béla Kun, who had been the most influential Communist member of the Hungarian communard government, as primarily responsible for the fall of the dictatorship of the proletariat. Party leaders and propaganda historians tried to transform Kun, who became a victim of the Stalinist reorganization and the subsequent virtual elimination of the Comintern during the 1930s, into the prefiguration of the Trotskyist-Bucharinist traitor and imperialist agent. In mid-century histories of 1919, he was normally accused of underestimating the power of counterrevolution and the bourgeoisie, making compromises with right-wing Social Democrats, undermining the party and preferring international proletarian solidarity over domestic support for the Communist cause. Kun, it was then claimed, misled even Lenin himself and pursued a criminal policy of easing class struggle and withdrawing the Hungarian Red Army from its victorious offensive. As a consequence, in the post-WWII years the actual Communist leadership of the dictatorship was practically replaced by Mátyás Rákosi, second-rank party leader in 1919. The one time leaders of the first Hungarian commune, who became nonpersons or, at best, were deemed to have failed in revolutionary Marxist theory and practice up until early 1956 (when Béla Kun was officially rehabilitated), could not be appropriated as the most significant forerunners of the glorious and successful Communist takeover.[94]

---

94 Miklós Szabó, 'A fegyverek kritikája', *Beszélő* 4 (March, 1999): 50–54. Aladár Mód's chapter on 1919 in the 1951 edition elucidates well the criticism on Kun: *400 év küzdelem*, 417–24. On Kun's rehabilitation, see the Politburo resolution on 6 March 1956, Central Organs, Politburo, MOL M-KS MDP 276/53/275, 72.

As a consequence, the history of the First Hungarian Soviet Republic remained an odd set of fragments of isolated occurrences: appropriate for drawing lessons mostly from its mistakes and failures. The history of the Soviet Republic was analysed in order to understand the reasons for its defeat. Rákosi created the archetype in his historical account of the republic in 1948, a narrative which was to eventually determine the official way in which the event was represented henceforth. Beginning with an account on the unification of the workers' parties, he unequivocally condemns the decision as a serious error. The second measure of the Soviet government was the organization of a state apparatus. Here the general secretary claims that it was a mistake for the Soviet Republic not to destroy the old bureaucracy. He then lists the proletarian regime's errors in this regard: the fact that the revolutionary law courts kept former judges on and maintained their influence; that in the industrial sphere the Soviet Republic nationalized production yet allowed the bourgeoisie to remain in their posts as state employees; and the ill-advised rearrangement of agriculture, chiefly the forced and rapid collectivization. Finally, after recounting the story of military success and retreat, Rákosi outlines the causes of defeat. He considers two main reasons: the numerical superiority of the international enemy and the treason of the Social Democrats. He concludes, however, that 'the experiences and the defeat, the successes and the failures of the First Hungarian Soviet Republic, provided lessons for the revolutionary workers' movement all over the world.'[95]

In general, the standard way of presenting the Hungarian commune was established by the proposal produced for the 30th anniversary by the Department for Propaganda together with the Institution for the History of the Workers' Movement. The first part of the document contains the 'political aspects' of the celebrations: the significance of the alliance between Western imperialists, Hungarian counterrevolutionaries and right-wing Social Democrats. It also states that serious mistakes were made due to the omission of Marxism–Leninism, such as the unification of the workers' parties without guiding principles, the neglect of the peasantry, the preservation of the old bourgeois bureaucracy and the unsatisfactory suppression of counterrevolution. These mistakes, combined with the inner activity of traitors and the inability to withstand aggression from outside owing to the absence of a Communist bloc, contributed to the downfall of the party.[96] In 1949, newspapers warned party leaders to avoid the superficial unity of the party accomplished by the merging of the Communist and Social Democratic parties in summer 1948, which was considered the main reason for the party's downfall in 1919. One of the articles even pronounced that the right-wing Social Democrats had capitalized on the unity by keeping the workers under right-wing influence and, hence, their tactic actually resulted in the liquidation of the Communist party.[97] The same principles were also inherent to

---

95 Rákosi, *A Kommunisták Magyarországi Pártjának*, 59.
96 MOL M-KS 276/54/28.
97 Erzsébet Andics, 'A jobboldali szociáldemokraták szerepe az 1919-es proletárforradalomban' (The role of right-wing Social Democrats in the proletarian revolution of 1919), SZN 13 March 1949. The Marxist historian Aladár Mód makes similar points in the relevant chapter of his comprehensive book on Hungarian history: *400 év küzdelem*, 391–9.

school textbooks. These all ended their narratives with an enumeration of the reasons for the downfall and by underscoring the appropriate lessons to be learnt.[98]

It was difficult to produce a chapter in the history of modern Hungary about the revolution in 1919 that was comparable to the story of 1848–49, the dominant reference point in this period. The centenary of the 1848 revolution in 1948 provided an excellent opportunity for the Hungarian Communist leaders to translate the national line of wartime and early postwar Stalinist tactics into vernacular propaganda. The years 1848–49 had been crucial in the genesis of modern Hungary and Hungarian national identity. In April 1848, the first parliamentary government had been set up and the representative national assembly had passed the first modern constitution of the country. Serfdom had been abolished and the general participation in the national fight for freedom against the Habsburg imperial armies had made the events into a sweeping experience of national solidarity and unity. In 1849, Lajos Kossuth had declared Hungary as an independent democratic republic, the first in Hungarian history. The symbols of the period – the tricolour, the army uniforms, the national anthem and Kossuth's coat-of-arms – have endured as the national symbols of the country to this day. Large and varying groups of Hungarian society had participated in the struggle, which made the idea of national unity and democratic participation a tangible experience. All these factors sustained the memory of 1848 as a broad popular historical myth.[99]

The postwar democratic coalition, which sought to create democratic political identity for Hungarian society, understood the importance of the legacy of 1848–49. Preparations for lavish celebrations of the 100th anniversary began soon after the war. Nonetheless, by the anniversary year, Communists had already become the dominant political force in the country, successfully dismembering their opponents, and were very close to an actual takeover. The party dominated the celebrations and turned the representations of 1848–49 into a prehistory of the Stalinist state. Stalinism was not inimical to nationalism: on the contrary, Stalinist propaganda in the USSR as well as in Eastern Europe strove to create unity based on nationalist sentiments, while presenting the Communist parties as the rightful successors of their respective national freedom fights and the fulfilment of their nationalist struggles. The revolution of 1848 could readily provide a powerful and nationally resonant historical prefiguration for the postwar Hungarian Communist dictatorship. The Hungarian party proclaimed itself the heir of the aspirations of 1848: national independence, popular politics, modernization and national unity. But it also saw itself as the fulfilment of 1848: the successor to an unfinished revolution. The events of 1848 only prefigured the goals the Communist party would attain in 1948: true national independence by seceding from capitalist powers, popular politics by representing workers and peasants, modernization by socialist industrialization, and true national unity based on the common interests of urban and rural proletariat. Hungarian Communists thus discovered that the true message of 1848 had manifested itself on 15

---

98 Karácsony, Feuer and Zsigmond, *Történelem VIII*, 181–91; and Kovács, Simon and Bellér, *Történelem IV*, 3–25.
99 András Gerő, *Imagined History: Chapters from Nineteenth- and Twentieth-century Hungarian Symbolic Politics* (Boulder: East European Monographs, 2006).

March, the day of popular protest initiated by radical young intellectuals against the Habsburg authorities. Previous to this, the official holiday was 11 April, the day the emperor had sanctioned the new Hungarian constitution, celebrated both by the late nineteenth-century dualists as well as in the conservative interwar period (though the interwar elites had already introduced 15 March celebrations to express a nationalist message). Likewise, they turned the Romantic poet and young hero of the revolution Sándor Petőfi into a prototype of the Communist fighter, leader of the freedom fight Lajos Kossuth into the prototype of a wise and cunning statesman, and defender of the rights of the poor Mihály Táncsics into the prototype of the working-class hero.[100]

Although not everyone believed that Communists were the only true heirs of 1848, it was possible for the events of the nineteenth-century revolution to be used or abused for such purposes. The democratic political aspects (i.e., the expansion of rights) and the progressive social components (i.e., the abolishment of serfdom and land reform) had been combined with national sentiments and with a broad unity in the struggle against Habsburg imperialism. Indeed, 15 March had been associated with protest, revolt and the protection of rights against oppressive powers long before the Communists. As before 1945 the state authorities had chosen 11 April as the official holiday to commemorate 1848 or chiefly emphasized the nationalist message of 15 March, radical social or political criticism were especially attached to 15 March. The memory of the experience of national unity one hundred years before the Communist takeover made it credible to interpret the failure of 1848 within the framework of a tragic plot structure, consisting of the glorious efforts of the nation and the overwhelming forces of external enemies. A similar narrative concerning the First Hungarian Soviet Republic had to cover the lack of genuine national unity, the opposition of propertied middle classes and, more importantly, the resistance of peasantry and the occasionally brutal suppression of dissent. The internal conflicts and bitter tensions within the leadership, the mutual accusations made by socialist and Communist participants that the other had betrayed the cause of the revolution and was responsible for the regime's collapse, made it difficult to represent the tragic story of the betrayal of a homogenous and resolute vanguard of unified progressive forces. The Soviet Republic led many instead to recall instances of the exploitation of the peasantry, the persecution of clerical and administrative classes, and the executions during the Red Terror. The memory of 1919 was too controversial to lay the foundations of a truly *national* historical myth.

The history of the First Hungarian Soviet Republic proved to be ineffective and troublesome. As its representations lacked actual data concerning many important participants of the dictatorship of the proletariat (such as Kun), as well as many of its events (such as particular revolts or conflicts), these didactic, moralizing narratives

---

100 András Gerő, *Az államosított forradalom* (Budapest: Új Mandátum, 1998), 9–19; Alice Freifeld, *Nationalism and the Crowd in Liberal Hungary, 1848–1914* (Washington, DC: Woodrow Wilson Center Press, 2000); György Gyarmati, *Március hatalma – a hatalom márciusa* (Budapest: Paginarium, 1998), 96–114; Balázs Apor, 'Hatalom és történelem', *Budapesti Jelenlét* 26–27 (2–3) (2000): 59–70; Róbert Szabó, 'Politikai propaganda és történelmi ünnep', *Történelmi Szemle* 40 (Autumn–Winter 1998): 215–27; Szabó, 'Pártok, politikai propaganda, történelmi ünnepek Magyarországon 1945–1948', *Sic Itur Ad Astra* (2–4) (1993): 261–72.

remained hopelessly abstract. Without proper names, places and events it was extremely difficult, if not impossible, to link the abstract ideological statements to comprehensible accounts. Without tangible details of the historical reality there was very little to remember in a commemorative ceremony and very little to experience in a historical festival. The attempt of Hungarian party leaders to attach their doctrine to actual events, persons or spaces failed. Hungarian Communists seemed to overestimate the representational capacity of historical festivals, or rather underestimate their relationship to the actual concrete past. Apparently, party leaders believed that a carefully planned festival which reflected preconstructed ideological metanarratives would effectively mediate the intended political message, as if representation could be divided into two distinct components: an abstract discernible form responsible for persuading the audience and concrete referents meant to actualize the metastructure. The failure of the Hungarian Communists sheds light on one of the more important components of successful rituals necessary for historical festivals.

Historical festivals had grown since the end of the eighteenth century. Initiated by the promoters of new French revolutionary civic culture, these festivals had become spectacular in their re-enactments of the past. These rituals were designed to manifest the ideal spatial and temporal order, which was made personal for individuals through their participation in the events. These commemorative ceremonies were shaped by their location and time: actual tangible spaces or standardized itineraries associated with the events of the revolution and the sequence of actual dates in one calendar year. It was difficult to conceive an abstract history of the revolution, as its representation was born as a personal experience. The memory of the revolution, or the political message concerning the history of the revolution, was never abstract: it was formed by firm connections to the experiences of actual tangible spaces, dates, persons and events.[101]

Arguably, historical memory – the shaping and keeping of the image of the past through social practices – has always been firmly related to cultural procedures aimed at the evocation of actual persons, events and spaces in the mind of the audience. 'A purely abstract truth is not a recollection; a recollection refers us to the past. An abstract truth, in contrast, has no hold on the succession of events; it is the order of a wish or of an aspiration', as Maurice Halbwachs observes in connection with the construction and preservation of the memory of the Holy Land.[102] These ceremonies fulfil their roles, provided they can turn the past into tangible present, as Jan Assmann puts it, concerning the practices of ancient high cultures, developed to preserve their cultural identities in time.[103] The sophisticated and intricate political rites of festivals create credible representations of history out of the set of events they evoke, as they are shaped by material objects, buildings or geographical landscapes, or tangible dates and persons, which make the historical interpretations presented both comprehensible and convincing.

---

101 Mona Ozouf, *Festivals and the French Revolution* (Cambridge, MA/London: Harvard University Press, 1988), 8; Paul Connerton, *How Societies Remember* (Cambridge: Cambridge University Press, 1989), 41–71.
102 Maurice Halbwachs, *On Collective Memory* (Chicago: Chicago University Press, 1992), 200.
103 Jan Assmann, *Das kulturelle Gedächtnis: Schrift, Erinnerung und politische Identität in frühen Hochkulturen* (Munich: Beck, 1992), 53.

Ironically, the abstract theoretical debates which the Communist leaders themselves believed to be crucial in confirming their historical theology had little resonance among ordinary party members and virtually no resonance at all among the wider Hungarian public. Choices that seemed crucial to them – such as that between Kun or Rákosi (a choice between a failed and persecuted leader and Stalin's faithful follower) – which were frequently matters of life and death for Communist Party cadres, remained utterly unimportant to ordinary Hungarians. The relevance of 1919, therefore, remained limited and fragmented and its memory was virtually confined to the membership of the Hungarian Communist Party. The First Hungarian Soviet Republic remained an event only of party history, and even here was described only in a fragmentary and partial way. In spite of the fact that the ceremonies of 1949 included a commemoration held in parliament, the installation of an exhibition in the Hungarian National Museum, the publication of a book of photographs and the broadcasting of a radio drama, the anniversary was for the most part regarded rather as a celebration only relevant for the Communist Party. A lecture was given at a ceremonial meeting of party workers, a party day was organized, the army celebrated in their barracks, and a special issue of the party's theoretical journal, the *Review of Society*, was published; in addition, a lecture by Rákosi on the subject was read and discussed in party schools.[104]

The efforts the Communist Party put into fostering broader public discussion of the First Hungarian Soviet Republic appears ridiculous in retrospect. Although 1919 was represented as an important step in the course of the struggle for national independence, the link between 1848 and 1948 overshadowed the connection between 1919 and 1949. The glorious but suppressed battle unifying the democratic and national cause of 1848 and its fulfilment in 1948 were considered more important than the failure of the socialist transformation in 1919 and its subsequent realization thirty years later. Although the Soviet Republic provided an instance of a usable past, the genuine *praefiguratio* of the postwar Communist dictatorship was not the 1919 commune. As such, the new Rákosi regime celebrated itself in 1948, prior to the 30th anniversary of 1919 in 1949.

4

The way the First Hungarian Soviet Republic was evoked remained unchanged throughout the 1950s. The directives that were written for the 35th anniversary in 1954 made it even more apparent that, notwithstanding the proposed fifteen- to twenty-minute-long commemorations at schools, the only community it concerned was Communist Party. Lectures were held in every important city, but only for party workers. The only newspapers to publish articles for the anniversary were those of the party: the daily *Free People*, the *Review of Society* and the *Propagandist*.[105]

During the Stalinist 1950s, commemorating the events of 1919 was framed as part of a transnational history and was used to evoke the meanings and concepts of anti-imperialism. The First Hungarian Soviet Republic was described as part of the global struggle between

---

104 MDP Central Organs, Secretariat, MOL M-KS 276/54/28.
105 MOL M-KS 276/89/21.

imperialism and the emerging new force of socialism headed by Soviet Russia. The collective volume that was published for the 35th anniversary stated frequently that events of 1919 had been influenced to a large extent by the Russian October Revolution, and called the First Hungarian Soviet Republic 'the child of October'.[106] Subsequent anniversaries of the Soviet Republic also provided opportunities to prove that the Hungarian regime was close to the archetype of Bolshevism: the USSR. Likewise, in 1955 the Communist Party's daily called the Soviet Republic 'the great tradition of Soviet–Hungarian friendship'.[107] The author states that the USSR is a natural ally against imperialists, apparently referring to the Cold War. According to the article the Soviet Union was the centre of the international revolution in 1919, therefore the Hungarian Communist regime aspired to establish a common border with it also in 1919. The statement is a clear reference to the new Hungarian–Soviet border that was formed after the annexation of the Carpathian Ukraine from Czechoslovakia to the USSR after WWII. Diplomatic relations were established due to the heroic flight of a Communist leader from Budapest to Moscow in 1919, through enemy lines, to meet Lenin personally. The two Communist systems supported each other even in arms, as stated the article: captives of both sides took part in each other's battles.[108]

The Entente's intervention in 1919 was compared with the current hostile relations between the two blocs in the Cold War. An article published in the newspaper of the Federation of the Working Youth revealed a covert plan of the American imperialists to overthrow the Soviet Republic in 1919. According to the author the US prepared a military intervention with the help of right-wing Social Democrats who served the American intelligence agencies. US leaders incited the armies of smaller imperialist states to war. The actual offensive, launched by Czechoslovak and Romanian military forces and advised by French and Italian officers, was connected also to the US: 'On 16 April the armed intervention against the Hungarian workers and peasants, organized and directed by Western imperialist powers and primarily by American billionaires, began.'[109] The article also attributed to the US leaders Clemenceau's promise to withdraw Romanian troops from eastern Hungary and invite representatives of the Soviet Republic for peace negotiations in return for evacuating Upper Hungary by the Red Army. Obviously, the author concludes that American imperialists had already aspired to overthrow Communism in 1919, as it did in the 1950s. Another context for evoking the First Hungarian Soviet Republic was the deep conflict between Tito's Yugoslavia and other countries of the Soviet bloc. Several articles called attention to the fact that in 1919 the armed intervention had been directed from Belgrade, and the authors were not reluctant to conclude, 'As in 1919, at Franchet d'Espèray's [French general, commander-in-chief of Entente forces in the Balkans] headquarters they are now hatching their murderous

---

106 *A Magyar Tanácsköztársaság hősi küzdelmeiről* (On the heroic struggles of the first proclamation of the First Hungarian Soviet Republic) (Budapest: Szikra, 1954), 70.
107 SZN, 21 March 1955, 3.
108 'A magyar Tanácsköztársaság kikiáltásának évfordulójára' (For the anniversary of the proclamation of the First Hungarian Soviet Republic), SZN, 21 March 1955.
109 'Az amerikai imperialisták – a Tanácsköztársaság hóhéra' (The American imperialists: The executioners of the First Hungarian Soviet Republic), *Szabad Ifjúság*, 17 October 1953, 3.

plot against us in Belgrade. Their agents, who are ready for every outrage, are lurking like hungry wolves by our borders and are called Tito and his gang.'[110]

During the subsequent years, commemorative articles repeatedly claimed that the major external contributor to the defeat of the Soviet Republic had been the attack by the Entente, completed in the absence of a 'socialist camp'. Therefore the Hungarian Soviet regime had to face being overpowered by hostile and imperialistic countries. Besides, it was stated that although the people and the intellectuals had supported the regime, Trotskyists and right-wing Social Democrats had overthrown it. The internal and external enemies of the proletariat were accompanied by the system's own failures, primarily those concerned with agriculture. The Soviet Republic rapidly nationalized the land and, hence, lost the support of the peasantry.[111]

In this mode, all characteristics of the first Soviet regime were presented as failures of a kind. Right-wing Social Democrats were able to betray the proletariat because the Communists did not pay enough attention to purge the Social Democratic Party. Social Democrats held their influence over workers because Communists let the trade unions remain independent. Class struggle was perpetuated within the party due to the presence of right-wing petit bourgeois Social Democrats. Communist compliance meant that old capitalists remained in leading positions of their once nationalized factories.[112] The relevance of 1919 was that it taught the post-1945 Communist regime how to avoid the pitfalls: 'From the past revolution we inherited invaluable political lessons, which we are going to apply to our ongoing victorious battles, exactly as we have always done. Thus the temporarily failed first proletarian revolution becomes a living and constituent part of the once-and-for-all victorious Hungarian people's democracy building socialism.'[113] Nonetheless, as the newspapers emphasized, 'The crucial reason of the downfall of the Soviet Republic was the imperialist intervention which attacked our country. From this fact our people draw important conclusions concerning the present.'[114]

László Réti, in a study written in 1954 for the 35th anniversary of the First Hungarian Soviet Republic, made this connection manifest. Firstly, Réti states that the Soviet Republic had fought alone against the enemies of Communism. The neighbouring countries were hostile towards Hungary, and the Soviet Union could not provide military assistance since she herself had to face interventions. Nevertheless, as he puts it, WWII altered the conditions fundamentally. Hungary became a member of a mighty socialist camp led by the most powerful country in the world. He concludes, 'Thus the first lesson drawn from the experiences of the First Hungarian Soviet Republic is to take care of, foster and fortify our indissoluble brotherly community with the other peoples of the socialist camp, since this is the guarantee of our further progress and victory, the secure basis of our

---

110 'A Tanácsköztársaság 34. évfordulóján' (On the 34th anniversary of the First Hungarian Soviet Republic), *Népszava*, 21 March 1953, 4.
111 'Harminckét évvel ezelőtt' (Thirty-two years ago), SZN, 21 March 1951.
112 SZN, 13 March 1949.
113 László Réti, 'A Magyar Tanácsköztársaság dicső példája' (The glorious example of the First Hungarian Soviet Republic), SZN, 21 March 1953, 3.
114 'Történelmi vizsga' (A history exam), SZN, 21 March 1954, 2.

socialist construction.'¹¹⁵ Secondly, Réti argues that the rapid collectivization prevented the formation of a stable alliance of workers and peasants in 1919. After 1945, however, Communists managed to engage with the peasantry with an immediate distribution of land: 'After the liberation our party learned from past mistakes and based the alliance of workers and peasants on stable grounds with the revolutionary land reform in 1945.'¹¹⁶ Accordingly, Communists considered it the task of historiography to draw appropriate lessons and, thus, to contribute to the establishment of appropriate political action:

> The existence, glorious fights, wonderful successes, but also the failures and defeat of the First Hungarian Soviet Republic provide an abundant treasury of lessons for our present work, for our present activity of constructing socialism. It is necessary to point out several of them, those which are perhaps the most significant from the point of view of our present work and can contribute most to the clarification and solution of the tasks we are about to face. The great historical experiences of the First Hungarian Soviet Republic can be found every time and everywhere in the work we have done since the liberation; we have managed to achieve our wonderful successes because we have learnt from the past. It is enough to refer, for instance, to the formation of the unified party of the working class. It is obvious that in 1948 we succeeded in realizing the final and indissoluble unity of the working class based on the right principles, implementing the instructions of Marxism–Leninism concerning the party; because we have learnt among others things from the history of the First Hungarian Soviet Republic and corrected the mistakes we made then.¹¹⁷

The politics of remembering 1919 was similarly Sovietized: it was justified if it could contribute to the carrying out of appropriate acts in the context of the present, 'The glorious, never-ending memory of the Hungarian Soviet Republic, the first Hungarian dictatorship of the proletariat, unceasingly inspires us to further strengthen the second, invincible power of the proletariat, the People's Republic of Hungary, for building socialism, for defending our peace and fatherland.'¹¹⁸

Evoking the First Hungarian Soviet Republic remained an important means to understand 'socialism' during the crisis of Communism in the mid-1950s. Stalin's death in 1953 led to increasing indeterminacy among the East-Central European parties. Although Khrushchev, Stalin's successor as secretary general, began to claim that Stalinist policy was a failure and devoted himself to correcting it, and urged other Communist leaders of the bloc to take anti-Stalinist measures, the admiration of Stalinist policy was not immediately discredited within the Soviet leadership. However, basic elements of the postwar Communist doctrine, like the use of violence, the primacy of industrialization or the style of leadership, were questioned, and Communist orthodoxy, in general, was challenged by revisionist attempts which stressed socialist democracy, the democratization

---

115 László Réti, 'Az első magyar proletárdiktatúra' (The first Hungarian dictatorship of the proletariat), *Társadalmi Szemle* 9 (March 1954): 10.
116 Réti, 'Az első magyar proletárdiktatúra', 12.
117 Réti, 'Az első magyar proletárdiktatúra', 8–9.
118 SZN, 21 March 1953, 3.

of the party and social consumption. This led to the rise of reformist Communist politicians; for instance, Imre Nagy's nomination as prime minister in Hungary for a short period. Tensions remained, however, as the gap between the Hungarian Workers' Party and Hungarian society became more apparent by 1956, partly due to Rákosi's reticence towards de-Stalinization.[119] In this context commemoration called attention to the fact that the Communist Party was able to reconsider its policy and regenerate its dynamism. Commemorative articles stressed that because the Communists were able to learn from the errors of the First Hungarian Soviet Republic, they did not make them again after the liberation in 1945. The newspapers also reiterated that the Hungarian Workers' Party adopted a resolution to correct the mistakes.[120]

Propaganda films based on historical comparison became the characteristic genre of this mode of representation, which identified historical analogies for the sake of contemporary political mobilization. The new Communist regimes of East-Central Europe could base their propaganda practices upon the features of Soviet films, in order to persuade the population to participate in the social and political efforts of the present government. The Bolshevik regime was among the first modern states to capitalize on the vast opportunities of the new technology. Stalinist historical films were born within this particular tradition. Historical films carried easily identifiable political messages, such as the anti-German sentiments in the 1938 feature *Alexander Nevsky*.[121] In Hungary, a typical work of this mode of representation was *I Defend the Homeland of Our People* (1955). The film adopted the new People's Army into a constructed national tradition of wars for independence, 1919 being a chapter in the sequence of Rákóczi's anti-Habsburg insurgents in 1703, the revolution in 1848 and the Soviet-like partisans of 1944. The final scenes, however, do not depict the soldier of the People's Army as simply a successor of the previous Hungarian freedom fighters. Emphasis is laid rather on how he can follow the lead of his historical counterparts – that is to say, how he can serve the interests of the people in the present. Apart from images of military training, the film therefore demonstrates how the army helped the population during floods and how it participated in construction works or at harvest time.[122]

---

119 On de-Stalinization and the conflict of orthodoxy and reformism in Hungary, see János M. Rainer, *Nagy Imre. Politikai életrajz. 1953–1958*, vol. 2 (Budapest: 1956-os Intézet, 1999), 9–233. On the trajectories of reformer thought between 1953–56, see Rainer, *Az író helye*.

120 Miklós Gárdos, 'A Magyar Tanácsköztársaság emlékére' (Commemorating the First Hungarian Soviet Republic), *Magyar Nemzet*, 21 March 1956.

121 Peter Kenez, *Cinema and Soviet Society, 1917–1953* (Cambridge: I. B. Tauris, 1992); Richard Taylor, *The Politics of the Soviet Cinema 1917–1929* (Cambridge: University Microfilms International, 1979). While there are no comprehensive studies on the interrelations of the genres of historical and propaganda films, the following article provides some insights: Richard Taylor, 'Red Stars, Positive Heroes and Personality Cults', in *Stalinism and Soviet Cinema*, ed. Richard Taylor and Derek Spring (London/New York: Routledge, 1993), 88. See also Graham Roberts, *Forward Soviet! History and Non-fiction Film in the USSR* (London/New York: I. B. Tauris, 1999). Political regimes based upon the conception of the end of history tend to use historical films in this way: Richard Taylor, *Film Propaganda: Soviet Russia and Nazi Germany* (London/New York: I. B. Tauris, 1998).

122 *Megvédem népünk otthonát!* Hadtörténelmi Levéltár (Archives for Military History), 5460–61.

Chapter 2

RESURRECTION: THE EMERGENCE OF 1919 AND THE COUNTERREVOLUTION AFTER 1956

1

Having succeeded the suppression of the revolution in October 1956, the first time that the new Communist regime evoked the events of 1919 was likely in the 21 November issue of the *Népszabadság* (People's freedom), the party's official daily. That day the editors published a letter, which had allegedly been sent to the government by an old worker. The author of this letter first gives an account of his life spent within the labour movement since 1917. The worker writes about his sufferings and privation during the previous regime, then recalls the happy years following the end of the war. The author then condemns the pre-1956 Communist leadership for distancing itself from the workers and their real life. He concludes that although the behaviour of the party elite contributed to the outburst of the rightful discontent in late October 1956, this was very soon appropriated by the 'bloody counterrevolution'. However, considering the fact that the worker's memories reflect the ideal Communist interpretation of history as well as the official depiction of the revolt in 1956 taking shape at that time, it is very probable that the 'old worker' is an editorial invention. 'He' creates a remarkable historical parallel when he reminds his comrades of the peril: 'Remember the bloody and cruel counterrevolution of 1919. Remember how many thousands and thousands of our innocent fellow workers and comrades met their death as martyrs, how many widows and orphans mourned their breadwinners and over many years how madly we were persecuted. Wake up, get on your feet again and defend the socialist power of the workers.'[1]

The new Communist government led by János Kádár that was established on 4 November 1956, following the Soviet Army's invasion of Hungary, was illegitimate. The overwhelming majority of society considered it to have betrayed a popular movement for democracy and independence and to have led a foreign army into the fatherland, and Kádár himself, formerly a member of Imre Nagy's government, was considered a traitor. His government was opposed by numerous social groups, including reform Communist and populist intellectuals, workers who had already set up their workers' councils and the provincial population who had established their local autonomies, the National Committees. Since the general idea of legitimacy for Communist parties rested on their identity as a revolutionary progressive movement, it was vital for the Hungarian Communists to prove that the insurrection in October 1956 against party rule had lacked progressive and revolutionary motives. In fact, as the new government tried to argue, it

---

1 NSZ, 21 November 1956, 4.

had been opposed to such goals, it had been a counterrevolution.[2] The relationship between 1919 and 1956 went through a gradual transformation from the winter of 1956 to the summer of 1958. The original pair of comparable analogies gradually began to reveal an essential temporal continuity, which seemed to guide Communists to realize a basic truth about the historical process. Recalling teleology, the chronology that those two dates signalled unexpectedly shed light on an apparent fact that history was moved by the constant struggle of revolution and counterrevolution.

The same issue of the *Népszabadság* also featured an account of the siege on the headquarters of the Greater Budapest Party Committee in Republic Square, set in parallel columns to the 'old man's' warning. On 30 October 1956, various armed groups initiated a common attack driven dominantly by the belief that the party's office was a centre of the security police. Most probably, the insurgents began the assault when shots were first fired at them from the party building. The struggle was eventually decided when an armoured military unit, sent from a provincial city to defend the Communist headquarters, arrived in the square and mistakenly bombarded the party building instead of firing at the attackers. After the occupation of the building, most of the defenders were executed, some of them lynched.[3]

The siege developed into crucial evidence in the construction of the counterrevolution during the autumn of 1956. János Kádár, prime minister of the Revolutionary Worker-Peasant Government, returned to Budapest in the morning of 7 November. In his radio speech transmitted on 11 November, he used the example of 'when the headquarters of the Budapest Party Committee in Republic Square was shot by cannons' as proof of the beginnings of the 'White Terror' and counterrevolution.[4] Kádár, who was also the first secretary of the newly created Hungarian Socialist Workers' Party clearly stated at one of the first meetings of the Provisional Executive Committee (21 November) that 30 October had been the start of the counterrevolutionary assault.[5] During party meetings on the following days (23 and 24 November) the first secretary reiterated that after 30 October the uprising had become a pure counterrevolution.[6]

The reasoning behind the establishment of the Revolutionary Worker-Peasant Government was based on the conviction that in the autumn of 1956 the danger of 'counterrevolution' was imminent. Meanwhile, Nagy's government was unable to resist this threat without the intervention of Soviet troops. Hence, Kádár returned to Budapest

---

2 Heino Nyyssönen, *The Presence of the Past in Politics: '1956' after 1956 in Hungary* (Jyväskylä, 1999); András Mink, 'The Revisions of the 1956 Hungarian Revolution', in *Past in the Making: Historical Revisionism in Central Europe after 1989*, ed. Michal Kopeček (Budapest/New York: CEU Press, 2008), 169–78; Zoltán Ripp, '1956 emlékezete és az MSZMP', in *Évköny X. Magyarország a jelenkorban*, ed. János M. Rainer and Éva Standeisky (Budapest: 1956-os Intézet, 2002), 233–50.

3 As a matter of fact, several of the executed defenders miraculously survived. The best account of the siege is László Eörsi, *Köztársaság tér, 1956* (Budapest: 1956-os Intézet, 2006). See also Péter Gosztonyi, 'A Köztársaság téri ostrom és a kazamaták mítosza', *Budapesti Negyed* 5 (Autumn 1994): 48–80.

4 *Hungarian Monitoring*, 11 November 1956, 981–2, OSA 300/40/1/1299.

5 MSZMP vol. 1, 77.

6 Meeting of the Provisional Executive Committee, 23 November 1956, and the meeting of the Provisional Central Committee, 24 November 1956, MSZMP vol. 1, 96.

with the intention of eliminating the 'counterrevolution'. While in Moscow between 2 and 4 November he was convinced of the impossibility of avoiding military intervention, and the Soviet party leaders persuaded him to personally take the presidency of the puppet government, legitimating the step.[7] In his 11 November radio address, Kádár forecasted the following gloomy vision on the future as an alternative to his government:

> Following the path of Imre Nagy's government leading to collapse, insisting on the withdrawal of Soviet troops, we'll only observe impotently as counterrevolutionary White Terror massacres the active masses of Communist workers, peasants and intellectuals, then those that sympathize with Communists, and finally all democratic patriots in the whole of Budapest, then in the countryside. Then the counterrevolution will throw away Imre Nagy's as well as all other governments based on democratic cooperation, in order to establish a pure counterrevolutionary government.[8]

The new Communist leadership was forged together by the commonly shared conviction of counterrevolutionary danger and the impotency of the Nagy government.

Nonetheless, during the first months following the suppression of the revolution, the new party leadership was characterized by uncertainty concerning the actual interpretation of the 'counterrevolution', and therefore, in this respect, it was far from being homogenous. On the one hand, the spectacle of the masses of people who took part in the revolutionary demonstration, whose legitimacy was admitted even by the old and the new party elite, remained an influential experience for many members of the new leadership. For Kádár himself, who participated in the work of the Imre Nagy government until 31 October, his personal involvement with the workers who joined the revolt was a lifelong influence. Kádár expounded his concerns even to his Soviet partners after accepting the military oppression of the revolution: 'I would like to say one thing: the whole people moved together. The people do not want to eliminate the people's democratic system.'[9] The first secretary maintained his ambivalent assessment of the revolution up until the meeting of the Provisional Executive Committee on 11 November: 'In the moment of the outbreak of the armed insurrection, it seemed clearly a counterrevolutionary movement. Later we saw that, especially in the countryside, huge working masses, labourers, miners, etc. moved with such demands – apart from social welfare demands, the withdrawal of the Soviet troops and the elimination of forced agricultural submission, which cannot be called counterrevolutionary demands.'[10] On the other hand, numerous leaders feared a repetition of the voluntaristic terror of the Rákosi regime against Communist Party members, which many of them – Kádár, Marosán, Aczél – had witnessed personally.

---

7 Tibor Huszár, *Kádár János politikai életrajza: 1912–1956*, vol. 1 (Budapest: Szabad Tér-Kossuth, 2003), 329–48.
8 *Hungarian Monitoring*, 11 November 1956, 983, OSA 300/40/1/1299.
9 Huszár, *Kádár*, vol. 1, 344 (329–48). Tibor Huszár provides a comprehensive description on Kádár's days in Moscow.
10 MSZMP vol. 1, 26.

The party leadership during these early postrevolutionary months disagreed even on policy. Originally, the members of the executive committee (anti-Stalinist but conservative Communists close to Kádár – György Aczél, Lajos Fehér, Antal Gyenes, József Köböl, Sándor Nógrádi) who favoured negotiation represented a majority. For Kádár the possession of actual power, and consequently the resolute elimination of the workers' councils and the nonparty opposition, was decisive since the beginning, though he would have preferred the negotiations to have provided a political solution.[11] But the new Communist government wanted to open the path of forgiveness for 'misled, but otherwise sincere people', too.

The siege of the party headquarters could serve at the same time as evidence for the alleged 'counterrevolutionary danger' that Communists recognized in the revolt and as an opportunity to maintain the narrative that many of the participants were actually 'honest workers' deceived by the counterrevolution. In its description of the events the article in the 21 November issue of the *Népszabadság* generally avoids the terms 'counterrevolution' or 'counterrevolutionaries', preferring to call the rebels 'armed men' or simply the 'crowd'. The nearly one-page-long report emphasizes the preparedness of the attackers. It also stresses the cruelty of the siege: firstly it calls attention to the fact that the negotiators sent by the defenders had been murdered. It goes on to describe in detail how the mostly unarmed defenders who had survived were beaten and executed by the attackers. A colonel was hanged upside down, soaked in petrol and set on fire. Even the barber of the party headquarters was killed because he was regarded a Communist. Although the article is not convinced that the attack consciously aimed at overthrowing the socialist system, it argues that eventually the fight weakened the workers' power: 'Armed White Terrorists and misguided rebels actually organized a cruel bloodbath against the faithful sons of the labour movement.'[12] On 1 December during his negotiations with Soviet party emissaries, János Kádár presented a two-stage history of the counterrevolution, with the siege in Republic Square as the turning point: 'The days between 23 and 30 October were characterized by the fact that the counterrevolutionary elements abused for their own purposes the just and instinctual discontent of the working masses. In the second stage – 31 October to 4 November – the reactionary attacks spread broadly throughout the country. Communists, progressive workers, the staff of state defence and the police were openly killed.'[13] This interpretation corresponded to Kádár's personal story: he stated that his participation in the revolt had lasted only as far as he believed he had stood rightly by the demands of the workers, while the widespread expansion of the counterrevolution had forced him to leave the Imre Nagy government.

---

11 Melinda Kalmár, *Ennivaló és hozomány* (Budapest: Magvető, 1998), 20–25; János M. Rainer, *Nagy Imre. Politikai életrajz*, vol. 2. 1953–1958 (Budapest: 1956-os Intézet, 1999), 375. In the 11 November meeting of the Provisional Executive Committee the possibility of negotiations even with Imre Nagy was raised: Éva Standeisky, *Az írók és a hatalom 1956–1963* (Budapest: 1956-os Intézet, 1996), 114.

12 'Mi történt a Köztársaság téren' (What happened at the Republic Square), NSZ, 21 November 1956, 4.

13 Huszár, *Kádár János politikai életrajza: 1957. november-1989. június*, vol. 2 (Budapest: Szabad Tér-Kossuth, 2003), 21.

In this context the events of 1919 were evoked to serve as a tangible warning of the threat of counterrevolution. The *Népszabadság* printed a report in its 28 November 1956 edition about Western publications concerning the 'counterrevolution', under the heading 'The memory of the Horthy putsch of 1919 haunts Hungary'.[14] The title comes from the coverage of the French AFP news agency on 31 October 1956. The party's newspaper relied on reports from the British Reuters in summarizing the essence of the uprising, 'The uprising has slipped into a situation when the victory of those elements that are acting for the Horthy restoration is not at all impossible. Manhunts have been carried out on the streets of Budapest since yesterday. Scenes that remind us the return of the Whites in 1919 are happening throughout the entire country.' The article concludes, however, that 'the Hungarian people are fed up with the twenty-five years of wallowing since the counterrevolution came into power in 1919. It won't swallow that again.'

The interpretive context of the First Hungarian Soviet Republic did not change significantly in the first months following the oppression of the 1956 revolution. It was evoked to understand crucial issues in the history of socialism, this time particularly the case of the 'counterrevolution'. As an analogy, the memory of 1919 was constantly available for Communist Party members of all types. In the summer of 1956, while discussing the experiences of the Petőfi Circle debate on the situation of the press, the anti-Stalinist György Aczél expressed his concerns about the increased tensions and a 'new "19"'.[15] On 26 October, in a meeting of the central leadership, Stalinist secretary and Rákosi's close collaborator, István Kovács, attacked the Imre Nagy government by arguing that it would fulfil a role similar to the Peidl government of August 1919, which succeeded the Communist regime in the hope of maintaining a social democratic system, but was soon overthrown by White forces.[16] Imre Mező, the leader of the defence of the Budapest party headquarters, recalled his experiences of the Peidl government, when Hungarian trade union representatives visited him demanding an increase of their governmental role.[17] The evocation of the First Hungarian Soviet Republic occurred within the context of coming to terms with the events of the revolution in 1956. The relationship with the past was based on conditions of similarity, whereas the history of the two events was described in commensurable terms. The representation of 1919 reflected the interpretation of 1956.

By early December, however, a considerable shift occurred in the interpretation of 1956. At that time, it became clear to the new party leadership and personally to János Kádár that the repression was unavoidable. First of all, there was nobody to negotiate with: neither would the Communist reformers of Imre Nagy's company, nor would the

---

14 NSZ, 28 November 1956. See also *Népakarat*, 18 December 1956. I have found statements on the White Terror from Western Europe exclusively in the Communist press. See, for example, 'Der Weisse Terror in Ungarn', *Volkstimme*, 20 November 1956; 'Die Konterrevolution in Ungarn 1919 und 1956', *Österreische Volkstimme*, 20 November 1956; '[…] a virtual White Terror reminiscent of 1919, wiping out the flower of Hungary's working class movement […]', *Daily Worker*, 7 November 1956.
15 Sándor Révész, *Aczél és korunk* (Budapest: Sík, 1997), 54.
16 Standeisky, *Az írók és a hatalom*, 43.
17 Eörsi, *Köztársaság-tér*, 26.

non-Communist intellectual opposition nor the workers' council accept the Kádár government as legitimate and so they were reluctant to engage in discussions with it. It also became clear that the reorganization of Communist power could be based predominantly upon reactivating the former Stalinist party cadres and the Soviet leadership urging the tough repression of the resistance. Kádár eventually let the Soviet pressure prevail and began to stress the aspects of conscious preparation and conspiracy in the interpretation of 1956.[18]

In December the Provisional Central Committee prepared a decision on the causes and nature of the happenings in October 1956. The proposition that was discussed on 2 and 3 December stated that the White Terror had appeared openly without masks in the assault against the Budapest party headquarters.[19] Kádár agreed with the formulation and added that the counterrevolution had always been a hidden possibility in the uprising. However, the attack against the party on 30 October was direct evidence for the counterrevolutionary essence of the events.[20] Thus, the decision that was accepted on 5 December 1956 pronounced that the counterrevolution that had masked itself before 30 October had openly organized the massacre at the party building.[21]

Thereby the attack lost its unintended character and became the malicious act of well-prepared counterrevolutionary troops. The new Communist government published its official interpretation of the revolution in 1956 in the so-called 'White Books'. The series of five volumes was prepared by the Information Office of the government in 1956–58 with the purpose of publishing evidence on the 'counterrevolutionary nature' of the events. The series was aimed at a broad public: the second edition in 1958 was planned to number 100,000 copies.[22] The evidence included photographs of the lynching of party members or security officers, alleged biographies of participants linking them to the interwar elite, and reports about atrocities or capitalist political programs that were supposedly taken from documents of post-1956 trials. The level of evidence, in reality, was rather uneven: photos documented real events, but they were not inimical to various techniques of manipulation, and many of the reports were tendentiously distorted and in some cases simply fictive. The first volume was issued in December not long after the events themselves. The publication firmly states that the uprising was a counterrevolution, namely a resolute attack directed against the institutions of the people's democracy. The introduction claims that the leading force of the people's power was the party of the working class, therefore the persecution of Communists evidently proved the reactionary aspirations of the rebels. Volume one mentions the siege of the Budapest party headquarters as the major sign of counterrevolution.[23] Communists

---

18 On the changes in Kádár's position see Rainer, *Nagy Imre*, vol. 2, 375–7; Huszár, *Kádár*, vol. 2, 20–25.
19 MSZMP vol. 1, 215.
20 MSZMP vol. 1, 144.
21 MSZMP vol. 1, 239. On the December party resolution, see also Kalmár, *Ennivaló és hozomány*, 25–9; Rainer, *Nagy Imre*, vol. 2, 377.
22 Decision of the party secretariat, 15 March 1958, MOL M-KS 288/7/2.
23 'A general chase started for the destruction of the leading force of people's power: the party of the working class. As a part of this chase the Budapest party headquarters in Republic Square was shot by artillery on 30 October' (WB vol. 1, 5).

perceived the siege as a genuine anti-Communist attack, equivalent to an attempt to destroy the fundamental institutions of the regime.

The evidence what the White Books accumulated soon after the suppression of the armed revolt contained a large number of photographs among the numerous testimonies and articles. A sizable proportion of them were shot by Western reporters who were staying in Budapest during the revolution, and were published in leading journals such as *Time*, *Life*, *Paris Match* or *Der Spiegel*.[24] The photos, which generally followed the generic features of photographic war documentation, concentrated on the crowd, violence, armed groups or the ruins of the city. These photographic images played a great role in constructing for the Western public a revolution, meaning a collective social deed, out of October 1956.[25] The way the Communist observers, who compiled the history of the counterrevolution, saw this documentation is eloquently reflected by the first volume of the White Books.[26] What dominates the leaflet even at first sight is the terrifying spectacle of physical violence. Pictures of bodies, beaten, tortured, executed and dismembered, appear one by one. Undoubtedly, one which depicts a young soldier stripped to the waist and hanged upside down has become one of the most telling (Fig. 4). The gaze of the viewer is drawn immediately to the body situated in the vertical axis of the picture, occupying it completely from top to bottom. Subsequently one notices the figures standing in the background of the illustration. A few people are watching the victim, others are talking to each other or paying attention to something outside the frame. The chief element of the story is clearly the tortured and hanged body. The event the picture wants to portray is not the action of lynching, but rather its result, frozen in time: the dismembered body. The cruelty that is made impersonal and atemporal in this way is transformed into a depiction of the barbarity concealed in the depths of human soul, but which on this horrific occasion has erupted onto the surface.

The image of the corpses of fallen soldiers laid down in a row inflicts similar effects on the observer (Fig. 5). No other human figure can be seen besides the dead, so the cause of death remains hidden. The subject is not human activity in this case, only its outcome. The photography that depicts the corpses of the executed in a perspectival point of view evokes the image of parallels leading to infinity: the viewer can imagine this spectacle of the dead to continue beyond the frame. The photo represents the impersonal nature of mass devastation and murderous cruelty. The stories told by the

---

24 István Rév, *Retroactive Justice: Prehistory of Post-Communism* (Stanford: Stanford University Press, 2005), 246–7.
25 Sándor Horváth, 'Kollektív erőszak és városi térhasználat 1956-ban: forradalmi terek elbeszélése', *Múltunk* 4 (2006), 281.
26 'Seeing', like reading, has its own historicity, it is itself also a sociocultural product. On the historical methodology of examining 'seeing', see Randolph Starn, 'Seeing Culture in a Room for a Renaissance Prince', in *The New Cultural History*, ed. Lynn Hunt (Berkeley: University of California Press, 1989), 205–32; Reinhart Koselleck, 'Modernity and the Planes of Historicity', in *Futures Past: On the Semantics of Historical Time* (Cambridge MA/London: Harvard University Press, 1985), 3–20; Carlo Ginzburg, 'Distance and Perspective: Two Metaphors', in *Wooden Eyes: Nine Reflections on Distance* (New York: Verso, 2001), 139–56. A general methodological introduction is provided by Peter Burke, *Eyewitnessing: The Uses of Images as Historical Evidence* (London: Reaktion Books, 2001).

Figure 4. 'Six members of the guard were hanged by their feet and beaten half to death following a firefight in Republic Square'. White Books, vol. 1, 14.

Figure 5. 'Corpses of the murdered in front of the party headquarters'. White Books, vol. 1, 21.

images attempt to depict violence in an abstract, allegorical manner, as illustrated by the picture of a group assaulting a woman lying on the ground (Fig. 6). The gaze of the viewer is drawn to the centre by the white blouse of the woman, which stands out of the grey-black background. Thus the viewer first encounters the fact of cruelty: the woman's body is surrounded by legs kicking her and hands twisting her arms. The picture, nonetheless, remains impersonal: neither the woman's nor the attackers' faces are visible. In fact, the members of the group committing the atrocity appear below the waist, merely as a mass of bodily members directly carrying out the violence. At the same time, the composition is loaded with symbolic meanings related to gender: the woman's white dress evokes concepts of defenceless innocence, whereas the darkly dressed male figures surrounding her represent images of the untamed violence hidden in man. The spectacle of pure cruelty dominates the publication: within its sixty-two pages, the thin leaflet features twenty-seven pictures of corpses, executions and other atrocities. Any logic among the photographs besides repetition is hard to detect: each illustration depicts a new instance of cruelty. The recurrent images of violence strengthen the impression of a flood of arbitrary mercilessness; the purposeless, unhindered violence evokes the notion of uncivilized barbarity. The crowd, raging wildly, showed no mercy and 'bestially

Figure 6. 'A female staff member of the party committee is kicked, beaten with a rifle butt and has her hands twisted'. White Books, vol. 1, 13.

Figure 7. 'A victim whose corpse was "bestially" dismembered'. White Books, vol. 1, 17.

dismembered' its victims: one of the photographs shows a naked upper body with its head and arms removed (Fig. 7).[27]

The volume, however, clearly localizes these manifestations of human cruelty. Almost half of the pictures published in the White Book (twelve of the total twenty-seven) were shot nearby the siege of the Party Committee headquarters in Republic Square. Accordingly, the first chapter is devoted to expounding the 'counterrevolutionary attack against the headquarters of the Budapest Party Committee of the Hungarian Workers' Party'. The description begins by calling attention to the fact that the siege was the start of the general charge of the counterrevolution against the Communist Party, and aimed at overthrowing the people's democracy and restoring the capitalist system. It also states that the attack was a tactical manoeuvre: the counterrevolutionaries who previously masked themselves took to the stage openly this time, proved by their merciless massacre of the captured Communist defenders. The booklet provides a detailed description of the torture and execution of the captives. The manslaughter began with the shooting of negotiators:

> Those leaving the house were received by a volley. Comrade Mező [secretary of the Budapest Party Committee and representative of the negotiators] wanted to persuade the attackers that the attack and further bloodshed was senseless. It did not come to

---

27 WB vol. 1, 17. The inscription reads: 'A victim whose corpse was bestially dismembered.'

that since all three persons were shot. Then the attackers crowded in, and tortured and murdered with horrific cruelty those who were inside. The persons in uniform, army officers, policemen, regulars doing their active military service in the security police, most of whom were workers or peasant boys around 20 years old, were hanged on the trees in Republic Square, some of them were beheaded after hanging, others' hearts were cut out. Imre Mező, the secretary of the Greater Budapest Party Committee, died in this way. The executioners cut out the heart of Colonel János Asztalos, the old, respected fighter of the labour movement. Colonels Papp and Szabó were then killed. Péter Lakatos, teacher of the party school, was shot also here. More than twenty sons of the Hungarian people were victimized by the massacre at the Republic Square.[28]

As the assault against the Budapest party building, characterized as an extremely brutal event, was used as evidence of the counterrevolution, descriptions of subsequent occurrences during revolt also focused on violence. The official line was that after the fall of the party headquarters the capital became a terrain of uncontrolled violence. It was emphasized that the city was subjected to shameless, indiscriminate killers. One witness testified the following:

> I witnessed the following event on 31 October 1956, standing at the corner of the Lenin Boulevard and 7 November Square in Budapest: somebody shouted to a man walking on the pavement opposite to the Művész cinema at Lenin Boulevard: 'You're a security policeman!' The crowd charged the person in question, who wore khaki-coloured trousers and a tracksuit blouse with the colour of the Dózsa sports club [violet], and began to assault him. Taking advantage of the tumult, somebody put a cable of coiled wire around the neck of the captured man. By this means the already unconscious person was hanged from the tree in front of the hardware shop at the corner of the Lenin Boulevard and the Aradi Street. A board was hung on the neck of the murdered person with the following inscription: 'Tóth security police captain. This is the fate of every security policeman.'[29]

The White Books are full of reports of uncontrolled and uncivilized violence, such as that of a group of rebels who occupied flats in Budapest on 2 and 3 November to carry out executions with poisoned syringes, or a commander who was always drunk and ordered his men to shoot indiscriminately. The publication quotes a sixteen-year-old boy who became involved with a counterrevolutionary group:

> I reported to a captain in civil dress and usually went to given addresses to settle old scores with security policemen and Communists. Once we went to the third floor of an address near to Hotel Royal. Our captain told us that we were going to a security policeman. We found him at home together with his wife and six-year-old daughter. The captain first beat the policeman up then tore his ears off and cut his nose with scissors.

---

28 WB vol. 1, 19.
29 WB vol. 1, 25.

Then he let a volley into him. In the meantime the policeman's wife tried to run away, but one of the members of our group brought her down with one shot. We thought about what to do with the small girl, then we killed her too.[30]

According to the official interpretation even the countryside fell into the hands of the bloody counterrevolution. The White Book features numerous reports of beatings of party secretaries, leaders of agricultural cooperatives, or executions of policemen and old Communists. The editors point out that arrests of Communist functionaries and the preparation of execution lists were widespread. For instance, the head of the council of Mezőtárkány village was assaulted seriously: the man's lung was severely damaged and two of his ribs fractured. Even his nine-year-old son was beaten. The booklet contains an account of the happenings in the industrial city of Miskolc as well, where on 3 November five police officers were assaulted and hanged on the Soviet memorial.[31]

Terrorist violence remained the fundamental element of the representation of the counterrevolution in the following months. The Budapest Central Police Station began to prosecute 'terrorist actions' committed during the revolt, and reported fifty assaults, robberies and murders on 14 December 1956.[32] The *Népszabadság* gives an account on the murder of a Communist commander, Sándor Sziklai, and his father-in-law: 'The old Communist was beaten to death. Then Sándor Sziklai's corpse was carried out to the street; his dead body was kicked and abused by the mob. They were shouting and searching the wife of comrade Sziklai. They cried that the woman would end up next to her husband. Then the flat was ravaged and robbed. Vandalism and walls splashed with blood bear the mark of the hands of counterrevolutionary evildoers.'[33] In the *Népakarat* (People's will), a report of the trial of one of the main rebel leaders, József Dudás, emphasizes that the defendant engaged himself with anti-Communism as a Horthyist spy and agent provocateur. It also states that the man had been arrested in 1946 because of counterrevolutionary conspiracy. The article mentions that Dudás's men put three persons to the sword in front of a department store, among other murders. One of his deputies led a special commando unit that was charged with searching out and arresting Communists. The report claims that the arrested were then tortured and some of them executed.[34] On 10 February 1957 the *Népszabadság* published a long report on the lynch law in Miskolc, where seven persons were killed. Two of them were hanged on the Soviet war memorial after having been tortured, and a third person was thrown off the balcony of the town hall. In the search for a proper attribute to classify the bloody events the journalist evokes a historical comparison. The article states, 'A sadist massacre was carried out on 26 and 27 October in Miskolc, the like of which can be done

---

30 WB vol. 1, 27–8.
31 WB vol. 1, 37–49.
32 MOL M-BP-1 1956/57/27.
33 NSZ, 5 December 1956, 5. Sziklai most probably committed suicide, after killing his father-in-law as the outcome of a harsh family quarrel. Before this, they had probably initiated the fight with the demonstrators by shooting at them.
34 *Népakarat*, 20 January 1957.

only by fascists.'³⁵ (Fascists usually meant Hitler's followers in Communist language.) Nonetheless, the author does not claim that the killers were fascists. The executions of the policemen are so extraordinary that ordinary language is inappropriate: 'Deliberate manslaughter! Though this term can be found in the police reports and in the indictments of the public prosecution as it is required by the law, to describe the outrage of the counterrevolutionaries in Miskolc other words have to be sought out.' Fascist barbarity seemed to be the appropriate term for the party journalist to describe the massacre of Communists. Another typical case representing counterrevolutionary bestiality was the trial of Ilona Tóth and her companions. The woman was accused of deliberately killing a man by using a poisoned syringe. According to the accusations, since Tóth failed to finish off the victim she stabbed him to death with a knife.³⁶

The cruelty of the counterrevolution was emphasized by reports describing how the rebels killed innocent and defenceless people. The party's daily, for instance, published an article on 30 March 1957 about the sad story of a small boy. It begins with a hospital scene, depicting a seriously injured four-year-old boy who could not sleep or speak, but was constantly weeping. The boy is the son of a security police officer. The article then emphasizes the harmony of the small family, who lived a quiet and modest life and were friendly towards everyone. The husband had to leave on 22 October 1956 and did not return. The author expressively describes the wife's fear and the attack by the counterrevolutionaries. According to the report the men were outrageously drunk, raped the woman and began to throw furniture out of the window. Eventually they threw out the body of the woman and the small boy who was watching the horrors in panic. The wife immediately died, her son however survived, but lost the ability to speak. The author concludes that his muteness is the strongest accusation against the merciless counterrevolution.³⁷ On 9 April a report about the siege of the Athenaeum print shop and the execution of its defenders was printed as well.³⁸

Communist interpreters who experienced the extraordinarily violent anti-Communist attacks were shocked by the perceived cruelty of the assaults. Thus it was logical for them that the uprising, initially supported by a considerable proportion of them, eventually aspired to destroy the dictatorship of the proletariat through a systematic elimination of the party. In an attempt to comprehend these terrible events they were connected to a more thoroughly understood violence. The horrors of 1956 reminded them of those in 1919: the massacre at the Republic Square was called 'the counterrevolutionary persecution similar to the White Terror of 1919'.³⁹ A folder of photographs taken at Republic Square, collected by Communist historians as evidence of the 'counterrevolution', is also titled

---

35 NSZ, 10 February 1957, 5.
36 *Népakarat*, 9 December 1956, 4; and 18 January 1957, 4; NSZ, 1 March 1957, 8. Ilona Tóth's case has remained a particularly controversial issue to this day. Many historians doubt if she actually committed the murders at all. See Réka Kiss and Sándor M. Kiss, *A csalogány elszállt: Tóth Ilona tragikuma* (Budapest: Kairosz, 2007).
37 Ferenc Vasvári, 'Vád' (Charge), NSZ, 30 March 1957.
38 Endre András, 'Hiteles történet az Atheneum Nyomda védőiről' (Authentic story about the defenders of the Atheneum print shop), NSZ, 9 April 1957.
39 WB vol. 1, 22.

'The terror of Siófok and Orgovány haunts!'[40] Thereby the mysterious was compared to the familiar in order to render the strange phenomenon easier to interpret. The first volume of the White Books does not base its argument solely on this specific historical analogy: 1919 is mentioned only twice in total. However, the memory of the White Terror seemed to provide a genuine opportunity to formulate a meaning from the happenings. Communist observers understood the attack against the people's democracy as an event that had 'happened in an astonishingly similar way to the counterrevolutionary attempt against the Soviet Republic in 1919'.[41]

In January and February 1957 the Hungarian Communist leadership decided to prepare trials against the participants of the uprising. In connection to this, the interpretation of the revolt in 1956 came closer to the hardliner position. A government programme published on 6 January had already mentioned Imre Nagy's treason: 'The treason of the Imre Nagy government opened the way for the counterrevolution, which during these days killed mercilessly the faithful sons and daughters of the socialist revolution.'[42] The meeting of the Provisional Executive Committee on 12 February defined the former prime minister and his fellows as an anti-Soviet and antiparty group.[43] The Provisional Central Committee accused Imre Nagy of organizing an independent faction and of consciously preparing the counterrevolution on 26 February.[44] Parallel to this, trials against those authors who took part in the revolution were prepared with the intention of revealing the role of the Authors' Association in 'directing the counterrevolution'.[45] Starting from the end of February, the party laid more stress on the measures against 'national Communism' and 'revisionism'.[46] By March the plan to begin legal proceedings against the Imre Nagy group, who were being kept in Romania, reached fruition, and on 14 April they were arrested.[47]

On 2 February 1957 László Réti, the director of the Institute for Party History during the Rákosi regime, published an article titled 'History teaches: August 1919' in the *Népszabadság*. The aim of the Communist historian was to accuse Imre Nagy of preparing the counterrevolution. The author stated that after 23 October a second Peidl government had been formed (Gyula Peidl had been a trade unionist Social Democratic leader who had presided over the six-day government that had followed the resignation of the Soviet government in 1919 and who had been forced to leave by counterrevolutionaries). The Peidl government in 1919 had deceived the workers by claiming that no counterrevolutionary menace had existed and therefore demanded a

---

40 Siófok and Orgovány were the sites of the most infamous White Terror massacres in 1919. The folder is in Állambiztonsági Szolgálatok Történeti Levéltára (Historical Archives of the State Security Services). 'Siófok, Orgovány réme kísért!' 4.1. A-220.
41 WB vol. 1, 3.
42 *Népakarat*, 6 January 1957; NSZ, 6 January 1957. On the program of the government, see Rainer, *Imre Nagy*, vol. 2, 378; Huszár, *Kádár*, vol. 2, 27.
43 MSZMP vol. 2, 114–21; Rainer, *Imre Nagy*, vol. 2, 379; Kalmár, *Ennivaló és hozomány*, 29.
44 MSZMP vol. 2, 219–21; Huszár, *Kádár*, vol. 2, 32; Rainer, *Imre Nagy*, vol. 2, 379.
45 Standeisky, *Az írók és a hatalom*, 208.
46 Standeisky, *Az írók és a hatalom*, 230, 235.
47 Rainer, *Nagy Imre*, vol. 2, 382–3; Huszár, *Kádár*, vol. 2, 39–46.

'bourgeois democracy'. Nevertheless, as Réti put it, the 'fascist counterrevolution' came into existence 'on the ruins of the dictatorship of the proletariat'. The article argues that Nagy apparently wanted a 'democracy' as well, but that the result of his politics would have also been the restoration of counterrevolution, unless the USSR could have intervened.[48] Academician Gyula Hevesi, former participant in the First Hungarian Soviet Republic, highlighted in his ceremonial address on 21 March that

> our present Revolutionary Worker-Peasant Government, after the recent unfortunate deviations, serves the cause of our people once again, following the path of the Hungarian revolutionary labour movement begun gloriously by the First Hungarian Soviet Republic. It drew all of its conclusions from the achievements as well as the failures of the Soviet Republic. This was already begun when the government recognized clearly and timely that the Imre Nagy government played exactly the same role as Gyula Peidl's right-wing government in 1919 after the fall of the workers' power, and it was virtually driving the country under the yoke of fascism. It was then continued when the government did what we would have also liked to have done at that time, in fact, had even attempted to do, but remained only an unrealized hope: to ask for the friendly help of the Soviet people to save the revolution.[49]

The memory of the counterrevolution in 1919 was easily available descriptive language for the Communist interpreters, which could connect familiar concepts with new experiences. Evoking the First Hungarian Soviet Republic at the turn of 1956 and 1957 provided an opportunity, first of all, for the Communist leadership to attempt to interpret the meaning of such notions as 'counterrevolution', 'White Terror', 'opportunism' or 'the people's power', which played a crucial role in the struggle to master the memory of 1956. The rethinking of the past meant a tangible help in understanding the present.[50] The discussion of 1919 thereby contributed to the Communist reading of 1956, meanwhile the problems of the present made it possible to summon the past. This condition increased the demand for historical knowledge related to the First Hungarian Soviet Republic. On 21 March 1957, in its ceremonial article the *Népakarat* put it as follows:

> And now, as we remember the 38th anniversary of the beginnings of the resolute struggle: the memory of the Hungarian proletariat and those fallen in the fight demand that we finally depict by Marxist methods the true face of the First Hungarian Soviet Republic for our people, purely, in its entire grandeur and sorrowful tragedy. Obviously, this is not the duty of a leading article and its author, but historians coming out of the fog of Byzantinism and ideologists tearing apart dogmatism.[51]

---

48 László Réti, 'Tanít a történelem 1919 augusztus' (History teaches August 1919), NSZ, 2 February 1957.
49 *Népakarat*, 22 March 1957.
50 In this period, the fate of 1919 in the Hungarian Communist remembrance was similar to that of the siege of Masada in Jewish memory: Barry Schwartz, Yael Zerubavel and Bernice M. Barnett, 'The Recovery of Masada: A Study in Collective Memory', *Sociological Quarterly* 27 (2) (1986): 147–64.
51 István Pikay, 'Tündököljék való fényében!' (Shine its true light!), *Népakarat*, 21 March 1957, 3.

This fact, however, did not immediately entail the elevation of the First Hungarian Soviet Republic. Though old party members became more and more respected, this happened in connection with the organization of the Workers' Guard during January and February 1957.[52] As the leadership searched for reliable membership its attention was turned towards the old party members, including partisans, organized workers from before 1944 and former Red Army soldiers from 1919. János Kádár even claimed that those persons would be the party's main force, since the younger members had become unsettled. In spite of the fact that the foundation of the Worker's Guard could have provided opportunities for comparing the regime with 1919, it could not create a historical context for its reappraisal. The Provisional Executive Committee accepted the idea of the Workers' Guard on 29 January 1957. Nonetheless, when it decided on the forthcoming spring political anniversaries on 12 February it did not include the proclamation of the First Hungarian Soviet Republic alongside the anniversaries of the 1848 revolution (15 March) and the end of the war in 1945 (4 April).[53] Only narrow circles of the party celebrated 21 March 1957: the Budapest Provisional Executive Committee accompanied by a group of hardliners and the Institute for Party History gathered in the Central Officers' Building of the People's Army of Hungary to organize a commemorative ceremony. At the same time, the chief leaders of the party and the government travelled to Moscow to participate in a formal meeting with the representatives of the Soviet party and state.[54]

2

The party's daily reported the arrest of Mihály Francia Kiss on 8 March 1957. The 70-year-old Francia Kiss was a well-known figure of the White Terror commandos, who had persecuted Communists, Jews and leftists after the collapse of the First Hungarian Soviet Republic in 1919 and 1920.[55] Francia Kiss was caught in 1957 after being spotted by a citizen, who informed the authorities. He was seen being driven on a Pobeda car to the president of the National Committee during the counterrevolution. Although this scene was used as an evidence for confirming that the old man played a counterrevolutionary role in October 1956, he was not sentenced for these crimes. Instead the judge upheld the statements of the People's Tribunal in 1947, in which he had been condemned in absentia for illegal tortures and executions. The accusations, however, were added to a series of others such as identity card forgery and illegal possession of

---

52 In 1957, for instance, the Executive Committee of the Communist Party of Baranya county demanded the honouring of those Communists of 1919 who 'gave proof of honest, party-like and brave behaviour during the events of the counterrevolution of 1956' (MOL M-KS 288/21/1957/3).
53 MSZMP vol. 2, 61–3, 109–10.
54 *Népakarat*, 19 March 1957, 21 March 1957, 22 March 1957.
55 The role of Francia Kiss's trial in the construction of the counterrevolution was brilliantly analysed recently by Rév, *Retroactive Justice*, 210–24. The translations are taken from here. The records of the trial are preserved in the City Archives of Budapest, BFL VII. 5e/20630/I–IV.

weapons. The court's intention was to prove that the once White Terrorist had pursued his counterrevolutionary activity and remained an enemy of the people's democracy: 'In addition to the crimes committed by Mihály Francia Kiss in 1919 and 1920, he also committed crimes following the liberation of Hungary in 1945.'[56] He was construed as a personality in perpetual criminality: the court stated that after the liberation the defendant realized the approaching threat of prosecution and tried to escape. He hid a Parabellum pistol on him and in 1954 forged an identity card, living under the name of József Kovács. The trial meant an opportunity for Communist observers to recognize that there prevailed, indeed, some form of temporal continuity between the instances of the counterrevolution in 1919 and the revolt in 1956. 'As if we are experiencing the first days of November 1956, [...] the methods of counterrevolution have not changed after 37 years', said the *Népszabadság* in its account of Francia Kiss's arrest.[57]

The December resolution of the party, while ranking the 'Horthy fascist and Hungarian capitalist landowner counterrevolution' in third place after the Rákosi clique and the Nagy group as the causes of the 1956 revolt, clearly maintained that the supporters of the previous regime did not give up their intention to restore their rule and had organized themselves illegally since 1945. As a matter of fact, the infamous document represented a history of deceit: first, the people took to the streets led by their just discontent towards the Rákosi regime; second, their benign intentions were abused by an apparently Communist government of the traitor Imre Nagy; while, third, in reality the events had already been directed by the supporters of the Horthy regime aspiring to restore the rule of capitalist and feudalist exploitation. The *continuity* of the counterrevolution thus formed an unavoidably necessary element in the construction of the 1956 revolt as an *essential* counterrevolution: if the uprising in terms of a higher historical reality had not been carried out by the 'people' who had actually participated in it, but by Horthyist supporters who had actually remained in the background, the only explanation for their capability of preparing the uprising was their constant presence as an *abstract* historical force throughout the recent period.[58] As a consequence, the crucial problem of the Kádárist Communist leadership and party elite was to prove the *actual* presence of Horthyist officers in the *actual* reality of the revolt of 1956.[59] The fact that the purpose of the anti-Communist persecution was the restoration of the Horthy regime was proved by the return of the figures of the prewar establishment. Communist interpreters of the uprising sought to prove that the principal force within the insurgents was the group of former landowners, capitalists and Horthyist officers whose main purpose was the resurrection of their previous rule over the Hungarian people.

---

56 Rév, *Retroactive Justice*, 211; BFL VII. 5e/20630/III.
57 NSZ, 13 March 1957.
58 MSZMP vol. 2, 239. This is the central argument in András Mink, 'The Fiction of the Counterrevolution', part of his PhD thesis 'The Kopjás: The Culture of the Counterrevolution' (Budapest: Central European University, 2003), CEU Library.
59 In this respect, the history of the Kádár era is the history of a constant historiographical project, focused on the documentation of the counterrevolution and its transformation into an intelligible narrative.

The White Books provided numerous examples describing how former Horthyist officers returned to their localities to claim leadership over the uprising in October 1956. It was stressed that the previous Horthyist administration was commissioned once more by the local revolutionary committees. The booklet supported with plenty of examples the statement that ex-owners of workshops or factories returned and began to command their workers again. At the end of January the *Népszabadság* also informed its readers that during October former Horthyist officers, gendarmes and a rich butcher had formed the workers' council in Esztergom.[60] The third volume of the official publications of the government laid greater stress on establishing the presence of supporters of the Horthy regime in the events of 1956. The publication devoted a chapter to the 'local revolutionary committees' of the revolution in 1956:

> The majority of the membership of the committees and especially the dominant leaders did not consist of the working peasantry that made up the overwhelming majority of the population, but of kulaks, former gendarmes, Horthyist officers and village notaries or mayors who allied with the criminal elements [...]. The working people of the villages were astonished by the fact that its well-known enemies – the kulaks, gendarmes, Horthyist village leaders and notaries – were regaining power.[61]

Evidence like this was not intended only to prove that the uprising aimed at a reactionary restoration of the old regime, but also to point at the constant anti-Communist activity of the counterrevolutionaries. As an example the booklet quotes the brief autobiography of the deputy head of the workers' council in the town of Mezőkövesd: 'I am an officer of the Horthy regime trained in the Ludovika Military Academy [the elite officer training centre of the prewar establishment which became the symbol of the old army during the Communist period]. I was punished many times for antiparty and antidemocratic instigation. I hid my weapons twelve years ago: a lot of handguns and a machine gun. Now I have taken them all out.'[62] One of the most instructive paragraphs in these regards describes the members of the National Committee in Monor.

László Szente, the head of the prewar county administration, who had been condemned for taking part in the antistate conspiracy of Ferenc Nagy (Nagy had been the smallholder prime minister of Hungary between 1946–1947; he had consistently opposed the Communist dictatorship and had been forced to leave the country due to the construction of the antidemocratic conspiracy in 1946) became the head of the National Committee in Monor. Ferenc Baranyi, former *Horthyist notary* became deputy and secretary, while the committee included Sándor Lengyel, *previously estate manager and the brother of a Horthyist general*, Ferenc Lilik, *organizer of the Arrow Cross party*, Imre Füzi, *kulak*, and Dr Antal Karbach, *Arrow Cross lawyer*. János Maróty, *Horthyist hussar captain*, became the commander of the National Guard, whereas Ferenc Mátyás, *former*

---

60 NSZ, 30 January 1957. See also radio broadcasts in February 1957, OSA 300/40/1/1299.
61 WB vol. 3, 12.
62 WB vol. 3, 13–15.

gendarme sergeant, became the leader of its political criminal section. His employees were József Wallner, *former gendarme lieutenant, counterintelligence officer*, Pál Kovács and Sándor Dávid, *former gendarme sergeants*, and Gábor Bara, *former gendarme lieutenant*. The 'National Committee' *gave the Factory of Monor over to its former owner*, Ferenc Kovács.[63]

Simultaneously with the publication of the White Books, the Communist government laid great emphasis on disseminating its evidence as broadly as possible. The Committee for Canvassing and Propaganda received a proposal on installing an exhibition on 'the counterrevolutionary attempt to overthrow the people's democracy' on 4 March. On its 15 March meeting the committee decided to open the exhibition on 1 May, to be organized by the Council of Ministers.[64] The exhibition aimed at increasing the moral authenticity of the official interpretation by artistic means, by displaying a considerable number of works of art; still, the main emphasis was not laid on these techniques of representation.[65] The propagandists who designed the exhibition, which was eventually opened in the Institute of Party History at the end of June, made great efforts to put a large number of photographs, original documents and objects – like weapons, communication technology, clothes of victims and gendarme uniforms – on display.[66] The party's daily gave an account of the preparations as follows:

> Pictures and documents depict October and November as it really happened in ten rooms [...]. There is the cover of US air photograph equipment no. 1102 among the displayed objects [...]. We can see the photocopy of the letter which a Hungarian fascist returned from a camp in Nuremberg, sent to his fellows who remained there. Cut and deranged flags show how the counterrevolutionaries burnt the red flags and dismembered the national flags by cutting out the emblem of the People's Republic.[67]

The purpose of the organizers was to bring the abstract interpretation of history tangibly close for the audience of the exhibition by means of building a direct relationship with the objects of the past.

The spatial organization of the exhibition also served this purpose, as demonstrated by a photograph taken at the opening in the provincial town of Ózd.[68] It is clearly visible in the picture that the boards could be studied next to each other, situated in a row on the wall of the exhibition room. Glass cases stand in front of the boards, arranged in

---

63   WB vol. 3, 18. Italics original.
64   MOL M-KS 288/22/1957/1.
65   Anna Oelmacher, 'A "Magyarországi ellenforradalom" kiállítás képzőművészeti anyagáról' (On the artistic material of the exhibition 'Counterrevolution in Hungary'), *Magyarország*, 28 August 1957.
66   A photograph kept in the Central Records Office of the Ministry of Interior shows the material evidence of the 'counterrevolution'. Online: http://w3.osaarchivum.org/galeria/index_hu/sites/ellenforradalom/ellenframes3.html (accessed: 30 September 2013).
67   NSZ, 29 May 1957, 5.
68   Historical Photographic Records of the Hungarian National Museum 48. ME/II/B, Box: Culture: Exhibitions, 1957–1962. Ózd. The exhibition on the counterrevolution. Martyrs. 1957. Registry no.: Hungarian Labour Movement Museum 86.11.

a similar manner in straight line. In front of the glass cases there is a roundtable and chairs belonging to it. The ordering of the furniture noticeably leaves very little room in between the cases, boards and the table, so that it would only be possible to stand in a line. This organization drove the audience to advance in a straight row that required them to constantly face the boards and objects displayed in the glass cases. In this way the exhibition demands from its audience a continuous assessment of the objects, documents and traces of the past, thereby imitating the method of the historian.

The historical evidence, however, was made available by the party and it was the party who revealed it to the intended audience in order to educate them about the past. The exhibition was thus meant to form the counterpart to the haunting nightmare of the revolting 1956 crowd: by constructing the social body of the ideal masses marching towards historical progress, organized, ordered and disciplined according to the instruction of the party. Museums make not only their collections, but also their visitors the object of display and the subjects of spectacle. Modern museums born at the beginning of the nineteenth century were established as special institutions of education and civilization: their purpose was to transform the uneducated, undisciplined and, therefore, terrifying crowd into cultured, civilized citizens. The spatial construction of exhibitions transformed the mob flowing disorderly in the streets into an observable, disciplinable and civilizable crowd.[69]

The public space of the room and the visitors' book of the exhibition offered the opportunity for a supervising gaze for the Communist authorities: the crowd which had flooded in disorder in the streets of October 1956, which hid in the urban jungle and was uncontrollable, now arrived in organized rows and in a disciplined manner to come to terms with the counterrevolution: 'A long queue is standing in front of the gate on József nádor Square. People are crowded up in the small rooms, too. It is true – who does not believe should look at it with his own eyes. This is the summer of 1957. It is not bad even as a symbol for foreign journalists or politicians: people are queuing in Budapest to visit the exhibition on the October counterrevolution.'[70] The exhibition room conveyed the power of transformation and the promise of purification: the chaotic, disordered, disorganized, barbaric 1956 crowd could become disciplined socialist man in front of the visitors' book:

> There is something really strange, extraordinarily shocking, in the way sixteen- to eighteen-year-old youngsters view the exhibition revealing the documents of the counterrevolution. The light of more and more shocking experiences is reflected on their faces than one would have thought possible: astonishment, horror and the recognition of something that almost drove their young lives into trouble. Something that tried to grab their youthful enthusiasm and something which they had to wake up from sooner or later – and it is right they woke up.[71]

---

69 About this process see: Tony Bennett, *The Birth of the Museum: History, Theory, Politics* (London/New York: Routledge, 1995), 72.

70 György Kalmár, 'Bejegyzés helyett az ellenforradalomról szóló kiállítás vendégkönyvébe' (Instead of making notes in the visitors' book of the exhibition about the counterrevolution), NSZ, 26 June 1957, 3.

71 Margit Várkonyi, 'Egy kiállítás látogatói…' (Visitors of an exhibition…), *Népakarat*, 4 July 1957, 3.

Historical museums were established during the turn of the eighteenth and nineteenth centuries in Europe. These historical exhibitions answered in a particular way the question of the qualities of the road towards the past. These collections were founded due to the conviction that images, photographs, graphic reconstructions and, most of all, objects enabled the visitor once more to truly experience the past. Historical museums were generated in the faith that objects of the past meant more authentic and direct connection to the experience of history than any text could. The artefacts represented relics of the past which through their physical identity with history bore a special power of resonance: they appeared to be able to directly summon the historical contexts and sociocultural webs that the objects themselves were derived from.[72]

Communist historical propaganda believed itself to be continuing this legacy. Relationships appearing among the objects raised the impression of a particular continuity. The gendarme uniforms and the weapons of the rebels in October, as well as the clothes attributed to victims (establishing spatial connection with them), uncovered the origins of 1956 directly in the history of the counterrevolutionary period. This effect was confirmed by the proportions of documents and photos installed in the exhibition. The thematic section 'The immediate open appearance of counterrevolutionary forces' had three times more than the depiction of the events of 23 October and almost six times more than the representation of the illegal measures of the Rákosi period.[73] These boards, which described the activity of returned émigrés or counterrevolutionary elements in the workers' councils, implied a direct connection between the 1956 October uprising and the sociopolitical conditions of the Horthy period.

These statements already implied a continuity of the counterrevolution: supporters of the regime established in 1919–20 after the fall of the Soviet Republic were allegedly the major delinquents in the counterrevolution of 1956. Communist interpreters believed they had touched upon the tangible evidence for this conception in the figure of Francia Kiss: 'The seeds Mihály Francia Kiss and company sowed in 1919 grew into a terrible harvest in the days of the counterrevolution on 23 October 1956.'[74] The fourth volume of the government's official interpretation, probably published in September after the trial, included a photo of the old defendant speaking in the courtroom with the following subtitle: 'Mihály Francia Kiss, the ill-famed mass murderer of the counterrevolution in 1919 had concealed himself under a pseudonym for 12 years. He saw his time had come in the days of October to leave his refuge and to take part in actions against Communists.'[75]

---

72 Stephen Bann, *The Clothing of Clio: A Study of the Representation of History in Nineteenth-Century Britain and France* (Cambridge: Cambridge University Press, 1984), 77–92; Susan M. Pearce, *Museums, Objects and Collections: A Cultural Study* (Washington, DC: Smithsonian Institution Press, 1992), 198; Stephen Greenblatt, 'Resonance and Wonder', in *Exhibiting Cultures: The Poetics and Politics of Museum Display*, ed. Ivan Karp and Steven D. Lavine (Washington, DC/London: Smithsonian Books, 1991), 42.
73 MOL M-KS 288/22/1957/1.
74 Rév, *Retroactive Justice*, 213; Court of the Capital, sentence of the first instance, 32. BFL VII. 5e/20630/III.
75 WB vol. 4, photo appendix.

The character of the relationship between 1919 and 1956 was thereby transformed, most probably largely unrecognized even for the Communist observers themselves. The similarity of the violence, which could be connected to one single individual, acquired a temporal dimension and, hence, suddenly revealed a historical continuity. As a matter of fact, this temporal identity shed light on the chronological sequence of 1919, 1956 and the mass murders committed by the Hungarian fascist Arrow Cross Party in between in 1944. The People's Tribunal formulated this reasoning in its sentence for the first instance, dated 13 June 1957:

> The detailed and well-established facts of the case are entirely recognizable in the acts of terror and mass murders committed by the Arrow Cross in 1944 and are also clearly visible in the movements which were committed against the faithful sons of the Hungarian People's Republic during the counterrevolution after 23 October 1956. The sadistic murders, skinning of humans alive, cutting out of sexual organs, and similar acts committed in Orgovány, Izsák and the region of Kecskemét in 1919 were not unknown to those who carried out similar murders in the Arrow Cross's Party Headquarters in Budapest. The murderers of our executed and mutilated martyrs on Republic Square and those who committed murders in front of the police department in Miskolc used the same methods and carried out their acts with the same sadistic cruelty as Mihály Francia Kiss and his terrorist companions did in 1919.[76]

Mihály Francia Kiss's case was the first in a series of arrests initiated by the Communist authorities in order reinstigate the prosecutions of criminals active in between the wars, but who did not go to trial due to political reasons. For that purpose, the People's Tribunals that ceased to function in 1950 were restarted and the investigations of numerous former gendarme officers were reopened. A local newspaper reported in August 1957 on the case of a 'former fascist gendarme sergeant, a murderer, a war criminal'. The journalist of the local paper attributed the killing of a fugitive Jew to the former officer in 1944. He was also claimed to have resumed his vicious crimes in October 1956 when he had allegedly been given weapons by the former village notary and stabbed one of his old enemies.[77] In May 1958 the minister of interior, Béla Biszku (a major proponent of hardliners during the Kádár era), commanded the Department of Investigations of his ministry to prosecute the cases of 385 persons who were suspected of having participated in the persecution of Communists or other left-wing people before or during WWII. Eventually, ninety-four of them were tried and thirty-six were executed. Like Francia Kiss, these mostly former gendarme officers were not called to account for deeds committed in 1956. These measures had different goals. On the one hand, the party leadership wanted to demonstrate conspicuously that it used violence in a significantly different way than its predecessor had done: it imprisoned no faithful Communists, but their previous

---

76 Rév, *Retroactive Justice*, 213; Court of the Capital, sentence of the first instance, 8. BFL VII. 5e/20630/III.
77 'Emlékezzünk... Tizenkét évi bujdosás után a népbíróság elé került a gyilkos csendőrfőtörzsőrmester' (Remember... after twelve years of hiding the murderer gendarme sergeant went on trial in front of the people's tribunal), *Kisalföld*, 9 August 1957, 7.

persecutors. On the other hand, it wanted to construct evidence for the alleged similarity of killings committed in 1956 and the war crimes carried out in 1944.[78]

The detailed descriptions of the violence and the shocking images added to them were not mere illustrations of the interpretation in these trials. The purpose of evoking terrible events was not only to condemn them as the consequence of cruel, violent and destructive movements. The bloody, materialistic and extremely naturalistic details of the violence occupy an essential and focal position in the narrative of the counterrevolution: these revealed the true characteristic of the happenings. The representation of violence was as shocking as it was extraordinary and unexpected. The outstanding cruelty of the executioners was barbarous and atavistic: nobody expected merciless deeds like these in twentieth-century Europe. The extraordinary nature of the violence provided the means to connect 1919, 1944 and 1956. The judge hereby linked 1919 to 1944, the war catastrophe, and then 1956, the counterrevolution. Thus, according to the judge, the similarities of the three events not only established a relationship between them. They proved that there had existed a constant threatening force throughout modern Hungarian history. Thereby, an understanding of modern Hungarian history as a constant struggle between revolution and counterrevolution was established. In order to forge together this conception the chronological distance between Horthy's coming into power in 1919 and Szálasi's takeover in 1944 was eliminated based on the violence that accompanied both events. The two regimes were understood as different historical manifestations of the rule of one same and continuous force. The Communist court believed that the counterrevolution in 1956 was also part of this continuous identity. The major problem of this abstract historical conception was the chronological gap between 1945, when according to official historiography the people's democracy successfully suppressed the remnants of the counterrevolutionary regime, and 1956, when it was allegedly still capable of striking back.

Family relations had played a role in constructing the continuity of agents between the elite of the Horthy regime and the participants in 1956 preceding Francia Kiss's trial. Probably the best depiction of the official representation was the case of the village of Csorna. The first volume of the White Books calls attention to the fact that the National Committee of the village was led by a former Arrow Cross administrator whose father had been a prominent figure of the White Terror in 1920. The man's younger brother had his own role: he began to reorganize the Gendarmerie in the settlement. The clan directed the local counterrevolution: they appointed an old Horthyist officer the head of the National Committee and started to raise White Terror commandos.[79] Though the story seems to be simply a weird chapter of the post-1956 repression, it contains

---

78 One of the main figures in these investigations, security officer and later propaganda historian Ervin Hollós, published the results of his former professional work in his *Kik voltak, mit akartak?* (Budapest: Kossuth, 1967), 301–9, in a typical chapter titled 'The reserve' (*A tartalék*). See also the report on the second half of 1959 of the Military High Prosecution, registry no. 0027/1960, in Sándor Révész, ed., *Beszélő évek. 1957–1968* (Budapest: Beszélő, 2000), 139–41. Four of these cases are described in detail in Attila Szakolczai, 'Háborús bűnösök elítélése az 1956-os forradalom után', *Évkönyv. Magyarország a jelenkorban, 1956-os Intézet* 13 (2004): 29–52.
79 WB vol. 1, 46.

a crucial element of the statements made on the counterrevolution. Although these descriptions do not state it definitively, they imply that the same forces and persons who created the Horthy regime in 1919 wanted to overthrow the Communist system in 1956. As the judge argued in Mihály Francia Kiss's trial, 'With no doubt Mihály Francia Kiss was and remains up to this day an individual with fascist sympathies.'[80] Communist historical interpreters tried to demonstrate that a tangible physical identity prevailed throughout the abstract historical continuity of 1919, 1944 and 1956. This physical continuity revealed the existence of a kind of essential historical identity for the Communist interpreters. Thereby, the three distinct historical events did not simply form a continuous chain, but became the individual manifestations of a temporally identical historical force. The court's historical interpretation did not argue simply for continuity, meaning subsequent casual links and relationships of historical origin and genesis. The continuity and likeness of action was explained through a representation of the actors as agents of the constantly identical historical force of fascism. The third volume of the government's White Books states that the rebels had started as Hitler had, by attacking Communists, and that they had had the same counterrevolutionary program as the Horthy fascists had in 1919.[81] The same perception of physical continuity drove the founders of the Federation of Communist Youth to formally establish the organization on 21 March 1957: 'Our Federation is a direct heir and successor of the Federation of Young Communist Workers founded in 1919 and was forced into illegality in between the two world wars and the years of World War II.'[82]

Although death means an end of earthly life, the body hides itself underground where it can preserve or develop that core of material identity that makes it possible to resurrect the same form of life.[83] Counterrevolution rested underground between its 1944–45 death and 1956 resurrection. The judge drew this conclusion at Mihály Francia Kiss's trial:

> His crimes point the way down a lasting trail leading to the next horrors and were a cradle to the deformity which was later called fascism. His behaviour laid its stamp on the quarter of a century of rule by Horthy fascism; it was to be found throughout the underground organization of the counterrevolutionary movement, throughout the period of the building of Socialism; and this same spirit eventually exploded with elementary power in the horrible days of the rebirth of the counterrevolution on 23 October 1956.[84]

---

80 Rév, *Retroactive Justice*, 211; Court of the Capital, sentence of the first instance, 3. BFL VII. 5e/20630/III.
81 WB vol. 3, 4, 10.
82 *Népakarat*, 22 March 1957, 3.
83 Caroline Walker Bynum, *The Resurrection of the Body in Western Christianity, 200–1336* (New York: Columbia University Press, 1995), 21–58.
84 Rév, *Retroactive Justice*, 213; Court of the Capital, sentence of the first instance, 32. BFL VII. 5e/20630/III.

Communist interpreters began to conceive the uprising in 1956 as a resurrection or revival of the White Terror in 1919. The fourth volume of the White Books contains a short chapter also about the White Terror which concludes that:

> The counterrevolutionary terror and formation of terror groups prove that the old Hungarian Gestapo of the Horthy–Szálasi era was under construction and it was preparing for a bloody persecution of the supporters of the Hungarian people's power, Communists and non-Communists, functionaries and tens of thousands of simple workers and peasants. The bloody White Terror of Horthy in 1919 began to gain new life. In certain places it was attempted to cover the true character of the 'freedom fight', while in other sites they appeared openly in the same form as in 1919 (officers' commandos).[85]

It is as if the party leaders were acting according to the spirit of the apostle Paul himself, who argued that the corpse was a kind of seed from which new life would grow. By insisting that the new comes from the old, Paul argued that a person has an identity before and after death.

Nonetheless, Communist leaders seemed to overlook the crucial feature of the belief in resurrection. Beginning with the second half of the thirteenth century, a remarkable transformation of the concept of the resurrection began, when dogma associated strongly with the recognizable and reproducible body. The Church condemned the propositions of clerical scholars concerning pure spiritual continuity in 1277 in Paris. The great scholastics of the late thirteenth century – Albert the Great, Thomas Aquinas and Giles of Rome – denied that the body equalled the person. They rather argued that the person formed a psychosomatic whole in which the soul played the crucial role. In fact, the soul alone secured identity, as it conveyed all the characteristics of the person which the body only expressed materially. Although this argument solved the problem of identity in a consistent way, all the authors (especially Aquinas) claimed that the perfection of the soul required the body. Thereby, the scholastics who generally resisted the idea of bodily resurrection retreated at this point. The clerical elite pronounced that the earthly body must return and thus opted for clear material continuity. Very likely, they were forced to do this by contemporary religious and pious practice. The thesis on spiritual identity implied that cadavers in the tomb and relics in reliquaries would not resurrect, and thereby it would have undermined the cult of the martyrs as well. The years around 1300 experienced an increased devotion to the body. Scientific interest was raised in examining and opening the body to learn the cause of the death, and bodies were dissected enthusiastically after death. In spite of the varied nature of burial customs and practices, all these agreed that what happened to the cadaver was an expression of the person. Bodily parts of saints and martyrs were treated as carriers of the whole personality and this habit influenced even the burial of laymen. The body was conceived as integral to

---

85 WB vol. 4, 84.

the person, and mainstream theology at the end of the thirteenth century defined resurrection as a reunion of the risen body and the soul.[86]

Contrary to this practice, Hungarian Communists were unable to demonstrate the direct tangible physical continuity between the actors of 1919 and 1956. Instead, they had to rely on vague implications of family relationships and blurred conceptions of blood ties. The first volume of the White Books called attention in its introduction to the fact that 'the government commissioned Béla Király, former Horthyist officer of the general commandment and relative of Gyula Gömbös [prime minister of Hungary 1933–36], the ill-famed fascist leader, as commander-in-chief of the armed forces'.[87] It is remarkable that the authors failed to indicate precisely the relationship and used the vague term 'relative' instead. The editors of the third volume of the government's White Books, which was probably issued in May soon after the arrest of Francia Kiss, considered it meaningful to publish a long quotation from the autobiography of Béla Király, who had been the commander-in-chief of the National Guard in 1956. Király mentions that his father had been the organizer of the governing party of the Horthy regime, and recalls his school years in the Ludovika Military Academy and his service on the Soviet front. The White Book considers a remarkable detail concerning the relationship of the author to the would-be Arrow Cross minister of defence. The booklet quotes in length the description of his duties and administrative activity in the ministry.[88]

In the absence of real corporeal continuity, claims made on the historical identity of 1919 and 1956 remained unconvincingly abstract, ineffective and, in fact, ridiculous. The *Népszabadság* reported on 14 March 1957 that a man called Béla Francia was arrested. The man was condemned for committing robbery, however he was released in 1963 as he was able to disprove the accusations. Béla Francia's fate was determined only by the similarity of his surname to Mihály Francia Kiss, who had been arrested a week before. The article that reported on Béla Francia's arrest printed in bold letters that 'the

---

86 Bynum, *The Resurrection of the Body*, esp. 256–78, 320–9. The body became a fundamental carrier of the self in Western culture. Modern novels and movies regularly approached the problem of identity through images of bodily sameness. The story of Dr Jekyll and Mr Hyde instigated a genre that elucidated the concept of the self through the disappearance, alteration or exchanging of personal bodies. Dilemmas over the modern scientific practice of organ transplantation also reflect the concerns on bodily continuity. Generally, in Western thinking there was and still is a fundamental agreement that there is no survival of identity without material continuity. Bynum, 'Material Continuity, Personal Survival and the Resurrection of the Body', in *Fragmentation and Redemption* (New York: Zone Books, 1992), 239–97.

87 WB vol. 1, 6. Béla Király indeed had a remarkable life. He began his military career in the 1930s, during the war became an officer in the General Staff, then volunteered to defend Kőszeg, a border town by Austria, against the Soviet troops. Subsequently, he decided to surrender to the Red Army and even joined the Hungarian Communist Party in 1945. Király became a high-ranking officer in the Communist army until his arrest in 1952 on false accusations. He was eventually released in September 1956. In the revolution, he became the commander of the revolutionary armed forces, the National Guard. Following the Soviet intervention he fled to Austria. In the sixties he obtained a PhD in history in the USA and became a respected historian.

88 WB vol. 3, 66.

offspring of Mihály Francia Kiss was captured'. Since accurate family relationships could not be detected, the press used the vague and archaic term 'offspring'. Another article definitively stated that 'Mihály Franczia Kiss's offspring was one of the leaders of the October counterrevolution'.[89]

Hungarian party leaders had but one choice: to represent their thesis on the historical continuity in a hopelessly allegoric manner. The case displaying gendarme uniforms in the exhibition of the counterrevolution demonstrates this aspiration well. No explanatory notes accompanied the clothes; the organizers described neither the social environment of the gendarmes nor the role they allegedly played in the events of October 1956. The representation of their objects did not serve the purpose of historical interpretation, instead it justified the statement on the theoretical possibility of their return. As one visitor of the exhibition wrote, 'Then there is another glass case: clothes lie in it. The uniform of Ferenc Fehér, gendarme sergeant from Somogy county, Zseliskisfalud village, which the man put on in haste. In haste? No way. There is no pleat on this uniform. No moth bit it, wetness did not attack it, sun did not burn it. It was carefully taken away, conserved, together with sword and decorations, for when the time comes.'[90] Objects, however, hardly speak for themselves.[91] The lack of explanatory texts, which would have situated the artefacts in the sociocultural totality that once belonged to them, clarified the aim of the organizers: it was not a representation of some actual structure of sociopolitical relationships, but rather the abstract evocation of the allegory of the 'counterrevolution'.

3

By the first anniversary of the siege of the Budapest party headquarters, the uprising in 1956 had become the 'second coming' or 'second edition' of the White Terror or counterrevolution in 1919:

> 30 October 1956 was the open reappearance of the saddest and most tragic period of Hungarian history: the Horthyist reaction was the political concept of killing Communists that was called 'the maintenance of the nation'. At the Republic Square *the counterrevolution stopped masking itself*. It attempted to do the same as it had done once before in the White August of 1919: it wanted a White October and a White November as well, as after the destruction of the first workers' power, in the bloody days of Siófok, Izsák and Orgovány.

---

89 NSZ, 14 March 1957, 8.
90 Kalmár, 'Bejegyzés helyett', 3. The Open Society Archives reconstructed the reconstruction of the 'gendarme uniform', in its exhibition 'The representation of the counterrevolution', which ran from 5 November to 1 December 1996. Online: http://www.osaarchivum.org/beta/galeria/index_hu/sites/ellenforradalom/ellenframes3.html (accessed 3 November 2009).
91 The role of inscriptions attached to museum objects in the establishment of a comprehensible link between representation and the metanarrative is emphasized by various authors. Greenblatt, 'Resonance and Wonder', 45; Spencer R. Crew and James E. Sims, 'Locating Authenticity: Fragments of a Dialogue', in *Exhibiting Cultures*, 171; Barbara Kirshenblatt-Gimblett, 'Objects of Ethnography', in *Exhibiting Cultures*, 387–96.

The anti-Communist atrocities in Republic Square turned into signs of a complex historical process. For Communists the siege provided an access to the meaning of history: 'Our predecessors have been facing the predecessors of the guns at Republic Square since the beginning of the century: the volley of the gendarmes which had been fired onto demonstrating workers by the *Kaiser und König* and later by Horthy's armed force *was the close relative of the thundering guns by the siege of the party headquarters.*'[92] History was seen as a continuing struggle between the rebellious people and its oppressors:

> Four hundred years ago the lords burnt György Dózsa [leader of the greatest peasant revolt in medieval Hungary in 1514] on a fiery throne and impaled his fellows. The ruling classes took revenge on every movement of the peasantry later on with similar ruthlessness. In 1919 after the fall of the First Hungarian Soviet Republic the capitalists and landlords paid with a cruelty never seen before for the few months of loss of their power. The lords' same fury raged in October 1956 as well.[93]

The historical context evoked through the First Soviet Republic of 1919 became the fundamental means to describe the events of 1956. The temporalization of the relationship of 1919 and 1956 that was based on the White Terror was gaining ground in historical common knowledge to the extent that it became an obvious reference of the representation of 1956. The proclamation of the Hungarian authors against the United Nations report on the 1956 revolution, which was prepared and manipulated through the writers by the party leadership in early September 1957, contained a condemnation of the uprising as follows: 'All the filth of fascism came to the surface: and produced conditions for a few days reminiscent to the White Terror in 1920.'[94] The publication of a book in December 1957 that described the history of 1956 in Miskolc, where the only truly cruel anti-Communist atrocities happened apart from in the capital, demonstrates remarkably how the comprehension of 1956 mobilized local memories of 1919. The booklet, which was edited by Communists in the county of Borsod and was issued by the publishing firm of the county party newspaper, puts enormous stress on demonstrating the cruelty and the dedicated anti-Communism of the 'counterrevolutionary terror groups' and, more importantly, their inherent connection to historical predecessors. The chapter describing the activity of the 'terror organization' concludes, 'They were worthy successors of the Miskolc executioners of the Horthy White Terror in 1920: the beasts of the "Szim sanatorium" [nickname of the prison in Miskolc in 1919–20].'[95]

The roof of the party headquarters in Republic Square thus gained particular significance: it became a point from which the direction and the starting point of history could be perceived. From there it could be seen that the beginning of the history of

---

92 *Népakarat*, 30 October 1957, 3. See also *Magyar Nemzet*, 31 October 1957, 1; and NSZ, 30 October 1957, 1.
93 *Magyar Nemzet*, 30 October 1957, 3.
94 Standeisky, *Az írók és a hatalom*, 275–86; Révész, *Aczél*, 84.
95 *Ez történt Borsodban* (This is what happened in Borsod County) (Miskolc: Északmagyarország, 1957), 107.

fascism and Communism was 1919. This view reduced the complexity of history to one straight thread which was seen to determine the trajectory of the past from its very beginning and, thus, precluded all other alternatives of history. The beginning of apocalyptic histories, however, can be detected only from these special points of view: without the privileged status of hindsight the starting point of the process does not exist. The formation of these peculiar narratives requires a point that appears to be the end of the historical process and from which the meaning of the entire sequence of events can be justified. From the prophetic point of view all visible and knowable events appear to run towards the position of the observer. From the point of view of Mount Sinai, which was the place of alliance between the Lord and the Jewish people, all previous occurrences could be seen as directly leading towards the outcome. From the point of view of Golgotha, which was the site of Christ's death on the crucifix, all former events were perceived as preparation for the only meaningful occurrence.[96] A similarly great narrative structure signified the position of 1919 in history. It was interesting as the starting point of a long-lasting fight and historical process which ended in 1956. This concept of history determined the true significance of 1919: in order to establish the perception of the historical struggle between revolution and counterrevolution the history of 1919 was required to create its genesis.

The first scholarly attempt to reappraise the history of the Soviet Republic was meant to reach primarily the Communist audience. The book that was issued for the first post-1956 academic year in August or September 1957 was a collective work of the Institute for Party History and was written as a textbook for the course in the history of the Hungarian labour movement. The publication covers the years between 1917 and 1919 and intended for the first time to provide an official interpretation of the Soviet Republic after 1956.[97] Communist historians sought to find answers for the question of the origins of both the Hungarian revolution and counterrevolution in general through research into the formative year of 1919. It is indicated also by the fact that more than half of the book is devoted to the prehistory of the first Communist regime and only forty pages of the total 108 concern its history proper. The collective of historians considered the primary reason and initiator of Hungarian Communism to be the effects of the Russian Revolution in October 1917. The authors argue that Hungary was ready to accept the ideas of the Russian revolt due to the general discontent of its people. The book states that whereas ordinary Hungarians like peasants and workers lived in want and privation due to the destruction of war, the members of the ruling classes were getting rich due to increasing exploitation. The burden of armed and bureaucratic oppression became heavier as well. Therefore the working class turned towards leftist ideas and two groups began to organize themselves: one among the old Social Democratic party as the

---

96 György Tatár, 'Történetírás és történetiség', in *Pompeji és a Titanic* (Budapest: Atlantisz, 1993), 129–39. The author here develops the metaphor of orienting heights from where the meaning and beginning of histories could be detected. On apocalyptic history writing, see Michael André Bernstein: *Foregone Conclusions: Against Apocalyptic History* (Berkeley/Los Angeles/London: University of California Press, 1994), 28.

97 *A magyarországi munkásmozgalom 1917–1919: A Magyar Tanácsköztársaság* (The labour movement in Hungary 1917–1919: The First Hungarian Soviet Republic) (Budapest: Kossuth, 1957).

opposition, while the other one remained an independent company of revolutionary socialists. The textbook points out that the Hungarian workers were already demanding in November 1917 to follow the Russian example and alludes to the growing discontent of the workers. Revolutionary activity increased among the prisoners of war in Russia as well as within the ranks of the Hungarian troops. The book considers the first significant result of the revolutionary wave to be the fall of the war cabinet and their replacement with a democratic government, led by Count Mihály Károlyi. As the king objected to the commission of the new prime minister, the people of Budapest, consisting of workers, soldiers and bourgeois, occupied strategic points in the capital and forced the deputy of the king to accept their demands on 31 October 1918.[98]

According to the Communist interpreters the victory of the October Revolution did not mean the final success of revolution in general. It provided a basis for progression, but at the same time it also increased the tension between the counterforces of revolution and counterrevolution. The historical argument implied that the heightening conflict resulted in the true manifestations of these general ideas: first of all in the foundation of the Communist Party of Hungary and secondly in the creation of reactionary organizations. The party textbook argues that the foundation of the party was necessary to drive the revolution forward. The authors call attention to the fact that although the principal carriers of the October revolt were the workers – the new government was still bourgeois and basically disinterested in improving their living conditions. Consequently, the revolution had to be pushed forward and the workers started to found their own institutions: the soviets. The book then describes the formation of the Communist Party of Hungary from the two leftist groups and the returning Communist prisoners of war. The authors do not neglect to mark the significance of this event and emphasize that the new party was the only truly revolutionary organ. It was reflected also by a transformation in the qualities of the revolutionary movements: the demands shifted from mere economics towards politics, from a wage increase to a socialist republic.[99]

The textbook outlines the centres of counterrevolutionary movement: reaction concentrated itself in Transdanubia (Dunántúl), where landlords and clerics played the major role. In Budapest the organization was taken into the hands of professional officers, who founded the Ébredő Magyarok Egyesülete (Association of Awakening Hungarians) and the Magyar Országos Véderő Egylet (National Association of Defence of Hungary). The book describes the atrocities committed by commandos and gendarmes against proletarians and Communists. The government also turned towards reactionary terror and ordered the arrests of the major Communist leaders in January 1919.[100]

The proclamation of the First Hungarian Soviet Republic on 21 March 1919 is interpreted as a consequence of the tense struggle between the agents of revolution

---

98 Ibid., 3–27.
99 Ibid., 28–55. Simultaneously, the genesis of the party became more and more significant: a year later on 20 November 1958 the old people's home of the party was named 21 March (the date of the proclamation of the Soviet Republic in 1919), and it was reported with great pride that 'currently it is inhabited by 17 comrades who feel themselves well: almost rejuvenated' (MOL M-KS 288/7/71).
100 Ibid., 55.

and counterrevolution. The authors consider the creation of the dictatorship of the proletariat as the decisive victory of revolution over reaction. The organization of the two opposing counterforces amplified the tension and the revolutionary crises. The authors call attention to the fact that from the end of February onwards the workers began to demonstrate for the release of the arrested Communist leaders. The Workers' Council of Budapest accepted the idea of social production and the power of the soviets. According to the textbook, on 20 March the masses were under complete Communist influence and were ready to overthrow the government. Consequently, when the cabinet met with a major crisis in its foreign relations on the same day it decided to resign and to assist the formation of a pure Social Democratic government. The authors emphasize that the Social Democrats, however, could not gain the support of the workers without an agreement with the Communists. The chapter concludes that the Soviet Republic was born on 21 March due to the insistence of the Communist leaders to proclaim the dictatorship of the proletariat and due to the general euphoria in society, which affected a lot of Social Democrats.[101]

Meanwhile the textbook endeavours to find the beginnings of the historical process; it presents 1919 as a projection of the interpretation of the conflict in 1956. Although the historians undoubtedly regarded the Soviet Republic as a great glory of the labour movement (as the book definitively states, 'In the history of our country power was taken by the people for the first time) they were also aware of the fact that its history was an ceaseless fight against counterrevolutionary aspirations:

> The counterrevolutionary conspiracy had already begun in the first days of the revolution. They sabotaged and obstructed the work of the proletarian state. They tried to get their own men involved in the soviets in several villages and even in some towns at the elections in April, successfully in a few of them. They attempted to break out armed rebellion in a few towns and villages in April and May. Counterrevolutionary governments were formed in territories occupied by Entente troops (in Arad, later in Szeged). The counterrevolutionaries who fled to Vienna created the Anti-Bolshevistic Committee (ABC). These organizations and the different agents of the Entente built their own connections in the territory of the Soviet Republic and fostered counterrevolutionary conspiracy and espionage. They succeeded in recruiting certain old officers who filled important positions in the Red Army. They also aspired to demoralize the masses in the hinterland with their propaganda, capitalizing on the economic hardships. On 1 June, two days after the beginning of the attack against the Czechoslovak army, they organized a railway strike in Transdanubia. Rich peasants attempted to revolt against the proletarian power in certain localities. Where the enemy troops marched into, Communist workers and members of the leadership were persecuted and denounced by them.[102]

While Communists were always resolute, the right-wing Social Democrats very frequently represented the interests of the counterrevolution. 'This double nature of the leadership

---

101 Ibid., 57–67.
102 Ibid., 68, 97–8.

leaves its mark on the history of the First Hungarian Soviet Republic.'[103] The textbook points out that this ambiguity determined the entire history of the dictatorship of the proletariat. Although the soviets were the true institutions of the people's rule, 'in many village councils the middle peasants and petite bourgeois formed a majority', and this contributed to a compliance towards reaction.[104] Apart from the examples above, the book mentions the case of the police, where the proletarian government maintained its former membership. The most difficult challenge, however, was the attack of the Czechoslovak and Romanian armies. Although the Red Army managed to resist these assaults, it was eventually defeated due to treason. The historians call attention to the fact, that precisely as the Soviet Republic was entering into a major military crisis, on 24 June 1919 the greatest and most well-prepared counterrevolutionary revolt broke out in Budapest. Officers occupied the battleship of the Danube fleet and other strategically important sites of the capital. The counterrevolutionaries tried to gain support from the workers but nonetheless failed, and the uprising was swiftly suppressed. The Communist interpreters consider it as evidence of the wide popular support of the workers. In spite of this, the numerical superiority of the enemy troops enabled them to make a decisive strike on the Soviet Republic, aided by treasonous military leaders. The collective of party historians conclude that the fall of the First Hungarian Soviet Republic meant the victory of counterrevolution: although it was destroyed by foreign troops its defeat was followed by the construction of a counterrevolutionary regime led by Hungarian landlords and capitalists.[105]

On 23 November 1957 an exhibition titled 'Hungarian Revolutionary Art' was opened in the Budapest Hall of Arts. The organizers displayed works by numerous important contemporary artists: Jenő Kerényi's *Celebrating Marchers*, Tamás Gyenes's *János Szántó Kovács* (a radical socialist peasant leader in the late nineteenth century), Sándor Mikus's *Woman with Snake*, Béla Kucs's *War: Never Again* and István Szabó Jr's *Resting Worker*. The central space of the exhibition was the circle room of the Hall of Arts, which featured statues of workers around the outside and a large statue of a worker in the centre. The background of these works of plastic art was provided by posters of the First Hungarian Soviet Republic hung on the walls. The order of the exhibition expressed the central message of the show by the means of the tenets of Marxist aesthetic ideology: revolutionary art was represented as an individual activity deriving from and manifesting its sociopolitical background.[106]

Jenő Kerényi's *Celebrating Marchers* is a glorious, dynamic, lively work of art, which expresses the organized, commonly shared and purposeful movement of the masses. The statue was to be seen in the foreground of a dark-toned painting with realist effects depicting the misery of workers. The spatial relationship of the picture – symbolizing privation and oppression – and the sculpture – showing the dynamism of advancement – formulated

---

103 Ibid., 69.
104 Ibid., 70.
105 Ibid., 68–108.
106 Historical Photographic Records of the Hungarian National Museum 48. ME/II/B, Culture: Exhibitions. Box 1957–1962. Pictures of registry numbers 58.145, 80.420.

the temporal connection of historical progress. Béla Kucs's *War: Never Again* represents a Pietà-like mother figure breastfeeding her baby. The statue itself is made of white stone: the mother defends her baby by raising her hands up to the sky, against air bombs as the title suggests. Posters of the First Hungarian Soviet Republic seen in the background of the work of art evoked the idea of socialism, which, thereby providing the sociopolitical context of the cry 'never again', appeared as the guarantee of this demand: peace. Thereby the First Hungarian Soviet Republic, rather than an individual event, referred to an abstract notion: the conceptualized theory of the revolutionary continuity of history.[107]

The First Hungarian Soviet Republic was beginning to be conceived as the starting point of the story of the continuous revolution and counterrevolution. This fact required the reassessment – the rehabilitation – of the Hungarian commune also in scholarly terms. At the beginning of the next year, 1958, the leadership of the party started to create the appropriate conditions for researching and writing on important topics from a relevant Communist point of view. The central organs of the party considered it a primary task to form an institution that would have the potential to direct all the workshops of historical research. The leaders were convinced that a full reorganization of the Institute for Party History would fulfil this function. Therefore the institute was required to produce a report on its status. The report was written on 8 January 1958 and stated that the institute had made considerable progress and formulated an essentially correct view on the history of the revolutionary labour movement. The report, however, defined further goals as well: 'It has to depict the history of the Hungarian revolutionary labour movement more authentically than it was doing previously in order to contribute to the idea that the wide working masses regard the past of the party with well-deserved respect.'[108] The call for reassessment of the revolutionary labour movement – that is to say, the proletarian revolution of 1919 – was completed with another major task. The documents of the counterrevolution would have to be collected in order to prepare a compilation of studies and to complete the series of the White Books with a publication exposing Imre Nagy. 1919 and 1956 were considered the two founding stones upon which the victorious road of the Hungarian Communists could be constructed: 'Our institution considers it its main task to publish as many works as possible as a result of its research which represents the glorious history of our party and the revolutionary Hungarian labour movement on a scientific level and with Communist partisanship.' A basic textbook on the history of the revolutionary labour movement, complete with original documents, was promised by 1962.

By the 39th anniversary in 1958, the discussion of the historical event of the 1919 dictatorship of the proletariat in Hungary began to dominate public speech on the counterrevolution. The increasing availability and interpretive potential of 1919 made the party leadership capable of talking about the counterrevolution without mentioning the actual uprising of October 1956. In the spring of 1958, the leaders of the Hungarian

---

107 Ibid.
108 Report on the Institution for Party History by Endre Kálmán, 8 January 1958. MOL M-KS 288/22/1958/7.

Communist Party began to feel uneasy about referring to the 1956 revolt and all its implications, and tended to prefer a politics of amnesia, offering the perspective of the future building of socialism in exchange. As Kádár put it, 'it is impossible to continuously repeat that achievement, failure, counterrevolution, etc. […] We should have this document start from the current situation and we should deal with the achievements of the past to the extent we have to, and with the failures of the past less than in September or December 1956. Our self-stigmatization is an outdated position.'[109]

The anniversary of the First Hungarian Soviet Republic in that year put the post-1956 Communist government in the context of the alleged history of the struggle between revolution and counterrevolution since 1919. On 21 March 1958, the day of the anniversary, the weekly *Élet és Irodalom* (Life and literature, then the organ of the Communist dominated Literary Council) published an interview with Prime Minister Ferenc Münnich on the relevance of the first Hungarian commune. Münnich, who became prime minister in January that year, was able to render the thesis of the continuity of revolutionary fight against counterrevolution authentic. The Communist leader was the 'hero of three revolutions', as his subsequent biographer characterized him. Münnich's official biography emphasized that his revolutionary career had started in 1919 as the political commissar of the Sixth Division of the Hungarian Red Army after he had returned from Soviet Russia, where he had participated in the civil war. Subsequent to the suppression of the First Hungarian Soviet Republic he lived in exile, mostly in the Soviet Union, until he joined the international brigades in the Spanish Civil War, where he became one of the most well-known Hungarian internationalists. He returned to Hungary after the war, but became a prominent party leader only in 1956 as a major figure in János Kádár's government: minister of the armed forces and supporter of the hardliner position. In his interview, Münnich expounded the historical continuity of the people's revolution, beginning with the early modern peasant leader György Dózsa, continued by the eighteenth-century anti-Habsburg prince in revolt Ferenc Rákóczi, and the nineteenth-century modern revolutionary Lajos Kossuth, culminating in the 1919 dictatorship of the proletariat. In the prime minister's view, 1919 meant at the same time the improvement of previous Hungarian freedom fights and the starting period of the struggle for Communism.[110]

On the same day, the *Népszava* (People's voice), the daily of the trade unions, quoted a long section from Béla Kun's speech delivered at the meeting of the Hungarian Soviets in June 1919:

> We will fight with the counterrevolution. It is an imperative never to shake, not even for a moment: this principle should lead the discussions of this congress of the Soviet

---

109 Kalmár, *Ennivaló és hozomány*, 158. See also Standeisky, *Az írók és a hatalom*, 390.
110 *Élet és Irodalom*, 21 March 1958. Münnich's official biography was written by one of his fellow fighters in 1919, Tibor Hetés. Its title, *Hero of three revolutions*, could be interpreted as 1917, 1919 and 1945, the liberation of Hungary by the Soviet Red Army, or even as 1919, 1945 and 1956, the establishment of Kádár's Revolutionary Worker-Peasant Government: Tibor Hetés, *Három forradalom hőse* (Budapest: Zrínyi, 1986), 5–23.

Republic. Hesitation and sabotage are the fatal enemies of the dictatorship, of socialism and Communism. As the only road towards socialism and Communism leads through the dictatorship, through the revolutionary dictatorship of the proletariat. We will fight with the counterrevolutions. We will crush the international counterrevolution as well as the national. We will crush them because we are helped by the historical vocation of the proletariat of other countries.[111]

Then the citation from Kun's text is explained by another quotation, this time from the official speech of a contemporary Communist historian:

> Hesitation may raise its head among those who joined the Communists before, but at the time of fierce struggle they became half-hearted. Their hesitation may drive them down the road of the absolute betrayal of the dictatorship of the proletariat, as it led the Kunfis and Böhms together with their Peyers. It is enough to refer to the experiences of 1956: the revisionism of the Communist Imre Nagy and his shameful role in preparing, carrying out and serving the counterrevolution.[112]

The clear reference to Imre Nagy also served the purpose of preparing the sentence in his forthcoming trial. Although the legal procedure was postponed in February 1958 due to the request of the Soviet leadership, which was concerned then with establishing its image in the Western public as the major force of world peace, the Hungarian party leadership and János Kádár personally had virtually already made the decision. Hungarian Communists had already started a press campaign against Marxist revisionist positions and the followers of Imre Nagy at the beginning of 1958. The scientific review of the party, *Társadalmi Szemle* (Social review) published a systematic critique of György Lukács's philosophy in its first 1958 issue. The study stressed that Lukács's 'revisionism' shared the same anti-Marxist and eventually anti-Communist political implications as Imre Nagy and his group.[113] After subsequent negotiations with the Soviet party in April, May and June, the Hungarian Communist leadership led Nagy's trial to its closure: the final verdict was brought on 15 June.[114] At dawn the following day Nagy and his two companions were hanged. The primary argumentation of the sentence was that the former Communist prime minister had been preparing the outbreak of the open counterrevolution while masking himself a faithful Communist. Nagy was accused of attempting to transform the proletarian regime into a restoration of capitalism. The judge condemned him for diminishing the fundamental institutions of the people's democracy step by step in the days of the uprising, and he was considered to be ready

---

111 *Népszava*, 21 March 1958, 2.
112 *Népszava*, 21 March 1958, 1. Zsigmond Kunfi and Peyer Károly were Social Democratic leaders who did not support the Communists in 1919, although Kunfi joined the Communist government. Vilmos Böhm was commander-in-chief of the Hungarian Red Army, but he started negotiations with Entente officials in the Summer of 1919 about the possibility of a democratic socialist government.
113 Kalmár, *Ennivaló és hozomány*, 213–15.
114 On the decision, see Rainer, *Nagy Imre*, vol. 2, 385–91.

by the beginning of November 1956 to transmit power to the representatives of the capitalist system.[115]

The interpretation of the historical relation between 1919 and 1956 provided a useful tool for Communist observers for understanding Nagy's role in 1956. The fifth volume of the White Books in 1956, which covers the trial of the former prime minister thoroughly, explains Nagy's function as follows:

> Hungary experienced a bloody counterrevolution for the second time in 1956. The darkest and most reactionary forces of the country set upon the lawful power, the free state of the people in Hungary in 1919, by the armed means of Western imperialists as well. Horthy and his company, with the help of foreign arms, succeeded in suppressing and crushing with ruthless violence the true revolution of the Hungarian people.
>
> The counterrevolution in 1956 also departed in this way: the way of the terrible White Terror in 1919, the service of the imperialists and the restoration of capitalist oppression. The tactic of camouflage was similar to that of 1919 too. Then Peidl's 'trade union government' accepted the role to hand the power over to fascism in seemingly democratic dress. Imre Nagy and his partners in crime accepted the role of the billeting officers of fascism in 1956. In 1919 the Peidl government attempted to deceive the masses with the slogan of 'socialism without dictatorship' while it opened the gates for the fascist White Terrorist dictatorship. Imre Nagy and his fellows followed their ignominious predecessor almost literally when they concealed the dark reactionary character of the attack against the state order of the people's democracy and assisted the gathering and forging ahead of open fascist forces with slogans like 'socialism without Stalinism' and 'democratic socialism'.[116]

The relationship of 1919 and 1956 based on the figure of Imre Nagy expanded the transnational implications of the narrative. It contained an explicit argument claiming that international imperialism tried to destroy socialism in Hungary in 1956 in the same way as it had successfully overthrown the first socialist state in the country in 1919. The narrative suggested that the struggle between revolution and counterrevolution was always inherently transnational. Any attempt in any nation to destroy socialism was a concerted act backed by international imperialism and simultaneously endangered the cause of socialism world wide. In fact, the struggle was fought globally. On the one hand, the fifth volume of the White Books claimed that the revolt in 1956 had been organized by Western imperialists who trained agents, sent weapons and provided financial support, particularly from the US and West Germany.[117] On the other hand, it emphasized that the real terror was not happening in post-1956 Hungary – on the contrary, it was happening in contemporary colonial wars. The volume provided textual and visual material to prove that the French in Algeria or the British in Cyprus executed and tortured revolutionary activists and ordinary workers and peasants who were fighting for independence from

---

115 WB vol. 5, 7–16. On Nagy's trial see Rainer, *Nagy Imre*, vol. 2, 373–431.
116 WB vol. 5, 5–6.
117 WB vol. 5., 90–110.

colonialism. The argument suggested that what had happened in Hungary had been only an episode in the global strike of imperialism against free or freedom-loving peoples of the earth.[118]

Nagy's trial forged together the history of the counterrevolution in 1919 and that of 1956 inseparably. The fifth volume of the White Books, the purpose of which was to demonstrate Nagy's guilt, contains a chapter which concerns 'The successors of the terrorists of 1919 in 1956'. It begins with the statement that, 'References are made in several places in this book to the fact that what happened in Hungary during the counterrevolution in 1956 could be compared only to the events of the terrible White Terror in 1919.'[119] The authors are shocked by the similarity of the two violent events: 'If we compare the deeds and terrorist actions of the bourgeois fascist counterrevolution that crushed the Soviet Republic in 1919 with the fury, the harsh measures and the brutal terror of the counterrevolution in October 1956, the astonishing similarity reveals itself even at first sight.' In order to prove this the booklet features five examples pairing one event from 1919 and the other from 1956. The first three instances concern the persecution and execution of Communists or supporters of the Communist regime. The last two examples highlight the ruthlessness of counterrevolutionaries by comparing detailed descriptions of tortures and cruel executions.

The shocking images of this violence published in the first volume of the White Books come into a peculiar relationship with other, apparently similar, pictures. The written accounts of atrocities in the fifth volume are accompanied by a few images. The first examples are placed on adjoining pages: the first page contains pictures from 1919, the second from 1956 (Fig. 8). The photos from 1919 depict when 'one of the leaders from the district of Tab was hanged in the main street of the village after crushing the Soviet Republic in 1919' and when 'White Terrorist officers executed a peasant on the outskirts of the village of Köröshegy'. The photos taken in 1956 show when 'the counterrevolutionaries carried off József Stefkó, a border guard lieutenant who was lying ill in hospital, and beat him to death then hanged him upside down'. The pictures taken in 1919 focus on hanged victims placed in the vertical axis of the composition. Framing the images one can see counterrevolutionary officers either posing proudly by their victim or observing with care the result of their activity. Both compositions thus emphasize the cold, merciless character of the counterrevolutionaries. The picture from 1956, placed next to the earlier ones, creates the impression of similarity by the commensurable composition, highlighting the hanged person in its vertical axis. The centre of the image is likewise juxtaposed by a raging crowd, thereby highlighting the contrast between the defenceless victim and the cruel counterrevolutionaries.

The second examples are printed on one page: the upper one depicts the 'Communists of Szekszárd in 1919', who are 'waiting the deadly bullets of Horthy's White Terrorists with their hands bound behind their back', whereas the picture below shows when 'the counterrevolutionary bandits shot the surrendered soldiers from behind at the Republic Square in October 1956'. Whereas the first picture focuses on the victims of the

---

118 WB vol. 5, 139–52.
119 WB vol. 5, 134.

Figure 8. 'In 1919... and in 1956'. White Books, vol. 5, 170–71.

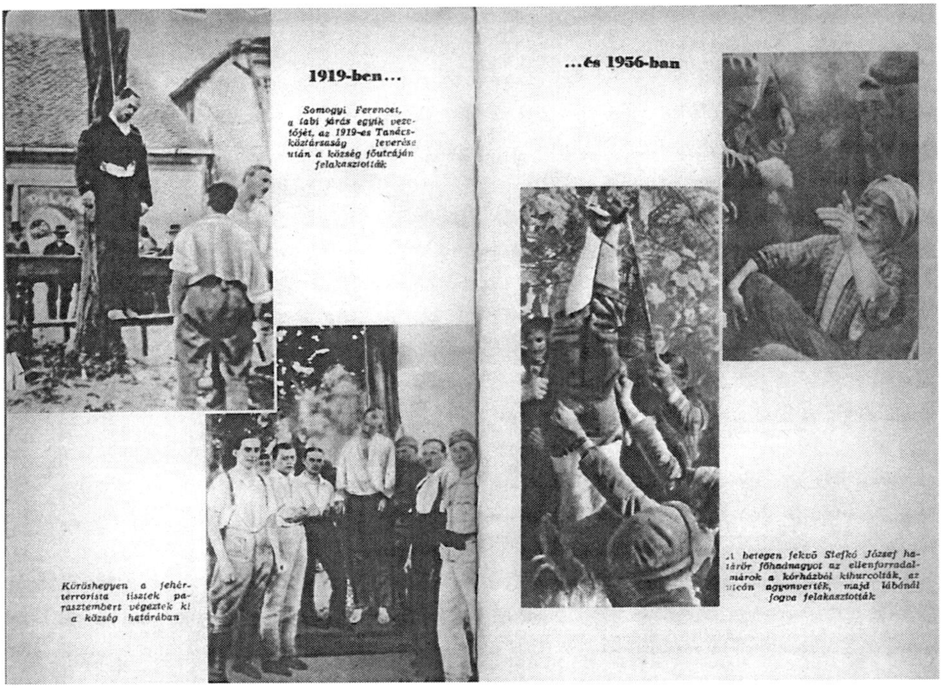

forthcoming execution, the second one places the executioners at its centre. Nonetheless, the differing compositions have a similar visual effect. The first picture shows the would-be executed persons – depicted as average ordinary people from all classes of society – in two rows silently and calmly waiting for the shots. These two rows occupy the entire picture, the depicted persons facing the viewer, with no visible sign of the execution squad. This photo thereby manages to emphasize the unarmed, nonviolent, defenceless state of the victims, giving also an impression of innocence. The second image taken in 1956 places a group of armed insurgents on the right hand side half of the composition, while the other side is occupied by two figures: a body lying on the ground, apparently dead, and a person seemingly trying to move away with his hands held up and showing his back to the group of insurgents. The gesture of this figure creates the impression that the armed group have already shot the surrendered combatants, which, as in the previous photo, builds its visual message on the contrast of innocence and mercilessness (Fig. 9).

The photos in the White Books are not illustrations – that is to say, they are not additions to or the direct representations of events described in the texts. They are presented independently, in themselves – even for themselves. Their role is to mediate the allegedly purified reality. Photography was endowed with the particular concept of objectivity during the second half of the nineteenth century. During these years, scientists started to look for methods of observation which could be made independent of the subjective points of view determined by individual value judgment, faith or conviction,

Figure 9. '1919 and 1956'. White Books, vol. 5, 172.

and were able to record the phenomena of the world in their pure reality. The mechanical recording of data appeared free of the fallibility of the human subject: machines do not tire, they are able to work continually without breaks and they do not make moral decisions and aesthetic judgments. Images recorded by photographic machines became the authentic representations of reality, free of subjective intervention and independent of human individuality. Photography, hence, is taken as the unquestioned evidence of objective reality: the imprint of truth beyond the human limits of perception.[120] Photos, thus, are believed to be able to reveal those aspects of reality which sometimes remain hidden from human eyes.[121] The similarity of the violence revealed something essential about historical continuity for the Communist editors:

---

120 Lorraine Daston and Peter Galison, 'The Image of Objectivity', *Representations* 40 (Fall 1992): 81–128. On the emergence of photography as means of accurate and cheap recording, see John Tagg, *The Burden of Representation: Essays on Photographies and Histories* (Minneapolis: University of Minnesota Press, 1993). The myth of images made without the touch of human hands as manifestations of the ultimate truth, however, arguably looks back on a longer tradition: 'In the Christian tradition this power to produce the visible without any manual technique is attributed to the direct imprint of God on cloth' (Marie José Mondzain, 'The Holy Shroud: How Invisible Hands Weave the Undecidable', in *Iconoclash: Beyond the Image Wars in Science, Religion and Art*, ed. Bruno Latour and Peter Weibel [Karlsruhe/Cambridge, MA: MIT Press, 2002], 324).

121 Thus, the photographs of the Shroud of Turin taken by Secondo Pia in 1898 revealed that the brownish traces on the cloth, hardly perceivable by the eyes, showed on the photonegative

The cruel, bloodthirsty White Terror in 1956 was reared by the White Terror of Horthy and his company. Fascists allied with criminals, former village leaders, gendarme officers and Horthy officers, Arrow Cross men attempted an attack the freedom of the Hungarian people and many brave sons of the Hungarian people. Although they felt in 1956 that they were just at the very beginning, the supporters of the fallen Horthy regime could not restrain themselves and tried to 'imitate' 1919 with the most open White Terror.[122]

Communist observers thus claimed that the images of similar violence revealed an unbroken historical continuity ranging from 1919 to 1956, as if one could foresee on the photos taken after the fall of the First Hungarian Soviet Republic what would occur in 1956.[123] The impressive photos taken as evidence of reality, free of human subjectivity, suggested the inherent homogeneity of the counterrevolution and, thereby, blurred and diminished its actual historical transformation from the White Terror through consolidation, crisis and war, to its eventual collapse and the coming to power of the Arrow Cross. In this context, a strange but largely forgotten history of 1919 obtained new relevance. Communist party leaders and historians rediscovered the all-but-forgotten postwar trials of war criminals, where People's Tribunals had created historical continuity between 1919 and 1944. The narrative of 1919 told in postwar trials had no interest in the First Hungarian Soviet Republic, however. It had focused instead on the follow-ups: the events of 1919–21, the White Terror and political persecution. The history of 1919 as that of the counterrevolution had remained virtually unconnected with the history of 1919 as that of the commune during the 1950s. The history of the White Terror had been told independently of the fragmented and isolated history of the Soviet Republic. It was only after 1956, when the perspective of the 'counterrevolution' shed new light on the relationship of 1919–44 as the continuity of counterrevolution, that links to the Soviet Republic were realized as the genesis of the twinned story of revolution and counterrevolution.

---

the positive image of a male body. Peter Geimer, 'Searching for Something: On Photographic Revelations', in *Iconoclash*, 143–5.
122 WB vol. 5, 139.
123 According to Georges Didi-Huberman, photography was regarded as evidence of events to come. The photographic process, which was more sensitive than human eyes, could detect deep features of the object that foreshadowed future events, e.g. the symptoms of future mental illness in a photo of the insane, the crime to be committed in a portrait of the criminal (Didi-Huberman, *Invention of Hysteria: Charcot and the Photographic Iconography of the Salpêtrière* [Cambridge, MA/London: MIT Press, 2003], 33).

Chapter 3

LIVES: 1919 IN THE POSTWAR TRIALS OF WAR CRIMINALS

1

The standard popular history book of the 1950s on the origins of the counterrevolutionary regime that ruled Hungary between 1919 and 1944 classified the Horthy regency as a fascist system:

> The Hungarian ruling class developed the first European fascism by applying old and new means of oppression, thereby showing – for the first time – what fascism, which would wildly ravage Europe two decades later and drive millions of people to war, looked like. One can hardly find a characteristic feature of Hitler's and Mussolini's dictatorships which cannot immediately be found in the Hungarian fascism. The fear of Bolshevism, the ruthless oppression of the working class and the wild racist incitement were the same in all these regimes. They all demonstrate the same unrestrained rule by the big capitalists and landowners, the same antiprogressive and anticultural attitudes, the same depreciation of the working man and the same social demagogy.
> Thus, in 1919 and 1920, it was not merely the seeds of fascism which appeared in Hungary, but rather fascism itself. In the Hungarian fascism of the twenties and forties, not only the fundamental idea but even the participants were the same. In 1919 in Orgovány, and in 1942 at the massacre in Újvidék, the same Horthy stands at the helm; in the middle of the thirties, it was the same Gyula Gömbös, who adjusted the Hungarian fascism to the newly emerged Nazi movement, who was the leader of the extreme right-wing MOVE in 1920. László Endre [a major figure in the Hungarian Holocaust], who was a brutal county leader in the Gödöllő district in 1920, and who became state secretary in the Ministry of Interior in 1944, threw hundreds of thousands of innocent people to the German fascist murderers. The same people, the same crimes: from 1920 to 1944, our history has a direct road to the reign of terror of the Arrow Cross hordes.[1]

The authors argued that the rule of the Hungarian fascist Arrow Cross Party in 1944 and 1945 had had its roots in the activity of the White Terror commandoes that persecuted Communists, Jews and leftist persons after the collapse of the short-lived First Hungarian Soviet Republic of 1919. The similarity of the violence convinced Communist historians that fascism in Hungary had been born in 1919. Thus, the interwar Hungarian system

---

1 Elek Karsai and Ervin Pamlényi, *Fehérterror* (White terror) (Budapest: Művelt Nép, 1951), 71–2.

was closely associated with the crimes committed by the Nazis and their companions throughout Europe. As a result, it was then possible to claim that the counterrevolutionary regime of Admiral Miklós Horthy was genuine fascism. At the same time, it was also claimed that fascism had emerged during the struggle against Communism, and was, in reality, nothing but anti-Communism. Consequently, Communism was the real opposition to fascism. This peculiar interpretation of history emerged to justify the power of the party, because the narrative entailed that the only genuine alternative to the Horthy regime was the Communist system. Moreover, since counterrevolution was equated with the rule of 'evil', Communism represented the rule of 'good'. This teleological interpretation of history that leads to the inevitable victory of the Communist Party is a typical example of Stalinist historical writing. In fact, this belief in historical inevitability had already featured in interpretations of the 1917 October Revolution and the fall of the Russian Provisional Government, which were regarded the results of historical laws. An attempt was made to adapt these principles – which were based upon a Manichean view of the struggle between light and darkness, good and evil, proletarian revolution and bourgeois reaction – to the particular records of contemporary Hungarian history.[2]

The official canon of the history of the counterrevolutionary regime, which featured the Stalinist 1950s in its historiography, archival research and education, was based directly on evidence and interpretation that had been produced in the postwar political trials. Communist and leftist intellectuals – after 1945 – first encountered a substantial amount of historical records and had to face the pressing challenge of interpreting the recent past during these trials. The newly founded People's Tribunals in 1945 called to account those who were accused of committing war crimes. This conformed to international expectations and was also required by the armistice agreement. In spite of the fact that the trials of the major war criminals ended in 1946, the people's courts had an unusual history thereafter. In 1946, they were authorized to deal with crimes committed 'against the order of the republic', one perpetrator of which was László Rajk, who would later become the most notorious victim of the Stalinist purges in 1949. After his trial, the courts were closed.[3]

---

2 The Communist way of thinking in contradictory counterconcepts such as fascism and reaction vs. democracy and its perils concerning Hungarian politics had been already recognized by István Bibó, lawyer and political scientist, in 1945 member of the National Peasant Party: 'A magyar demokrácia válsága', in his *Válogatott tanulmányok, vol. 2: 1945–1949* (Budapest: Magvető, 1986), 13–79. On the first five decades of Soviet historiography, see Konstantin F. Shteppa, *Russian Historians and the Soviet State* (New Brunswick: Rutgers University Press, 1962). On early Soviet historical scholarship, see John Barber, *Soviet Historians in Crisis, 1928–1932* (New York: Holmes and Meier Publishers, 1981). An intriguing recent work is David Brandenberger, *National Bolshevism: Stalinist Mass Culture and the Formation of Modern Russian National Identity, 1931–1956* (Cambridge MA/London: Harvard University Press, 2002).
3 On the system of the People's Tribunals in Hungary, see Tibor Lukács, *A magyar népbírósági jog és a népbíróságok* (Budapest: Közgazdasági- és Jogi Könyvkiadó, 1979); Tibor Zinner, 'Adalékok az antifasiszta számonkéréshez és a népi demokrácia védelméhez különös tekintettel a budapesti népbíróságra', *Budapest Főváros Levéltára Közleményei '84* (1985): 137–69; Zinner, 'Háborús bűnösök perei. Internálások, kitelepítések és igazoló eljárások 1945–1949', *Történelmi Szemle* (Spring 1985): 118–40; Sándor Szakács and Tibor Zinner, *A háború 'megváltozott természete'* (Budapest: Genius Gold, 1997), 182–93; Károly Szerencsés, *'Az ítélet: halál'* (Budapest: Kairosz, 2002), 29–53.

Using the records of a local trial which ended with capital punishment, this chapter concentrates on the procedures and practices of connecting abstract historical constructions to actual individual lives in order to render them tangible and provide evidence for their authenticity and credibility. It also seeks to demonstrate that popular forms of memory-biased and politically biased history writing both contributed to a peculiar way of individualizing history. Focusing on the method of proof, the chapter draws conclusions concerning the form, as well as the structure, of Communist historical representations.[1]

2

At the beginning of 1947, Lőrinc Latorczay, whose original family name was Szim, was denounced for various assaults in 1920 when he had been the commander of the Military Department of Investigations in Northern Hungary. He was apprehended and tried at the People's Tribunal in the provincial city of Miskolc in 1947–48 and was sentenced to death as a war criminal. The People's Tribunal condemned Szim for crimes committed in 1919 and 1920.[5] In spite of the fact that he was charged with war crimes, this was an obvious legal error. Although political crimes committed in 1919 and the following years began to lapse only in 1944, and could, therefore, be tried by the People's Tribunals, these acts were not classified as war crimes.[6]

There were ninety-six witnesses present at the court and most of them accused Szim of murder and assault. As one of them put it, 'there were serious beatings' in the cells of his headquarters.[7] Another witness, who had been in jail there for two days, had seen a lot of people covered in blood. When he was beaten he had 'wailed so much that it could be heard even on the street'.[8] A third witness had been assaulted so badly that he lay ill for three months. One of the witnesses gave evidence that beatings had happened daily. Even more cruel tortures had been inflicted. According to one witness, the defendant had hit one of his victims in the face 140 times and knocked out all of his teeth. One man testified that he had received twenty-six beatings in a month and said that Szim had hit him even with a seal ring.

   On the armistice, see Mihály Korom, *Magyarország Ideiglenes Nemzeti Kormánya és a fegyverszünet* (Budapest: Akadémiai, 1981). The best comprehensive work on the history of the legal system is Mária Palasik, *A jogállamiság megteremtésének kísérlete és kudarca Magyarországon, 1944–1949* (Budapest: Napvilág, 2000), esp. 41–5.
4 My intention, however, is by no means to identify a 'paradigmatic case in order to illustrate broad general 'historical tendencies'. My choice in a certain way is rather random: to depart from an individual case, to investigate it thoroughly and to establish its meaning in its particular historical context. As Carlo Ginzburg remarks, 'A life chosen at random can make concretely visible the attempt to unify the world, as well as some of its implications' ('Latitude, Slaves, and the Bible: An Experiment in Microhistory', *Critical Inquiry* 31 (Spring 2005): 682).
5 BAZ ML, Records of the People's Prosecution 1038/1949. On Szim's role in the war, see Péter Bokor, 'Egy ezredes két halála', *Élet és Irodalom*, 14 May 1982, 3–4; and 'Egy lázadás története', *Magyar Hírlap*, 15 October 1993, 8.
6 The act on the People's Tribunals is in: *Magyar Törvénytár. 1943–1945. évi törvénycikkek* (Budapest: Franklin-Társulat, 1946), 93.
7 BAZ ML, Minutes of the hearing, 16.
8 Ibid., 36.

On one occasion, he had been bound to a chair, his mouth wedged open and Szim's men had spat into it; they had torn his hair out and hit his head with a stick, creating a wound that did not heal for ten years. Another witness stated that he had seen a person whose face had been torn to pieces. One of the testimonies claimed that Szim and his subordinates had beaten a war invalid who was amputated below the knees. Another of the ex-prisoners remembered how one victim's nose had been bleeding after the 'treatment'; the blood had been collected in a glass and he had been forced to drink it. Several statements claimed that people had been killed during their interrogation, and that Szim had personally shot two men. Another recalled a case in which Szim had killed a person because he had struck back. A third witness gave an account of the extrajudicial murder of a railwayman, in which the victim had begged for his life, but the lieutenant had given the order to fire.[9]

These testimonies characterized the defendant as a disgustingly violent person: 'Szim subjected a thirteen-year-old child, women and even a seventy-one-year-old man to satisfy his sadistic propensity.'[10] One of the witnesses recounted how his fifteen-year-old brother had been taken away and had returned home severely bruised. Another witness recalled the times when, as a twelve-year-old, he had delivered cigarettes and meals to the inmates. Szim had disliked this and so had ordered him to be beaten up. The officer had pulled his ears until they started bleeding. Another testified that a woman had been beaten with an iron bar. Another had seen that 'women were treated in the same way as male captives'.[11] One of the testimonies described how Szim had shown no mercy even to elderly women; the witness recalled that the officer had kicked his fifty-five-year-old mother. Often, prisoners were not fed. Moreover, one witness remembered that, if a relative brought a meal, it would be overturned, and the captive would have to lick the food up from the ground. The same witness also said that, due to the mental suffering his wife had endured from her visits to the police station, his baby had 'suckled milk poisoned by his wife's nerves' and the child had died in its fifth year.[12] Szim preferred to interrogate his victims at night. One of the victims remembered the rumour that Szim and his men investigated by day and interrogated at night. Another witness recounted that he had been taken to Szim for a beating at night. A third remembered that screaming could be heard every night. Executions were generally carried out at night: 'One night somebody cried, then I heard a shot and the crying stopped. I was taken to Szim for interrogation twice late at night.'[13] The popular memory formulated by the witnesses during the trial took on the character of a thriller. One could construct the blurb of a pulp fiction from the text of the testimonies. This was 'the horror story of the Szim nursing home': 'In the cell of his institution, called the house of terror', sat Szim, 'the monster of the *Csabai kapu* [the street where the building stood]'. 'Those caught in his grasp' were tortured cruelly. 'It is impossible to sleep here due to the constant wailing; corpses are transported weekly' from the prison.[14]

---

9   Ibid., 28.
10 BAZ ML, Detective report, Ernő Páricsi, 14 June 1947.
11 BAZ ML, Minutes of interrogation, János Vanyó, 20 May 1947.
12 BAZ ML, Minutes of interrogation, Árpád Sviderszky, 21 April 1947.
13 BAZ ML, Minutes of interrogation, János Béres.
14 BAZ ML, Minutes of interrogation, Imre Kosziner, 16 May 1947, Lajos Márkus.

The tropes by which Szim was characterized by the witnesses are not new. Take the accusations of child cruelty, for example. The early Christians were accused of slaughtering children as well as Jews. In Roman times, Christians were frequently accused of sacrificing children and of drinking their blood during their ceremonies. In the Middle Ages, the murder and sacrifice of children repeatedly appeared in charges against heretics and witches: in the eighth century against the Paulicians, in the twelfth century against the Cathars, and in the fourteenth century against the Waldensians. The motif of baking babies featured among the tales told of the Knights Templar, while witches were considered to be experts in child killing. The murdering of children is generally considered by every society to be a crime that breaks very basic norms. Therefore, a group which denies or is believed to deny the fundamental rules of its society is usually accused of killing children. Szim's night activity has similarly ancient implications. Those who act at night, under the veil of darkness, are usually suspicious characters. The trials of the Knights Templar called attention to their practices at nightfall; witches flew and also held their meetings at night. The night evokes an alien, unknown world full of danger. The night is the world of monsters.[15]

The narrative presented by the witnesses was the narrative of a monster, of a cold-blooded resolute killer. He 'subjected large masses of people to long-lasting torture, revealing unrestrained cruelty, with which he aimed to kill his victims. Only persons of very strong constitutions and mental strength could withstand such treatment.'[16] Such bloodlust triggers an extreme sense of danger: 'When Lőrinc Latorczay-Szim, once an officer of Horthy's clique, was escorted from the Military Political Department [Department of Political Investigations for Army Personnel] to the juridical lock-up, the detective who accompanied him witnessed a shocking scene. A dog was sitting in front of the gate of the County Hall. When it saw Szim, it started to whimper showing its teeth, then it ran away in fear. Even the dumb animal suspected the bloodhound in him.'[17] The figure of Szim, as formed by the witnesses, obviously meant a significant danger to normal people; they are the enemies of every society.

Some of the testimonies connected general popular understanding with politically more meaningful concepts. A musician remembered that he had played a song recalling Béla Kun at the beginning of 1920 and that, as a result, he had been taken in and beaten with a stick. A witness recalled that, when he had stood before Szim in November 1920, the lieutenant had shouted at him, 'So, you are that renowned Communist' and had beaten him up. Others were allegedly taken away, either for abusing the Horthy army or singing 'La Marseillaise'. One of the testimonies claimed that the victim had been beaten because he had delivered a speech by the grave of a Red Army soldier. Another man was convinced that he had been victimized because he had participated in suppressing the counterrevolutionary uprising of the Ludovika Academy during the Soviet Republic.

---

15 See Norman Cohn, *Europe's Inner Demons* (London: Pimlico, 1993); and Gábor Klaniczay, 'Az orgiavádak nyomában', in *A civilizáció peremén* (Budapest: Magvető, 1990), 194–208.
16 BAZ ML.
17 SZM, 28 September 1947, 3.

A third remembered that Szim's men had raided his premises searching for a red flag, a typewriter and leaflets. During the house search, he had been beaten and kicked with a spur. The defendant was characterized as a fanatical anti-Communist. According to one statement, he had remarked after killing a person, 'This is your common fate, dirty Communists!' Szim was also said to have shouted: 'I will kill all of you like flies in autumn, bloody Communists!'[18]

Other witnesses attributed more direct political leanings to the defendant. As one of them put it, 'Szim was a lieutenant with a crane feather who acted on Horthy's highest order with unlimited power.' The crane feather was the symbol of Horthy's 'national army' which distinguished the soldiers from the Red Army troops who wore the red star. Another witness claimed, 'I definitely remember that the defendant was mounted on a white horse at the corner of the engine house.'[19] The colour of the horse was not an incidental element in this description: it recalled the well-known scene of Miklós Horthy marching into Budapest on a white horse. The witnesses thus posited the defendant as a typical member of the Horthy regime. Such political meaning was amplified by the politically conscious People's Tribunal and the left-wing press. In their perception:

> Lőrinc Szim was Horthy's bloody handed henchman in Miskolc.[20]
>
> He was a wicked murderer of the counterrevolution who became a colonel due to his brutality in the Horthy regime.[21]
>
> He appeared in Miskolc with a special commission after the takeover of the White Terror. He was granted an absolutely free hand to crack down on the leftists; he had unlimited power to achieve his goal. The place of his operation was the so-called Szim sanatorium where, together with his subordinates, he interrogated the leftist people who came into his hands in the cruellest manner.[22]
>
> His aim was to silence every freedom-loving Hungarian by causing fear and dread, and to lead the murderous counterrevolution to power.[23]

Thus Szim was depicted as a brutal criminal, who in addition had made the profound reality of the Horthy regime tangible: 'Lőrinc Latorczai-Szim was the epitome of the regime knight, of this darkest type of human being that was produced by the previous decades.'[24] 'This defendant let the children of the people languish, he is the counterrevolution and the Hungarian terror.'[25] In the courtroom, Szim embodied the alleged brutality of the Horthy regime in its entirety.

The report of the investigation labelled Szim a cruel anti-Communist and associated him with the White Terrorists: 'The White Terror commando committed a series of

---

18 BAZ ML, Minutes of the hearing, 16, 18, 19, 21, 29, 32, 38.
19 BAZ ML, Minutes of interrogation, Károly Losonczy.
20 FN, 17 March 1948, 1.
21 SZM, 7 April 1948, 3.
22 SZM, 29 May 1947, 3.
23 SZM, 7 April 1948, 3.
24 FN, 7 April 1948, 1.
25 BAZ ML, Minutes of the hearing, 122.

brutal tortures and executions. All the responsibility is Szim's, he was the leader; left-wing people were tortured in his lock-up.'[26] The description of Szim as a White Terrorist helped to explain his deeds. On the other hand, his figure personalized the crimes of the group. Numerous witnesses believed that they could explain Szim's cruelty. As one of them put it, Szim had been the cruellest figure of White Terror in Miskolc. White Terrorists played a significant role in the establishment of the counterrevolutionary system. They were usually recruited from the officers of the Hungarian army in WWI and, after the fall of the First Hungarian Soviet Republic, they persecuted Communists and Jews. Such groups are generally described as 'officer commandos'. One of the witnesses remembered that the defendant 'had also been the commander of the widely known Szim commandos'. Nevertheless, Szim's unit was not a military detachment like the officer commandos. His men were regular military troops, who conducted political investigations between 1919 and 1921. Nevertheless, the witnesses remembered that he had been a bloodthirsty sadist who had gained a reputation in Borsod county equal to that of Iván Héjjas in the Trans-Tisza region.[27]

Iván Héjjas himself, together with his companions, was tried at the end of 1946. Héjjas was one of the most notorious figures of the White Terror officers' detachments that had carried out numerous robberies, tortures and killings between 1919 and 1921 in the region of Kecskemét. Although Héjjas himself and Mihály Francia Kiss, one of his main followers, were not caught the trial encompassed more than forty defendants. The legal proceedings began in January 1947 in front of the Budapest People's Tribunal and the sentence for the first instance was issued on 13 May 1947.[28] Héjjas's name in the Szim trial invoked a particular understanding of interpreting cruelty:

> Anti-Semitism [...] appeared in the practice of the Héjjas detachment in the atrocities of prefascism to the extent that it was a worthy counterpart to the fascist vandalism of the 1940s. [...] They bound their captives with the preference that they were bound together by wires pulled through their palms. The splitting off of their skin, the piercing of their eyes, the cutting off of their penis, the mutilation of the women's breasts, the sawing of persons into two and the use of the *Horthy-kalincs* [a whip] were prescribed as a matter of fact.[29]

Atrocities committed with special ruthlessness emerged as a characteristic feature of the Nazi system in the Nuremberg Trials. The judges in Nuremberg argued that the specificity of the newly formulated concept of the crimes against humanity was not the enormous size or industrial mode of killing, but rather its connection to atavistic practice. Nazi violence was represented as a return to primitivism in the heart of modern civilized Europe.

---

26 BAZ ML, Detective report, Ernő Páricsi, 14 June 1947.
27 BAZ ML, Minutes of interrogation, Sándor Dakó, 29 April 1947. On the investigation of military organizations, see Dr Vargyai Gyula, *katonai közigazgatás és kormányzói jogkör (1919–1921)* (Budapest: Közgazdasági és Jogi Könyvkiadó, 1971), 104–46.
28 BFL VII 5e/20630/I.
29 BFL VII 5e/20630/I. Sentence of the first instance, 6.

The prosecution thus exhibited the shrunken head of a prisoner of war that was found in the Buchenwald camp. The head shocked the audience, bringing to mind the practice of head shrinking by the Latin American Jivaros that came to be widely known in the Western world a few years before the war. This depiction of primitive violence was accompanied by a constant description of uncontrolled instinctive anti-Jewish atrocities – a conscious reference to medieval pogroms. The spatial and temporal distancing of uncivilized, barbarous violence presented the Nazi atrocities as peculiar – unexpected and unimaginable in modern Europe.[30]

Hereby, the judge in the Héjjas trial considered the White Terror in 1919 not only a prehistory of the actual fascist movement and regimes, but rather the birth and beginning of fascism itself: 'It was this Idea of Szeged which Miklós Kállay [then prime minister] referred to in 1943 in his unfortunate speech as a theory predating the idea of National Socialism by more than a decade, and yet being essentially identical to it and having a major influence on it. This Idea from Szeged was the first sprout of the enormous tree of fascism.'[31] In the manner of apocalyptic history the sentence articulated a very forceful notion of continuity: 'The reasoning behind the accusation treats Hitler and Szálasi as if there had been no other historical alternative to fascism after 1919; events that followed the logic of history had to lead to 1944, then to 1947, and finally to the courtroom where these events and their consequences were being discussed. Thus, the executioner, Mihály Francia Kiss, was in fact already a member of the Arrow Cross in 1919, long before the party was set up, and perhaps even then knew Hitler.'[32]

The peculiar historical continuity of 1919 and 1944 appeared for the first time in the trial of former prime minister László Bárdossy. The verdict in his case brought down on 2 November 1945 argued for a historical continuity and pronounced that the events of 1944 had begun in 1919 in a certain way. The court intended to demonstrate that the counterrevolutionary regime begun in 1919 was fostered by individual actions of certain persons instead of abstract motives. The sentence argued that the ultimate reason for the catastrophic war in the country had been the foundation of the counterrevolutionary regime led by Admiral Horthy in 1919. The system followed an identical road of politics during its existence and Bárdossy was only one person in a series of its carriers: 'From the point of view of the judge, the Hungarian system of government took the direction in the summer 1919 in Szeged that straightforwardly led the nation to WWII, namely the historical catastrophe that struck the Hungarian people.'[33] The sentence connected the Hungarian fascist dictatorship of the Arrow Cross Party in 1944 to 1919 and claimed that the foundation of the counterrevolutionary regime was actually the birth of a fascist power: 'The Hungarian counterrevolution created the first fascist dictatorship in Europe. The counterrevolutionary leaders themselves boasted many times that the Szeged Idea

---

30 Lawrence Douglas, 'The Shrunken Head of Buchenwald: Icons of Atrocity at Nuremberg', *Representations* 63 (Summer 1998): 39–64.
31 BFL VII 5e/20630/I.
32 István Rév, 'Counterrevolution', in *Between Past and Future*, ed. Sorin Antohi and Vladimir Tismaneu, 247–71 (Budapest: CEU Press, 2000), 250.
33 Pál Pritz, ed., *Bárdossy László a népbíróság előtt* (László Bárdossy in front of the People's Tribunal) (Budapest: Maecenas, 1991), 242.

was the pioneer of fascism in Europe. This political system was essentially fascist: it was characterized by the suppression of civil rights, social and nationalist demagogy and anti-Semitism. The workers were treated as enemies, thus the system was in a constant struggle with them.'[34]

According to the act on the People's Tribunals the 'illegal execution and torturing of people' – which could not be persecuted in the previous regime – had to be investigated and punished as 'crimes against the people and humanity'. In describing Szim, the judge made reference to this act, and did not utilize the term 'war crime'. Nevertheless, the reasoning of the verdict consistently stated that the defendant's deeds were tantamount to all the criteria of a war crime. According to the act of the People's Tribunals, a war criminal was a person who promoted the expansion of the war to Hungary in 1939, or the involvement of Hungary in the war. The question was thus how political crimes committed in 1919 had contributed to Hungary's catastrophic war. The sentence argued,

> After the fall of the Hungarian Soviet Republic on 1 August 1919, the counterrevolution that spread over its ruins wrote the most baneful and disgraceful pages in Hungarian history.
> This is the first page in a chapter that was concluded by Ferenc Szálasi's insensate reign of terror at the end of the year 1944 and the spring of 1945 as the Russian Red Army of liberation was forging ahead.
> The war against the Hungarian people was started by Miklós Horthy in his sanguinary frenzy in the year 1919 on behalf of his class and clique with his slayer henchmen, and was pursued by him through various means during the next 25 years, when he imbecilely passed the murderous weapon into Ferenc Szálasi's hands in shameful conditions on 15 October 1945, who cut the last strokes with it on the Hungarian people until the liberation.
> This war, the struggle of the counterrevolution against the Hungarian people, was constant during a period of a quarter of a century. It was waged by the same forces, was motivated by the same goals; the only difference was its means according to the circumstances of the ages.[35]

The history here ended with a real 'apocalypse': the catastrophe and destruction of WWII. The collapse, however, was attributed to one single cause by the judge: the fall of the First Hungarian Soviet Republic. According to the sentence, the road from 1919 towards 1944 was straight and clear: history left no alternative but war after the defeat of the proletarian regime.

> There passed twenty-five years between 1919 and 1944. The oppression, the struggle of the reaction against the Hungarian people, started in 1919. In the year of 1945, the glorious soldiers of the Red Army liberated the country under oppression and subjugation. Essentially, throughout the twenty-five years, the reaction continued its

---

34 Pritz, *Bárdossy*, 244.
35 BAZ ML, Sentence of the People's Tribunal in Miskolc.

struggle against the Hungarian people with the same means in 1919 and in 1944. [...] Here is a politically uniform process which started in 1919 and ended at the time of the liberation.[36]

Apocalyptic or prophetic histories see in the past only prehistories and prefigurations, and attempt to represent inevitability and dismiss all alternative possibilities. They are usually based upon the rhetorical device of mirroring back the knowledge of the present into the past, which seeks the signs of events in the past to prove that the eventual outcome was the only possible historical outcome.[37] The historical interpretation of the People's Tribunal implied that the war catastrophe had been the inevitable consequence of the defeat of the revolutionary forces; namely, the Soviet Republic. As the Horthy regime had been born to crush the genuine movement of the people, it had to maintain a constant struggle against the people. The judge argued that the war itself had been nothing other than another means of fighting against the Hungarian people. From this point of view, the only satisfactory explanation of Hungary's participation in the war was that it was a means of perpetuating the survival of the Horthy regime. The counterrevolution in 1919 had been the beginning of this political system; thus, it was also the start of the war.

In the interpretation of the People's Tribunal, the collapse of the First Hungarian Soviet Republic was the cause of the war catastrophe, since it was in 1919 that the fascist regime of 1944 had been born in Hungary: 'Not without grounds, Horthy boasted that the first manifestation of fascism appeared in Hungary in 1919, while Hitler and Mussolini admitted the fact resignedly. This fascist era continued during the next twenty-five years.'[38]

The events of 1919 convinced the court that the 'Horthyist fascist dictatorship' had come to power with the single purpose of eliminating Communism; therefore, it concluded that Communism was the only true enemy of fascism. The essence of the fascist systems was to fight Communism. Consequently, the inevitable fall of fascist powers meant the inevitable triumph of Communism, because, besides these two historical forces, there were no other alternatives. In turn, this straightforward historical interpretation was a powerful means of justifying Communist rule. The judge argued that the defeat in the war had become unavoidable from the very moment that the first Communist regime in 1919 was overthrown. Furthermore, as the war resulted in the destruction of the counterrevolutionary system, its fall had been encoded at the time of its genesis. With this reasoning, the sentence sought to demonstrate the thesis of the inevitable downfall of all non-Communist social and political structures. The judge believed that, by such a historical argument, the thesis of the inevitable victory of Communist systems could be justified.

The purpose of the trials of war criminals in Hungary was, from the beginning, the creation of historical narratives. The foundations of this peculiar representation of the recent past were laid down by the Communist or leftist political attempts to discredit the constructed history of the Horthy regime in order to bolster the legitimacy of the new

---

36 Ibid.
37 Michael André Bernstein, *Foregone Conclusions* (Berkeley/London: University of California Press, 1994), 16.
38 BAZ ML, Sentence of the People's Tribunal in Miskolc.

political system.³⁹ The preface to the decree on the People's Tribunals in 1945, written by István Ries, then Social Democrat minister of justice, claimed that the beginnings of the road leading to the war catastrophe had to be sought in the events of 1919: 'The destruction of Hungary had little to do with Hungary's drifting into the war and less with Sztójay's or Szálasi's Arrow Cross rule. The counterrevolution succeeding the revolution of 1919 laid the grounds for the Hungarian catastrophe. […] It could almost be foreseen that they would set the country on fire. They systematically prepared the Hungarian people for suicide.'⁴⁰

The political prosecutor in the trial of another former prime minister called for a clear differentiation between guilty individuals and the rest of the people. He claimed very powerfully that it was possible to identify the criminals and crimes could be avoided. The prosecutor argued that the only appropriate punishment that could equal the character of the culprits was their complete exclusion from the community. They required the completion of the social drama – that is to say, legal confirmation of the irremediable break in society and the final expulsion of the ill-doers:⁴¹

> The tribunal of the Hungarian people must condemn in front of the whole world the man who became traitor of his nation and people and who pushed this country into the deepest abyss of its history, and the sentence must excommunicate him from the body of this nation. The sentence of the People's Tribunal must shout from the housetops that neither the working Hungarian people nor the Hungarian nation are guilty, but this man and those who after betraying humanity, culture and human morality shamefully put the whole Hungarian nation on the market. This is the defendant's crime and of those lackeys who accompanied him. Let the tribunal of the Hungarian people condemn them according to their crimes.⁴²

The political prosecutor in Bárdossy's trial requested that the judges act in the same way: 'Dear Sir People's Judges! Now there is nothing else to do but to point out that the Hungarian people that were eventually given a voice – for the first time in history – have nothing to do with these masters. You must expel, deny and exterminate them.'⁴³

At this moment the way of forgetting WWII did not differ from the general European attempts to come to terms with the past. The immediate reaction in 1945 was the cry of 'never again!' which signalled the inherent demand for forgetting. In most parts of Europe the suppression was carried out by turning the crimes onto the Germans. Histories of German

---

39 See László Karsai, 'The People's Courts and Revolutionary Justice in Hungary, 1945–46', in *The Politics of Retribution: World War II and Its Aftermath*, ed. István Deák, Jan T. Gross and Tony Judt (Princeton: Princeton University Press, 2000), 233–51; László Varga, '"Forradalmi törvényesség": Jogszolgáltatás 1945 után Magyarországon', *Beszélő* 4 (November 1999): 57–73.
40 The Decree on the People's Tribunals, no. ME 81/1945, 6, *Magyar Törvénytár. 1943–45. évi törvénycikkek* (Budapest: Révai, 1946), 93.
41 The concept of 'social drama' is from Victor Turner, *Dramas, Fields, and Metaphors* (Ithaca/London: Cornell University Press, 1974), 35–42.
42 Péter Sipos and András Sipos, eds, *Imrédy Béla a vádlottak padján* (Béla Imrédy in the prisoners' box) (Budapest: Osiris, 1999), 360.
43 Pritz, *Bárdossy*, 203.

occupation and legends of national resistance were born immediately parallel to the trials, which were designed to identify the group of traitors as real persons. In Germany society was divided between the perpetrators and an innocent (in fact, victimized) population. The narrative of Hitler and his vicious clique that terrorized the majority of the people coincided with the immediate postwar experience of most of the ordinary Germans who felt themselves victims of air raids, destruction and privation. The process of denazification created the category of *Mitläufer*, who were not considered real perpetrators in spite of their affiliation with the regime. This fact made the collective forgetting of participation and cooperation all the more easy due to their subsequent reintegration into the public sphere after 1948. Commemoration in Germany focused on anti-Nazi resistance and avoided including survivors, whereas the mass extermination of the Jews was encircled in silence.[11]

Originally, 1919 played a similar role in Hungary: the event was recollected in order to obtain a historical explanation for the division of the society into perpetrators and victims. According to the prosecution, the separate history of the masters and the people did not begin with Bárdossy. The prosecutors argued that, basically, Hungarian history had been divided into two since 1919. The judge argued that in 1919 power had passed into the hands of a well-defined system of governance. By these means the court hoped to decline the stigma of collective guilt. The events of 1919 were evoked to demonstrate that from there onwards the Hungarian people had lost their sovereignty and the country was basically ruled by selfish adventurer politicians; as a result it suffered the effects of 1944. The First Hungarian Soviet Republic in 1919, paradoxically, was seen from this point of view as a democratic regime and a forerunner of democracy that served the national interests: 'The workers took the power in their own hands in Hungary in 1919 and organized the national resistance against the demands of our neighbours.'[15] The sentence pointed out that in 1919 Hungary was faced with two opportunities: either it would become a democratic country or feudalism would prevail. Although the judge argued that the war catastrophe was a logical consequence of the counterrevolutionary rule, he did not attempt to make out that all other alternatives were erased from Hungarian history afterwards. The history that had begun in 1919 was a constant struggle between the evil leaders and the aspirations of the people, which always carried the opportunity of change. According to the historical interpretation of the sentence the tragedy of Hungary was precisely the fact that its leaders always ignored the interests of the people. According to the charge, the history of the ruling class meant the continuity of the politics that eventually resulted in the catastrophe. Bárdossy was accused of

> executing consistently the politics of the masters' Hungary, the Hungary of lords. He defended the politics that was begun by Horthy in '19 and was consolidated by Bethlen, which eventually passed through Bárdossy. All these lead straightforwardly to the same

---

44 On forgetting WWII, see Tony Judt, 'The Past is Another Country: Myth and Memory in Postwar Europe', *Daedalus* 121 (4) (1992): 83–97. The German case is in Alf Lüdtke, 'Coming to Terms with the Past: Illusions of Remembering, Ways of Forgetting Nazism in West Germany', *Journal of Modern History* 65 (Summer, 1993): 542–72.
45 Pritz, *Bárdossy*, 242.

conclusion. This is the politics of the twenty-five-year-long regime, to where Szálasi's bandit politics, the politics of this political adventurer loafing about the regime: to 15 October [the day of the failed armistice and the beginning of the Arrow Cross rule] and to the activity directed to the obstruction of the armistice.[46]

In this regard, however, the Hungarian trials and their similar Central and Eastern European counterparts diverged from the Western European pattern from the beginning. In the West, the postwar trials of those accused of war crimes were principally aimed at making amends for the wartime suffering of their victims, without any explicit claim to the construction of overarching historical interpretations.[47]

The formal similarity of the legal and historical practices seemed to authorize the judge's claim to make historical statements. History and jurisprudence share common epistemological roots: in fact, both historiography and legal proceedings originated in the demand to establish the reality of the past. Generally speaking, a juridical verdict needs the notion of the past in order to make statements on the present. This means that, in order to claim titles, rights or judgments in a legally appropriate way, one has to know the preceding events of the case in question. In order to claim these rights or the basis for legal action, one has to prove that something actually took place. Thus, it is necessary to demonstrate the actual *reality* of a event. Legal reasoning in Western law ordinarily takes the following form: the established facts indicate a plot that is always related to the past, whereas the proven events are organized in a chronological order. The argumentation is always retroactive: an action that is known by the judge is conceived of as having been done because of certain reasons which, however, are only assumed to be probable. This is also the way modern historiography operates.[48]

Szim personified and tangibly realized the narrative described above. The sentence declared: 'The defendant was one of the outstanding leaders of this exterminating war led by executioners.'[49] One of the newspapers claimed that 'the Hungarian people were offended by the activity of the defendant!'[50] Another paper wrote that 'the honour

---

46 Pritz, *Bárdossy*, 202. The political prosecutor in Imrédy's trial began his historical narrative with the events of 1919 as well. Nonetheless his precise argument cannot be discovered due to the fragmentation of the sources. See Sipos and Sipos, *Imrédy*, 356.

47 See Deák, Gross and Judt, *The Politics of Retribution*; Henry Rousso, *The Vichy Syndrome: History and Memory in France since 1944* (Cambridge, MA: Harvard University Press, 1991); Pieter Lagrou, *The Legacy of Nazi Occupation: Patriotic Memory and National Recovery in Western Europe, 1945–1965* (Cambridge, Cambridge University Press, 2000); and Bernhard Giesen, 'National Identity as Trauma: The German Case', in *Myth and Memory in the Construction of Community*, ed. Bo Stråth (Brussels: PIE/Peter Lang, 2000), 240–47. On Sweden in the same volume, see Bo Stråth, 'Poverty, Neutrality and Welfare: Three Key Concepts in the Modern Foundation Myth of Sweden', 393–4. For the Hungarian case, see István Rév, 'Miért győzhetett oly elviselhetetlenül könnyen a kommunizmus Magyarországon?', *Rubicon* (July 1989): 4–6.

48 Michel Foucault, 'Truth and Juridical Forms', in *Power* (New York: New Press, 2000), 46–7; Patrick Nerhot, *Law, Writing, Meaning: An Essay in Legal Hermeneutics* (Edinburgh: Edinburgh University Press, 1992), 24–109. See Carlo Ginzburg, *The Judge and the Historian* (London/New York: Verso, 1999), 12–14.

49 BAZ ML.

50 SZM, 7 April 1948, 3.

of the Hungarian people requires Lőrinc Szim to suffer for the crimes committed against the people!' 'The People's Tribunal in Miskolc sentenced the bloody-handed executioner of the workers and peasants in Upper Hungary to death', it informed the population. 'The terrifying crimes of the counterrevolution have been revealed during the trial. The true face of the counterrevolution born in crime and blood, and which perpetrated the killing of peasants and workers, was shown in its own nakedness.'[51]

The public trial itself was abundant in horrific details. The court attempted to show tangible or visible evidence wherever possible. One of the witnesses stated that 'the defendant even kicked the flesh from my chest'. At which point, 'according to the people's prosecutor's proposal the witness takes off his coat and, pulling up his shirt, shows his chest. The chairman and the people's judges inspect the witness's breast and state that a mark from a bruise can be seen on it.' Later, the 'witness takes his upper set of teeth [a dental plate], shows it and declares: all of my teeth were knocked out'.[52] These details had no direct relationship with the course of the historical narrative. They played no role in advancing the story. According to the judge, the existence of counterrevolution would have resulted in the downfall of the regime during WWII even without the committing of ruthless crimes. Such particulars fulfilled no narrative function. Having no symbolic function, such details could only state and indicate that the story *really happened*.[53] Articles in the press also emphasized the horrifying details, bearing titles such as: 'Horrors of the Szim trial', 'Witnesses confess of brutal torture in Szim's trial', 'Gruesome confessions of terrors in the Szim sanatorium', 'Szim knocked out all the teeth of a craftsman with his own hands', 'First blow given by Lőrinc Szim to victims taken to the house of terrors in Csabai-kapu, old handicapped invalid beaten until he was covered with blood'.[54] Further gory details were provided within the articles: 'The henchmen of the Szim sanatorium hanged their victim by his hair.'[55] One article quoted a witness who 'had seen in the cell that a man rolled about in his own blood as the nails had been torn from his toes by Szim's executioners'.[56] The newspapers attempted to capture the attention of their readers with brief, shocking front page headlines: 'Blood-curdling details on the horrors of the Szim sanatorium', 'Lőrinc Szim's henchmen started their carefully chosen tortures at the evening peal of bells', 'Lőrinc Szim was Horthy's bloody-handed henchman in Miskolc'.[57] Popular trials are stages where complicated notions of social reality are re-enacted in palpable ways and, hence, rendered easily comprehensible.[58]

---

51 FN, 7 April 1948, 1.
52 BAZ ML, Minutes of the hearing, 30.
53 Roland Barthes created the concept of 'reality effect' to signify these apparently unimportant particulars in narratives. See his 'The Reality Effect', in *The Rustle of Language* (Oxford: Blackwell, 1986), 141–8.
54 SZM, 24 March 1948; SZM, 25 March 1948; FN, 18 February 1948; SZM, 23 March 1948; FN, 23 March 1948.
55 SZM, 21 March 1948.
56 FN, 24 March 1948.
57 SZM, 20 March 1948; FN, 17 March 1948.
58 Robert Hariman, ed., *Popular Trials* (London/Tuscaloosa: University of Alabama Press, 1990), 1–16.

Szim and his defence lawyer attempted to rebut the accusations. Their tactic was directed against the charge of war crimes. Nevertheless, they did not challenge the thesis that the political crimes committed in 1919 and 1920 had been war crimes, but instead sought to prove that Szim had not actually carried out the actions attributed to him. The defendant plead not guilty to the spreading of fascism. Denying this, he claimed that he had prevented the persecuted persons from being carried away by the authorities and that he had opposed the Germans and the Arrow Cross. However, he had not opposed the Russian army, which had made an effort to liberate the Hungarian people from German subjugation. Szim presented himself as a resistance fighter, who had kept the oath he had sworn to the regent by not handing the barracks over to the Arrow Cross. He summed up his arguments in the following way: 'In the hardest and most crucial period in the history of the Hungarian people, I was already advancing on the way as ordered by the laws of humanity and democratic ideals.'[59] Basically, he was only a soldier, who had fought when the people demanded it, as in 1919 or during WWII.

According to the logic of the court, Szim, who was portrayed as a typical figure of the Horthy regime, could not have prevented or reduced the devastation of the war. The acquittal of the defendant would have meant that the Horthy regime had survived the war, and this was impossible to countenance. If the reason for the war was the Horthy regime, then Szim could only be a war criminal. In order to justify this interpretation, the People's Tribunal tried to prove that the defendant was not a resistance fighter:

> According to the defendant's own presentation, he, as a resistance fighter, gained no significant merits that could be adduced as a considerable mitigating circumstance. He did not suffer any legal disadvantages by the Arrow Cross rule, except for having been wounded, which would have been inconceivable if his resistance had been of great value. His injury was instead the consequence of the misunderstanding of the situation.[60]

This perception denied that Szim had actually resisted the Arrow Cross. In another statement, however, the court argued that it was theoretically impossible for a Horthy officer to resist: 'The Hungarian people have nothing to do with the fact that these two beasts of prey, the Arrow Cross and the Horthy henchmen, were wrangling over the bones.'[61] The People's Tribunal at this point demonstrated an attitude similar to that of certain inquisitors during witch trials; all kinds of behaviour of the defendant could prove his or her guilt. The way in which Szim's wounds demonstrated his war crimes was the same way in which the inquisitors condemned suspected witches on the basis of the literature of demonology: if the defendant 'were to confess, she was guilty; if she remained silent, even under torture, she did so by virtue of an enchantment (the so-called *maleficium taciturnitatis*); if she denied being a witch, then she lied, seduced by the Devil, the father of lies'.[62]

---

59 BAZ ML, Petition for a reprieve, June 1948.
60 BAZ ML, Decision of the National Council of People's Tribunals.
61 BAZ ML, Minutes of the hearing, 123.
62 Ginzburg, *The Judge and the Historian*, 103.

Secondly, the sentence proved that Szim had led the life of a counterrevolutionary. In spite of the fact that he fought in the Hungarian Red Army, he had 'secretly' prepared himself for the coming of the counterrevolutionary regime. The prosecutor articulated this narrative in the following way:

> The defendant displayed a unity of desire and decision in the summer of 1919. The defendant started his activity before his capture; namely, he surrendered the company he commanded into the hands of the Czechs. He pursued this in captivity in Bohemia, when he organized people for the White Terror. When he arrived home, it was a natural outcome that he, as a White Terrorist officer, was put at the head of this commando.

The sentence accepted this interpretation as true and argued the following:

> His counterrevolutionary aspirations had already manifested themselves during the existence of the Soviet Republic. He had been the commander of one of the companies of the Hungarian Red Army, of the Red Army, which had defended Hungarian territories against the surrounding states that would subsequently organize themselves into the Little Entente in the spring and summer of 1919. The defendant believed that he could serve the so-called 'national idea' manifested in the damned 'Idea of Szeged', which would later direct our foreign policy towards the national disaster with its extreme irredentism, by surrendering together with his troops to the Czech army and, thus, he himself poured murderous machine gun fire onto his own soldiers who were fighting against the Czechs around Miskolc.
>
> It is obvious that he owed his honourable position to the full confidence of Horthy and his clique, who appreciated his merits in leading the counterrevolution to victory. He obtained the post of the commander of the so-called Department of Military Investigation – since he was the ardent supporter of the 'White Terror' which was the ground of the counterrevolution – which was created to terrorize and ravage the counties of *Borsod, Gömör, Abaúj, Zemplén* and *Heves*.[63]

Courts detect the connection between the past of the accused and his or her crime, as well as the expectations of his or her future. The legal procedure is interested in the origins of the crime within the criminal, be it the result of an instinct, the unconscious, the environment or family heritage. Crime is regarded as a consequence of the specific character of the individual, the way of life, or the thinking of the criminal. In reality, the trials themselves shape the subjects of the committed crimes in order to establish the most appropriate and effective punishment for the criminals.[64] The biography is a means of maintaining an identity that has already been formed. Life narratives reflect and reveal the character and essence of their bearers. These stories are able to demonstrate that the

---

63 BAZ ML, Minutes of the hearing, 118; Sentence of the People's Tribunal in Miskolc (emphasis added).
64 Michel Foucault, *Discipline and Punish* (New York: Random House, 1979), 17–22, 99–101, 189–94; Foucault, 'Truth and Juridical Forms', 56–7, 83–4.

attitudes that caused the present behaviour of a person were already present in his or her past. In mental hospitals, the case records play this role.[65] Prisons construct the essential character of the convict, the *criminal*, through an observance and recording of his or her life story. Penal institutions are convinced that the personality of the criminal can be identified with his or her crime, since malicious acts are the result of the past lives of the individual: crimes are born in life stories.[66]

Biographical records play a role similar to that of certain rituals in tribal societies where ambiguous identities are fixed. During these rites, entities that cannot be categorized without doubts are usually imposed to occupy one prescribed position in the taxonomy, or are simply eliminated through a ceremonial meal. Anthropological data testify to the way in which a system of categories attempts to deal with ambiguity or anomaly. A well-ordered structure of classifications tries to encompass all the phenomena of the surrounding world, whereas an ambiguous or anomalous event entails a challenge to it due to the invitation of more than one interpretation. The experience that does not conform to the previously set system is ordinarily considered 'impure' or dangerous. In other words, an indefinable event spoils the pattern and causes pollution. In order to dissolve the confusion the maintainers of the structure may choose to control the danger physically and to aim at excluding any plurality of meaning by settling for one or the other interpretation.[67]

If the defendant aspired to lead the system to victory, which was the reason for the war catastrophe, then the statement that he was a war criminal seemed to be logical for the People's Tribunal: 'Thus, in this light, the defendant's acts met the criteria of war crimes. The connection to war is not excluded by the longer period passed between the time of committing the acts and the actual breaking out of the war.'[68]

Regarding the narrative described above, Szim did not merely symbolize the Horthy regime as a social and political system, but symbolized its history from its beginning to its inevitable end. To the court, his life narrative represented the history of the downfall: his destiny shed light on the fate of a whole social system. Szim's actual person represented the historical continuity between White Terror and the war catastrophe, while his figure brought an abstract process to life. By staging him in the court, it was demonstrated that the stories told in general terms actually occurred. He was the commander of 'a commando called the Department of Military Investigation; actions like these are ranked among the first phenomena of the reaction in Hungary, and, as such, they prevailed in the series of events which led necessarily to Hungary's drifting into the war and later

---

65 Erving Goffman, *Asylums: Essays on the Social Situation of Mental Patients and Other Inmates* (London: Penguin, 1991), 155–6, 375–7, 87.
66 Foucault, *Discipline and Punish*, 251–2. On biography as evidence, see István Rév, 'In Mendacio Veritas', *Representations* 35 (Summer 1991): 1–20.
67 For example, a monstrous childbirth may threaten the cultural order of a society. The Nuer cope with this anomaly by secluding the possibility of manifold interpretations. They treat the children as baby hippopotamuses born to humans accidentally and drive them back to their proper place among animals: the river. See Mary Douglas, *Purity and Danger* (London: Routledge, 1966), 37–40, 49–53, 94–5.
68 BAZ ML, Decision of the National Council of People's Tribunals.

to the fatal downfall'.⁶⁹ Thereby, a retrospective view of the happenings of 1919 made it possible to create a historical interpretation based upon individual actions. This fact provided the People's Tribunal with the proper conditions to fulfil its duty and to make statements that could be accepted as a sentence. Lawful sentences justify individuals and their personal deeds, whereas legal proceedings deal with individual activities.⁷⁰ Consequently, utterances are not valid sentences unless they meet these requirements. A trial is a place where it is not sufficient to say certain things in order for them to be accepted: the conditions have to be appropriate and the participants have to follow the expected procedural routine.⁷¹ In this way, the People's Tribunal successfully performed the act of sentencing people. As a valid sentence, however, or as an accepted truth, it verified an abstract historical representation, the only evidence of which was the biography of the defendant constructed by legal means.⁷² Consequently, the trials of war criminals did not prove the representation of an abstract historical process – the continuity of the events of 1919 and 1944 – based upon comprehensive research, but rendered them tangible through the construction of individual personalities.⁷³

---

69 Ibid.
70 Jurisdiction and historiography, despite all their epistemological similarities, represent different genres. Legal procedures establish individual responsibility upon the scrutiny of the past of the defendant, historians examine temporal processes of political communities and societies from a critical perspective, but in theory having no intention to judge them. As Henry Rousso argues, historians are not witnesses. Probably, the reverse is equally true: witnesses are not historians (*The Haunting Past: History, Memory, and Justice in Contemporary France* (Philadelphia: University of Pennsylvania Press, 2002), 60.)
71 See John L. Austin, *How to Do Things with Words* (Oxford: Oxford University Press, 1975), 14–15.
72 Mark J. Osiel also claims that the formation of collective memory in court is unintentional. The author also expresses doubts concerning the success of history writing in legal proceedings: 'Ever Again: Legal Remembrance of Administrative Massacre', *University of Pennsylvania Law Review* (1995): 463–74. For a comprehensive view on the structure of retrospective justice, see Stanley Cohen, 'State Crimes of Previous Regimes: Knowledge, Accountability, and the Policing of the Past', *Law and Social Inquiry* 20 (Winter 1995): 7–50.
73 Therefore, contrary to the opinion of most of the historians, these trials concerned themselves with individualization rather than abstraction. According to the previous interpretations, the purpose of these legal acts was to produce an abstract image of a historical phenomenon all in all through the symbolic persons of the defendants. A recent study on the case of László Bárdossy, who was the first prewar prime minister to be condemned to death, pronounces that: 'The whole trial, but especially the sentence for the first instance shows a very definite effort to establish a then profoundly new conception of history. In the spirit of this conception not only Bárdossy was condemned devastatingly but also the quarter of a century between 1919 and 1944' (Pál Pritz, 'Bevezetés', in *Bárdossy*, 16). See also his *A Bárdossy-per* (Budapest: Kossuth, 2001). In a similar manner the editor of the records of another prominent ex–prime minister's case states that: 'The trials held in front of the People's Tribunals and especially those public criminal proceedings that were carried out against persons occupying the office of the prime minister or leader of the state had the important designation to represent pejoratively and to deny unambiguously and definitely the history of that quarter of century passed between the two world wars' (Péter Sipos, 'Imrédy Béla pere a népbíróság előtt', in *Imrédy Béla a vádlottak padján*, 68).

3

Postwar political trials seemed to prove the Soviet type of teleological narrative about the inevitable victory of Communism by generating actual life courses that were directly tangible in the courtroom. Thus, it is hardly surprising that this peculiar mode of historical representation began to dominate Communist interpretations of the recent past. The first published history textbook for the eighth class of the primary schools in 1948 begins the history of the counterrevolutionary regime by focusing upon the brutal persecution of Communists by 'Horthy's gangs':

> The counterrevolutionary hordes were authorized to massacre anyone labelled as 'Communist conspirator' without a legal sentence in the street. The officer commandos situated in hotels Gellért and Britannia and in various barracks terrified the capital. The situation was the same throughout the whole country. In Kecskemét, about one hundred persons were caught and killed in the Orgovány woods under the direction of Iván Héjjas. The real masters of the country were the bloodthirsty Prónay, Ostenburg and other detachments.[74]

The authors are convinced that the nature of the violence reflected the fascist essence of the system. The textbook claims that, in December 1919, 'The fascist terror continued to collect its victims'. The second edition of the schoolbook in 1950 states that 1919 meant the birth of a system that was inherently against the people, since Horthy's group aimed at 'restoring the rule of the great landowners and capitalists, diminishing the achievements of the revolution and taking bloody revenge on the Hungarian people'.[75] The historical interpretations emphasized the foundation of the putative fascist regime in Hungary.

Apart from highlighting the fact that Hungary had been the first fascist dictatorship, scholarly attempts to understand the counterrevolution provided more sophisticated explanations for the foundations of fascism. In a 1951 book on the White Terror, two young historians argue that the system of brutal oppression was formed as a result of the resistance of the Hungarian people. The authors point out that, once they had experienced the benefits of a socialist regime, the Hungarian workers would no longer tolerate the restoration of capitalism. The combination of the techniques of suppression was the crucial factor in the genesis of Hungarian fascism.[76] The emphasis on violence and oppression is hardly astonishing. For Communist scholars, the history of the interwar regime was a genuine indictment that could be represented most adequately by following the pattern of the postwar trials of war criminals. The form of historical narrative did, in reality, include legal texts.

The indictment-like form of Communist historical interpretation, however, had further important consequences. In fact, official historical representations were based

---

74 *Történelem VIII* (Budapest: VKM, 1948), 64–5.
75 *Történelem VIII* (Budapest: Tankönyvkiadó, 1950), 186.
76 Karsai and Pamlényi, *Fehérterror*.

upon a carefully selected pool of data isolated from their related contexts cautiously. This technique of manipulating historical evidence was completed by the regular use of abstract, unclarified categories like 'capitalist classes' in general. This mode of description left significant blanks, disconnected chronologies and recognizable silences in the narrative, leaving its audience puzzled and lost. In 1953, the first volume of a series of source publications was published by Dezső Nemes, a research fellow at the Institute for Party History. The title of the book was *Az ellenforradalom hatalomrajutása és rémuralma Magyarországon 1919–1921* (The coming to power and the reign of terror of the counterrevolution in Hungary).[77] The editor contributed to the volume with a lengthy study entitled 'For the history of the bloodthirsty counterrevolution'. The author rearticulates the standardized opinions on the violent nature of the counterrevolution as a proof of its fascist essence and the inevitability of the foundation of the 'fascist dictatorship'. Besides this, he tries to elaborate a complex historical explanation concerning the necessary participation of the putative Hungarian fascist system in the war. Nemes argues that, although the Social Democrat government that succeeded the dictatorship of the proletariat on 1 August 1919 advanced the restoration of capitalism, the bourgeoisie did not trust it. According to the article, the 'capitalist classes' preferred a counterrevolutionary dictatorship in order to secure their interests. Nonetheless, Nemes leaves his readers in complete disorientation about who or what the 'capitalist classes' actually were. There are no references to the actual social and political composition of those groups who allegedly demanded the dictatorship. Besides, no evidence is quoted that could prove the general will to introduce a White Terror dictatorship. The author simply concludes *in abstracto* that it was logical that the massacres committed by Horthy's troops against the Communists had increased confidence in him on the part of the imperialists. They perceived the activity of the 'robber and murderer detachments' as the policy of the 'strong hand' that was needed to restore capitalism:

> The counterrevolution gave power to the most bloodthirsty beasts of capitalism, to the most bloodthirsty representatives of the great capitalists and landlords. The Hungarian great capitalists and landlords, however, supported the coming to power of precisely these representatives, which was not only acknowledged by the Entente imperialists, but was also endorsed by them. Horthy's army gained the trust of the industrialists by the bestial terror directed against the workers.[78]

Nemes points out that the Horthy regime had lived up to the expectations of its sponsor, the capitalist class – the governments always acted on behalf of the capitalists. They reduced wages and tolerated a high level of unemployment, inflation and speculation. Nevertheless, the policy of unrestrained exploitation could only be maintained by means of sheer terror

---

77 Dezső Nemes, ed., *Az ellenforradalom hatalomrajutása és rémuralma Magyarországon 1919–1921* (*Iratok az ellenforradalom történetéhez*, vol. 1) (The coming into power and terror rule of the counterrevolution in Hungary 1919–1921 [Records of the history of counterrevolution, vol. 1]) (Budapest, Szikra, 1953).
78 Dezső Nemes, 'A vérengző ellenforradalom történetéhez' (To the history of the bloodthirsty counterrevolution), in *Iratok az ellenforradalom történetéhez*, 7–144.

because of the desperate resistance of the workers. The author demonstrates the intensity of discontent by describing various miner strikes and referring to the high membership of the trade unions. As a result, according to the study, the reign of terror came to an end: the massacre was the means designed to restore and maintain capitalist power after the Communist experience. The terrorist regime developed logically, since the old means of suppression could no longer fulfil their task. Consequently, the counterrevolutionary regime employed a wide variety of measures in order to establish a profound system of oppression. The various governments introduced summary jurisdiction, political prisons, internment camps and frequent executions. Nemes claims that the 'fascist dictatorship' was established as the only possible tool to eliminate Communism and thereby preserve capitalism. In reality, Nemes ignores evidence of the attempts of the successive governments to consolidate the regime by introducing a variety of social welfare measures. Although these remained confined to a limited group of mostly urban working classes and were far from truly democratic emancipation, they reflected an intention to incorporate lower classes into an authoritarian corporate society in a fairly peaceful way. In general then, Nemes, while highlighting the facts of exclusion and secession, is silent about the instances of inclusion and integration.

This ignorance, however, results in puzzlement and loss of orientation as he tries to explain the historically necessary collapse of the Horthy regime. Nemes presents his evidence in order to prove that 'fascism' had inevitably led to war. Firstly, the exploitation of the workers had resulted in privation and serious economic hardships. Although the profit of capitalists rose, productivity declined. The author stresses that, in this situation, capitalism could only be saved by foreign loans. Nevertheless, repayments could be achieved through even more ruthless exploitation. Since the territory of exploitation had been narrowed, the Hungarian capitalist class had begun to search for new areas. Nemes concludes that this inevitably results in a policy of revision and war. Secondly, foreign loans raised the dependency of the country on foreign capital, mainly on German economic and political interests. Thus, the 'adventure politics' of war of the counterrevolutionary regime had inevitably led to the destruction of the Horthy regime:

> Eventually, during the 1930s, and especially at the time of WWII, Horthy and his fellows 'successfully' transformed the country into Hitler's colony and the monopoly territory for the expansion of the German imperialist great capital, and resulted in Hungary's participation in the anti-Soviet imperialist war of robbery. They pushed the country into a new catastrophic war of robbery, which destroyed the Horthy regime. Its fall was as shameful and disgraceful as its coming into existence.[79]

The highlighting of instances of privation, exploitation and terror marking the beginning and end of the interwar period in Hungary serves to directly connect the White Terror to the collapse of the Horthy regime and, thus, by turning the era in between into an irrelevant historical episode in the dominant temporal continuity of capitalist dictatorship, also serves to bridge the chronological gap in between these two violent epochs. However, a historical account in which 1919 is virtually followed immediately by 1944 triggers

---

79 Nemes, 'A vérengző ellenforradalom', 108.

disorder in the perception of historical time: it poses questions about the events of the period in between, but offers no comforting answers. Therefore, it causes puzzlement rather than orienting its reader. Communist propaganda historians apparently believed that by simply establishing legal evidence they could also authenticate by their historical interpretations the indictment-based form of historical representation. However, instead of constructing a comprehensible historical interpretation of causes and consequences, they brought forward loosely connected instances of atrocities in a vaguely defined explanatory framework.

It resulted in an abstract, barely tangible historical account, whereas in its form, it ended as a counterhistory. Counterhistory writing is a peculiar mode of historical representation: it aims at depriving the target group of its self-identity by constructing a counteridentity. Counterhistories reverse the positive self-assessment of the adversary in order to substitute it with a negative image.[80] The constructed continuity between 1919 and 1944 made it possible to imagine WWII as the world wide collision of fascism and Communism. Party historians emphasized the details of White Terror and the persecutions against Communists. They also claimed that the Nazi system had been the direct consequence of 1919. Thus, the White Terror of 1919 overshadowed the memory of the genocide of the 1940s: the horrors of the counterrevolution eclipsed the abyss of the Hitlerite extermination. As a prelude, 1919 expelled the Jews and other victims from the narrative: it was claimed that the real victims of the death camps of fascism had been the Communists.[81] Thereby, it became possible to suggest that the only purpose of the Nazis had been the elimination of Communists and that all anti-Communist regimes were actually fascist. Party historians constructed a rigid interpretation of history that consisted exclusively of two factors: fascism and Communism. All events of the past could be comprehended with the help of this scheme. The Communist narrative of WWII did not make a development similar to that of the West possible. In the West, from the end of the 1950s, and after the Eichmann trial in particular, the memory of the war was inseparably linked to the Holocaust. Thus, the notion of fascism began to be used to educate Western European peoples from committing mass extermination once again. In the Soviet bloc, by way of contrast, the concept was exploited to justify Communist rule.

Counterhistories, however, generally fail to produce the positive self-image of their supporters. They focus on the image of the adversary and construct the self-image in contrast with the image of the enemy group. In practice, this meant that Communist historians hoped to prove the necessary victory of Communism by demonstrating the inevitable fall of the Horthy system. The narrative of the necessary victory of Communism, nonetheless, proved to be fairly fragile. Constructing a counterhistory, Communist

---

80 Amos Funkenstein, 'History, Counterhistory, and Narrative', in *Probing the Limits of Representation*, ed. Saul Friedlander (Cambridge MA/London: Harvard University Press, 1992), 66–81.

81 On the controversial politics of memory in Poland, see: James E. Young, *The Texture of Memory* (New Haven/London: Yale University Press, 1993), 119–54. The Communist interpretation managed to construct a narrative of the post-1945 anti-Semitic pogroms and their connection to the Holocaust in Hungary, astonishingly, without the Jews. See Péter Apor, 'The Lost Deportations and the Lost People of Kunmadaras: A Pogrom in Hungary, 1946', *Hungarian Historical Review* 2 (3) (2013): 566–604.

historians used a type of historical narrative, the accepted truth of which was based upon no historical proof. Built upon legal authority and vested with the political authority of partisanship, Communist historiography claimed the truth of these representations without the verification of historical narratives. Soviet-type historiography thus shifted the authority of historical representations from its regular basis of independent research and the interpretation of evidence towards political devotion and partisanship.[82] The counterhistory of the Horthy regime consciously suppressed any relevant available evidence that contradicted its narrative, with the intention of erasing the histories and memories attached to them. However, it was precisely these still-living histories and memories which were attached to the evidence that led to the narrative always remaining a source of doubt and, consequently, an ineffective foundation of faith. To base the history of inevitable victory solely upon the history of the inevitable fall foreshadowed its very own inevitable fall.

The history of 1919 that these trials produced was not about the First Hungarian Soviet Republic, but focused rather on the White Terror that had followed the fall of Béla Kun's regime. During the Rákosi regime, this narrative had an important role in creating a certain antifascist myth, but it could not impact the problematic, isolated and fragmented story of the Hungarian commune. Besides the troubles which Kun, the Social Democrats or the peasants possibly created for any public interpretation of the Soviet Republic, the relationship between 1919 and 1944, the history of fascism, did not need to talk about the commune. The imagined continuity of fascism had no relevance to the study of the Soviet Republic. The narrative of the continuity of 1919 and 1944 affected considerably, though somewhat unexpectedly, the narrative of the Soviet Republic only after 1956 when it became relevant as part of the counterrevolutionary continuity of 1919, 1944 and 1956 constructed by Kádár's propaganda historians. The role that this narrative could play was partly connected to the fact that the People's Tribunals were resurrected after the uprising in 1956, when crimes against the people's democracy were dealt with once again.

---

82 Thus, the Sovietization of history domesticated a pattern of historiographical authority that preceded the formation of modern historical scholarship. The modernization of historical studies took place as a result of the rejection of historical interpretations as articulated by traditional institutions of authority, such as the Church and the prince, and the endowment of organizations, such as universities, which possessed the potential to define the criteria of proper scholarship. On the institutional segments of the modernization of history see Gerard Noiriel, *Sur la 'crise' de l'histoire* (Paris, Éditions Belin, 1996).

Chapter 4

FUNERAL: THE BIRTH OF THE PANTHEON OF THE LABOUR MOVEMENT IN BUDAPEST

1

For many decades, the Pantheon of the Labour Movement situated in the Kerepesi Cemetery of Budapest was regarded by the then ruling Hungarian Communist Party as one of its principal commemorative constructions. Nowadays, the building stands abandoned. On the one hand, while the era of the Communist politics of history seems to be over forever, this is precisely why the monument's megalomaniac attempt to reinterpret the national past may seem familiar to us. On the other hand, this monumentality is exactly what renders the story of the pantheon distant and unfamiliar: what could be the origins of this obsession towards the dead?

The memorial, as we know it today, gained its form in 1959 with the inauguration of its most significant and architecturally monumental part: the Mausoleum of the Labour Movement. The mausoleum itself consists of different elements. Its central building is the mausoleum proper, containing urns of cremated corpses; it is completed by six pillars designed to commemorate those who were buried outside the cemetery. A row of honorary graves, considered to be the most prestigious burial site for those who were not cremated, is situated in front of the central building. A plot by the side of the mausoleum was opened to receive the remnants of less significant persons, while four other plots and a so-called 'heroes' plot' were counted among the parts of the Pantheon of the Labour Movement as well. Although the mausoleum was inaugurated in 1959, the final shape of the pantheon is the result of an ongoing process that lasted until the middle of the 1960s: partly because of construction works, and also because of the reburial of corpses in order to attach them to the pantheon. In its final form the Communist pantheon in the Kerepesi Cemetery consists of approximately five hundred tombs. Apparently, the ultimate purpose of the creation of the pantheon was to gather the graves of all significant Communist personalities in one place in order to form one outstanding site of cult and memory.[1]

The idea of a martyrs' sepulchre derived from the classical Communist period that preceded the outbreak of the popular anti-Stalinist revolution in Budapest on 23 October 1956. Remembering the martyrs was an important issue in the Communist Party even before the establishment of the dictatorship. The Hungarian Communist Party organized a commemoration for its wartime martyrs on 27 July 1945 where the

---

1 Vilmos Tóth, 'A Kerepesi úti temető másfél évszázada' (The one-and-a-half centuries of the Kerepesi Road Cemetery) *Budapesti Negyed* 24 (Summer 1999): 97–103.

idea of their reburial and provisional sepulchre was raised, followed by the proposal of a memorial site for Communist martyrs a year later, in spring 1946. A list of victims that highlighted the role of Communist resistance fighters during the war was established, while the five Communist martyrs of the period between 1919 and 1944 were to receive a common grave and an honorary reburial.[2] A competition for a martyrs' sepulchre was advertised in 1947. Nonetheless, its winning work was deemed inappropriate to be raised in a cemetery, and the National Propaganda Department renewed the competition on 13 July 1948.[3] The leadership of the Hungarian Workers' Party proposed on 18 January 1949 – soon after its eventual takeover in 1948 – that a common sepulchre for five great martyrs of the party together with the victims of the First Hungarian Soviet Republic in 1919 should be raised. The proposition did not specify the names of the five great persons, but stressed that the monument ought to occupy a busy public square in a proletarian district.[4] The memorial was to be bestowed in the cemetery in a separate plot with life-size statues. A four-week deadline was stipulated to accomplish the construction work, and János Kádár and György Marosán were appointed as the supervisors.[5] The building of the martyrs' sepulchre was considered a task of party propaganda in order to diminish the widespread ignorance of the Communist martyrs. The party leadership planned to issue an illustrated publication commemorating 145 fighters of the movement in autumn 1950, and the following April the Institute for Party History was instructed to elaborate a proposal concerning the commemoration of several heroes and martyrs of the First Hungarian Soviet Republic.[6] In 1955, an open competition for designing the memorial was advertised; however, with no success. Therefore, the party leadership decided to restart the procedure in early 1956 with the participation of invited designers and architects.[7] The intention of the party was to cover a wide range of martyrs, and the sepulchre was planned to include various periods. Due to the political crisis and the subsequent eruption of the revolution in October 1956, the Stalinist leadership could not realize their plans. When the new party leadership returned to the idea, the original meaning of the monument was profoundly reinterpreted in close connection with the anti-Stalinist revolution itself.

The actual construction of the burial site began after 1956, with the pressing problem of finding an appropriate place for the Communists who died during the revolution of 1956. The party leadership considered these persons the great heroes of the nation, and

---

[2] PIL 274/4/41, 274/4/136, 274/4/138, 274/4/140, 274/4/142, 274/4/145, 274/4/149. Martin Mevius argues that the emergence of the Communist martyr cult occurred in connection with the attempt of the party to obtain national legitimacy: *Agents of Moscow: The Hungarian Communist Party and the Origins of Socialist Patriotism* (Oxford: Oxford University Press, 2005), 192–5.
[3] MOL M-KS 276/55/10.
[4] MOL M-KS 276/86/14. See also Mevius, *Agents of Moscow*, 252–3.
[5] MOL M-KS 276/54/26.
[6] MOL M-KS 276/86/73; MOL M-KS 276/86/75.
[7] MOL M-KS 288/7/11. *A Magyar Szocialista Munkáspárt Központi Bizottsága Titkárságának jegyzőkönyvei. 1957. július 1. – december 31.* (Minutes of Secretariat of the Central Committee of the Hungarian Socialist Workers' Party, 1 July–31 December 1957), ed. István Feitl (Budapest: Napvilág, 2000) (hereafter: Secretariat), 112.

therefore decided to bury them in the Kerepesi Cemetery, which was, and still is today, the most prestigious national site of burial. The cemetery has been regarded as the virtual pantheon of the Hungarian nation and the honorary resting place of the great dead of the political community for some time. Here rest the most significant actors of the history of the nation, among them politicians, authors, poets, actors and actresses, composers, artists, diplomats and military commanders. These outstanding personalities range from the era of 'national awakening' at the turn of the eighteenth and nineteenth centuries, the reform period and the birth of modern Hungary in the first half of the nineteenth century, the revolution and war of independence in 1848–49, the great modernization era in the second half of the nineteenth century, to the turbulent twentieth century. In short, the Kerepesi Cemetery unfolds the great narrative of national history.

Consequently, since the Communist dead in the pantheon were necessarily related to other corpses and tombs in the cemetery, these penetrated into the field of historical representation. The Communist construction of the memorial site inherently conveyed in itself the intention to reinterpret national history symbolically and generate a new type of historical continuity. This interpretation was originated in the gradually emerging relationship of the dead of 1956 to the fallen victims of the First Hungarian Soviet Republic in 1919. The Pantheon of the Labour Movement was the logical and indispensable realization of this particular history.

2

When the newly organized institutions of the Communist Party acquired a relatively stable form, the issue of the fallen of 1956 was raised. The initiative came from the Budapest organs of the party that remembered the siege of their main building – the core event of the counterrevolution – as their own sacrifice. The corpses of the defenders of the Budapest party headquarters were exhumed on 5 March 1957 in order to be identified and reburied as heroes. Apart from the armed defenders of the party building, the Communist leadership also considered Imre Mező, the secretary of the Budapest Party Committee who had been killed as one of the negotiators in the battle of Republic Square. Two other persons, Sándor Sziklai and Lajos Kiss, were mentioned as well.[8] Their deaths were covered in the first volume of the government's White Book; thus it became well known to the Communist public. The official booklet described the siege of their family house (Kiss was actually Sziklai's father-in-law) and the battle between the old Communists and the attacking 'bandits'.[9] On 9 March the party's Provisional Executive Committee in Budapest submitted a proposal to the Central Committee to renovate the graves of Communist martyrs and raising a provisional sepulchre.[10] It stated that, 'The graves of the martyrs of the counterrevolution in 1956 are treated in a manner unfair to their struggles and to victims of the labour movement.' The graves were

---

8 Open Society Archives 300/40/1/1300. *Hungarian Monitoring*, 5 March 1957; NSZ, 5 March 1957.
9 WB vol. 1, 27.
10 MOL M-KS 288/7/3.

considered inappropriate as they had fallen into extreme disrepair. Therefore the report put great emphasis on repairing the burial sites of the martyrs of the counterrevolution. This renovation, however, was regarded only a provisional solution, as the aim was to give the martyrs of the counterrevolution their appropriate burials in two months. The real issue, however, was revealed in a letter to the first secretary of the Budapest Provisional Executive Committee from the party secretary of a factory in Budapest. It pronounced, 'The fact that our comrades are buried together with their murderers revolted us deeply.'[11] Then he demanded, 'Our martyrs have to be buried thoroughly isolated from counterrevolutionaries in an honorary plot that is their due.' The letter clearly expounded the idea that the Communist victims of 1956 could not rest together with the bodies of counterrevolutionaries. Death and the funeral are among the most powerful social and cultural borders. Death eliminates in a moment the complex social being carried by the physical individuality. The social body of the person is constructed through long and complicated social mechanisms and its social deconstruction requires a similar process. Death as a social and cultural act ends when the deceased individual finds their appropriate place among their companions, and this demands an appropriate funeral and resting place. The deceased passes over to the world of the dead and rests in peace after having an appropriate ceremony. The funeral is a community ritual in which the survivors accept the place and mode of burial as appropriate and the person is given their final passage.[12]

For Communist interpreters the anti-Communist revolt in 1956 was not an isolated event. In fact, they perceived it as part of the historical continuity of the counterrevolution that had begun in 1919, had persisted during the existence of the counterrevolutionary Horthy regime culminating in 1944, and finally had erupted once more in 1956. Therefore, the Communist fallen of 1956 represented only one group of the victims of the counterrevolution for the party and it seemed adequate for the Communist leaders to commemorate these persons together. The 9 March proposal of the Budapest party leadership presented a plan of erecting a monument for the Communist martyrs of 1956, those of the First Hungarian Soviet Republic in 1919 and the interwar Horthy era. This sort of design for a different class of dead created a peculiar historical interpretation. The dead, first of all, set 1919 and 1956 in a particular relationship to each other: the message of the common memorial was that the incorporated people were connected by the mode of their death. All of them were comprehended as manifestations of a violent anti-Communist counterrevolution: 'Holocaust monuments are produced specifically to be historically referential, to lead viewers beyond themselves to an understanding or evocation of events', writes James E. Young.[13] Likewise, the interpretation of 1956 attached tangible historical meaning to the memorial: the popular anti-Stalinist uprising was characterized by features similar to the White Terror persecutions against Communists in 1919 or the executions of illegal Communist Party leaders during the

---

11 MOL M-BP-1-1. Secretaries 1956/57/18. Mrs József Csikesz's papers.
12 Robert Hertz, 'A Contribution to the Study of the Collective Representation of Death', in *Death and the Right Hand* (Aberdeen: Free Press, 1960), 36–7.
13 James E. Young, *The Texture of Memory* (New Haven/London: Yale University Press, 1993), 12.

Horthy regency. This interpretation provided evidence for claiming that the revolution in 1956 had been a genuine counterrevolution. On the other hand, the representation encompassed 1919, the Horthy regime and 1956 into one historical continuity based on the putative unbroken nature of counterrevolution.

Eventually a committee for the martyrs' sepulchre was raised to solve these issues. The proposal set the committee the task of calling for applications to design the memorial. By April 1957, the secretariat had already decided over the submission. This document formulated the idea of a common sepulchre for all the martyrs, namely the Communist fallen of the First Hungarian Soviet Republic in 1919, those of the interwar regime and the Communist heroes of 1956. The plan for a martyrs' sepulchre was accepted by the leadership of the party by July. The committee required the placement of tables for the martyrs of 'the proletarian revolution in 1919, the struggle against fascism and of the counterrevolution in 1956'.[14]

Meanwhile, as the Communist Party made an effort to bury its dead, a peculiar separation began to crystallize around the corpses. The third volume of the White Books included a chapter that contained names and brief biographies of 200 Communist victims in order to distinguish the revolutionary fighters.[15] The significance of the martyrs was stressed further by the simultaneous opening of an exhibition on the counterrevolution, which received growing public attention between the end of May and July according to newspaper articles of the time. The reports were aware primarily of the violent nature of the uprising, which reflected the organizers' original intention.[16] The Budapest Provisional Executive Committee prepared a report that was received on 5 July 1957 by the party secretariat. The document states that on 1 November 1956 the Revolutionary Committee of the Council of the Capital, an organization of the freedom fighters, had attempted to build a common honorary grave for the fallen. The Communist members of the council, however, had succeeded in burying the corpses together with those members of the Department of State Security who had 'fallen defending the people's republic'.[17] Thus, those who had been 'fighting with arms in their hands against our people's republic', those who had fallen defending it and those who had died as a result of an accident had been buried in the same place. Therefore, the author of the report concludes, those who had fallen in the fight against the counterrevolution had to be separated by a garden setting – a hedgerow – that would constitute an appropriate resting place.

---

14 MOL M-KS 288/7/11; Secretariat 112.
15 WB vol. 3, 125–42.
16 NSZ, 29 May 1957; György Kalmár, 'Bejegyzés helyett az ellenforradalomról szóló kiállítás vendégkönyvébe' (Instead of noting the guestbook of the exhibition on the counterrevolution), NSZ, 26 June 1957; Margit Várkonyi, 'Egy kiállítás látogatói...' (Visitors of an exhibition...), Népakarat, 4 July 1957. Cruelty was also represented by sorrowful stories like that of the death of a nine-month-old son of a Communist village leader. The small child died because of the delay of medical assistance since the Communist person's family had to run away from counterrevolutionaries: Jenő Gerencséri, 'Élt 9 hónapot' (He lived for nine months), NSZ, 27 July 1957.
17 MOL M-KS 288/7/11. Secretariat 112–13.

Rites of separation are those which disconnect their subjects from their previously occupied social position in order to annul their former identities and produce new ones.[18] One of the primary consequences of the rites of separation is the construction of borders. These ceremonies do not simply indicate that an individual moves from one social group to another; they also state that there is a clear border to be crossed between certain statuses and positions. Almost an entire year later, a document of 5 May 1958 that was submitted by the Administrative Department of the Central Committee to the secretariat elaborated the plan of division. The approximately eighty to one hundred dead Communist heroes would receive clearly separated burial sites. The proposal assigned a terrain of fifty-six metres by sixty-three metres to the left-hand side from the main road of the cemetery. It would be lined with an avenue, and the entrance was to be formed by two five-metre-wide winged iron gates. The whole site would be fenced in with a fifty-cm-high hard limestone wall. The submission described the plan for a common burial site for those partisans, soldiers and security policemen who 'were killed in action during the armed struggle against the counterrevolution'.[19] On 16 June 1958, approximately one month after the report, the prime minister during the 1956 revolution, Imre Nagy, and his two companions – Miklós Gimes, leader of the postrevolutionary intellectual resistance and Pál Maléter, minister of defence in Nagy's government – were hanged. At first, they were buried in unmarked graves in the courtyard of the prison, covered with shabby furniture and refuse. Three years later the remains were transported to a remote plot in what was at that time a remote cemetery of Budapest and buried under fake names. In that plot, there already rested two other victims of Nagy's 1956 government: the fourth defendant of the Imre Nagy trial, Géza Losonczy (minister of state in Nagy's government), who had died earlier in prison during interrogation, and József Szilágyi (former chief of Nagy's secretariat), who had been executed in April, earlier than his former fellow defendants in the Imre Nagy trial.[20] Their burial was a real rite of exit: they had no ceremony, no tombstones and no inscriptions. Besides, the victims lost their identifications: their proper names. By the two complementary rites of initiation and exit the Communist Party indicated clearly the borders of two opposing groups: that of revolutionaries and counterrevolutionaries. Revolutionaries were and could be identified as victims of the counterrevolution, whereas the continuity of counterrevolution rested upon the constant sequence of revolutionary victims. This fact led to an important consequence.

---

18 Arnold van Gennep, *Rites of Passage* (Chicago: University of Chicago Press, 1960); Sir James George Frazer, *The Golden Bough*, abridged edition (London: Macmillan, 1987), 595–607; Zoltán Fejős, 'Az átmeneti rítusok' (The rites of passage), *Ethnographia* 90 (Autumn 1979): 409–10; Victor Turner, *The Ritual Process* (New York: Aldine de Gruyter, 1995), 95–6. See also Mary Douglas, *Purity and Danger* (London: Routledge, 1966), 96–7.
19 MOL M-KS 288/7/27.
20 István Rév, 'Parallel Autopsies', *Representations* 49 (Winter 1995): 19–20. See also János M. Rainer, *Nagy Imre: Politikai életrajz, 1953–1958* (Imre Nagy: Political biography) vol. 2 (Budapest: 1956-os Intézet, 1999), 436; György Kövér, *Losonczy Géza, 1917–1957* (Budapest: 1956-os Intézet, 1998), 337–54. On the search for the corpses after the fall of Communism, see József Pajcsics, 'A 301-es parcella titkai', *Magyar Hírlap*, 16 June 1999.

The demand of making the continuity of martyrs palpable resulted in the physical continuity of their bodies: their actual common grave. On 17 June 1958, the day after the execution of the Communist leaders of the 1956 revolution, the issue of the sepulchre was raised again at the meeting of the Politburo and the idea was set up. The committee for the martyrs' sepulchre also proposed a list of names of those who should be placed in the memorial.[21] Five well-known martyrs of 1956 closed the roll of names. In spite of the fact that the document failed to mention the cause of their death, it became widely known among the public from other sources and the media. Three of them – Imre Mező, János Asztalos, and Éva Kállai – were killed at Republic Square during the siege of the Budapest party headquarters on 30 October 1956.[22] Sándor Sziklai was shot when the rebels attacked his house. The fifth person was party secretary in Csepel, an industrial district of the capital that was seen as a traditional Communist base. The First Hungarian Soviet Republic was represented by eight persons including the once chief of the General Staff of the Hungarian Red Army and one of the main leaders of the Communist Young Workers' Movement founded in 1919. The remaining six men were executed in 1919 and 1920 during the anti-Communist reprisals carried out by the counterrevolutionary regime. The fall of the Soviet Republic represented the beginning of anti-Communist violence. Their biographies emphasized their Communist allegiances and characterized them as the firmest fighters of the revolutionary elite: the first was the head of the Department of Political Investigations of the Commissariat of Interior; the second was one of the political leaders of the revolutionary law court; the third and forth were commanders of the Communist Party troops; the fifth was a political deputy in the Red Army; and the last was a commander of the Communist police, the Red Guard. Recalling the memory of these men as executed martyrs fulfilled another function apart from stressing the closeness of 1919 to 1956. It served as a means to forget the Red Terror, which corrupted the otherwise pure image of the Soviet Republic. The biographical notes, which consisted simply of two contrasting statements – one about the person's revolutionary commitment and the other on his death – revealed the men's commitment to an idea and execution of their convictions, and otherwise concealed the ruthless Red Terror. A typical one, for example, stated, 'He defended the power of the workers armed with a gun in Székesfehérvár until 4 August 1919. He was executed in December 1919.'[23] The design of the sepulchre clarified that the party leadership considered the appropriate resting place of the Communist fallen of 1956 not together with the other victims of the conflict, but next to the martyrs of the Soviet Republic in 1919.

The original idea of the sepulchre was to incorporate the Communist victims of the interwar period. Among them were secretaries of the illegal Communist Party, the party press and the Kommunista Ifjúsági Szövetség (Communist Youth Federation). Sometimes these figures led trade unions and organized strikes. Often they fought in

---

21 MOL M-KS 288/5/83.
22 Imre Mező's official, but unpublished, biography describes how he had been shot during the siege of the party headquarters. As a lesson, the biography prescribed his sacrifice as a model for survivors. MOL M-BB-1-21 (1956–57), 37. Imre Mező's biography, 8.
23 MOL M-KS 288/5/83.

various places in Europe. Some of them were members of the internationalist brigades during the Spanish Civil War. A few persons were resistance fighters in France against the Nazis. The brief biographical notes attributed great significance to the mode of death of the persons included. Almost all of them died a violent death: one was beaten to death during interrogation, another was murdered after his arrest and a third was shot in a fight with the police. Others were executed in the war as Communist partisans. Thereby, the dead demonstrated that the extermination and persecution of Communists was not suspended between 1919 and 1956. In reality, the killings by counterrevolution continued. For instance, the biographical note of one of the Communist martyrs of the Horthy regime began by mentioning that the woman had been a member of the Budapest Workers' Council in 1919. Three other persons performed various leading functions in the government of the proletarian state. 1919 eventually reached 1956: the biography of the party secretary of Csepel who had been killed in 1956 pointed to the fact that he had started his revolutionary career in 1919 as member of the Communist directorate of Csepel.

The register that proposed those who would be buried in the sepulchre contained not only the names that were supposed to represent the martyrs of 1919, the Horthy regime, and 1956: one of the most exciting facts in the history of the Pantheon of the Labour Movement is that the historical connection between the bodies of the martyrs of 1919 and 1956 attracted many other cadavers even before the First Hungarian Soviet Republic. The sepulchre incorporated five dead workers from the genesis of the Hungarian labour movement. These figures were considered as representatives of the revolutionary leaders of the late nineteenth-century workers' parties. One of them was described as 'the leader of the opposition acted against opportunism in the General Workers' Party of Hungary during the 1880s'. The list contained an ironworker who had been a pioneer in the socialist movement of Hungary, and one of his fellow workers who was considered the main figure in the emergence of trade unions. The classical period of the Hungarian labour movement was represented by a Social Democrat who 'was the leader of the trend of class struggle in the party during the 1890s'. The demands of the gigantic tomb extended over even remnants of heroes of 1848. The register started with Mihály Táncsics, who had been a radical plebeian during the 1848 revolution. His figure was inherited by the Kádár regime of the 1950s. During this time Táncsics had been represented as the archetype of the revolutionary Communist worker and had been made part of a revolutionary holy trinity together with Lajos Kossuth, the politician, and Sándor Petőfi, the poet.[24] However, in the context of the relationship between the martyrs of 1919 and 1956, Táncsics's corpse created a mythical genesis of the Hungarian labour movement and demonstrated that in reality Hungarian history had always been driven by the workers' aspirations. Every Hungarian schoolboy and schoolgirl knew the story

---

24 The canonical formulation was provided by József Révai, chief party ideologue, in 1948 on the occasion of the 100th anniversary of the 1848 revolution: 'Kossuth, Petőfi, Táncsics öröksége', originally published in *1848–1948. Száz év a szabadságért* (1848–1948: One hundred years for freedom) (Budapest: Szikra, 1948). It was reprinted in András Gerő, *Az államosított forradalom. 1848 centenáriuma* (Budapest: Új Mandátum, 1998), 25–31.

of the beginnings of the revolution in 1848 in Pest-Buda, which had been initiated, according to common historical knowledge, through the release of Táncsics from his prison by the revolutionary crowd led by Petőfi.

The proposal for the martyrs' sepulchre thereby deviated from the original intention. János Kádár, secretary general of the party, realized the nature of the alteration and claimed that there was a confusion of ideas in the proposal. Kádár stated that while the submission spoke about a martyrs' sepulchre, it contained persons most of whom had died in bed. He concluded that either those people had nothing to do with the memorial or the name of the monument was not appropriate. Nevertheless, he accepted the idea of a common resting place for great Communist figures. The secretary general argued that 'this should be the memorial and burial site of those persons who gave their lives to the cause of the working class'.[25] He was convinced that it did not matter how the person had died or whether they had been a martyr or not; what counted was only the role which they had filled in the movement during their life. The martyrs' sepulchre, therefore, had to be renamed as a memorial for the great dead of the workers' movement. The majority of the leadership of the party shared his opinion.

On 29 July in the Politburo another leading Communist returned to the idea of the continuity of martyrdom. He proposed that the sepulchre would be dedicated to the martyrs of 1919, the interwar period, WWII and 1956. He argued, 'This memorial must feature accusations against the counterrevolution!'[26] Nevertheless, Kádár's intervention was decisive. He insisted on the double function of the construction as a memorial and a place of burial. It seems that the debate ended with the decision to gather enough corpses so as to arrange them into an uninterrupted historical continuity, supported by the majority of the leadership of the party. Eventually they opted for the construction of a memorial for the great dead of the workers' movement instead of a simple martyrs' sepulchre. The inscription of the pantheon apparently refers to this fact: 'They were living for Communism, for the people'.[27]

3

A member of the Politburo presented the plans for the sepulchre at the meeting, expressing that the building was designed for the future as well as the past. The basement would not be completed at that time, since it would be the burial place of the future. This conception created continuity between past and present Communists. In this sense the pantheon mediated between dead and living party members. In its original decision on 9 August 1957, the secretariat chose to inaugurate the memorial on 20 November 1958, the 40th anniversary of the foundation of the Communist Party of Hungary. This was a clear indication of continuity.[28] The sepulchre fulfilled a function similar to that of the tombs of saints in early Christianity. Heaven and Earth were perceived to meet at

---

25 MOL M-KS 288/5/83.
26 MOL M-KS 288/5/88.
27 MOL M-KS 288/22/1963/14 and 7/171.
28 MOL M-KS 288/7/11.

the grave of saints. The saints' souls stayed above the sky whereas their corpses rested under the ground. The saints, who stood close to God, could mediate between him and human beings. The grave was considered to be the saint's place on earth, therefore one of the channels of communication with Heaven became the tombs of the exceptional dead. Cultural anthropology testifies that the dead are generally thought to be concerned with two sorts of entity: material and spiritual. According to their double nature they are considered to be able to mediate between dead ancestors and living members of the community. Continuity of rulership was occasionally assured by visiting a predecessor's tomb in the medieval Germanic tradition. Entering the graves of previous kings was conceived as a passage into the other world and a form of communication with the dead ruler himself, and taking his sword meant to return to this world as his successor. Inheriting power from the other world created continuity between the dead and the living.[29] The possibility of transition secured the continuity of the political corporation. The pantheon, which contained the future tombs of still living Communists, ensured that the body politic of the party would not die since there would always be physical bodies in which it could be resurrected.

A similar material representation was unveiled in the USSR approximately ten years after the first decision on the martyrs' sepulchre in Hungary. On 9 May 1967 (Victory Day), the eternal flame of Leningrad that immortalized the martyrs of the revolution in 1917 was transported to Piskaryovskoye Cemetery, which contained the tombs of the dead of WWII. This symbolic action implied continuity between the fighters of October 1917 and those of the world war. This continuity was stressed further on 8 May 1967, on the arrival of the eternal flame in Moscow at the Tomb of the Unknown Soldier. The ceremony alluded to the notion that the soldiers of the two events had fought for the same cause, and, what is more, they formed one eternal army. N. G. Yegorichev, first secretary of the Moscow Committee of the Communist Party of the Soviet Union, stated as much in his inauguration speech: 'It is as if the soldiers of the revolution and the soldiers of the Great Patriotic War have closed ranks into one immortal rank, illuminated by the eternal flame of glory, lit by the living honour of the fallen who will always live.'[30]

The Communist veneration of martyrs capitalized on components of the modern cult of the dead. The form of the pantheon in Budapest on the one hand recreated the shape of other typical world war monuments with tables of individual names and, on the other, tried to reproduce the meaning the fallen were endowed with as sacrifices for the greater good of their communities. During and following WWI the traditional military and political cult of the great dead was transformed to a significant degree. The veneration of exceptional heroes and military leaders was replaced by a massive cult of ordinary individuals as a consequence of the previously unprecedented scale of mass death on

---

29 Peter Brown, *The Cult of the Saints* (Chicago: University of Chicago Press, 1981), 3–4; Victor Turner, 'Death and the Dead in the Pilgrimage Process', in *Blazing the Trail* (Tucson/London: University of Arizona Press, 1992), 29–47; Patrick J. Geary, 'Germanic Tradition and Royal Ideology in the Ninth Century: The Visio Karoli Magni', in *Living with the Dead in the Middle Ages* (Ithaca/London: Cornell University Press, 1994), 49–76.
30 Nina Tumarkin, *The Living and the Dead* (New York: Basic Books, 1994), 128.

the front lines. As communities were searching for modes of making sense of individual loss and of creating political meanings, they produced memorials with lists of their dead, identified and individualized by proper names. The commitment, which communities took on themselves, to record each and every individual, resulted in the extensive multiplication of monuments as numerous local constructs were raised instead of central national ones. In the quest for coming to terms with the unexpected, Europeans utilized traditional forms of representing war sacrifice in terms of religion and martial virtues.[31] WWI as an experience of immense sacrifice resulted in similar commemorative practices and in raising similar monuments enumerating the names of dead in each community in Eastern Europe in general and in Hungary in particular.[32] WWI monuments shaped the content and form of commemorating the fallen as the disaster of mass death returned in 1939–45.[33] The cult of the dead had religious and political aspects: it mediated a mystical knowledge of the other world and ideas about the ideal society of survivors.[34] Meanwhile, constructing their own pantheon, Communists in Budapest benefitted from the political and transcendent implications of war monuments to the fallen. Still, their sepulchre for the martyrs mobilized a tradition much further in the past.

The gradually broadening circle of corpses related to each other led to a particular effect: the abstract organization, the party seemed to be immortal as a corporation since it constantly reproduced itself within the physical bodies of its mortal members. The Communist Party apparently achieved its own corporate body – *Corpus Communismi Mysticum* – the eternity of which was independent of the death of individual Communists.[35] The idea of physical continuity was forcibly described by a newspaper article recollecting the lynching of a security police officer after the siege of the Budapest party headquarters:

> The Heart was beating in the breast of a man who devoted all his life to the cause of the workers. The Heart loved and hated and gave one's share according to one's merit. It

---

31 On the shift in the culture of mourning and commemorating, see Thomas W. Laquer, 'Memory and Naming in the Great War', in *Commemorations: The Politics of National Identity*, ed. John R. Gillis (Princeton: Princeton University Press, 1994), 150–67. WWI modalities of coming to terms with the unprecedented scale of casualties in Western Europe have been analysed by Jay Winter, *Sites of Memory, Sites of Mourning* (Cambridge: Cambridge University Press, 1995). The role and stake of local communities has been explored by Alex King, *Memorials of the Great War in Britain: The Symbolism and Politics of Remembrance* (New York: Berg, 1998).
32 See for example Maria Bucur, *Heroes and Victims: Remembering War in Twentieth-Century Romania* (Bloomington: Indiana University Press, 2009), 49–72. For the Hungarian case, see Ákos Kovács, ed., *Monumentumok az első háborúból* (Budapest: Corvina, 1991).
33 George L. Mosse devoted a book to study the ways WWII preserved and transformed the tradition: *Fallen Soldiers: Reshaping the Memory of the World Wars* (New York: Oxford University Press, 1990).
34 Reinhart Koselleck, 'Einleitung', in *Der Politische Totenkult*, ed. Reinhart Koselleck and Michael Jeismann (Munich: Fink, 1994), 9–20; and *Zur politischen Ikonologie des gewaltsamen Todes* (Basel: Schwabe, 1998).
35 The replacement of Christian religiosity with political mysticism can be regarded an element of the 'political religion'. The concept was developed by Emilio Gentile in the context of Italian fascism: 'Fascism as Political Religion', *Journal of Contemporary History* 25 (May–June 1990): 229–51.

loved life, honest people, those who finally threw off the yoke twelve years ago. It hated those who put that yoke on the people, death and its carriers. That Heart was torn out of the body on 30 October 1956. It beat for the party's cause and suffered for others even in its last moments.[36]

The following paragraphs contain an interview with one of the murderers. The author concludes that the killers could not understand why the party did not want to revenge itself: 'How can she understand that the Heart which she tore out with her fellows still continues to beat? It lives within those who took the flag again which was painted red by the martyrs' blood.'[37] The party had nothing to revenge. Although it had losses, the continuity of its life suffered no rupture. The theme appeared also in fiction of the time. A novel that was highly appreciated by the Communist literary critique as one of the best works on the First Hungarian Soviet Republic included a fictional discussion between a leading Communist functionary and a common member of the party. The discussion takes place in prison while the two men are waiting for their execution.

'Sometimes' – said Küvir [an ordinary party member] silently, and once more smoothed down his forehead – 'it comes to your mind that if you die it is all the same.' – 'What, comrade Küvir?' – and now Korvin's [a Communist leader] brown hawk eyes were shining with sorrow. – 'And what about our children, or if not ours then the children of others? Thoughts like this lead to where poor Jóska Cserny [a traitor] is now. Life did not begin with us. It does not end with us. All of our deeds will survive us, both the right ones and the wrong ones, as well as all of our thoughts. Everything points further… We revolutionaries have the vocation to provide examples.'[38]

It seems as if Communist Party leaders had found a solution for the pressing problem of the continuity of political institutions and communities similar to that which the German American historian Ernst Kantorowicz detects in the strange medieval practices concerning the two bodies of kings: 'Undoubtedly the concept of the "king's two bodies" camouflaged a problem of continuity.'[39] How to preserve the temporal identity of a political institution, the kingdom, despite constant change: despite the regular passing of individual kings? By the seventeenth century, lawyers of the English royal court elaborated a highly sophisticated theory of the double nature of the king's body to be employed in legal reasoning. Legal theorists distinguished between an immortal body politic and a mortal 'body natural': whereas the king as a natural person was doomed to die, his rights and claims were never to be declined since his body politic never died. Kantorowicz identifies the roots of this theory and practice in the medieval ideas

---

36 István Pintér, 'Bosszúért lihegve' (Panting for revenge), NSZ, 22 March 1957, 8.
37 Ibid.
38 József Lengyel, *Prenn Ferenc hányatott élete avagy minden tovább mutat* (Ferenc Prenn's life of vicissitudes or Everything points further) (Budapest: Szépirodalmi Kiadó, 1958). A television series based on the novel was broadcast for the 50th anniversary in 1969.
39 Ernst H. Kantorowicz, *The King's Two Bodies* (Princeton: Princeton University Press, 1957), 273.

concerning the double nature of the ruler's body. Kings had two bodies: a physical body that was subjected to all natural consequences and a mystical immortal body of abstract dignity, a *corpus mysticum* that incorporated the entire body of citizens. The king in his body politic served as the head of the political corporation of his subjects, while due to his immortality it guaranteed stability to the entire community.

Kantorowicz believes to have discovered the impact of the ideas of this particular political theology in the strange practices of medieval royal funerals. Rulers, writes Kantorowicz, had two deaths, at least in fourteenth- and fifteenth-century England and France. The death of the body natural did not mean the end of the body politic, since during the transitory period before the coronation of the new ruler it would have endangered the continuity of the political institution. The body politic, therefore, had to live on symbolically, argues Kantorowicz, up until it could be transferred to the new body natural of the succeeding king. The historian discovers the representation of this argument in the strange fact that until the final burial an effigy of the deceased ruler would substitute the physical body, which was vested with full regalia and honoured as if living. At the funeral ceremony the supra-individual body politic was separated from its old body natural to be resurrected in the new physical body of the succeeding king during the coronation ritual.[40] The burial sites that royal dynasties constructed in the eleventh and twelfth centuries seemed an appropriate representation of the continuity of the body politic despite the temporal change of individual physical bodies. In St Denis Basilica in France or in Westminster Abbey in England, tombs of dead kings and queens followed each other. Dynastic burial sites became a common European practice. The Přemysl kings of medieval Bohemia formed their dynastic cemetery in St Vitus Cathedral in Prague, whereas the Polish House of Piast did the same in Wawel Cathedral in Kraków. In medieval Hungary, the kings from the House of Árpád buried themselves in the Cathedral of Székesfehérvár, virtually a royal capital until the mid-thirteenth century.[11] It seems as if the spectacle of medieval royal tombs impacted both political practice in Eastern Europe and historical interpretation as well. It seems that the troubles with the search for communities in the late 1950s (Kantorowicz's book was published in 1957, the same year that plans for the pantheon in Budapest began) resulted in similar ideas in diverse contexts: the idea that the mere gathering of individuals in some mystical way shaped by the power of religion, law or politics could be transformed into a thoroughly distinct quality, a genuine community.

4

The martyrs of the First Hungarian Soviet Republic in 1919 achieved new significance. Their violent death marked and proved the historical origins of the anti-Communist

---

40 Kantorowicz, *The King's Two Bodies*, 409–19; Ralph E. Giesey, 'Models of Rulership in French Royal Ceremonial', in *Rites of Power*, ed. Sean Wilentz (Philadelphia: University of Pennsylvania Press, 1985), 41–64.
41 Gábor Klaniczay, *Holy Rulers and Blessed Princesses: Dynastic Cults in Medieval Central Europe* (Cambridge: Cambridge University Press, 2002), 342–7; Colette Beaune, 'Les sanctuaries royaux', in *Les lieux des mémoire*, vol. 2, ed. Pierre Nora (Paris: Gallimard, 1986), 57–87.

counterrevolution. The proposal received by the Politburo on 17 June 1958 from the committee of the martyrs' sepulchre defined the names of those who the pantheon should commemorate.[42] Among the seventy-two proper names that would be inscribed on six columns, eighteen persons would represent the history of the First Hungarian Soviet Republic, including six martyrs and leaders like Béla Kun. The monument included the proper names of those persons as well who turned to Communism in Russia during the revolution and were fighting as internationalists for Soviet power. This group established firm connections between the dead of the revolutionary labour movement before WWI and the founding fathers of the Communist Party of Hungary. All those people who preceded 1919 in the common grave and memorial built their relationship first of all with the Soviet Republic. They obtained their place as perpetuators of the revolution and victims of the counterforces.

The Committee for Canvassing and Propaganda submitted a proposal for celebrating the 40th anniversary of the Soviet Republic of 1919 on 16 July 1958. It referred to the decision of the secretariat of 31 January which had called attention to the importance of commemorating the 40th anniversary. The submission suggested several persons to be members of the preparatory committee, among them leading figures of the party including the secretary general, popular actors and writers. The intention of the party was to organize a nationwide celebration and considered the event as extremely significant in the sequence of national anniversaries. As Kádár said, 'Let the anniversaries mean an event of the Hungarian nation.'[43]

Preparations started at the end of the year. The event itself was intended to be a colossal celebration. The reception was to be organized for between eight hundred and a thousand persons and to include guests from the Communist Party of the USSR and from the Central Committee of the Communist Youth of Hungary. The National Council of the Trade Unions called for a day of so-called revolutionary shifts, where the income earned was offered for the revolutionary cause. The 21st of March was declared a public holiday. Artistic performances were also taken care of; new operas by prominent contemporary composers evoking scenes of peasant life were to be played in the opera house. The theatre of the People's Army was to stage a play by one of the major Communist playwrights of the Soviet Republic. The party leadership assigned the role of each social group in the commemoration. A festival of revolutionary songs performed by workers' choirs was to be held. The Communist Youth introduced a spring cultural muster of the young people, and the National Council of Women issued a poster that depicted the relationship between children and the dictatorship of the proletariat. The army arranged a friendly meeting with the Czechoslovak People's Army.[44]

During the summer of 1958 a spectacular ideological offensive started to unfold in postrevolutionary Hungary. This was a period when many great ideological resolutions were published that determined the framework of exercising politics in the subsequent decades. These measures were first introduced by the party's resolution concerning

---

42 MOL M-KS 288/5/83.
43 MOL M-KS 288/5/87.
44 MOL M-KS 288/54/109.

the 'populist authors' – which themselves were a diverse group consisting of leftist peasant democrats, rightist peasant romanticists or anticapitalists inclined towards the Communists. It was followed by the publication of the principles of cultural policy, a resolution of the Central Committee of the Hungarian Socialist Workers' Party (HSWP) which formulated a flexible framework for the subsequent political intervention and party direction. The commonly shared feature of these documents was that they, in general, tried to avoid direct confrontation with non-Communist ideas or groups. The party rather aspired to differentiate various subgroups and to define its policy towards them according to the extent the individual subgroups were inclined to accept collaboration with the Communist leadership or not. This tactic resulted in the dissolution of alternative political identities without the necessity of administrative intervention. This relatively flexible political tactic reflected the recognition of postrevolutionary Communist leaders that the struggle between Communism and alternative political visions was far from being over. The Communists realized that there remained various strong non-Communist social and cultural ideas and identities, which they still had to deal with. Although the party now considered the Communist takeover after 1945 an important opportunity to dominate the political arena, following the crisis of 1956 they began to increasingly see themselves in the midst of a still undetermined historical process. The ideological offensive was a means to move the fulfilment of this process closer to the Communist cause.[15] The First Hungarian Soviet Republic had a prominent role in this policy as an embodiment of the revolutionary traditions of the labour movement, which was believed to be capable of counterweighing the alleged bourgeois intellectual pathos of 1848. On 25 July 1958, in the meeting of the Central Committee, István Tömpe argued passionately for a spectacular celebration of the 40th anniversary: 'Now the 40th anniversary is coming, do not we do the same with 21 March as it was done many years ago, where a few Communists gathered in a small room and celebrated? And one ceremony is not enough for the 40th anniversary, there have to be more such movements, which will elevate 1919 to the appropriate level of our revolutionary traditions.'[46]

For Communists, the First Hungarian Soviet Republic was relevant as the culmination of that historical process that had led precisely to its proclamation. At the meeting of the Politburo on 22 July 1958, the Communist Party leaders discussed for the first time the issue of celebrating the 40th anniversary of the revolutions in 1918 and 1919. During the meeting, János Kádár argued for presenting the events of October 1918 and the foundation of the party as a process that culminated in the proclamation of the Soviet Republic.[47] The celebrations occurred according to the first secretary's wishes. The series of ceremonies started with the commemoration of the revolution of October 1918. On 31 October 1958 the Patriotic People's Front inaugurated a memorial table at the Eastern Railway Station remembering those soldiers who joined the revolution

---

45 On the aspects of the ideological offensive, see Kalmár, *Ennivaló és hozomány* (Budapest: Magvető, 1998), 134–89; Révész, *Aczél és korunk* (Budapest: Sík, 1997), 96–103; Standeisky, *Az írók és a hatalom 1956–1963* (Budapest: 1956-os Intézet, 1996), 371–9C.
46 Kalmár, *Ennivaló és hozomány*, 156.
47 MOL M-KS 288/5/87.

just before their departure toward the battlefield. The Scholarly Educational Association held a scientific conference on the revolution.[48] From the new perspective, the democratic revolution in October 1918 was retrospectively conceived merely as a preparation for the true fulfilment of human progress. The statement on the connection of October 1918 and March 1919 was confirmed by professional argument. Tibor Hajdú, who ten years later would become the leading scholar in the field, devoted an original interpretation to explain why the October Republic had to be regarded a preparatory phase for the Soviet Republic. The historian, who began his research on 1918–19 in 1951, concerned himself with the problem of the soviets in the two revolutions. His main argument was that the soviets had been the true institutions of the revolutionary masses and, therefore, the absolute power of the soviets had meant the genuine victory of revolution. Hajdú explained that the soviets in Hungary had been formed according to the example of the Russian Revolution, proving that those organs had been the exclusive way to revolution. According to Hajdú, the rebellion in October 1918 prepared the victory of the soviets, since Károlyi's government came to power by the powerful assistance of the councils of workers and soldiers. Nevertheless, as he stressed, the bourgeois regime could not have led the revolution to fulfil itself as it constantly opposed the power of the soviets. Consequently, the Communist Party had to be founded in order to create a truly revolutionary centre, and eventually the party fulfilled the expectations and brought all power to the soviets.[49]

In autumn 1958, the publishing house of the party launched a volume containing Béla Kun's selected writings on the dictatorship of the proletariat. The preface, which was Kun's biography, was formulated by the prime minister Ferenc Münnich, himself a participant in the Soviet Republic and Kun's comrade. This fact did not only signal Kun's rehabilitation as a genuine and respected Communist leader, but also the increased significance of his regime in 1919 for Communist leaders after 1956.[50] The increase in significance of the First Hungarian Soviet Republic is well reflected in the submission of the Committee for Canvassing and Propaganda on 22 January 1959, which proposed the publication of a series of portraits of warriors and martyrs of the workers' movement. The Politburo accepted the proposition on 27 January. There are no surprises in the list of persons; it contains basically the same names as the pantheon, surveying all the heroic periods of Hungarian Communism from the ancient times of founding the workers' parties through the dictatorship of the proletariat and the illegal activity of the party until the resistance. However, the memory of 1919 weighs even heavier on this representation of Communist martyrs. The register contains eighty names and almost half of them (thirty-seven persons) are directly connected to the dictatorship of the proletariat. Besides those the document mentions in six cases that the beginning of the revolutionary career was 1919, the Soviet regime.[51]

48　MOL M-KS 288/5/94.
49　Tibor Hajdú, *Tanácsok Magyarországon 1918–1919-ben* (Soviets in Hungary in 1918–1919) (Budapest: Kossuth, 1958).
50　Béla Kun, *A Magyar Tanácsköztársaságról* (About the First Hungarian Socialist Republic) (Budapest: Kossuth, 1958).
51　MOL M-KS 288/5/115.

Modern Hungarian history was arranged into a continuous narrative. The past was imagined as a gigantic competitive strategic game; each step of the revolutionary Communists was followed by a countermeasure of the adversary, which in turn produced subsequent actions on the previous side. The party developed its first coherent historical interpretation in this manner for the 40th anniversary of the Hungarian Communist movement. The document, which is a fine piece of dialectic analysis of action and reaction, was discussed on 16 September 1958.[52] According to the basic perception, the course of party history began with the first upswing of revolutionary movements. The document states that the birth of the workers' movement meant the formation of the new revolutionary class that was destined to carry on the cause of progress. The revolutionary boom, however, could not reach its goal, since the world war was triggered by the imperialists. The Social Democrats betrayed the workers; they supported the government in its war efforts. The revolutionary movement could react only in January 1918 by going on a massive strike for the acceptance of the Russian Soviet government's peace proposal. This meant again the turn of the progressive forces. On 31 October 1918 the workers of Budapest went on a general strike led by the left-wing Social Democrats and revolutionary socialists that developed into a victorious armed revolt.[53] Revolution, however, culminated in the birth of the Communist Party of Hungary on 20 November 1918: 'By the foundation of the Communist Party the organized vanguard of the forces of socialist revolution appeared on the scene of political struggles to lead out the nation by bringing the workers into power from that whirlpool into which it was pushed by the power of capitalists and landlords.'[54]

The proclamation of the First Hungarian Soviet Republic was a final result and the peak of the steps taken by revolutionary forces: 'The Communist Party made fundamental revolutionary propaganda for the creation of the Soviet Republic, the oppression of counterrevolutionary aspirations of monarchists who began to organize themselves.' Although 'the bourgeois–Social Democratic coalition attempted to stop the revolution and against the radicalized masses intended to reach an agreement with the class of monarchist landlords and to secure the support of the monarchist grand bourgeoisie', the only way out of the crisis was the formation of the Soviet Republic, concluded by the historical analysis of the party. The organized workers joined the Communist Party and forced the Social Democrats to associate with the Communists. The narrative considers the peak of the revolutionary movement the birth of the dictatorship: 'The creation of the First Hungarian Soviet Republic was an outstanding victory of the international Communist movement as well as of the Hungarian Communist movement, obviously, which was able to lead the working class into proletariat power.'[55] The proclamation of the dictatorship of the proletariat meant only the provisional glory of revolution, however. As a response, the counterrevolution gathered its forces and carried out a successful counterattack. Their representatives left the country to form an alliance with

---

52 MOL M-KS 288/5/94.
53 Ibid., 16.
54 Ibid., 17.
55 Ibid., 18.

the enemy, the Entente imperialists, while their inner allies, the traitorous right-wing Social Democrats, disrupted the Soviet regime from within.

As a reaction to the revolutionary upswing, the alliance of bourgeois and landlords reconstructed their oppressive regime. The response of revolution on the success of counterrevolution came with the economic world crisis, which resulted in the radicalization of the masses and a colossal strike on 1 September 1930, driven by the Communists. The official interpretation claims that Communists were able to defeat reaction by creating a nationwide democratic ground during the 1930s, which took over government in 1945, following the war. The historical interpretation begins with a section on postwar events, enumerating the progressive steps of the new Communist directed government: 'The democratic forces led by the Communist Party created the new democratic state of Hungary, basically solved the task of appropriating the land and the distribution of big estates, and realized the workers' control over production.'[56] This fundamental victory provided the ground for increasing industrial and agricultural production as well as the standard of living, pronounce the authors. Socialism was well on its way, until the next action of counterrevolution. This time it was initiated by Imre Nagy, seemingly a faithful Communist who became prime minister in 1953. The traitorous leader urged the kulaks to attack the agricultural cooperatives, attempted to reduce industrial production, aspired to weaken the leading role of the party, and intended to support the petit bourgeoisie. His measures resulted in the increase of the power of counterrevolution:

> The counterrevolutionary forces triggered an armed revolt to overthrow the people's democracy in October 1956. They carried out the most double-dealing counterrevolution in history by letting the revisionist betrayals into the fore as a battering ram following the callings and instruction of the Radio Free Europe of the American imperialists. By unprecedented hypocrisy, Imre Nagy and his fellows achieved co-option into the Central Leadership and managed to enter the government. They even issued martial law against counterrevolutionaries only to be able to dissolve and paralyse the forces of the revolution, to pass the government over to the counterrevolution and more easily eliminate the dictatorship of the proletariat. The fascist counterrevolution appeared with an eager rapidity from the counterrevolutionary uprising, at first masking itself as democratic, and the rage of the White Terror began. The revisionists masked themselves as 'Communists' and the right-wing Social Democrats activated by the counterrevolution assisted the re-formation and appearance of reactionary bourgeois parties and the open appearance and rage of fascist forces [...]. On 4 November 1956 the new revolutionary centre, the Revolutionary Worker-Peasant Government led by János Kádár, was formed. It provided clear revolutionary instructions for the struggle against the counterrevolution: for saving the workers' power, restoring the lawful order of the people's democracy.[57]

The party's historical analysis concludes that the victory of Communists over the counterrevolution meant the final clash of those opposing forces. Counterrevolution

---

56 Ibid., 39.
57 Ibid., 44–5.

suffered an ultimate defeat, thereby leading history to come to a rest: 'Hungary as a country of the irresistibly advancing socialist world system came to the fore of international progress and will stay there forever.'[58] In the party history the event of the First Hungarian Soviet Republic played an extraordinary role. The preceding events appeared to direct themselves towards the revolution as preparatory occurrences, whereas the subsequent periods seemed to have their roots in 1919.

On 23 January 1959 the leadership announced that the Pantheon of the Labour Movement would be unveiled on 21 March 1959, on the 40th anniversary of the First Hungarian Soviet Republic. The document calls attention to the fact that the ceremony would be treated as one of the events of the anniversary; the inauguration was to be published in the press and included within the documentary of the celebrations.[59] The firm connection between the anniversary of 1919 revealing the meaning of the modern history of the Hungarian Communist movement and the Pantheon of the Labour Movement was not accidental. For the Communists, the historical process that was crystallized around 1919 had become palpable through the sepulchre and the monument. Through the pantheon and the surrounding Kerepesi Cemetery the continuity of the Hungarian past could be experienced and relived by the party as the pantheon spatially organized other tombs around itself within the Kerepesi Cemetery.

The Communists actually conceived the pantheon together with its historical environment. Sándor Szerényi's guidebook to the mausoleum believes in the necessity of incorporating the sepulchre into the wider context of the cemetery. He calls attention to the graves of other – non-Communist – outstanding persons of Hungarian history, such as Kossuth, Táncsics and Károlyi. The brief book also includes photos of the tombs of these men together with images of the pantheon.[60] Powerful spatial links were established between the graves during the construction of this part of the Kerepesi Cemetery. Although the mausoleum can be approached directly through an independent gateway, the ordinary way begins by the main entrance (Fig. 10). This road passes by different tombs and sepulchres of varying significance. The main entrance leads toward the first actual graves of the cemetery, to the heroes' plot on the left-hand side of the road, which was dedicated to the Communist martyrs of 1956. The visitor can still observe the heroes plot together with the honorary resting place of Soviet soldiers fallen in WWII in the background (Fig. 11). This particular setting creates the visual impression as if the Hungarian victims of the counterrevolution have been embraced by the greater eternity of Soviet revolution. In fact, from 1958 until 1989, the official commemoration of the fallen Communist heroes took place on 4 November, the day of the Soviet invasion in 1956, instead of 30 October, the day of the bloody attack against the Communist Party headquarters in Budapest. The ceremonies, which started on Republic Square, ended by laying wreath on the Soviet Army Memorial on Liberty Square (Szabadság tér), which commemorated the fallen of the Red Army in 1944–45. Besides evoking the abstract

---

58 Ibid., 47.
59 MOL M-KS 288/21/1959/6.
60 Sándor Szerényi, *Ismertető a Mező Imre úti temető Munkásmozgalmi Panteonjáról* (A guide to the Pantheon of the Workers' Movement in the cemetery at Imre Mező street) (Budapest: Fővárosi Temetkezési Intézet, 1977), 11.

Figure 10. The road leading to the mausoleum. Author's drawing based on the map in the *Guidebook to Fiumei úti sírkert (Kerepesi temető)* (Budapest: Budapesti Temetkezési Vállalat, 2007), 12.

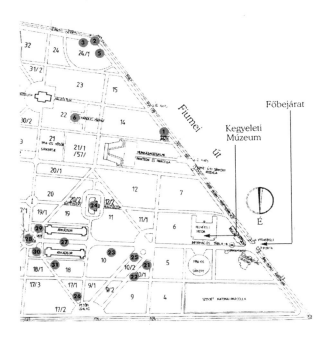

Figure 11. The heroes' plot. Courtesy of the author.

Figure 12. The sepulchre of the Jacobins. Courtesy of the author.

revolutionary brotherhood, the ritual had a concrete meaning: to commemorate the Soviet assistance in crushing the revolt of 1956 without setting up a special memorial, to link 1956 to 1944 and to equate counterrevolution with fascism.[61]

The path then turns to the right toward the mausoleum. At the crossroads is situated the sepulchre of the seven Hungarian Jacobins who were executed in 1795 in Buda (Fig. 12). The Jacobins formulated ideas on the reformation of Hungarian politics and society influenced by the French revolution; in reality, they formed a small and isolated conspirator group. After the plot was revealed by the Habsburg secret police, they were condemned to be beheaded, and were buried in anonymous graves after their execution. Their bodies were found in 1914 and taken into the City Archives to be preserved in small wooden caskets. After being buried anonymously in the Kerepesi Cemetery in 1926 the Jacobins were rediscovered and reburied in the same cemetery during the planning of the pantheon in 1959. They received a sepulchre a year after its inauguration, on 20 May 1960.[62] The next stop on the walk toward the memorial of the great dead of the workers' movement is Count Lajos Batthyány's mausoleum. Batthyány was the prime minister of the revolution in 1848 and was the first constitutional prime minister of the country. He was executed in Pest in 1849. Although he was not a popular and still less a charismatic leader, the bullets of the firing squad transformed him into a martyr of the nation.

---

61 István Rév, *Retroactive Justice: Prehistory of Post-Communism* (Stanford: Stanford University Press, 2005), 144, 194.
62 *Népakarat*, 28 November 1957; *Magyar Nemzet*, 20 May 1960; Rév, *Retroactive Justice*, 110–14.

Figure 13. The sepulchre of the martyrs of the Hungarian Soviet Republic. Courtesy of the author.

His reburial in 1870 opened a series of great burial ceremonies of national heroes in the Hungary of the monarchy. The count's mausoleum was inaugurated in 1874.[63]

The promenade ends in a square, the biggest part of which is occupied by the building of the mausoleum. On the other side, however, is situated a sepulchre for the martyrs of the proletarian regime in 1919 (Fig. 13). The memorial was erected for the 30th anniversary of the First Hungarian Soviet Republic in 1949, and inaugurated by János Kádár. Behind the mausoleum of the workers' movement two other great sepulchres can be found. The first belongs to Lajos Kossuth, leader of the revolution in 1848–49 who died in exile in Turin in 1894. He was buried in the Kerepesi Cemetery two weeks after his death, but his mausoleum was completed only in 1909. The second sepulchre is dedicated to Count Mihály Károlyi, the prime minister of the revolution in 1918, considered by the Communist leaders as a mediator between the bourgeois and proletarian revolutionary regimes. Károlyi's democratic republic of October 1918 was considered a preparatory phase or a prehistory of the genuine realization of the revolution. Károlyi's widow visited the country with the agreement of the Communist leadership at the beginning of 1961.[64] Mrs Károlyi's intention was also to begin negotiations with the Communist authorities over a possible reburial of her husband, who had been buried in the United Kingdom.

---

63 Ildikó Stéfán, 'Gróf Batthyány Lajos halála és temetései' (The death and funerals of Count Lajos Batthyány), *Sic Itur Ad Astra* 4 (2–4) (1993): 6–17.
64 MOL M-KS 288/7/98.

At the end of November the British officials granted permission to exhume and transport the ashes of the late prime minister.[65] The remains were reburied in Budapest on 18 March 1962. In the preceding half year, however, Károlyi's figure went through an odd metamorphosis: the first justifications for his reburial stressed the honesty of the 'radical democrat politician', while just before the ceremony the newspapers spoke about the 'faithful son of socialist Hungary'.[66] The Communist state thus rehabilitated Károlyi. Their intention was not, however, to pay respect to his democratic ideals, but rather to testify to the continuity of revolution.[67]

The Pantheon of the Labour Movement is situated at the end of the road. James E. Young claims that the monument and its geographical environment are interrelated. A memorial is a point of reference within the surrounding landscape, while its meaning is appropriated in connection to its neighbourhood: 'A stainless steel obelisk situated in an empty field, for example, generates different meanings from that situated in a neighbourhood shopping mall.'[68] On Louis XIV's palace and garden in Versailles, Louis Marin writes,

> It is, in effect, easy to perceive that the 'narrative', by inscribing a pathway, passes through the *voyage* in all senses of this term: it institutes its moments as notable events of the past and dissipates the mobility of its performance, paradoxically, in the stability of traces that construct the order of places traversed. Thus the narrative constructs a configuration of places as the inscription of a pathway. It is a kind of map, a topography, just as, inversely, the map, which as a configuration of inscribed sites in the proper order of a coexistence without faults, implies in its very inscription the virtual syntagmas of narratives insisting in the discreet form of possible pathways.[69]

Following the route from the entrance to the mausoleum, in the cemetery Hungarian history was physically seen from the perspective of the great dead of the workers' movement. The avenue leading from the sepulchre of the Hungarian Jacobins creates the visual effect of straightforward progression (Fig. 14), as if modern Hungarian history began with the rather underdeveloped initiative of the Jacobins to modernize the country. The modernizing efforts culminated in the bourgeois revolution of 1848, whereas the Károlyi regime of 1918 attempted to correct its failures. The republic could not meet the requirements of the age, however; therefore a Communist revolution broke out. Its defeat

---

65 MOL M-KS 288/5/252.
66 Balázs Varga, 'Károlyi Mihály újratemetése', *Sic Itur Ad Astra* 4 (2–4) (1993): 43–56.
67 The plan for celebrating the 50th anniversary of both the revolution in 1918 and the soviet system in 1919, written in September 1967, spoke already about the revolutions of 1918–19 and called for the celebration of the events as one single unity. Communist leaders regarded them as one single historical process or occurrence that began on 30 October 1918 and culminated on 21 March 1919. Later on these were ordinarily mentioned as the revolutions of 1918–19 and historical accounts dealing with the First Hungarian Soviet Republic started with the story of the 'bourgeois democratic revolution'. MOL M-KS 288/41/83.
68 Young, *The Texture*, 7–8.
69 Louis Marin, *Portrait of the King* (Minneapolis: University of Minnesota Press, 1988), 184.

Figure 14. The walkway to the mausoleum. Courtesy of the author.

meant only a short pause in history as the existing Communist system gloriously fulfilled the historical destiny. Accordingly, the memorial could be exploited in commemorations of different historical anniversaries since it is not connected to any specific event, but rather a thorough context of history. On 4 November 1965, for instance, the party laid a wreath by the sepulchre in remembrance of the anniversary of the Soviet invasion in 1956.[70] In 1967 the wreath laying ceremony for the 48th anniversary of the First Hungarian Soviet Republic was situated by the pantheon.[71]

The architectural design of the sepulchre prompted continuity as well. The parallel tombs of the honorary plot in front of the main building lead the eyes straight ahead to the entrance of the mausoleum. A drawing that was published in the official daily of the trade unions during the designing stage of the pantheon demonstrates the way the audience would have seen the construction (Fig. 15). The six pillars, situated in couples, form the optical shape of parallels disappearing into the distance, and produce the effect of linearity. The architect confirmed this perception, explaining that a modern architectural form had been chosen since a classical line of columns could not have expressed the message of the monument properly. Therefore, the sepulchre had been constructed from basic ancient elements to expound the contrast between the cemetery, looking to the past, and the monument, opening up for the future. Thus, the monument symbolized beginning, not mortality. The sepulchre was intended to form the beginning of the future for which many Hungarian martyrs of progress sacrificed their lives.[72]

---

70 MOL M-KS 288/22/1965/1.
71 MOL M-KS 288/7/276.
72 Mária Dutka, 'A jövőbe néznek' (Looking at the future), *Magyar Nemzet*, 15 March 1959.

Figure 15. 'More than 2 billion forints have been accumulated for the memorial of the great dead of the labour movement'. *Népszava*, 20 March 1958, 3.

In his ceremonial speech delivered on the 40th anniversary of the proclamation of the First Hungarian Republic, Prime Minister Münnich interpreted modern Hungarian history as a continuous struggle of revolution and counterrevolution. As on the 39th anniversary, the ceremonial speaker himself contributed to render the historical interpretation authentic, since Münnich was an active participant in the dictatorship of the proletariat and fought in the Hungarian Red Army. The party leader conceived of the revolution of 1848 as the definitive starting point of the process leading up to 1919. Since the revolution of 1848 had not solved all the problems of social progress, revolution remained an issue for Hungarian politics. However, in 1919 the appropriate revolutionary measure was not to form a capitalistic bourgeois society as in 1848, but to destroy capitalism in favour of socialism. The proclamation of the dictatorship of the proletariat hence became the true action of the revolutionary movement, and its leader, the Communist Party, was the legitimate representative of progress. Münnich stressed that:

> The Hungarian working class was the rightful heir and worthy follower of the centuries-old tradition of revolution and freedom fighting of the Hungarian people. This meant first of all to solve the problems that remained after the fall of the revolution and war of independence in 1848–49, namely to perish the feudalistic remnants, to achieve and defend the independence of the country. The Hungarian people led by the working class stopped the imperialist war, overthrew the rule of the Habsburgs in our country and created the republic in October 1918. The working class, however, would not be satisfied with a repetition of the demands of 1848: with the making of a bourgeois democracy. The world had developed a lot and considerable changes had occurred also in Hungarian society since 1848. In 1848 progress required the clearing away of those obstructions that blocked the development of capitalism, in 1919 capitalism itself became the obstacle of social development. The First Hungarian Soviet Republic would have not finished the uncompleted work of 1848 unless it had improved to a great extent the program of 1848.[73]

---

73 NSZ, 21 March 1959, 2.

Münnich's speech was one of the first attempts to link 1848 and 1919 together and to establish a historical continuity around these dates, which would become one of the central features of Communist historical culture in Hungary during the late 1960s. What Münnich realized was that the new conception of the First Hungarian Soviet Republic as a social revolution that had been simply adequate to the demands of its own historical period opened up new possibilities to interpret broader historical processes. 1848 had already been transformed during the 1950s as a step in the history of social revolutions just preceding the alleged socialist transformation. Nonetheless, since 1919 had been a largely controversial event during the 1950s and mostly conceived by the party as a dead end for the revolutionary program, the connection between 1848 and 1919 could not be made. This started to change after 1956: since the failure of the Soviet Republic could be related to counterrevolution and dissociated from the contemporary Communist leadership itself, the event could be seen as a proper, albeit tragic, revolutionary experiment. In Münnich's point of view, the Entente powers were forced to concentrate greater military forces against socialist Hungary due to the unexpected success of the revolutionary armies. Counterrevolution united its forces, armies and members of the fallen ruling classes and opportunistic revisionists to oppress the regime of the workers. The downfall of the Soviet Republic pointed to 1956:

> The 'democratic' counterrevolution led into fascism. The *reality* of humanist phrases became Siófok and Orgovány, the cruelty of the officers of the Hotel Britannia [the Budapest headquarters of White Terrorists], the twenty-five years of official terror that almost pushed the nation to catastrophe. The counterrevolutionary uprising of October 1956 attempted to repeat with the help of international imperialism what Horthy fascism accomplished in 1919: to restore capitalism… In 1919, at the time of the overthrow of the dictatorship of the proletariat in our country, the trade unionist government led by Peidl paved the way for the overcoming of Horthy fascism. In 1956 the double-dealing group of revisionists led by Imre Nagy played a major role in preparing and disguising the preparation of the counterrevolution. The billeting officers of Horthy's company in 1919 as well as the Hungarian revisionists in 1956 masked their disgraceful betrayal with democratic phrases. The accusations that Communists were antinational, the democratic and chauvinist phrases that played a principal role in the official ideology of Horthy fascism, surfaced again in 1956 and were heard in a modernized form in the incitements of the revisionist enemies of the Hungarian Communist movement.[74]

According to Münnich, Hungarian history revolved around the axis of 1919 and 'the Soviet Republic brought about a historical turn in spite of its defeat with the help of forces without'. Not independently of what Communist leaders saw in the pantheon and in the Kerepesi Cemetery, 1919 was now seen as important not only as the origin of a process that led to 1956, but also as having retrospective implications: it seemed to reveal an essential message of modern history for Communist leaders.

Various social and political organizations created exhibitions to commemorate the 40th anniversary of the Soviet Republic. These strove to bring the memory of 1919

---

74 NSZ, 21 March 1959.

Figure 16. 'To Arms! To Arms!' OKISZ Commemorative Exhibition for the Soviet Republic. Historical Photographic Records of the Hungarian National Museum 48. ME/II/B, Culture: Exhibitions 1957–62. Registry no. 59.233.

close to the audience by the means of a diversity of techniques of representation. The exhibition, organized by OKISZ (an organ for small industries), chose the medium of folkloric stylization to achieve this objective. The exhibition displayed objects that typically were used to evoke the stereotypical image of nineteenth-century peasant households. These household objects, however, recreated the iconic, commonly known images of the Soviet Republic. Visitors could encounter the Red soldier of the famous 1919 poster 'To Arms! To Arms!' in a novel environment, within a folk gobelin (Fig. 16), or the scene of the march of the Hungarian Red Army on the side of a peasant jug. In a similar manner, the figure of a typical peasant doll completed by a globe attached to its head referred to the familiar visual representation of socialist world revolution (Fig. 17).[75]

To dress the symbols of the 1919 revolution in a mask of stylized folk art evoked the revolutionary traditions of the 1848–49 freedom fight. The various symbols of the fight – Kossuth's national emblem, the tricolour, portraits of Petőfi, Kossuth and other leaders – were integrated into the culture of peasants, lower middle class and middle class, and they became the recurring decorative elements of a diversity of everyday articles and ornaments. The Soviet Republic memorial exhibition of OKISZ projected 1919 onto

---

75 The Historical Photograph Archives of the Hungarian National Museum keeps many images of the exhibition: Box 48. ME/II/B, Culture: Exhibitions 1957–1962. The inventory numbers of the photographs: 59.233, 59.234, 59.235, 59.236.

Figure 17. OKISZ Commemorative Exhibition for the Soviet Republic. Historical Photographic Records of the Hungarian National Museum 48. ME/II/B, Culture: Exhibitions 1957–62. Registry no. 59.235.

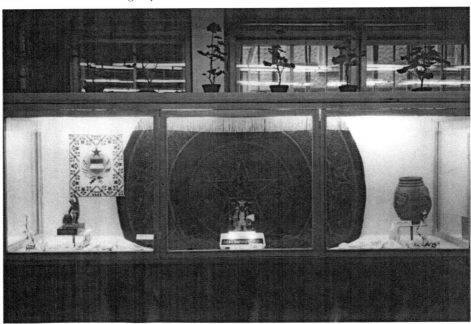

the memory of 1848 by blurring these two time layers and hence endowing the Soviet Republic with national significance attached to the nineteenth-century revolution and freedom fight. In turn, the integration of the symbols of the Soviet Republic into folklore traditions created the illusion of broad social awareness associated with the memory of 1919. The amalgamation of the spectacle of peasant artefacts with the images of the Soviet Republic produced the semblance of spontaneous civic activism, which, in fact, substituted real social traditions. The OKISZ as an apparent civic organization simulated social activism aimed at the preservation of the memory of the Soviet Republic.

The genre of representation used by the OKISZ exhibition, the simulation of social traditions, the invention of such traditions, the dressing up of the self-identity of the political elite in the accessories of folk traditions, culture or art obtained particular meaning during the nineteenth century. National elites transformed their own particular historical concepts successfully into historical narratives valid for the entire political community by the means of mixing them with elements of different kinds of fictive peasant culture.[76] The transformation of individual historical events into 'folk tradition' fabricated their 'national' relevance. The OKISZ memorial exhibition strove to achieve similar objectives: the spatial relationship between the gobelin presenting the red star of the Soviet Republic and the embroidery wearing the Kádárist national emblem created

---

76 On this process: Eric J. Hobsbawm and Terence Rangers, eds, *The Invention of Tradition* (Cambridge: Cambridge University Press, 1983).

the illusion of a temporal relationship, of the historical continuity of national community.

Historical continuity rendered it appropriate for international deputies of socialist countries to lay wreaths at the memorial table of the party headquarters on Republic Square on the 40th anniversary of the Soviet Republic on 21 March 1959.[77] Newspaper front pages on the day of the 40th anniversary indicated that the post-1956 Communist regime perceived itself as a successor of 1919. The front page of the party's daily depicted a member of the newly founded Communist armed force, the Workers' Guard, whereas the background of the picture was provided by a recruitment poster from 1919 (Fig. 18). The poster represents a Red Army soldier carrying a flag with the inscription '1919–59'. The front page of the peasant daily Szabad Föld (Free land) was not as explicit; it published a photograph of a workers' guard, but without a background (Fig. 19). The relationship was constructed by the fact that the picture was placed within the editorial commemorating the Soviet Republic.

Figure 18. '1919–1959'. *Népszabadság*, 21 March 1959, cover page.

Communist interpreters conceived of the Soviet Republic as an event that revealed the unbroken continuity of modern Hungarian history. The revolution in 1919 was meant to be an axis around which history revolved and to which the chronological series could bound back and forth in time. Preceding events could be connected to the history of the first proletarian regime as a sort of prehistory, whereas succeeding occurrences directly led up to 1956, which, in turn, originated from 1919. The revolution of 1919 was thereby conceived of simultaneously as a beginning and also a fulfilment. The revolutionary workers' state fulfilled the aspirations of the nineteenth-century labour movement and at the same time generated an expectation for the second and final coming of the dictatorship of the proletariat. Regarding this, the role of 1919 in the post-1956 Communist historical consciousness was similar to that of Christ's materialization in the Christian eschatology. The earthly presence of Jesus Christ was perceived as both the fulfilment of the coming of the Messiah and the promise of the Last Judgement. Thus, Jesus' life in this world determined the past retrospectively and the future foreseeably.[78] The decisive difference is, however, that whereas Christians did not expect any historically new event in the future, according to the post-1956 Communist interpretation, the dialectics of revolution and counterrevolution moved history forward even after 1919.

---

77 MRA News, 21 March 1959.
78 Karl Löwith, *Meaning in History* (Chicago: University of Chicago Press, 1949).

Figure 19. 'A néphatalom hű őrzője' (The true guardian of people's power). *Szabad Föld*, 22 March 1959, cover page.

The proclamation of the first dictatorship of the proletariat thus meant a real historic event. Historic events are dissimilar to historical events: the term historical has a neutral meaning and merely refers to the fact that an occurrence is perceived within the process of history; the concept of historic, on the contrary, entails that the event has a special significance in history – it is generally considered to change and also to reveal the meaning of history. Communists saw the Russian Revolution in 1917 as a historic event concerning universal history. Likewise Italian fascists held that the *Marcia su Roma* in 1922 had a similar significance.[79] In the Communist version of Hungarian history, 1919 gained a special historic importance. The proclamation of the First Hungarian Soviet Republic appeared to be the greatest event in Hungarian history. The Communist legislation decided to enact this recognition, and an act was planned to codify the memory of the Soviet Republic. Originally the parliament was to be convoked on 18 March 1959; however, the secretariat objected to this idea. It argued that on that day there would be numerous other speeches as important as the report of the government and the proposal of the budget; the submission on the Soviet Republic would lose its significance. There would be twenty speakers and only one of them would address the issue of the Soviet Republic, which would overshadow the importance of the event in public opinion.

---

79 Claudio Fogu, 'Fascism and *Historic* Representation: The 1932 Garibaldian Celebrations', *Journal of Contemporary History* 31 (April 1996): 317–45.

Consequently, the party leadership decided to hold the ceremonial meeting on the day of the anniversary, 21 March. The secretariat considered that day appropriate, as there appeared to be no other issues on the agenda.[80] Eventually, the proposal for the act was delivered by the survivor of the Hungarian commune, Prime Minister Münnich, who stressed that 'we took on and pursued the legacy of 1919 when we fought for dictatorship of the proletariat and defended it against the counterrevolutionary attack'.[81] In his speech, 1919 made it possible for Hungarian Communists to establish the appropriate road towards socialism in the country. Communist historiography devoted a particular monograph to the crucial day. Tibor Hajdú once again was called to write a book on 21 March 1919 for the 40th anniversary, although the volume did not appear until early 1960. His *21 March* finely demonstrates the preparation and gathering of revolutionary forces and the maturing of revolution itself in spite of the inertia of the government, which objectively supported the counterrevolution in the preceding months. The book vividly depicts the eventual triumphal march of Communism and the union with the Social Democrats.[82]

Within the two and a half years that passed between October 1956 and March 1959, from the Communist perspective the Soviet Republic was transformed from a relatively insignificant event in the party's own history into the most important anniversary of the nation. Although 1919 had already become important in 1956–57 for providing the linkages to 1956, its role in 1959 was something completely new. Whereas in the previous few years the Soviet Republic had been used to interpret and to condemn the revolt of 1956, even though it also connected the 1944 Hungarian fascism to the temporal chain, during 1958–59 it started to shed new light on a broader set of events, including 1848 or even further back in time. Looking from the perspective of 1919, Hungarian history was seen as a constant fight for progress full of tragic failures and counterrevolutionary revenge up until 1956, when the Kádárist leadership smashed counterrevolution forever.

5

The corporate continuity of the party had somewhat strange but important implications. Károly Kiss aptly formulated it in his inauguration speech: 'And if we made mistakes or stopped short during the fight, it was not the party who was wrong; it was us, individual persons who proved to be feeble.'[83] After 1956 the new Communist Party's primary problem with self-representation was its trouble with continuity. On the one hand, the party professed itself to be the successor of the previous Communist regime. On the other, by declaring 1956 a counterrevolution it claimed itself to be a restoration of the

---

80 MOL M-KS 288/5/117; NSZ 21 March 1959.
81 NSZ, 21 March 1959.
82 Tibor Hajdú, *Március huszonegyedike* (21 March) (Budapest: Kossuth, 1959). The book was published in the series *Értekezések a történettudományok köréből* (Treatises in historical studies). The director of the series, István Barta, personally asked Hajdú to write this book as the 40th anniversary of the First Hungarian Soviet Republic was approaching. Personal communication with Tibor Hajdú, autumn 2007.
83 NSZ, 22 March 1959, 2.

Communist regime. The HSWP demanded the right to be the heir of the transition that began in 1945:

> Everything that the party accomplished in the last one and a half decades – concerning the revolutionary leadership and the development of class consciousness of the working class; the education of tens and hundreds of thousands of Communists; the assistance to the whole Hungarian working people to find its consciousness, to improve its spiritual and material conditions; the revealing and destruction of squads of reactionary landlords and grand bourgeoisie masking themselves under various veils; the creation, improvement and stabilization of democratic and socialist achievements of the Hungarian people – belong inseparably to the last three years of our party.[84]

This statement comes from the report composed by the Central Committee for the party congress in 1959. The document pronounces in the subsequent sections,

> We have to consider the development of our party and the people's democracy a homogeneous process from the liberation onwards; we profess and pronounce that the successes our party has gained in the last few years are based on the achievements that were accomplished during the more than one-decade-long period preceding 1956; we profess the continuity of the struggles of our party, those struggles due to which we led to victory the people's democratic revolution heading the progressive forces of the nation and capitalized on the liberating victory of the Soviet Union over fascism, which also liberated our country; we realized the reconstruction of the country, the distribution of land, the democratic transformation of our state and social life at a rapid pace, fighting against the reactionary forces, and accomplished the creation of the dictatorship of the proletariat and the beginning of socialist construction in our country in a peaceful way by gaining the support of the majority of the working masses.[85]

On the other hand Kádár's Communist Party had to distance itself from the terrors of its predecessor. The report composed by the Central Committee for the party congress in 1959 states that, 'The leadership of the Hungarian Workers' Party [pre-1956 Hungarian Communist Party] committed many failures during the building of socialism which prevented the enforcement of proletarian power, withdrew socialist construction and weakened its social bases.'[86] The report attributes errors to the former leader of the party, Mátyás Rákosi. The former secretary general is accused of insisting on his sectarianism and resisting the definitive correction of failures. The former leadership is collectively condemned by the new party: 'The serious failure of the old leadership of the party was that it avoided the struggle based on principles and replaced it with tactics without principles, complete with an application of mere administrative measures.'[87]

---

84 MOL M-KS 288/21/1959/62, 10.
85 Ibid., 11.
86 Ibid., 13.
87 Ibid., 17.

The previous leadership resisted the solution offered by the 20th Congress of the Communist Party of the Soviet Union because of their sectarianism, indecisiveness and inactivity.

The identity of the party despite its members' individual deeds was able to solve the dilemma of continuity and discontinuity. The new Communist Party found a way in which its continuity could remain unbroken without having the burden of identifying itself with the unpopular oppression of its predecessor. The continuity of Communism remained unbroken while certain attitudes and deeds of its individual heirs were excluded from the tradition. The party as a community of individuals travelling on the road towards Communism would always serve as a source of truth that points towards the final goal in spite of occasional individual failures along the way. In the report, wrong decisions are attributed to individual actors such as Rákosi, whereas the right measures were taken by the party as such. Although individuals would commit failures, the 'party' would always correct them: 'The party openly detected these failures in June 1953 and aimed at correcting them. [...] These decisions were basically right [..] and were capable of bringing positive changes to the life of the party and the country.' The Communist Party is considered identical with its essence – the revolutionary centre. Although the pre-1956 Communist organ was dissolved and the new HSWP was basically a new foundation, the period is characterized in the report on the party's past activity as being 'marked by the forging together of party unity'.[88] The document ignores discontinuity by emphasizing identity over difference. The perpetuity of the Communist Party is elucidated by the manner of naming the forthcoming congress. It was obvious for the leadership to count their meetings starting from the foundation of the Communist movement in Hungary in spite of the constant dissolution and reorganization of parties. The leaders stressed that the meeting in 1959 would be the Seventh Congress of the party since its existence had been continuous for four decades:

> It was justified, just because of the necessity of taking these four decades into consideration, to call our congress the seventh congress of the Hungarian Socialist Workers' Party. Of course, there are certain contradictions in this title at first sight since this congress actually is the first and not seventh congress of the HSWP, reorganizing itself after 1 November 1956. However, by calling this congress the first we would deny the origins of the HSWP from the single and homogeneous Hungarian Workers' Party, the HWP, formed by the unity of the Communist Party and the Social Democratic Party in 1948, then we would deny our conviction that the HSWP is following and improving the great deeds and revolutionary traditions of the Hungarian Workers' Party. However, we cannot call this congress simply the fourth congress of our party, even though it is the fourth congress succeeding the 1954 third congress of the HWP. We cannot start listing the congresses of the Hungarian revolutionary workers' party, truly the milestones of the revolutionary workers' movement, with the HWP. Thereby, we would isolate the development of the HWP from the entire history and chronology of the Hungarian revolutionary workers' party, in fact, from the true history of the Communist movement. The HSWP is a Communist Party, even according to its party rules, that from its formation onwards

---

88 Ibid., 13, 18.

pursued and furthered the politics, programme, goals and ideas of the Communist Party. The HSWP is the party of Marxism–Leninism, namely the party of the struggle for Communism, therefore it is the successor of only the true revolutionary traditions of the Hungarian workers' movement. It denies everything in the past of the Hungarian workers' movement that meant an opportunistic, reformist attraction and turns against them. Therefore, we cannot count the congresses of the old Social Democratic party in forming the chronology of our revolutionary Marxist–Leninist party. The HSWP was formed and organized to be the leading mass party of the Hungarian people's democracy, building socialism on the grounds of drawing the lessons of the counterrevolution in 1956 and the union with the Social Democratic party; nevertheless the roots of the HSWP go back to the past of the Hungarian Communist movement and it is an inseparable part of the Hungarian Communist movement. We call this congress the seventh congress of our party. Since the revolutionary, namely Marxist–Leninist, workers' party in our country was founded, which happened exactly forty years ago, the deputies of the revolutionary workers' party in Hungary have gathered seven times to assess its history, to analyse the lessons of the past and to define the tasks for the forthcoming period.[89]

6

The inauguration ceremony of the memorial was an attempt to forcefully connect the abstract historical narrative to the real presence of actual corpses. The intention of the organizers was to enact the ritual in a similar way to Catholic masses, in which the crucial historical narrative of Christ's death and resurrection is connected to the Sacrament, the real presence of the Saviour. The Eucharist is forceful and tangible evidence of the recollection of an event that occurred a long time ago.[90] The speaker by the pantheon formulated the intended connection as follows:

> Be this memorial an eternal symbol and let it remind us of those thousands and tens of thousands of other people whose names cannot be read here, who possessed neither title nor rank, who died as regulars of the workers' movement. Be they either the unanimous soldiers of the proletarian revolution in 1919, or those who gave their lives for the idea as volunteers of the Russian Civil War or the Spanish War of Independence; they rose to the highest rank of man: they were revolutionaries, heralds and creators of the future. […] Let us remember those heroes and martyrs who gave their lives for the socialist future at home during the first decades of the formation of the workers' movement, on Soviet land during the Great October Socialist Revolution and the civil war or in the prisons of Horthy fascism.[91]

The Communist leadership wanted to construct a place where 'history comes close to man, or rather more precisely, man comes to a direct closeness to history', as a journalist

---

89 Ibid., 1–2.
90 Marin, *Portrait of the King*, 12.
91 Magyar Rádió Archívuma (Archives of Hungarian Radio, hereafter: MRA), News, 21 March 1959, 10 pm; NSZ, 22 March 1959.

of a county newspaper perceived several years later in 1971.[92] Sándor Szerényi, secretary of the Committee for Piety, which was responsible for Communist burials from 1964 onwards, formulated his thoughts in a similar manner: 'Two centuries of Hungarian history are here together.'[93] The narrative on history that was recapitulated in the inauguration ceremony obtained its persuasive force from the real environment of the cemetery; the real presence of tombs and bodily remnants made the account convincing and authentic.

This peculiar mode of representation provides a highly personalized vision of history. The six pillars standing in front of the mausoleum of the memorial contain names of the dead organized into chronologically ordered groups. The groups were intended to represent the different periods of the Hungarian-related workers' movement in chronological order. Although the pillars include no inscriptions apart from the names, the plan of the memorial specifies the historical eras.[94] The first eight persons form the pioneers of the Hungarian workers' movement, whereas the next eight are called the Hungarian heroes of the Great October Socialist Revolution in Russia. Twenty-nine outstanding fighters of the First Hungarian Soviet Republic succeed them. The next forty-two persons represent the illegal Communist Party, who worked underground between the wars. The plan for the memorial refers to them as the heroes of the fight of the Hungarian workers' movement against fascism. Fifteen other men are grouped separately as the outstanding heroes of the armed struggle of the Hungarian workers' movement against fascism. Similarly, six names represent the Hungarian heroes of the struggle of the international workers' movement against fascism. The series ends with the martyrs of the fight against the counterrevolution in 1956 and the great dead of the workers' movement of the socialist Hungary. The honorary enumeration of great Communist heroes is actually an abstract sequence: whereas the entire construction of the pantheon commemorates 144 persons, it includes only thirty-one actual corpses, as the list carved onto the pillars refers to actual tombs elsewhere – outside of the cemetery and in many cases even outside the country. This is the case with Leó Frankel, founder of the first workers' party in Hungary, then leader of the Paris Commune, who was resting in France when the pantheon was inaugurated. Many leaders of the First Hungarian Soviet Republic, like Jenő Landler or Károly Vántus, were buried in the Soviet Union, while Tibor Szamuely (the commander of Hungarian Red Terror troops) was still unidentified in 1959. Besides, numerous Communist Party members who died during the interwar period (called the victims of the struggle against fascism) were resting in Germany or in the Soviet Union.

It seems clear that the party leaders and architects of the pantheon tried to found their project on the referential capacity of proper names in order to substitute missing bodies and, thus, fill in the blanks of the imagined historical continuity. The engraved names as referents identify a certain number of life narratives that unfold in the obituaries and biographical collections of deceased party members. Thus, for example, the biography of Imre Mező, the most well-known Communist to fall in the fights of October 1956, that was compiled shortly after his death builds firm connections to general abstract

---

92 Iván Ordas, 'Séta a panteonban' (A tour in the pantheon), *Tolnai népújság*, 1 November 1971, 3.
93 Szerényi, *Ismertető*, 5.
94 MOL M-KS 288/22/1963/14; Szerényi, *Ismertető*, 12–14.

historical notions. The very first date mentioned in the biography, thus ignoring his birth date, is 1914, the beginning of WWI. According to the authors, as a consequence of the war the young nine-year-old had to earn a living for his family. This detail reflects the historical theses of the war as the cause of the impoverishment and privation of the society. The next date is 1927, when the young worker left Hungary, due to the hopeless unemployment, to find a job in Belgium. At this point the biography connects his life to his revolutionary predecessors. In Antwerp the would-be Communist settled down and received his first political lessons from Hungarian leftist émigrés. Whereas the hero's youth connects to previous lives within the movement, his death establishes links toward the present and the future. The biography describes how Mező was shot during the siege of the party headquarters in Budapest in 1956. In the conclusion the paper relates the self-sacrifice to the survivors: 'His life is exemplary, his martyr death is a reminder, a warning for our people constructing the new world.'[95] Individual life narratives are never singular or isolated: they necessarily refer to other lives by the means of other proper names appearing in the account. Biographies evoked by proper names define the identity of persons marked by these names, which in turn obtain their meaning in relationship to other proper names.[96] The names that are engraved on the pantheon achieve their meaning in comparison to the whole series of dead bearing proper names. The personal acts these embody follow each other and thus form a continuous flow of actions. Revolutionaries come one after another, standing on each other's shoulders, and the revolution is imagined permanent. It is as if the architectural construction in the Kerepesi Cemetery was imagined as a special kind of simulacrum, where the virtual common resting place would produce a hyperreal body politic substituting bodies natural, dispersed far away in 'real' reality.[97]

Nonetheless, there are many aspects in the design of the pantheon that eventually dismantle the desired undisturbed perception of historical continuity. The sheer amount of missing bodies raises a number of troubling questions. What were the historical misfortunes or disasters that prevented heroes of liberation and emancipation struggles to be honoured by a resting place they deserved after the victory of revolution? (These were questions puzzled even Communist Party leaders, who in the 1960s made strenuous efforts to transport Frankel's and Communist poet Aladár Komját's bodies from France and rebury them in Budapest, and who launched a time- and money-consuming quest for Szamuely's body, shot near the Austrian border while he tried to escape from counterrevolutionary troops in 1919.)[98] The missing bodies, in fact, revealed many discontinuities in the history of the Communist revolutionary movement.

---

95 MOL M-BB-1-21 (1956–57), 37; Imre Mező's biography, 8.
96 István Rév, 'The Necronym', *Representations* 64 (Autumn 1998): 76–108.
97 Jean Baudrillard, 'Simulacra and Simulations', in *Selected Writings* (Cambridge: Cambridge University Press, 1988), 166–84; Jean Baudrillard, *Symbolic Exchange and Death* (London/Thousand Oaks/New Delhi: Sage, 1993), 51–86; F. R. Ankersmit, 'A Phenomenology of Historical Experience', in *History and Tropology* (Berkeley/Los Angeles/London: University of California Press, 1994), 188–94.
98 MOL M-KS 288/5/238; and MRA, News, 11 February 1966.

The frequency of dates of death in 1937, 1938 and 1939 of persons identified as victims of the struggle against fascism or participants in the Spanish Civil War but who died in the Soviet Union, and particularly Béla Kun, raises doubts that the simple dates on the pillars try to cover, but cannot satisfactorily answer. The cases of persons whose dates of death occur following the Communist takeover (such as László Sólyom, identified as a fighter against fascism but who died in 1949 following a show trial, or István Ries, the former Social Democrat politician who died in a similar way) could pose even more embarrassing questions. But when the unprepared visitor meets Sándor Zöld's alleged tomb twice, he or she could feel totally lost in the labyrinth of the past. Zöld was first entombed together with his family, which already triggers considerable puzzlement as all the dates of death are written as 1951, including those of his children. Second, his name is included in the list on one of the pillars commemorating the great dead of socialist Hungary. Zöld's double funeral reveals a puzzlement concerning appropriate burial, which eventually the party leaders could not solve or cover unambiguously. Zöld, former minister of interior, committed suicide in fear of the purges among Hungarian Communist Party cadres in the 1950s, after killing his entire family.[99] Eventually, despite the great efforts of the Communist authorities, it proved to be extremely difficult to construct a legible and intelligible historical narrative in the absence of tangible references to the past. It proved to be extremely difficult to construct the understanding of a political community in the absence of actual bodies, but substituting those with abstract markers.

Communist authorities considered the crucial component of constructing concepts of continuity for political institutions to be the political will of actors and the creative imagination of the intellectuals, ideologists, legal theorists or historians involved. Such concepts created funeral rites and the cult of the dead as their symbolic representations. The Pantheon of the Labour Movement seemed to follow the ideals of mystical corporate identities in a way Ernst Kantorowicz and a few of his followers understood it roughly in the same period.[100] It was the abstract that created the concrete; it was the idea that produced the thing.

Apparently, an important feature of the process remained hidden for the Communist leaders, designers and speakers, and, albeit implicitly, probably even Kantorowicz himself. For Kantorowicz the truly important aspect was the transcendent mystical quality of

---

99 Rév, *Retroactive Justice*, 120–21. On the afterlife of Sándor Zöld's death, see György Majtényi, 'Zöld Sándor tragédiája. Emlékezés, emlékezet, egy történet elbeszélése' (Sándor Zöld's tragedy: Remembering, memory, narrating a story), in *Megtalálható-e a múlt? Tanulmányok Gyáni Gábor 60. születésnapjára* (Is it possible to find the past? Studies in honour of Gábor Gyáni's 60th birthday), ed. Zsombor Bódy, Sándor Horváth and Tibor Valuch (Budapest: Argumentum, 2010), 447–58.

100 Giesey provides a minutely detailed analytical description of French royal funeral ceremonies in his *The Royal Funerary Ceremony in Renaissance France* (Geneva: Librairie Droz, 1960). See also Sarah Hanley, 'Legend, Ritual, and Discourse in the *Lit de Justice* Assembly: French Constitutional Ideology, 1527–1641', in *Rites of Power*, 65–106; and *The Lit de justice of the Kings of France: Constitutional Ideology in Legend, Ritual, and Discourse* (Princeton: Princeton University Press, 1983), 230–55.

genuine communities, which was thought to be able to enable individual characteristics to melt together in the immortal supraindividual entity.[101] Although the understanding of the supraindividual body of the party emerged through actual funeral practices, the concept eventually deceived perhaps even the designers of the Pantheon of the Labour Movement, since, probably, the process of constructing medieval political bodies was exactly the opposite.

The theological transformation of the Eucharist during the twelfth and thirteenth centuries had far-reaching consequences for the production of continuity of abstract corporations. Until the Carolingian Age the term *corpus mysticum* was used to describe the Eucharist. It was a mystical body of Christ, whereas the Church was simply called *corpus Christi*. During the twelfth and thirteenth centuries, however, the meaning of the concept turned upside down. The dogma of transubstantiation in 1215 proclaimed the Eucharist as the real body of the Saviour, while the Church, the community of believers, became the mystical body. As a consequence, the understanding of a community, a mystical body, was firmly linked to the real presence of physical bodies. Since then the idea of the mystical body of Church community was based on social and cultural practices: the act of Communion which unified the physical bodies of Christ and believers.[102] The idea of *praesentia* – real presence – and the practice of the Communion shaped political institutions in the medieval West. Through the real presence of the king by acts of power, jurisdiction, constitutional affairs and warfare, and his Communion with his subjects, the state and political communities became understood as the real continuities and connection of physical bodies.[103] Funeral rites of kings and the cult of the dead were shaped according to the religious practice of constructing communities. The central element was the real presence – the corpse and the effigy – and the communion of knights, nobles and Church authorities who were present there. Similar to how the abstract community of the Church was thought of in terms of the physical bodies of believers and Christ, the abstract continuity of kingdom was thought of in terms of the physical bodies of the king and his subjects, the state was thought of in terms of citizens and political communities and parties in terms of their real members. The relevance of abstract concepts and the theoretical understanding of the state, the community and the temporal identity of political bodies were built on already existing social and cultural practices: rituals, bodies and objects.

7

The heroes' plot was inaugurated in the Kerepesi Cemetery at the end of 1960. The plot contains graves of fallen men who were members of the Communist governed armed forces and were killed during the 1956 uprising. The fallen are buried in order of rank in a circle. Those who enter the burial site will notice in the centre the grave of

---

101 Alain Boureau, *Kantorowicz: Stories of a Historian* (Baltimore/London: Johns Hopkins University Press, 2001).
102 Carlo Ginzburg, 'Representation: The Word, the Idea, the Thing', in *Wooden Eyes* (New York: Columbia University Press, 2001), 63–78.
103 David Starkey, 'Representation through Intimacy: A Study in the Symbolism of Monarchy and Court Office in Early-Modern England', in *Symbols and Sentiments: Cross-Cultural Studies in Symbolism*, ed. Ioan M. Lewis (London: Academic Press, 1977), 187–224.

Figure 20. Colonel László Lukács's tomb. Courtesy of the author.

Colonel László Lukács. On the tombstone the inscription only has two dates: 1919 and 1956 (Fig. 20). Walking around the circus one recognizes four similar gravestones. The fallen were considered heroes, persons who did their duty fighting against the enemies of Communism and did more by giving their lives for Communism. However, their status as heroes was confirmed, their lives gained their meaning, only in the light of their death, being killed by counterrevolutionaries. A martyr becomes a martyr only after his or her death; a martyr's death makes a martyr's life. An inscription on a tombstone is a biography compressed into two dates, that of birth and death. The biography on a martyr's gravestone is interpreted by the fact that he or she died a martyr. Born in 1919 – without any political intention – Colonel Lukács and his fellow officers were killed during a counterrevolution, which gave new meaning to their birth. The year 1919 meant the beginning of martyrdom, thus the dead incorporated history. The corpses embodied and personified a historical continuity. According to Communist interpretations, 1919 meant the beginning of Communist martyrdom as the Horthy regime, which came into power after the fall of the First Hungarian Soviet Republic, executed some of the prominent figures of the former Communist government.[104]

The heroes' plot was ready in 1960 and thus its inauguration took place only three weeks later than that of the monument on Republic Square, a memorial dedicated to

---

104 An extremely revealing interpretation on the heroic and saintly social behaviour is in: James O. Urmson, 'Saints and Heroes', in *Essays in Moral Philosophy*, ed. A. J. Melden (Seattle: University of Washington Press, 1958), 198–216. On the connection of martyr and his or her death, see Brown, *The Cult of the Saints*, 71–6. On martyrdom in the Hungarian context of 1989, see Rév, 'Parallel Autopsies', 15–39.

the victims of the counterrevolution. The secretariat received a proposition containing a model of the artistic arrangement of the site. The proposition stated that the most appropriate date of inauguration would be 4 November.[105] On that day in 1956 János Kádár had declared in a radio speech the foundation of the new Revolutionary Worker-Peasant Government. On that day Soviet troops entered Budapest and helped Kádár to re-establish Communist power in the country. Nonetheless, as the heroes' plot would not be ready until 6 September 1960, as the administrative department reported, the inauguration was postponed until 10 December.[106] The proposal of the dedication stated clearly that the fallen were considered martyrs of the Communist movement. As they were armed men, their memory was honoured with the highest military respect and the minister of defence addressed the memorial speech. Members of the armed forces, workers of prominent factories, and representatives of a few pioneer teams formed the audience. Organs of the Communist Party – armed forces and the Communist Youth – were expected to lay wreaths. Plans were made to broadcast the event via the press, radio, television and newsreel. The death of the honoured Communists was considered a revolutionary action: during the wreath-laying ceremony the orchestra planned to play revolutionary marches and to finish the performance with 'The Internationale'.[107]

The post-1956 authorities never erected any memorials to those who suppressed the counterrevolution, only to those whom they considered as having been killed by it. The inauguration of the monument in Republic Square that took place on 30 October 1960 was planned to be a colossal performance, as the headquarters of the Party Committee of Budapest passed through a heavy siege on 30 October 1956, at the end of which the insurgents executed the captured security policemen. The proposal intended to gather 50,000 people for the opening ceremony, though this number was reduced later to 500. Speakers were members of both the government and the Politburo. Party and governmental organs as well as the Communist Youth laid wreaths. Great attention was paid to the preparation, and the submission proposed even that spotlights should be placed on the roof of the party headquarters to provide the most advantageous illumination of the monument. The fallen were incorporated into the caste of revolutionary martyrs. The existence of an abstract continuity, called the idea of Communism, was aptly expressed by the address given at the inauguration ceremony of the memorial at Republic Square: 'The bronze statue of the monumental memorial demonstrates precisely the message of the memorial: the fighter can be killed, but the idea is triumphant.'[108] However, living party members, active fighters against the revolt in 1956, made no sense as parts of a temporal continuity. It was only the dead, the Communists that had been killed, who could render the linkages between various periods and generations of revolution tangible. As the inscription of the memorial reads, 'In memoriam of those who fell for the freedom of the Hungarian working people.'[109]

---

105 MOL M-KS 288/7/74.
106 MOL M-KS 288/7/89.
107 MOL M-KS 288/7/94.
108 MRA News, 31 October 1960.
109 MOL 288/21/1960/1, 7/90 and 5/206.

Chapter 5

NARRATION: HISTORY, FICTION AND PROOF IN THE REPRESENTATION OF THE FIRST HUNGARIAN SOVIET REPUBLIC, 1959–1965

1

The Czech emigrant writer Milan Kundera provided the following spectacular description of the Eastern European Communist construction of history:

> In February 1948, Communist leader Klement Gottwald stepped out on the balcony of a Baroque palace in Prague to address the hundreds of thousands of his fellow citizens packed into Old Town Square. It was a crucial moment in Czech history – a fateful moment of the kind that occurs once or twice in a millennium.
>
> Gottwald was flanked by his comrades, with Clementis standing next to him. There were snow flurries, it was cold, and Gottwald was bareheaded. The solicitous Clementis took off his own fur cap and set it on Gottwald's head.
>
> The Party propaganda section put out hundreds of thousands of copies of a photograph of that balcony with Gottwald, a fur cap on his head and comrades at his side, speaking to the nation. On that balcony the history of Communist Czechoslovakia was born. Every child knew the photograph from posters, schoolbooks, and museums.
>
> Four years later Clementis was charged with treason and hanged. The propaganda section immediately airbrushed him out of history and, obviously, out of all the photographs as well. Ever since, Gottwald has stood on that balcony alone. Where Clementis once stood, there is only bare palace wall. All that remains of Clementis is the cap on Gottwald's head.[1]

Kundera eloquently addressed the problematic, deeply ambiguous relationship of Communist Party propaganda historians to the historical record: on the one hand, their rather easy-going voluntaristic abuse of the means of historical authenticity according to higher political commitments and, on the other hand, their fetishistic insistence on binding political objectives and historical legitimacy to the strong aura of original evidence.

The problem of evidence or proofs is present in historiographies of Communist historical writings to a remarkably insignificant extent due to specific but typical ideological and intellectual backgrounds. During the Cold War, when non-Communist

---

1 Milan Kundera, *The Book of Laughter and Forgetting*, trans. by Michael Henry Heim (New York/London: Penguin, 1986), 3.

interpreters of Communist historical production were largely interested in deconstructing and dismantling statements on the past by Eastern Bloc authors, critical historiography, not groundlessly, but probably too easily, disqualified these scholarships as falsification and ideological distortion of evidence; consequently it had very little stake to analyse the modes of dealing with original documents and genuine historical records. As a consequence, this tendency of scholarship could not make sense of the admiration of original historical documents that was so typical of most of the official historical production during the Eastern European socialist dictatorships.[2] Contrary to the mainstream Cold War explorations, post-1989 analyses of Communist historiographies tend to regard these predominantly as means of constructing narrative legitimacy. In this perspective, the association of modes of emplotment and generic structures with political and cultural implications seems sufficient to understand the characteristics of Communist historical representation. As a consequence, these interpretations risk equating the practice of Communist propaganda histories with normal historical scholarship, and therefore hardly provide any means to critically assess the ways and extent to which ideological historiography deviates from proper historical investigation.[3] This chapter suggests a different path and examines a case of Communist historical writing, the representations of the First Hungarian Soviet Republic of 1919 following 1956, where the appropriation of original historical records, the burden of proof and authenticity played an important role. As I demonstrate the mode of narrative emplotment, its moral implications and political context, I will seek to answer how the ideological prescriptions shaped the use and function of evidence in these historiographies. As a conclusion, I will argue that the eventual failure of party historians to establish any proper evidential paradigm rendered their narrative prefigurations ineffective and their moral-political implications inauthentic.[1]

---

2 Matthew P. Gallagher, *The Soviet History of World War II: Myths, Memories, and Realities* (Westport: Greenwood Press, 1976); John Keep, ed., *Contemporary History in the Soviet Mirror* (London: George Allen and Unwin, 1964); Nancy Whittier Heer, *Politics and History in the Soviet Union* (Cambridge, MA/London: MIT Press, 1971); Michael J. Rura, *Reinterpretation of History as a Method of Furthering Communism in Rumania: A Study in Comparative Historiography* (Washington, DC: Georgetown University Press, 1961); Samuel H. Barron and Nancy W. Heer, eds, *Windows on the Russian Past: Essays on Soviet Historiography since Stalin* (Columbus, OH: American Association for the Advancement of Slavic Studies, 1977).
3 Georg Iggers, Konrad Jarausch, Matthias Middel and Martin Sabrow, eds, *Die DDR-Geschichtswissenschaft als Forschungsproblem* (Munich: Oldenbourg, 1998); Konrad Jarausch and Martin Sabrow, eds, *Die historische Meistererzählung: Deutungslinien der deutschen Nationalgeschichte nach 1945* (Göttingen: Vandenhoeck und Ruprecht, 2002); Rainer Eckert and Bernd Faulenbach, eds, *Halbherziger Revisionismus: Zum Postkommunistischen Geschichtsbild* (Munich/Landberg am Lech: Olzog/Aktuell GmbH, 1996), esp. 11–23, 69–82; Joachim Hösler, *Die Sowjetische Geschichtswissenschaft 1953 bis 1991: Studien zur Methodologie und Organisationsgeschichte* (Munich: Sagner, 1995).
4 From various perspectives, numerous authors have argued for incorporating the practice of research back into the description of historical creative work: Paul Ricoeur, 'Histoire et rhétorique', *Diogène* 168 (October–December 1994): 9–26. See also David Carr, 'Die Realität der Geschichte', in Klaus E. Müller and Jörn Rüsen, eds, *Historische Sinnbildung* (Hamburg: Rowohlt Tb., 1997), 309–28.

2

After 1959, the 40th anniversary of the First Hungarian Soviet Republic in 1919, numerous narrative representations on the history of the first Hungarian Communist state began to appear, in a richness of form and style. At that time the memory of the Soviet system began to spectacularly dominate the public discourse on the past. Novels, scholarly publications and works of art were issued to an unprecedented degree. In the year of the anniversary alone, ten memoirs, twelve collections of documents, twenty-five books concerning regional and local history, ten monographs on various aspects of the historical event, eight greater official pieces of appreciation, two books providing an overall review, approximately five fictions, and hundreds of studies and minor articles were published.[5]

Starting from 1959, the Hungarian Communist Party began to pursue a characteristic politics of bargaining. By the beginning of 1959 the party leadership had already made the borders clear for any possible ideological and political discussion. The crucial element of these limitations concerned the exclusion of all alternative interpretations of the 1956 revolt contrary to the official view of the 'counterrevolution'. Nonetheless, the Communist leadership also made it clear that its interest was directed rather towards the future, the building of socialism. These ideological-political frames provided the opportunity for those intellectuals who aspired to return to the public sphere to accomplish it in exchange for demonstrating their loyalty to the cause of socialism. This concerned mostly literary authors, who traditionally were dominant intellectual figures in Hungarian public life and usually played active roles in the revolution in 1956. Many of them, including leading 'populist' writers Gyula Illyés and László Németh, made public declarations in which they acclaimed the achievements of the socialist system under János Kádár since 1956. In return, from the beginning of the 1960s the authorities proved to be flexible and guaranteed vast publishing opportunities for them. The process of rapprochement and compromise culminated in 1962 when the HSWP formally excluded Mátyás Rákosi, the symbolic figure of pre-1956 repressions, from its membership. The fundamental precondition of this move was the mutual amnesty of 1956. On the one hand, literary authors and non-Communist intellectuals in general remained withdrawn from politics and virtually never raised the theme of the revolution. On the other hand, the Communist Party steered public discussion away from the question of the counterrevolution.[6]

A major lesson that the Kádárist leadership drew from the experience of 1956 was that the Communist Party needed broader social support for running the system. Kádár's strategy was to establish pacts of alliance with several social groups other than intellectuals and to make his system acceptable, or at least not radically intolerable, for as many

---

5 András Siklós, *Az 1918–1919. évi magyarországi forradalmak* (The revolutions of Hungary in 1918–1919) (Budapest: Tankönyvkiadó, 1964), 186–90.

6 On the compromise between public intellectuals and Communist authorities orchestrated mostly by György Aczél, leading party official in cultural matters, see Standeisky, *Az írók és a hatalom 1956–1963* (Budapest: 1956-os Intézet, 1996), 444–61; Révész, *Aczél és korunk* (Budapest: Sík, 1997), 113–32. On Rákosi's exclusion, see also Tibor Huszár, *Kádár János politikai életrajza: 1912–1956*, vol. 2 (Budapest: Szabad Tér-Kossuth, 2003), 93.

citizens as possible. A general amnesty for political prisoners was introduced in 1963, which concerned many of the participants of 1956, though not everyone. Kádár's main target, however, was the lower class, the socialist *menu peuple*, whom the regime sought to benefit with increasing opportunities for consumption, travel and popular culture. The authorities sought to base legitimacy on an image of power, which was able to secure peaceful life by containing both inside and outside troubles. The regime depicted itself as granting predictable everyday life for all loyal citizens, free of major troubles, and also as keeping the turmoil of the modern world outside of the country. Radicalism and heterodoxy both inside and outside the country were seen as major enemies of the largely conservative culture in late socialist Hungary.[7] The politics of integration and compromise, initiated mostly by the pragmatist Kádár but shaped and realized in the field of culture by the equally pragmatic György Aczél, found a genuine treasure chest in the already flourishing public memory of 1919. The theme of the First Hungarian Soviet Republic provided a perfect means to clarify basic ideological-political issues related to the interpretation of revolution and counterrevolution, Communist revisionism, nationalism and socialist patriotism without the need to openly address the revolt in 1956. Via 1919, it was possible to talk about 1956 without actually talking about it.

The central committee of the HSWP prepared an outline for ceremonial speeches in January 1959 that provided the keynote for further representation. The history of the revolution began with a positive representation as it contributed to the development of the country: 'By the declaration of the First Hungarian Soviet Republic the working people led by the working class came to power for the first time in the history of our people and by this our country came to the fore of international social progress.'[8] This statement was followed by an enumeration of the 'historical' deeds of the Soviet Republic. The historical outline emphasized that the dictatorship of the proletariat had overthrown the oppressors of the Hungarian people, therefore it had created real democracy for the working masses, as they had been involved in governing the country through the system of councils. It was stressed that in spite of the extremely serious hardships, the regime had made great efforts to improve the living conditions of the people. The document pointed out that the Soviet Republic had been the only real power that had fought for national independence, as the previous ruling classes had betrayed the country. In addition the proletarian state secured the right of self-determination for nationalities. In sum, the authors pronounced, 'The First Hungarian Soviet Republic was characterized primarily, not by the undoubtedly committed failures, but by great historical deeds.'[9] The history of the Soviet Republic was presented as a glorious event that opened up a bright future for the whole of society.

The editorial in the ceremonial issue of *Szabad Föld* (the weekly of the 'working peasantry') on 22 March 1959 stated openly and categorically that essentially the history of the first dictatorship of the proletariat had been glorious but also tragic:

---

7 János M. Rainer, *Bevezetés a kádárizmusba* (Budapest: 1956-os Intézet, 2011), 95–184.
8 MOL M-KS 288/22/1959/9.
9 Ibid., 4.

We were the first to follow the glorious, great October socialist revolution. This fact should mean an eternal pride for the Hungarian working class and peasantry, who should also be proud of gaining victory after victory while being surrounded by imperialist armed forces ready for attack, and laying the grounds of a world in which, if it had been successfully established, workers and peasants and men of mind would have found their prosperity and happiness. Perfidy, vileness and treason hit the weapons and the tools of creation out of the hands of workers and peasants and the short, overall 133 days-long dictatorship of the proletariat decayed. The rising, shining dawn was followed by a dark night full of tortures that lasted for twenty-five years. A sea of pain washed over the people. The rule of magnates with a thousand acres, of bankers, of capitalists, returned together with the even crueller rule of the gendarmes. Tens of thousands were taken into prison and many more tens of thousands into internment camps: the best of workers and peasants, the bravest sons of the fatherland. An era of manslaughter followed, like that after the peasant revolt of Dózsa in 1514. Gallows trees were raised towards the sky to serve the death of workers and peasant heroes. A sea of blood covered the Hungarian land; the name of Orgovány and Siófok gained a very bad reputation. Thousands of martyrs sacrificed their precious lives since they had the revolutionary courage of attempting to realize the idea of a new world order here in this land of the servants.[10]

Around 1959 the depiction of the events of the first dictatorship of the proletariat was unfolded in the form of a tragedy: between 1958 and 1962 four important new historical novels were published which were preceded and completed by new or first domestic prints of exile literature on 1919.[11] Frequently the narratives are divided into two major parts: the first gives an account on the victorious advance of revolution and its heroic struggle, whereas the second is devoted to the signs of counterrevolution and the sad downfall. In a tragedy the horrific end usually juxtaposes a magnificent success. Therefore, these narratives usually have a double character: their first part contains a period of ascent that tells the story of how the hero emerges, while the second part gives an account of how the harmony breaks apart. This is the structure of Miklós Gárdos's novel from 1959, *Két ősz között* (Between two autumns), which was the first historical novel to cover the whole period of the revolutionary years in 1918 and 1919.[12] The novel begins with the defeat in October 1918, the ground zero from which the steps leading upwards began. Gárdos represents the first such step as the appointment of the opposition politician count Mihály Károlyi as prime minister. His appointment is depicted having been coerced by the irresistible power of the people's movement. From here onwards the plot follows two parallel lines up until the proclamation of the Soviet Republic, the real goal of the revolution. The first is constructed from the machinations of the government and

---

10 Árpád Szakasits, 'Felejthetetlen március' (Unforgettable March), *Szabad Föld*, 22 March 1959, 1.
11 József Lengyel, *Visegrádi utca* (Visegrádi street) (Budapest: Kossuth, 1957), 4th edition; Béla Illés, *Ég a Tisza* (River Tisza is on fire) (Budapest: Zrínyi, 1957), 2nd edition; Sándor Szatmári, *Históriás ének. 1919* (A saga: 1919) (Budapest: Zrínyi, 1959).
12 Miklós Gárdos, *két ősz között* (Between two autumns) (Budapest: Kossuth, 1959), 367.

its parties to freeze the reformation of the country, while the second is carried by the increasing signs of the insurmountable power of socialist revolution. On the one hand, the author describes the desperate attempts of the Károlyi government to save bourgeois power in Hungary: all the reforms the leadership implement are regarded as having been forced by the labour movement. First of all, the government aspires to maintain the rule of the Habsburg dynasty in the country: Prime Minister Károlyi gives guarantees to the king that he is not a supporter of the republic. Nevertheless, thousands of workers demand the immediate proclamation of the republic. Then the novel provides a vivid description of the drama between the inability of the government to make decisions and the increasing reports of the enthusiasm of the masses for the republic. Gárdos calls attention to the fact that although the Károlyi leadership had dethroned the king it had been intended only to save the order of exploitation. The book contains a characteristic scene in which the ministers declare the new form of state; however, together with a call for stopping the 'class struggle' that had been initiated by a Social Democrat politician. The novel underlines that the attempt was futile: the workers did not abandon the fight for their real interests. The chapter ends with a leaflet, written by young revolutionaries while they had been listening to the Social Democrat minister, which clearly states, 'Our real interest is the Communist republic!'[13]

On the other hand, the signs of the approaching victory of revolution appear throughout the novel. Thus, the author includes a chapter on a rebellion in a mine where the workers form a council and take the organization of production into their own hands. The miners march in front of the offices of the mine and urge the director and his secretary to agree, at least verbally, to join the revolution. The rapid success of the newly founded Communist Party is used also to represent the accumulation of the forces of revolution. The author states that although the party had only been created at the end of November 1918 it had already attracted huge masses: 'The worker members of the Social Democrat Party, having revolutionary emotions, left the party in crowds from the beginning of November until the end of December. And, besides, new masses who never participated in politics formed ranks with the Communists: the new party that stepped into publicity in the beginning of November conquered more and more thousands, hour by hour.'[14] The book does not fail to emphasize that the only measure that had remained for the government to take in this situation was to imprison the Communist leaders. This step, nonetheless, could not prevent the revolutionary masses from realizing their aims: Social Democrats were soon astonished by the fact that the Communist Party could operate effectively even without its first-rank leaders. Social Democrat politicians were forced to negotiate with their Communist counterparts since they learned that the workers were to rescue the Bolsheviks. According to the novel, the Communists entered into government due to the massive support of the working class. In this perspective the formation of the Bolshevik dictatorship seemed a genuine triumph: the stubborn persistence and self-sacrificing struggle of the workers in spite of the government's hindrance resulted in the birth of their true political representation and leadership.

---

13 Ibid., 83.
14 Ibid., 133.

The author vividly demonstrates the atmosphere of triumph in a scene where the news of the dictatorship is introduced for the Workers' Council:

> Garbai [the speaker] was still speaking. But for the hall it was already unimportant what he was talking about. Kun was cheered; the new united labour party was cheered. Suddenly someone started to sing. First, the melody of 'La Marseillaise', its stirring first verse flew over the hall [...]. By the last words a woman on the gallery from the group of the workers of Csepel in a sonorous voice had already begun a new song. Many of the old Social Democrats already knew this song, though they could rarely hear its text [...]. First, the song was coming only from the gallery, from the mouths of the Communists of Csepel. [The first verse of 'The Internationale' then follows.] However, the flying melody of the refrain absorbed the voice of the majority in the hall. When it was sung for the second time, most of them were already standing.[15]

This is the zenith of the novel: from here onwards a story of decline begins. Although the book concentrates on the achievements of the dictatorship of the proletariat, the descriptions of the efforts feature positive results and an increasing number of bad omens alike. Two characteristic parts elucidate this especially well. The first is the summary of the advantages of the new regime that appears at the end of the chapter on the takeover and the first measures of the Soviet Republic:

> Two weeks in a country in revolution is an extraordinarily little time. But the first two weeks, the first two weeks of the dictatorship of the proletariat, demonstrated that Communists wanted to proceed fast and determinedly in the construction of the new society. The measures that signified the new era were born after each other following the victorious night of 21 March. The main tools of exploitation were nationalized, namely factories, banks, mines, means of transportation and the great estates. The eight-hour working day was introduced, wages were raised by thirty per cent, women were secured with equal wages for equal work. Rents were decreased by twenty per cent; insurance was extended to all workers: even to workers of the land. The state of the proletariat took the schools into its own hands: all private institutions of education were nationalized. There passed no day during these two weeks without lots of new steps that attempted to help and improve the conditions of working men. Newspapers informed the public about the organized holiday of proletarian children or the new worker inhabitants of the superfluous rooms of bourgeois apartments or cheap theatre tickets or raising the benefits of widows and orphans three times more.
>
> However, in these two weeks serious and dark troubles ripened as well. It was impossible to perish all the misery and poverty of the four years' war and the difficulties flooding the suddenly shrivelled country in two weeks. In the lands of nationalities that were torn apart from the old Hungary, new states were being formed now – and the capitalists and landlords of the new states viewed Soviet Hungary with hungry eyes. The Entente, the officers of which commanded the Romanian, Czech and Serbian

---

15 Ibid., 208.

bourgeois armies as absolute masters, were watching with increasing anger how the state of workers and peasants was settling down in the middle of Europe.[16]

The second citation comes from the description of the event that was generally considered the greatest military and moral success of the First Hungarian Soviet Republic, namely the occupation of Kassa (now Košice in Slovakia): 'The Red Army moved forward. In Kassa the news of the proclamation of the Slovak Soviet Republic in Eperjes [now Prešov in Slovakia] a few day ago was declared in a mass meeting. Hungarians and Slovaks demonstrated for the dictatorship of the proletariat [...]. But behind the frontlines, in the back of the fighting Red Army the woodworm of counterrevolution was gnawing.'[17] The history of the First Hungarian Soviet Republic is imagined as an instance of the struggle of abstract ideas and historical forces, shining glory meaning the advance of revolution and gloomy downfall, namely the catastrophe of counterrevolution.

Although there is no main figure in the novel, the story could be followed along through the character of a young revolutionary, Ottó Korvin. He was a real historical person: the young man worked as a clerk in a bank during the war and became a resolute antimilitarist. Korvin formed a group of revolutionary socialists and struggled against the war and for social revolution. They supported the revolution of October 1918, but not the government, which for them was simply another form of bourgeois oppression. Korvin's figure is used to symbolize the general meaning of the novel: his personal fate seems appropriate for reflecting the general history of the First Hungarian Soviet Republic. The young man worked as the head of the Department of Political Investigations of the People's Commissariat of Interior; he was later accused of manslaughter and executed after the fall. In Miklós Gárdos's novel the very last pages are devoted to a scene where Korvin and one of his fellow prisoners are led to the prison after interrogation. The description is preceded by another about Béla Kun, who gave an interview on the situation in Hungary. The Hungarian Bolshevik leader spoke in Vienna while he was in internment: 'I know what happens in Hungary. The White Terror is raging. [...] Officer bandits are killing hundreds of people.'[18] In this context Korvin's capture and torture, being only one among many others, symbolizes the counterrevolution:

> During these weeks spectacles like this were frequently seen in the streets of Pest. After Horthy marched in, when the crane-feathered commander-in-chief talked about 'the guilty Budapest' in his speech stammered in broken Hungarian, the manhunt for Communists accelerated. In the cellar of Hotel Britannia, in the barracks in Kelenföld, everywhere where the ill-famed White commandos stayed, Communists were killed. And the prisons were full of workers, as well – White courts passed sentences in summary proceedings.[19]

---

16 Ibid., 237–8.
17 Ibid., 294.
18 Ibid., 362.
19 Ibid., 363.

Korvin's figure became a canonized detail in representing the counterrevolutionary terror that followed the dictatorship of the proletariat. The figure and fate of the young revolutionary expressed more than revolutionary continuity. Ottó Korvin also appears at the end of Péter Földes's novel published in 1962, depicting the struggles of the Hungarian Red Army. After Kun predicts the coming of White Terror at the last meeting of the Workers' Council, out of all the leading figures of the Soviet regime only Korvin is featured. The young man represents the nascent illegal activity in the circumstances of persecution. In the last pages he is sitting in camouflage on a bench in a park and searching for other comrades who are forced to hide themselves as well.[20] The figure of the revolutionary leader embodies the imagination of the dynamics of history. As the chief political prosecutor of the Soviet Republic, he investigates the counterrevolutionary conspirators, who manifest the historical force of reaction, then after its takeover begins to organize revolutionary conspiracy, rescuing the possibility of progress. Korvin's personality represents the birth of the two opposing secret conspiracies at the same time. Behind the fall of the Communist prosecutor and his regime the secret group of counterrevolutionaries takes shape, whereas his own activism means the origins of revolutionary conspiracy.

In Gárdos's novel, a scene in which revolutionaries – representatives of the Soldiers' and Workers' Council and radicals from factory trade unions – gather in a secret meeting gives an account on the first steps of revolution, namely the organization of armed uprising. They decide here to launch the insurrection and arrange weapons for workers. The other component of preparing the revolution is the Revolutionary Socialists' (Korvin's organization) illegal underground activity, which originally is directed at antiwar propaganda, then at the creation of the Socialist Republic. The crucial step, however, is the foundation of the Communist Party of Hungary, which begins with only a few persons meeting in a private apartment in Pest, after the secret return of Hungarian Bolshevik leaders. Remarkably, the other side was described also in terms of conspiracy. The first sign of counterrevolutionary plot in the novel is the putsch in June 1919, prepared in secret by professional military officers, which the Red troops quickly suppress. The conspiracy of high officers, nevertheless, stab the Soviet Republic in the back. Julier, chief of the General Staff, reveals the operational plan of the Red Army for the enemy and, when in spite of this the offensive succeeds, he orders retreat. This finally demoralizes the army, while the organization of new troops fails due to the betrayal of Social Democrats in the government. After the defeat Korvin begins to illegally organize the new party, which starts in an secret underground meeting.

The nostalgic dream about revolutionary conspiracies became a typical and inevitable component of these works. One chapter in János Gyetvai's autobiographical novel *Fegyverek és emberek* (Weapons and persons) has the telling title 'The secret company'. This part gives an account on how the narrator gains revolutionary consciousness and joins the labour movement. The participants are boys from secondary school and worker apprentices, who found a secret organization to fight against exploitation and prepare the

---

20 Péter Földes, *Mennyei páncélvonat* (Armoured train from heaven) (Budapest: Móra, 1962), 432–3.

revolution. The plot of the novel is constructed through the related fate of the members: various life trajectories meet eventually in the Soviet Republic, where each of them participates in various roles. This period, however, brings with it not only the birth of the revolutionary organization:

> We observed suspicious movements in the city on 24 June. Richer bourgeois and propertied persons grouped together and were conversing, whispering in fever. Soon our telegraph received a message about the outbreak of counterrevolution in Pest. The commandeering old officers took the monitor fleet in the Óbuda harbour and had the entire river fleet in their command. So, they started to flow down the Danube. At first it struck no one, as those who saw the boats believed they were on patrol. When the boats arrived at the House of Soviets on the bank of the Danube, they took to a shooting position and began to fire their guns at the headquarters of the Communist Party and the government. At the same time, apparently according to the well-prepared plan of their far-reaching conspiracy, officers and disciples of the former Ludovika Military Academy also went into action.[21]

The June counterrevolutionary putsch, however, was not simply an isolated historical event, as the novel itself makes clear. In reality, it meant the first action of counterrevolutionary conspiracy that eventually destroyed the First Hungarian Soviet Republic, followed by White Terror after the defeat. In White Terror, however, it was a long-term historical actor, the modern twentieth-century face of counterrevolution, the real adversary of Communism, fascism that stepped into the foreground: 'And then blood was flowing everywhere at the street crossing, as if it had been the bloody cradle of history where the new monster was born and where Man and humanity was disgraced to a terrible extent heretofore never experienced. We were as yet unaware then that this monster was called fascism.'[22] Parallel to the birth of evil, the crystallization of the forces of good was also occurring. The resignation of the Soviet government, though, meant the fall of the dictatorship of the proletariat, not the end of fight: 'But we continue the struggle! We shall return! Anger was fired on everyone's faces and there was an unbreakable belief in our souls...'[23]

This dichotomous structure dominated the narrative form of historical works published after 1959 on the First Hungarian Soviet Republic. *A Magyar Tanácsköztársaság* (The First Hungarian Soviet Republic), by the leading military historian of the period, Ervin Liptai, was the first to realize in a comprehensive scholarly form the statements made on 1919. His 1965 work is dedicated to the description of the causes of the destruction of the revolution and the victory of the counterrevolution. Liptai begins with a description of the desperate social, political and economic conditions of prerevolutionary Hungary, underlining the glory of the ensuing revolution. The profound discussion of the troubles creates a point of departure juxtaposed by the subsequently victorious Communist regime. The monograph

---

21 János Gyetvai, *Fegyverek és emberek. Regényes korrajz* (Weapons and people: A fantastic portrait of an age) (Budapest: Zrínyi, 1959), 255.
22 Gyetvai, *Fegyverek és emberek*, 273.
23 Gyetvai, *Fegyverek és emberek*, 265.

begins its enumeration of the flaws of the contemporary Hungarian political and social system with the assertion that the country had been bound to a state, the Austrian–Hungarian Monarchy, that was determined to collapse, since its various parts had been connected neither by common traditions, economic interest nor by political aspirations. Secondly, the author emphasizes that the oppression of the nationalities had forced them to develop ideas and plans of independence. Thirdly, the book discusses the social conditions in agriculture and presents statistical data to depict the poverty of small peasants:

> Apart from dwarf holders and half-proletarians scraping by on a patch of soil, the forty-five per cent of agricultural population made up of approximately six million people together with family members got not even a hoeful of land. In the shadow of great estates poverty was breeding freely. For the majority of peasants the basic elements of knowledge, the appropriation of writing and reading skills, were as inaccessible as medical assistance or hospital nursing in case of sickness. Whereas the income of fifty great landlords exceeded 100,000 forints per year, the income coming from the farms of the eighty-eight per cent of those who owned property did not reach even fifty forints. Fifty forints per year could not save a family consisting of several members even from death of starvation. Peasants either begged for work from great estates, from great holders or tried to get communal work. Hundreds of thousands of families scraped by from hand to mouth without any prospect for improving their conditions.[24]

In this situation the new regime, which promised to radically improve all the aspects of Hungarian society, obviously seemed glorious. Liptai considers the revolutionary government of October 1918 as having benign intentions, but no means to govern the country. The troubles and difficulties that had been sharpened by the war defeat could be overcome solely by a Socialist–Communist dictatorship. The author is convinced that only a thorough restructuring of society could have made it possible for the country to leave the past behind for the future:

> Thus the struggle was decided: the dictatorship of the proletariat was born. For the first time in the history of Hungary the workers took power into their hands. A new era began in the life of the Hungarian people: the era of freedom. The hearts of the proletarians of factories and land were filled with happiness never felt before, having shaken off the thousand-year-old chains of exploitation. The perspectives of a bright future free of exploitation and oppression were drawn for a starving and weak country corrupted by the crimes of the classes of the lords.[25]

The perception of triumph dominates the subsequent discussion of events as well. The book gives an account of how the various social classes and groups had joined the new regime with genuine enthusiasm and expectation. The chapter reaches its emotional

---

24 Ervin Liptai, *A Magyar Tanácsköztársaság* (The First Hungarian Soviet Republic) (Budapest: Kossuth, 1965), 8.
25 Ibid., 132.

peak when Liptai describes the communication by telegraph between Lenin and Béla Kun, when the leader of the Russian Revolution mediated the greetings of the Bolshevik Party. The First Hungarian Soviet Republic appeared to be a victorious regime: the book discusses the measures of the government to improve the living conditions of the majority of the population. Meanwhile, the army was successfully braving the imperialist aggressors, as revealed in the description of the Northern Campaign of the Red Army.

The author introduces the origins of the downfall with the allegation that certain counterrevolutionaries in fact joined the proletarian government. Liptai argues that since the revolution appeared to be victorious once and for all, Communists did not pay enough attention to isolate opportunistic and irresolute leaders: 'On 21 March the leaders of the Communist Party were not yet aware that an element of the Social Democrat Party and trade union leaders would bring the counterrevolution in their minds into the crucial positions of the First Hungarian Soviet Republic. They did not know that the dictatorship of the proletariat would pay an enormous price for their compliance regarding the Social Democrats.'[26] Liptai forecasts the ensuing tragedy for the first time in the case of the counterrevolutionary revolt on 24 June 1919. On that day several professional officers and their troops attacked the headquarters of the people's commissars and other crucial buildings. The riot, however, failed rapidly: virtually in a couple of hours the counterrevolutionaries were deprived of mass support. Liptai interprets the event as evidence that the Soviet government had not adequately suppressed the bourgeoisie, and this fact resulted in the relative freedom of counterrevolutionary organization. The chapter concludes that, unfortunately, nothing happened to change this sorrowful situation. The fact that counterrevolution remained a considerable force allowed the possibility of a second and successful revolt.

3

Although Liptai's comprehensive book ends without a detailed discussion of the White Terror, its readers had not even the slightest doubt concerning the sense of the tragic downfall. The last chapter of the book is imbued with impermeable sadness and sorrow: 'The defeat of the betrayed and corrupted Red Army dealt the dictatorship of the proletariat a deadly blow. Despair and bitterness seized the masses.'[27] After learning the news of the defeat, the people's commissars first were thinking of fortifying the capital and pursuing the armed resistance. Nonetheless, this time the government was not unified and the Communists decided to resign. Then the author continues with a description of the final meeting of the revolutionary leadership: 'The same persons gathered once again who on 21 March had approved with enthusiasm the decision to proclaim the dictatorship of the proletariat, who had given a new turn to the events by their brave defence of the Soviet Republic on 2 May. This time no inspiring words were heard. The Budapest Central Workers' and Soldiers' Council mourned: they came to bury the dictatorship of the proletariat.'[28] The description is a vivid re-enactment: one

---

26 Ibid., 136.
27 Ibid., 446.
28 Ibid., 456.

can imagine the members of the council slowly entering the meeting hall, burdened with heavy thoughts and feeling remorse, to listen in silence to the speakers. According to Liptai they had very good reasons to do this. The historian ends his book with the conclusion that the downfall of the Communist regime would be succeeded by merciless oppression: 'Twenty-five years passed within dark oppression and a sea of suffering.'[29] Liptai also has an explanation for the woeful outcome of the events: all the troubles were derived from the possibility of counterrevolutionary conspiracy, stemming from within the leadership of the army and even within the government, where right-wing Social Democrats plotted against the dictatorship of the proletariat. These two centres of conspiracy managed to drive the army into a poorly prepared campaign against Entente troops where the General Staff itself betrayed its own soldiers and maliciously exposed them to defeat and dissolution. According to Liptai, this retreat sealed the doom of the dictatorship: at the last meeting of the revolutionary leaders the right-wing traitors within the government undermined the determination of the government to resist the interventionist troops and forced the Communists to resign and to go into exile.

The predominance of the tragic narrative form reflected an overwhelming interest in the end of the history of the First Hungarian Soviet Republic. The aura of sorrow and despair permeated historical representations, as eloquently demonstrated by *39-es dandár* (39th Brigade), a costume drama from 1959 filmed by the formidable Hungarian art director Károly Makk. The black-and-white film, characterized by long, slow-moving camera shots and scenes of dialogue emphasizing the individual personality and emotions of the main characters, starts with a sequence of swirling dark clouds above the Hungarian plains, while an inscription informs the audience about the counterrevolutionary betrayal that resulted in the collapse of the Hungarian Red Army in April 1919. The plot focuses on the resurrection of revolution subsequent to raising a new army in early May, and the victorious offensive. Nonetheless, the fate of individual characters unfolds to demonstrate the catastrophic tragedy of various classes of Hungarian society after the fall of the dictatorship of the proletariat. The film has three main protagonists: a young political commissar, Frigyes Karikás (whose autobiographical short stories of the same name inspired the film), an old veteran of WWI recruited from a peasant family, and a young romantic revolutionary worker depicted as spontaneous but politically uneducated. The three men meet for the last time in the film following the defeat of the Red Army in July 1919. The retreating troops enter the village of the peasant veteran, where the seriously wounded young worker is tended to. Here the old peasant learns about the fate of his father, killed by White Terror troops, and his wife, taken away by counterrevolutionaries. However, in spite of his personal tragedy the old veteran is concerned more with the fate of his dying young fellow fighter, who asks in desperation if the collapse of the dictatorship is true. The old man confirms the fact of the defeat on the battlefield, but reassures the young worker that the cause would not be defeated: 'It is impossible to defeat us forever…'. Following this scene, the political commissar and the old peasant leave the house for a cigarette, where the veteran soldier asks if he was right. Karikás, the party member, can do nothing but assure him once again. The film ends with a

---

29 Ibid., 459.

symbolic dialogue between the two men: 'The night is very dark', says the peasant. But, the commissar answers, 'The day is breaking soon.'[30]

Novels about the dictatorship of the proletariat invariably end with a minutely detailed description of the White Terrorist bloodshed. The last section of Gyetvai's work, a chapter titled 'In memoriam', depicts the campaign of vengeance of counterrevolution marching in the capital. In József Lengyel's book, Ferenc Prenn discusses in length the fate of Korvin and the terror commando led by József Cserny. One particular chapter presents the cruelty of White Terrorists taking vengeance on peasants. Korvin's destiny is also included in the final chapters of a book written by a group of journalists in 1959, *133 nap* (133 days). Korvin's torture is included to dramatically signify the start of counterrevolutionary rule, which inherently entailed the most brutal White Terror according to Communist journalists. The paragraph on Korvin's interrogation is followed by the sentence 'Terror flooded the city'.[31] The events of the White Terror occupy almost one-fifth of the whole work: forty-three pages of the total 220. The relatively great proportion of the articles devoted to the violence is even more striking when one considers that the history of the Communist regime proper is told in barely more than a double the length: 109 pages. The remaining chapters describe the preparation of the revolution.

It is obvious that the glory of the First Hungarian Soviet Republic was inseparable from its tragic destiny: the history of the soviet regime was as glorious as it was tragic. For Communist observers the history of the dictatorship of the proletariat could be comprehended from the point of view of its horrific downfall. It seemed that the government of the First Hungarian Soviet Republic committed a series of genuine great deeds even in an absolutely hopeless situation: 'In 1919 the international revolutionary movement was not powerful enough to provide discernable assistance for Soviet Hungary, encircled by enemies', states the outline for ceremonial speeches in 1959.[32] It was precisely the fall foreshadowing itself that made the deeds 'historical' and glorious. For Communist interpreters the history of the First Soviet Hungarian Republic was inseparable from the coming into power of the White Terror. Essentially, the history of 1919 meant the sorrowful and tragic history of the birth of the counterrevolution. The perception and description in which the sequence of events of 1919 appeared a contrast between a triumphant beginning and the subsequent fall was generated by means of the catastrophic ending.[33] The definition of a certain ending provides narrative cohesion to the sequence of events: the end of a story is the culmination of the occurrences in which the conflict ordering the emplotment is resolved.[34]

---

30 *39-es dandár* (39th Brigade) (Hunnia Film Studio, 1959), dir.: Károly Makk.
31 József Horváth, Gyula Kékesdi, János Nemes and Nándor Ordas, *133 nap* (133 days) (Budapest: Táncsics, 1959), 185.
32 MOL M-KS 288-22/1959/9.
33 On the concept of tragedy see Bernstein, *Foregone Conclusions*, 11. On catastrophe cf. Hayden White, 'Catastrophe, Communal Memory and Mythic Discourse', in *Myth and Memory in the Construction of Community*, ed. Bo Stråth (Brussels: PIE/Peter Lang, 2000), 57.
34 Hayden White, 'The Value of Narrativity in Historical Representation', in *The Content of the Form* (Baltimore: Johns Hopkins University Press, 1987), 133 (1–25).

In the postscript of his novel, Miklós Gárdos explains his motivations to write the novel: 'Since I thought that I would try to demonstrate how the woeful alliance of bourgeois counterrevolution and the traitors of the working class, the inner and outer enemy incessantly laid mines in the way of Hungarian Communists to being victorious in their struggles and heavy battles. Today, in the Hungary of 1959, this lesson is fresh and vivid again: after October 1956 it calls attention to the White August of 1919 once more.'[35] The fall of the first dictatorship of the proletariat as a conclusion that prescribed the mode of its historical representation was born due to a specific political point of view in the present: the Communist experience of the counterrevolution in 1956. The perspective of 1956 provided the tragic end for the history of 1919.

Actually, all interpretations on the history of the First Hungarian Soviet Republic that were produced during this period foreshadow the post-1956 present. For instance, Tibor Hetés's monograph on the worker regiments is finished by a quotation from prison diary of Aurél Stromfeld, former chief of the General Staff of the Hungarian Red Army: 'If today nobody else thinks about you except your imprisoned leader, still you died for progress and the wellness of the nation, and time will come when the grateful posterity offers you, just you, a handshake.'[36] Then the author concludes: 'The time has come. Today our people think with love and appreciation about those who were fighting for our happy future, of whom many gave their lives for the power of the proletariat, but many others are still working among us, together with us to realize our common goals.' The existing Communist power was conceived as the result of those past struggles. Liptai's work sheds light on this fact. The Communist historian quotes Kun's final speech in the last pages of his book on the Soviet Republic: 'Now we leave the country only to start a new struggle for the dictatorship of the proletariat, to start a new phase of international proletarian revolution with renewed effort, being richer of experience and in more realistic conditions, with a more mature proletariat.'[37] On the last page of the book, the author refers to the re-formation of Communist power in Hungary and concludes, 'Béla Kun was right: the best of the working class, the working people started a new struggle for the dictatorship of the proletariat in the "new phase" of the international proletarian revolution with "renewed effort, being richer of experience, in more realistic conditions, with more mature proletariat."' However, he also expounds that the new Communist state was the result, the direct successor of the first: 'The experience and memory of the first Hungarian dictatorship of the proletariat, the Hungarian Soviet Republic, which heated the hearts of the workers, contributed to a great extent to the victorious completion of this struggle.'[38]

Histories of 1919, in turn, were read from the perspective of 1956. One of the most popular thrillers of the period, *Kopjások* (Spearmen), begins in 1956, after the restoration of Communist power in Hungary.[39] Following their final victory, the most important duty

---

35 Gárdos, *Két ősz között*, 369.
36 Tibor Hetés, *Munkásezredek előre!* (Worker regiments, forward!) (Budapest: Táncsics, 1960), 141.
37 Liptai, *Magyar Tanácsköztársaság*, 457.
38 Ibid., 459.
39 András Berkesi and György Kardos, *Kopjások* (Budapest: Szépirodalmi, 1959).

of the Communist police was to destroy entirely counterrevolutionaries. In the novel, the Communist intelligence services make strenuous efforts to detect the secret organization seen as responsible for the preparation of the counterrevolutionary revolt. A former counterrevolutionary agent then returns to Hungary from West Germany, bringing the secret diary of one of the leaders of the movement. The diary proves to be particularly valuable for the Communist intelligence services, as it reveals the entire history of the organization. According to one entry, the movement was founded in 1919 in order to fight against the dictatorship of the proletariat. During the First Hungarian Soviet Republic the conspiracy pursued secret illegal activities. The memoir also clarifies that following the victory of the counterrevolution this illegal movement became the leading organization of the regime and directed politics from the background. The covert activity of the organization was necessary even during the counterrevolutionary government in order to pursue the merciless hunt of Communists undisturbed. Though this was the essence of the regime, it would have caused troubles for a legitimate government aspiring for international approval. The idea of the existence of an secret underground elite organization guaranteed firm continuity for the concept of counterrevolution, since in reality the same conspiracy appeared to hide behind the diverse shapes the political regime took.

This continuity survived the fall of the counterrevolutionary system, as the conspiracy already hiding itself underground could conveniently conceal itself during the people's democratic government and continue its anti-Communist activity. The memoir gives an account of how the counterrevolutionaries, who remained illegally in Hungary after 1945, organized a conspiracy against the republic. The novel here refers to the 1946 trial of an alleged anti-republican plot. In reality, these 'conspirators' formed a small isolated group which discussed political issues in friendly circles. According to the novel, however, the counterrevolutionary movement continued its activity underground so that it could come into the open again in 1956. The work claims that the illegal 'spearmen' actually organized the counterrevolution in 1956. Since the aging counterrevolutionary leader could not come to the fore, his son and successor accept the duty. The most important purpose of the novel, obviously, was to prove the historical continuity between 1919 and 1956. According to the authors, the counterrevolution in 1956 was prepared by the counterrevolutionary White Terror that succeeded the collapse of the First Hungarian Soviet Republic in 1919. Thereby, the book states that the uprising in 1956 was a genuine counterrevolution led by the same people.

An unexpected turn in the novel creates continuity on the other side as well: it is revealed that a young officer in the Communist intelligence service is the son of one of the last victims of the counterrevolutionary leader. This personal relationship elucidates the belief that the true meaning and aim of the counterrevolution was the struggle against Communists: counterrevolutionaries had been killing Communists since 1919, as they were in 1956. This statement proves to be crucial as it demonstrates the continuous presence of Communism throughout modern Hungarian history. While the Communist Party worked legally above ground in 1919 and following 1945, between 1919 and 1945 it pursued its activity underground, illegally. Thereby, the novel represents modern history in a particular way, a process made to move by two opposing forces: one of these ruling openly above the ground and forcing the other into illegal underground conspiracy. The dynamics of history was determined by two antagonistic conspiratorial movements, which exercised political power in shifts. The ultimate reason for historical change, thereby, can always be connected to the success or failure of one of the conspiring group or organization. The dialectics of progress and reaction, revolution and counterrevolution, became comprehensible according to a weird conspiratorial logic. In this imagination, revolution and counterrevolution ceased to be abstract notions. In the most literal sense, they took actual shape: behind the events of history and the phenomena of the surrounding world there acted conspirator organizations clearly demarcated by the frontlines of good and evil, but which were bound to actual persons working consciously for clear purposes.

The authors of this political pulp fiction, András Berkesi and György Kardos, began their careers in the 1950s as detectives in the Department of Army Politics of the Communist intelligence services, which was founded to detect (and invent) and reveal counterrevolutionary plots within the ranks of the army.[40] The conspiracy theory structuring the work, however, was not only the fiction that directed the activity of the Communist intelligence service. The party elite itself, which was educated in politics in the conspiratorial spirit of the illegal interwar period and various émigré organizations, experienced the dynamics of history as a struggle between rival conspiracies and spying agencies. This particular experience, on the one hand, reproduced and confirmed the centuries-long tradition concerning the origin of revolutions. According to this comprehension, mysterious, consciously organized small conspiracies are responsible for movements undermining social order. This imagination gained a lot from the history of the 'Illuminati', a philosophical society of the Enlightenment period in Germany, which cultivated ideals of thorough moral and social reform, and was close to the Freemason organizations. Authoritarian principalities exiled from political publicity the criticism of the regimes, which, as a consequence, aimed at representing itself as principally a moral humanist discourse, whereas companies committed to this discourse were born as organizations associated with mysterious rites of initiation and secret regulations. Both the anti-revolutionary and idealized revolutionary traditions inherited the myth of Freemasons as it sprung from this context.[41] On the other hand, the interwar Communist experience confirmed the idea that the struggle against counterrevolution essentially meant the fight against its police and secret police organizations.

After 1959, the authorities tried to popularize the vision of history read backwards from 1956 also by visual means. The typical example of these propaganda films is titled *Az eskü* (The oath), which was shot in 1962.[42] This work is a feature film about the oaths

---

40 András Mink, 'Kopjások', in *Beszélő évek, 1957–1968*, ed. Sándor Révész (Budapest: Beszélő, 2000), 137–8.

41 Reinhart Koselleck, *Critique and Crisis: Enlightenment and the Pathogenesis of Modern Society* (Oxford/ New York/Hamburg: MIT Press, 1988), esp. 86–97.

42 *Az eskü* (The oath) (1962). Collection of military propaganda films of the Museum of Military History. HL 10038. Open Society Archives VHS no. 39. The following book provided profound assistance in reading filmic language: James Monaco, *How to Read a Film: The World of Movies, Media and Multimedia: Language, History, Theory* (New York/Oxford: Oxford University Press, 2000).

taken by an army unit. The main character in the movie is a captain who has to take over the duty of managing the procedure due to the abrupt departure of his superior. After the commander leaves the barracks, the captain is left to meditate alone in the commander's office. The camera centres on the officer's face from a close distance, emphasizing his concentration and his uncertainty about what to say to the troops. The camera moves slowly around the captain, suggesting his state of mind, while the audience hears his thoughts: should he talk about his own life, his childhood, about the bitterness of daywork and privation? The camera then shows the captain from behind, positioning him in the bottom right of the frame, whereas the gaze of the audience is attracted to the portrait of Lenin fixed in the top left. The visual relationship of the soldier turning to Lenin and the Bolshevik leader looking down on the officer evokes the image of the believer asking for help from the source of knowledge.

During this scene, the captain meditates on the importance of the oath for a soldier left to his own devices. The significance of the oath is confirmed by his own example: in the next cut the officer remembers his personal experiences from October 1956. His task was to deliver a goods train to a barracks, however it seems impossible due to the railway workers' strike. Meanwhile, armed 'counterrevolutionaries' gather around the train. While the main character negotiates with the railway workers, the armed men try to get a hold of the train's load. Nonetheless, the soldiers guarding the wagons defend the train, following the command of their oath, even in the absence of their actual commander.

Memories from 1956 provide the moment of enlightenment: in one blow they elucidate the meaning of the oath – to be faithful to the idea – while at the same time also reveal the sense of Hungarian history – a continuous struggle between the tyranny of the masters and the oppressed people. The retrospective of 1956 evokes, one after the other, the memories of the historical past. The scene of 1956, by the means of a quick cut, imitating the rhythm of abrupt, flashing memories, is followed by a series of graphics from the well-known Hungarian Communist artist Gyula Derkovits on György Dózsa, leader of the great peasant revolt in 1514. The film generates the impression of a story occurring in time by the means of images merging into each other and panning the camera within individual frames. The captain's interpretive commentary – as if it is the voice of the person who is remembering – qualifies this visual movement as instances of the antagonism between master and peasant. The process of recollection connects the individual historical events: following the meditation of the officer the spectator learns that Dózsa's downfall in reality meant an alarm signal for Rákóczi's horsemen (anti-Habsburg rebels in the early eighteenth century). The scene depicting Rákóczi's war of independence emphasizes the popular descent of the rebels, their reluctance to fight in the service of noble commanders and enthusiasm in the camp of the popular leader Bottyán.

By evoking these memories of history, the captain draws the conclusion that the Hungarian Jacobean conspirators (a small republican conspiracy influenced by the French revolution), although they followed Rákóczi's rebels in the series of popular freedom fights, made one step forward and pursued this struggle for the republic. Memories of Habsburg oppression follow the execution of the Jacobeans in the film. Historical scenes depict the sufferings of the people, then the revolutionary crowd in

Pest taking an oath of freedom in 1848. The First Hungarian Soviet Republic appears as a chapter of these popular freedom fights in the film. Images evoking the event show a popular festival, thus emphasizing the joy felt by the proclamation of the dictatorship, which are succeeded by pictures of battles and speeches urging to fight.[43] The part that represents the dictatorship of the proletariat corresponds to the tension reflecting the state of mind of the captain: by a quick cut the scene continues with the officer stepping up to the speakers' platform. The period subsequent to the Hungarian Soviet Republic appears as the age of darkness and suffering in the film. The images depicting the Horthy era show the execution of two captive men accompanied by gendarmes. The captain's voice, occupying the narrator's position, calls attention to the idea that during this dark age the power of the people was defended by the Communists, who then guaranteed its victory after WWII. The concluding message of the film is that it is the task of future generations to defend this power.

Az eskü consists of long scenes and a limited number of cuts: the slow, relaxed tempo of nostalgic recollection provides the rhythm of the work. The captains role as narrator renders the contemporary perspective of 1956 in order to guarantee the abstract historicizing frame for memories. The practice of the film in evoking the past apparently follows the method of the historian: following the gathering of data concerning the event under scrutiny, the interpretation of the entire occurrence begins. The apparent purpose of historical investigation is Marxist analysis: to inquire into the meaning of history in general based on individual events. The documentary-like moving pictures are meant to guarantee the authenticity of the historical account. These frames provide recognizably distinct spectacles to the visual settings of the overall story: whereas the scenes showing the hesitation of the captain are based on fluid shots typical of the 1960s and a relatively low-key acting performance, the images evoking the past consist of fragmented shots which bring the archaic impressions and expressive acting style to the foreground. Clearly, the film is designed for impact, as if the past has been reconstructed from contemporary sources, like a documentary. In fact, the authorities encouraged the production of films on the period which applied documentary techniques.

---

43 The film in this respect followed the traditional canon of military propaganda films ordered by the Hungarian People's Army throughout the entire socialist period. The canonical scheme of these films was the historical tableau which depicted in recurrent chapters the freedom fights of the Hungarian people like the peasant rebellion of 1514, Rákóczi's insurrection, the war for independence in 1848–49, the First Hungarian Soviet Republic in 1919 and the victory of Soviet troops in 1945. This concept of history, which was most of all the visual display of Aladár Mód's historical book, *400 év küzdelem az önálló Magyarországért* (400-year struggle for freedom, Budapest: Szikra, 1951), was easily recognizable in works recorded after 1956. The message of the film *Szabadságharcos elődeink* (Our Freedom Fighter Predecessors) from 1958 was to highlight German imperialism as the main threat against Hungarian freedom. The directors contrasted this menace with the longing for freedom of the people which they supported by showing recurrent episodes of freedom fights. The film focused on the crucial role the people played in these struggles, which it intended to illustrate from historical costume dramas and mass spectacles taken from documentaries recorded in 1919 and 1945 (Collection of military propaganda films of the Museum of Military History. HL 10010. CSA VHS no. 66).

The guiding light of the 1963 historical documentary film *Elárult ország* (The country betrayed), which aimed at depicting the political elite of the interwar Horthy regime, is provided by portraits of the regent, Miklós Horthy, and prime minister, Gyula Gömbös situated next to each other.[44] The narrator explains these images, calling Gömbös the executor of the German imperial alliance, who subsequently led the country into disaster. Following an abrupt cut, the film continues with Mihály Francia Kiss's trial in 1957. The appearance of this judicial process secures the function of 1956, similarly to *Az eskü*, as the point of departure for historical reconstruction and the fixing of the fall of the 1919 Soviet Republic as the turning point in history. The historical conception is similar as well: according to the film the Hungarian ruling classes had been pursuing an opportunistic politics due to their fear of the people since 1849, which resulted in the service of German imperialism.

The First Hungarian Soviet Republic was depicted as a significant episode of this historical struggle conceived in terms of social conflicts. The documentary titled *Landler Jenő: A forradalom jogásza* (Jenő Landler: The lawyer of revolution) attempted to render this statement plausible.[45] The work represents Landler's activity in the labour movement, the culmination of which was the chief commandership of the Hungarian Red Army in 1919, with various photographs instead of contemporary moving images. The film is composed of slow panning camera movements, which imitate the slow, contemplating gaze of an observer immersed in the surrounding social world. The movement of the camera represents the meticulous scrutiny of society, making it clear that the represented historical processes are to be understood as the result of various social components. According to the film, this societal surrounding is marked by tension and social conflict, illustrated by images of light and darkness. The documentary describes the story of society running into revolution by means of photographs depicting striking and demonstrating crowds, making the Soviet Republic tangible as a social revolution.

The film *Az elárult ország* (The country betrayed) tries to integrate this narrow historical interpretation into a broader context. The work clearly meets the formal criterion for documentaries to use cuts from various contemporary films. The logic of the visual display evokes the perspective of an objective observer, thereby putting the filmic documents forward as evidence for investigation.[46] The shaping of the Austrian–Hungarian and German militarist political alliance is represented by images of military inspection and units from the end of the nineteenth century. The filmmakers believe to have detected the real purpose of war, depicted by pictures of cavalry troops put into action against workers on strike. This method features throughout the entire documentary: images of balls and hunts representing the luxurious lifestyle and irresponsible behaviour of the political elite and ruling classes are juxtaposed by visual displays of privation and oppression.

---

44 *Elárult ország* (The country betrayed), 1963, dir.: László Bokor. Collection of military propaganda films of the Museum of Military History. HL 3058–3060. OSA VHS no. 64.

45 *Landler Jenő: A forradalom jogásza* (Jenő Landler: Lawyer of the revolution), dir.: János Lestár. Collection of military propaganda films of the Museum of Military History. HL 3204–3205. OSA VHS no. 66.

46 Bill Nichols, *Representing Reality: Issues and Concepts in Documentary* (Bloomington/Indianapolis: Indiana University Press, 1991), 18–29.

Shots taken of birth and death registers, which aspire to demonstrate mortality by means of evoking the concepts of archives and statistics, reinforce the aura of documentary-like historical authenticity.

At first sight, there is nothing extraordinary in this practice. As if Communist propaganda historians are interested in the same questions as every other historian: How was the state of his or her point of view formed? What was the historical process that led to the conditions of the present?[17] Communists saw their present determined by the conflict of revolution and counterrevolution. Historians hence behaved as if they were searching for the historical origins of this struggle, believing that they had discovered its archetypal event in the history of the Soviet Republic. In order to find answers to the question, partisan scholars meant to imitate the method of investigation: they felt they were looking sources that would answer their questions and might reveal the secrets of the past. During their investigation these propaganda historians acted as if they had been exploiting their sources as clues: based upon these clues researchers believed they were deducing what past occurrences the remnants reflected, creating the impression that it had been the reading of evidence that shaped the narrative.

4

The certainty of a tragic ending, however, confined historical sources to a curious role in representations of the First Hungarian Soviet Republic. The editing techniques of *Az elárult ország* are marked by rapid shifts of sharply cut frames, which make the profound encounter and working with the presented documents barely possible. In fact, by applying this method the film specifically attempts to hinder a comprehensive and profound appropriation of history. The short, rapidly changing images and simple narration following this rhythm are aimed at stirring emotions: contrapuntal frames quickly follow each other, leading the audience towards emotional identification with the oppressed. The film is apparently a documentary, though in fact it is a propaganda work, the primary goal of which is the deconstruction of critical distance from the message, suppressing the voice of contradictory evidence. The real purpose of the procession of images is actually nothing else than to justify emotional proximity and to simultaneously suspend critical distance.

---

47 The importance of the questions of the historian in shaping the plot and the narrative has been argued by various scholars with many different backgrounds and interests, e.g.: Paul Ricoeur, *Time and Narrative*, vols 1–3 (Chicago/London: University of Chicago Press, 1984–85), esp. I: 52–87. See also his 'Narrative Time', *Critical Inquiry* 7 (1) (1980); and 'The Narrative Function', in *Hermeneutics and The Human Sciences* (Cambridge/Paris: Cambridge University Press, 1981), 274–96. This last piece is basically a summary of the three volumes. See also Christopher R. Browning, 'German Memory, Judicial Interrogation, and Historical Reconstruction in Writing Perpetrator History from Postwar Testimony', in *Probing the Limits of Representation: Nazism and the 'Final Solution'*, ed. Saul Friedlander (Cambridge, MA/London: Harvard University Press, 1992), 31; but also the early piece by Hayden White, 'The Burden of History', *History and Theory* 5 (1966): 111–34.

Az elárult ország tells the story of the interwar period by means of corresponding frames on Hungarian politics and German military preparations succeeding one another, which makes it possible to represent these historical events, otherwise lacking sufficient narrative explanation, as being parallel occurrences. A typical example of this practice is the quick, sharp cuts between scenes that depict recordings of the Nuremberg NS Party days and the Hungarian prime minister Gyula Gömbös in national-style festive costume. The Hungarian foreign policy of the 1930s thereby entered into a direct relationship with the goals of Nazi politics without any particular explanation or justification. Another scene that juxtaposes the Hungarian rearmament program of the 1930s with the German *Anschluß* of Austria plays a similar role. Corresponding parallel images, thus, integrate contemporary Hungarian politics into the context of German imperial expansion without any profound historical investigation. Images edited next to each other in these Hungarian military propaganda films summon a sense of affinity and initiate particular historical associations. The similarity of spectacle connects the historical events, persons and data depicted by these pictures, while the temporal succession of moving images transform them into a narrative.

The spectacle of this historical continuity features the memorial exhibition opened on the 40th anniversary of the Soviet Republic, which was organized by the Trade Union of Railway Workers. The workers wanted to install a genuine historical exhibition representing the past by means of original documents. According to this intention, clearly visible on preserved photographs, some boards did not simply show copies of contemporary historical sources, but the actual documents themselves stuck to the boards in their physical entirety. The volume titled *The Establishment of Organizations*, which describes the history of the railway workers' trade unions in between the wars, was put on display to be opened and leafed through by the visitors (Fig. 21).[48]

This direct encounter with the traces of the past, however, concealed the fact that, rather than being an accurate descriptive explanation, the sequence of the display defined the nature of the relationship among these historical documents. The exposition made its objects available for the public in a montage-like arrangement (Fig. 22). Documents of the counterrevolution following the fall of the Soviet Republic can be seen on a background made of graphical works of art. This background is dominated by a gallows tree and the figures of a gendarme and a village notary grasping a whip. These iconic images attempt to refer to the existence of a deeper, profound historical continuity, but which remains barely explicated. The inscription 'Year 1932', visible on boards representing the history of the interwar period, is succeeded by an image of the German imperial eagle, and the visual series is completed by a depiction of a Hungarian fascist Arrow Cross armband. The portrait of Hitler situated above the series of images, in turn, appears to reveal the essence of the power domineering the events in reality.[49] The exhibition in this way actually represented the historical allegory of counterrevolution, of downfall and continuity replacing genuine historical explanation.

---

48 Historical Photographic Records of the Hungarian National Museum 48. ME/II/B, Box: Culture: Exhibitions 1957–1962. Registry no.: 59.524, 59.525.

49 Historical Photographic Records of the Hungarian National Museum 48. ME/II/B, Box: Culture: Exhibitions 1957–1962. Registry no.: 59.523.

Figure 21. 'The Establishment of Organizations'. Historical Photographic Records of the Hungarian National Museum 48. ME/II/B, Culture: Exhibitions 1957–62. Registry no. 59.525.

Figure 22. The exhibition of the railworkers' union for the 40th anniversary of the First Hungarian Soviet Republic. Historical Photographic Records of the Hungarian National Museum 48. ME/II/B, Culture: Exhibitions 1957–62. Registry no. 59.524.

Apparently, historical representations of the Soviet Republic that followed the party line put very little effort into establishing critical relationships between historical evidence and narrative claims on the past. Documentary films commissioned by the authorities in general were disinterested in creating particular indexical relationships with reality, where images mediate the authentic sense of being there and of direct experience by means of accurate references to the represented actions and events.[50] In a similar vein, historical works in printed media seem to disregard the traditional function of the footnote as a method of critical reflection on the sources of knowledge on the past. Historians ordinarily are expected to go to the archives, dig up sources and reveal their findings, together with the process of investigation, to the public. Communist Party historians ignored the fact that footnotes does not simply claim that the evidence exists, but also prove that the historian was there, meeting and working with the records and has drawn conclusions from the direct experience of them. These works on 1919 had no concern for turning footnotes into tools for demonstrating the outcomes of obligatory critical work and testifying to the ability of the historian.[51] All these expectations, however, constrain a peculiar status of uncertainty for the historian: he or she is required to reach conclusions, make claims and arguments, end the narrative and construct the ending of the plot structure together with its broader moral, political and cultural implications after meticulous engagement with the evidence. Since no pool of sources is entire and no interpretations are final, there is always a certain level of uncertainty in the historian's work. Historians are inherently dependant on the contingency of archives and the uncertainty of evidence. Historical authenticity rests on the certainty of uncertainty: an accurate description of inaccuracy and absences of evidence and a sincere declaration of the reasons why a particular interpretation is preferred.

The intention of demonstrating evidence in these historical representations was not to reflect uncertainty by answering questions: on the contrary, the use of historical records was reduced to illustrate the given certainty of abstract prescribed statements on the past. At the end of his book, military historian Ervin Liptai depicts the Workers' Council's mourning of the resignation of the Communist government. The source of the description is Kun's last speech there. The essence of Kun's message was that he would have preferred a different outcome. The revolutionary leader expressed his desire for fighting on barricades instead of silent resignation. Kun also said that the Communists would withdraw from the country in order to prepare themselves for the next battle. Liptai reads it as a text expressing despair and accusation: 'In his despair and desperation he also accused the masses of leaving the dictatorship of the proletariat in the lurch.'[52] The lesson Liptai draws from the perception of Kun's despair is that the revolutionary leader was mourning the sorrowful downfall of the Soviet Republic. The text, however, is loaded with a richer variety of implications. The speech also urged Communists onto further illegal resistance; it was the last plea of a fallen dictator to incite his faithful

---

50 Nichols, *Representing Reality*, 108–18.
51 Anthony Grafton, 'The Footnote from de Thou to Ranke', *History and Theory* 33 (December 1994): 53–76; Carlo Ginzburg, 'Just One Witness', in *Probing the Limits of Representation*, 96.
52 Liptai, *A Magyar Tanácsköztársaság*, 456.

followers to the final battle. What is more, Kun was desperately disappointed with the masses who no longer wanted to fight for his regime. Kun's sorrow is the only element in this text to relate to the conviction that the end of the Soviet Republic meant the tragic destruction of revolution by the rule of counterrevolution.

Historical works of various modes of representation ordinarily sought out signs and precedence of the future catastrophe. In fact, historical works of the more traditional printed media dealt with their sources in a way similar to contemporary historical films. *Munkásezredek előre!* (Worker regiments, forward!) from 1960, written by military historian and veteran of the 1919 Red Army Tibor Hetés, is devoted to the worker regiments of the Hungarian Red Army. The author predicts in advance the future betrayal of the most revolutionary troops in the beginning of his work. The historian juxtaposes the intention of the Communists, who had wanted to form a determined revolutionary army based on the worker units, with the policy of the Social Democrats, who had constantly obstructed the organization, since they wanted to avoid the arming of the workers. Later, when the regiments were formed, Social Democrat leadership decided to deploy them solely in the hinterland. Apart from that, Social Democrat leaders appointed professional officers and ignored the worker commanders. This conflict foreshadowed the later withdrawal of these companies from the Red Army. Hetés, however, argues that the Social Democrats could have not reached their purpose until the army had advanced victoriously. Nevertheless, when the troops received the first command to retreat in June the opportunistic views of the Social Democrats began to influence the soldiers. The book claims that because the worker regiments were not led by Communists, their members tended to accept the view of capitulation coming from Social Democrat circles, and occasionally even declined to fight. The effect of opportunism contributed to the failure of the Communists to preserve the bellicose spirit of the army and, eventually, led to the final defeat of the Red Army in July. Hetés describes the failure of the offensive against the Romanian army in July 1919, which resulted in the dissolution of the Red troops: 'The majority of the worker regiments did not take part in it due to the sabotage of the officers.'[53] Liptai implies, therefore, that the military leadership consciously deprived the army of those troops that were most fit for action. He goes on to claim, 'The fall of the first Hungarian dictatorship of the proletariat was not hinged on the workers' resoluteness for standing their ground, it happened rather as a result of the actions of the outer enemy, having numerical superiority, and those of the inner opportunists and traitors.'[54] Thereby, the author concludes that at the end of the story it was fulfilled what even could be expected at the beginning: the betrayal and corruption of the revolutionary worker regiments.

Historical works usually claimed to recognize the clues of revolution or counterrevolution in every historical record. In one such book describing the history of 1919 in the Transdanubian region, published in 1961 by the young scholar Zsuzsa L. Nagy (who went on to become a leading intellectual historian within two decades, travelling far from ideological confines), the work starts by establishing that Transdanubia became the hinterland of the Soviet Republic, undertaking the revolutionary fight for

---

53 Hetés, *Munkásezredek előre!*, 140.
54 Ibid.

social progress and national subsistence. The author then calls attention to the fact that this struggle meant a constant conflict with counterrevolution, which appeared in various forms apart from open riot. As Nagy argues,

> We would be wrong if we thought that the counterrevolution took merely armed steps under the wings of the Entente against the Hungarian Soviet Republic. Nationalistic and anti-Semitic slogans spread by whispering propaganda, propagation of the compromise with the Entente, sermons from the pulpit, speculation with banknotes, the abuse of bureaucracy and expertise belonged to the war properties of counterrevolution as well as the weapons received from Vienna, the activity of right-wing Social Democrats or the work of the Entente officers on mission. The struggle against counterrevolution meant not only to suppress the strike of railworkers and armed uprisings, but also to defend the green corn from being cut, the ripe grain from being set on fire, to throw out the inappropriate persons from the soviets and to begin a movement in the plants for raising productivity.[55]

The book discovers the traces of counterrevolution in very different sources. For instance, the historian manages to identify the signs of counterrevolution in the records of the trial of the Hungarian people's commissars that followed the fall of the Soviet Republic in 1920. During the process a witness stated that they had rebelled against the Soviet Republic in 1919 in the village of Tolnatamási because 'they could not stand the rule of the Reds'. The author concludes from the account that it was 'an open counterrevolutionary uprising'.[56] The peasants' aversion to state power is interpreted as evidence of counterrevolutionary practice. What is more, the author finds evidence that counterrevolutionary activity had constantly threatened the Soviet Republic. For instance, the book points out that although there was no open resistance against the appropriation of big estates and the creation of cooperatives, the owners obstructed and attempted to hinder the entire process. Later, many of them were kept on as directors of their nationalized estates; however, they were reluctant to make any bigger investments, thereby they were considered saboteurs. Likewise, the reluctance of well-to-do peasants to carry out the necessary agricultural work is interpreted as an action directed against the revolution. The book asserts that these were genuine counterrevolutionary attempts since they were capable of dissolving the alliance of workers and peasants. Peasants who were accustomed to selling their products on the market usually objected to the mandatory delivery of agricultural goods. This behaviour is also coined as anti-Communist resistance by the author. Later, the historian states that the revolution had had to fight even for the new crop against counterrevolution. Nevertheless, the behaviour of the peasants could be described in terms of political support for the Communist regime as well. For instance, the scholar perceives the popular land-occupying movement that spread among poor peasants, which aimed at the seizure of big estates, as a driving force of the revolution.

---

55 Zsuzsa L. Nagy, *Forradalom és ellenforradalom a Dunántúlon 1919* (Revolution and counterrevolution in the Transdanubia, 1919) (Budapest: Kossuth, 1961), 5–6.
56 Nagy, *Forradalom és ellenforradalom*, 134.

The most important criterion of authentic historical interpretations, as György Lukács claims in his treatise on the historical novel published in Russian in 1937, then in Hungarian in 1947, is if they are able to represent the tendencies of development that shape the present. The Marxist philosopher expects historical novels to demonstrate how society came to its contemporary form and which historical processes determined its contemporary state: 'Without a felt relationship to the present, a portrayal of history is impossible. But this relationship, in the case of really great historical art, does not consist in alluding to contemporary events, but in bringing the past to life as the prehistory of the present, in giving poetic life to those historical, social and human forces which, in the course of a long evolution, have made our present-day life what it is and as we experience it.'[57] Lukács believes that precisely because the purpose of historical representations is to detect processes leading to the present, many historically relevant tendencies reveal themselves only for the retrospective gaze into the past. Numerous components of the historical development remained hidden for contemporaries, which, nonetheless, became recognizable for succeeding observers. Lukács, however, is searching for more than the relevance of historical explorations as tools to understand the present. The Marxist philosopher is arguing that since the genuine essence of historical reality is made of those processes that lead towards the present, this reality becomes accessible through an adequate assessment of the present. The appropriate understanding of the historical process is dependent on the correct moral-political commitment and cultural-ideological consciousness of the observer-interpreter of the past. The purpose of authentic historical representation, thus, is to document the process of historical necessity as understood retrospectively: 'Measured against this authentic reproduction of the real components of historical necessity, it matters little whether individual details, individual facts are historically correct or not. [...] Detail is only a means for achieving the historical faithfulness here described, for making concretely clear the historical necessity of a concrete situation.'[58]

It is as if the construction of narratives about the past, namely historical interpretation, was the result of an imagination independent of reading the sources. Apparently, historians willing to meet the official expectations of the party considered historical research as the value-free and interpretation-less activity of selecting and collecting facts from an unprocessed historical field that had nothing to do with genuine historical understanding. It was as if evidence could automatically establish, by the mere virtue of its existence, a relationship with reality; as if it constituted a positive store of facts, independent of and unchanged by the interpreter, but which was at the historian's disposal to be selected freely according to the needs of demonstration.[59] The unquestioned, naïve belief in the mystical power of records ended in a weird fetishistic admiration of historical

---

57 Georg Lukacs, *The Historical Novel* (Boston: Beacon Press, 1963), 53.
58 Ibid., 59.
59 On the distinction of narrative interpretation and positive factual historical data in contemporary historical theory, see Martin Jay, 'Of Plots, Witnesses, and Judgements', in *Probing the Limits of Representation*, 91–107; Chris Lorenz, 'Can Histories Be True?', *History and Theory* 37 (3) (1998): 287–309.

documents. Communist authors of historical representations laid great stress on working in archives, detecting newer and newer documents and supporting their argument with exhaustive knowledge of evidence. Tibor Hetés felt it necessary to announce, 'I used contemporary documents preserved in the Archives for Military History, contemporary press material and memoirs of contemporaries for writing this book.'[60] The popular comprehensive narrative by Ervin Liptai contains 346 footnotes for 459 pages including published memoirs, press articles and unpublished archival sources.[61] The same author, in his book concerning the history of the Hungarian Red Army, emphasizes his usage of non-Hungarian sources that were formerly unknown to the Hungarian public in order to produce a better and profound understanding of the campaigns of the army.[62]

Remarkably, despite the many differences between Communist and fascist understandings of history, in this respect Hungarian party historians share the epistemological, sceptical conviction of the *Mostra della rivoluzione fascista* (Exhibition of the fascist revolution) opened on 28 October 1932 in Rome. The exhibition aimed at a painstakingly minute reconstruction of the atmosphere of the period of Mussolini's *Marcia su Roma*, the takeover of the Italian Fascist Party in 1922. The organizers, led by Dino Alfieri, emphasized the focus on an 'objective, faithful, chronological reconstruction' and put great efforts into securing abundant documentation for this purpose. Local party activists were mobilized for researching and collecting original evidence, photographs, medals, postcards and other types of artefacts in order to tangibly demonstrate the historical origins of fascism.[63] Nonetheless, the sheer abundance of objects hindered the audience's ability to appropriately assess the historical events displayed in the exhibition. The visitors encountered a flood of images, artefacts, symbols, signs and documents, which overwhelmed them with information and contributed to their complete disorientation, confusion and loss of focus. The exhibition consciously mixed objects of art with original historical evidence, blurring the distinction between fiction and investigation, aiming at the denial of the critical distance necessary to establish rational appropriation, instead cultivating an emotional reaction among the audience.[64]

5

In representations of the Soviet Republic the distinction of fiction and investigative narrative was loosened, blurred, confused and, eventually, undermined. Miklós Gárdos calls *Két ősz között* a chronicle, differentiating it from historical scholarship.[65] Nonetheless,

---

60 Hetés, *Munkásezredek előre!*, 141.
61 Liptai, *A Magyar Tanácsköztársaság*, 461–73.
62 Liptai, *A Magyar Vörös Hadsereg harcai* (The battles of the Hungarian Red Army) (Budapest: Zrínyi, 1960).
63 Simonetta Falasca-Zamponi, 'Of Storytellers and Master Narratives: Modernity, Memory, and History in Fascist Italy', in *States of Memory: Continuities, Conflicts, and Transformation in National Retrospection*, ed. Jeffrey K. Olick (Durham, NC/London: Duke University Press, 2003), 57–61.
64 Marla Susan Stone, *The Patron State: Culture and Politics in Fascist Italy* (Princeton: Princeton University Press, 1998), 131–62.
65 Gárdos, *Két ősz között*, 367–8.

he states that all the details in his work are authentic and faithful to historical reality, though he treated the topic in the manner of a chronicle or reportage. The term is meant rather to refer to the readable and personal style than the strict chronological sequence of events. The notion of the chronicle is exploited by him to separate his work from normal historical science; however, not in the sense of a protohistory, but rather as a true representation of the events from a different point of view. Gárdos concentrates on the actors, uses a close description of their personal feelings and motives, and does not aim to establish general social tendencies within the events. In spite of his aim to build his narrative upon 'true facts', the writer consciously fictionalizes his work by using conventional techniques of constructing fiction, such as conversations which move the plot forward, inner monologues of actors and imagined conflicts in the agents' minds. The purpose of referring to original evidence is to pretend the fictional narrative is a result of historical investigation. The other book published on the Soviet Republic in 1959, *133 nap*, which consists of a collection of reportages, also calls itself a chronicle. The purpose of the distinction is to justify the adversarial choice of topics, the lowering down the scale towards ordinary people, the powerful subjective voice and the absence of footnotes and general conclusions that were presumed to be the requirements of real historical scholarship. Yet the team emphasize that their work is based on original documents; as their foreword states, the book describes the revolutionary activity of proletarians 'in the light of facts'.[66] Arguably, party historians perceived the function of evidence simply as a means of demonstrating the connection between representations of the past and the historical field.

In fact, the manipulation of historical authenticity is detectable behind the appearance of authentic historical representation: the evocation of the past in works which call themselves historical documentaries aims at effects similar to those in historical costume dramas. Obviously, the majority of historical scenes represented by moving images could not be produced according to original documents. In *Az eskü*, the peasant rebellion of 1514 is depicted by art graphics, and the Rákóczi insurrection and the war for independence in 1848–49 are shown by frames from a feature film produced in the 1950s.[67] The proclamation of the Soviet Republic and the struggles of the Red Army are illustrated by contemporary documentary shots; however, the fall of the dictatorship is depicted by images from a feature film. Historical feature film, however, is a particular genre: it represents the events of the past overwhelmingly via individual fates and trajectories. Individual deeds stand in the focus of historical processes, while social conflicts and ruptures are conceived through individual mental and emotional reactions.[68] Historical dramas do not present historical evidence for the spectators in order to drive them to consider, come to terms with and perform interpretive work with this proof. The purpose

---

66 Horváth, Kékesdi, Nemes and Ordas, *133 nap*, 6.
67 1848 was represented by images taken from the well-known historical drama *Föltámadott a tenger* (The raging sea).
68 Natalie Zemon Davis, *Slaves on Screen: Film and Historical Vision* (Cambridge, MA: Harvard University Press, 2000); Robert A. Rosenstone, *History on Film/Film on History* (Harlem/London: Pearson Education, 2006), 15, 38–48; Leger Grindon, *Shadows on the Past: Studies in the Historical Fiction Film* (Philadelphia: Temple University Press, 1994).

of historical feature films is to encourage emotional identification with abstract, positively depicted forces and values symbolized by the events of the past by means of establishing particular relationships to individual characters.

Post-1956 narratives of the history of 1919 were meant to mobilize a broader cultural tradition of historical storytelling. During the nineteenth century the battle of Mohács in 1526 (in which the army of Hungarian noblemen were almost destroyed by the Osman Turks – even the king lost his life while running away from the battlefield) acquired a special significance for the history of the nation. It began to be considered as the decisive tragic event of the country, which separated the preceding glory of the medieval kingdom from the subsequent period of national decline. The ancient kingdom was usually characterized as a flourishing empire ruling 'the three seas' and its kings were regarded as triumphant conquerors. The succeeding centuries, however, were ordered into the master narrative of heroic but tragic wars for national integration and independence.[69] The legend of Mohács subsisted during the years of Communism as well. One popular history book that discusses the history of late medieval (fourteenth and fifteenth centuries) Hungary bore the title *Hungary's Flourishing and Deterioration*. The glory is depicted through the construction of the royal castle by the great medieval king, Mathias:

> Meanwhile the castle was built as well. Mathias made new palaces, raising one after the other with spacious dining halls and superb sleeping areas that were differentiated by their variedly decorated gilded ceilings. A chapel was also built on the side of the Danube with a water organ and a double baptismal font made from marble and silver. The library stood next to it, having on its shelves heaps of Greek and Latin books, handwritten, beautifully illustrated *Corvinas* [codices of Mathias Corvinus] with splendid binding and among them modest printed volumes. From here opened the large vaulted room, displaying the copy of the starlit sky. Elsewhere golden reception halls were built, council and meeting halls, hidden deep niches, cold and warm bathrooms. High stairs, covered passages, terraces.[70]

This picture is juxtaposed by that of the destruction: 'Turkish troops, however, raided the defenceless country. They killed, plundered and set fires, took and drove captives: masters and servants.'[71] The book discusses the process that led from the beginning triumph to the final corruption. Although it is true that Hungarian Marxist historiography broke with the concept of Mohács as the ultimate decisive battle, historical scholarship still considered the clash a border of periods. Historical interpretation regarded the event as part of a larger context: that of the decay of feudalism and the 'feudal ruling classes'. The battle of Mohács was seen as an accidental but inescapable point of culmination in this process of destruction of Hungarian feudalism. According to the Marxist approach,

---

69 Ferenc Szakály, *A mohácsi csata* (The battle of Mohács) (Budapest: Akadémiai, 1975).
70 Domokos Varga, *Magyarország virágzása és romlása* (Hungary's flourishing and deterioration) (Budapest: Móra, 1974), 115–16.
71 Varga, *Magyarország virágzása és romlása*, 153.

the battle ended the age of the mature feudal state in Hungary and began a new era of dependence, semicolonization and the deadlock of social development.[72] Another characteristic monograph that concerned the foundation and discontinuance of the Principality of Transylvania after Mohács (sixteenth and seventeenth centuries) was published as the *Corruption of the Fairy Garden*, referring to the contemporary naming of Transylvania.[73]

The juxtaposition of promising prospective for historical progress and the tragedy of the failure of these expectations was a theme which frequently appeared in contemporary historical novels besides those which took the Soviet Republic as their topic. King Mathias is the central character in the Ferenc Jankovich trilogy published in 1965, which focuses on the conflict of the enlightened ruler and his reactionary noblemen crew. The king appears in the novel as the major agency of historical change, attempting to move his backward country, ruling class and people closer towards Europe, culture and civilization. Mathias's progressive political project, however, is hindered by constant conspiracy in the secular and clerical elite of the country, which is depicted as cultivating only its selfish interests. The novel ends with a succession of fights following the great king's death, which result in the dominance of reactionary lords and priests, leading the country towards backwardness and the ultimate collapse in the battlefield of Mohács. The tragic fate of progressive political projects motivated other authors interested in much earlier periods as well. In 1959, Géza Hegedűs published a novel on the Egyptian ruler Akhenaten, which represents the pharaoh's rule as a brave attempt in modernization, enlightenment and social progress. His aspirations are claimed to be resisted by the reactionary clerical elite of the arch-god Amen. It is remarkable that this conflict is emplotted as the struggle between two opposing conspiracies – that of the backward priests and the supporters of the progressive ruler – mirroring the struggle between revolution and counterrevolution.[74]

The generic structure of the dichotomy of glory and destruction is a fundamental aspect of historical tradition in East-Central Europe. This is a peculiar mode of historical discourse and a specific genre of storytelling that has a long tradition in East-Central European national historical representation. The foundation and institutionalization of professional historiography took place in the second half of the nineteenth century, when the peoples of the region experienced an era of decline. The point of view from where their past was seen was basically the failure of national aspirations for independence and liberty manifested in the revolutions of 1848. Czechs, Poles and Hungarians were all defeated in their armed struggles. Poland's next uprising in 1863 also failed, and

---

72 See, for example, Szakály, *A mohácsi csata*.
73 János Barta, *A 'Tündérkert' romlása* (The corruption of the fairy garden) (Budapest: Móra, 1983).
74 Ferenc Jankovich, *Világverő Mátyás király* (King Mathias, conqueror of the world) (Budapest: Szépirodalmi, 1982), 5th edition; Géza Hegedűs, *Az írnok és fáraó* (The clerk and the pharaoh) (Budapest: Móra, 1983), 3rd edition. I have written in more detail on this particular literary genre and its relationship to historical novels on the First Hungarian Soviet Republic: 'A konspiráció dialektikája' (The dialectics of conspiracy), in Tamás Kisantal and Anna Menyhért, eds, *Művészet és hatalom. A Kádár-korszak művészete* (Art and power: The art of the Kádár period) (Budapest: Petőfi Irodalmi Múzeum, 2005), 157–80.

while Hungary agreed on a pact with Austria in 1867, the country still lacked profound independence from the state. It is true that the pact was depicted as a triumph, a reconcilement between the nation and the king, but the tragic consciousness of history remained lively, however. Polish historical consciousness ordinarily views the past of the country as a cycle of catastrophes. Events are usually ordered according to the master narrative of destruction and renewal. A characteristic and determining episode of this history is the partition of the early modern Polish state that occurred between 1772 and 1795. In between those years the territory of the country was divided among the contemporary great powers of Prussia, Austria and Russia. Quotidian historical sense as well as scholarly representation hold that this event has to be regarded as a tragic downfall of a flourishing empire. The sixteenth and seventeenth centuries generally are described as the golden age of Polish spirit and nationality: the exceptionality of the Polish people was expounded perfectly during this period. Poles formed a unique shape of the state, a republic of nobles, Catholicism prevailed over the country, and Poland was the shield of Christian Europe and the great mill of the continent. The partition ruined this perfection of national spirit and pushed the country into the abyss of oppression, where no feature of its character could be expressed.[75]

Remarkably, in several Eastern European countries, especially in Poland and Hungary, WWII was also framed as a tragedy, in accordance with the legacy of narrative canons. In Poland, where Nazi occupation, Sovietization, the collapse of the nation state in barely more than twenty years and the massive loss of human lives rendered the war a broad traumatic experience, the genres of Polish cultural tradition were mobilized. The long-established canons of national martyrology and a narrative of victimization provided the framework to make sense of the war in the decades following 1945.[76] In Hungary, during the postwar trials of several wartime prime ministers and German collaborators, a concept of the war emerged that highlighted the tragedy of the 'Hungarian people'. The trials, which sought to establish tangible individual guilt, conceptualized the people – workers, peasants, lower middle classes and intellectuals – as innocent, helpless means in the hands of their masters who betrayed and sacrificed their own nation for the interests of Nazi imperialism.[77]

These works belong to a generic tradition, the 'history of downfall', which carries particular moral implications with itself. This genre generally consists of two distinct elements: the beginning part usually tells the story of a flourishing realm that brings prosperity to all of its citizens and where law and order are encompassed by material richness; the second part, however, ordinarily gives an account on the gathering of stormy

---

75 Ewa Domańska, '(Re)Creative Myths and Constructed History: The Case of Poland', in *Myth and Memory*, 249–62.
76 Annamaria Orla-Bukowska, 'New Threads on an Old Loom: National Memory and Social Identity in Postwar and Post-Communist Poland', in *The Politics of Memory in Postwar Europe*, ed. Richard Ned Lebow, Wulf Kansteiner and Claudio Fogu (Durham, NC/London: Duke University Press, 2006), 177–209.
77 See for example the trial of Prime Minister László Bárdossy who was executed for declaring war both on the USSR and the USA: Pál Pritz, ed., *Bárdossy László a népbíróság előtt* (Budapest: Maecenas, 1991).

clouds and the spreading of darkness. At the end the good empire is destroyed after a long and desperate fight, while its collapse results in the suffering and servitude of its inhabitants. Emotional proximity, grounded in this way, is meant to lay the foundations for obtaining certain moral-political conclusions.

6

For Communist propaganda historians the structure of glory and downfall managed to coherently account for a huge corpus of available sources and successfully mobilize traditional moral concerns: the plot of triumph and downfall portrayed the heroic struggle for the liberation of the working class and the sorrowful suffering of Communist fighters. This form of historical representation was regarded by propaganda historians as having incorporated evidence into a comprehensive and comprehensible narrative, and thus was capable of supporting their political project, effectively representing the 'truth' of Communism.[78] Communist propaganda historians seemed to consider the authenticity of historical accounts the result of the success of representing cultural-philosophical concepts by means of various forms of art. The artificial division of the interpretation of sources and the creative narrative process had convinced them that the validity and credibility of historical interpretation was bound to coherent narratives embedded in a cultural context of narrative tradition. Communist authorities shaping the politics of history tended to believe that the credibility of historical representations was grounded if they acquired meaning as narratives. The validity of historical interpretation was well founded if it was related to a culturally accessible set of narratives. They expected readers to perceive the correspondence between narrative forms and genres, whereas the form of the particular historical account was to remind them of those kinds of story structures which generally were already available in society.[79]

Nonetheless, the effectiveness of the abstract history of the First Hungarian Soviet Republic remained deeply doubtful. Instead of accurate references to particular individual phenomena, these works referred to general moral and cultural positions in order to draw (political) lessons and provide judgement. As a consequence of this use of evidence to invoke moral judgement, political commitment or ideological notions,

---

78 Hayden White assumes that the truth of historical interpretations can be measured according to the effectiveness these are able to support various political projects that enhance the security of communities: 'The Politics of Historical Interpretation: Discipline and De-Sublimation', in *The Content of the Form* (Baltimore: Johns Hopkins University Press, 1987), 58–83.
79 Narrativist historical theory describes genuine historical interpretation as an activity of relating accounts on the past to narrative traditions: Hayden White, 'Interpretation in History', in *Tropics of Discourse* (Baltimore: Johns Hopkins University Press, 1978), 51–80; Louis O. Mink, 'Narrative Form as a Cognitive Instrument', in *The Writing of History*. ed. Robert H. Canary and Henry Kozicki (Madison: University of Wisconsin Press, 1978), 143–4. Departing from this point, Hayden White calls the narrative account an inherently figurative account that endows real events with meaning by poetic means: 'The Question of Narrative in Contemporary Historical Theory', in *The Content of the Form*, 26–57; Frank R. Ankersmit, 'Six Theses on Narrativist Philosophy of History', in *History and Tropology* (Berkeley: University of California Press, 1994), 40–41.

the abstract narrative of the Soviet Republic was conceived as it really was: a means to cover and conceal the fact that the Communist fighters of 1919 had directly or indirectly contributed to the suffering of those people who were objectors or obstructions to their program of political and social transformation.[80] These representations of the past appeared to be tools of a particular 'rhetoric against the evidence': the rhetorical means of suppressing evidence.[81] Communist representations of the Soviet Republic represented no evidential paradigm, no mode of reading the evidence, but realized an artistic modality: fiction that transformed the evocation of reality into aesthetic quality to reflect abstract world views, moral structures or ideological constructions. The mode of uploading evidence into prefigured narrative constructs made the representations of the Soviet Republic appear as they really were: fictions exploiting original documents to illustrate the abstract fictive concept of the counterrevolution.

---

80 Communist terror troops executed several hundred people for 'counterrevolutionary' activity. Exact details will probably never be available. Péter Gosztonyi, *A magyar Golgota* (Budapest: Heltai Gáspár Kft., 1993), 24–30; Péter Konok, 'Az erőszak kérdései 1919–1920-ban. Vörösterror–fehérterror', *Múltunk* 55 (3) (2010): 72–91; István I. Mócsy, *The Effects of World War I* (New York: Social Science Monographs, 1983), 99, 102; Nicholas Nagy-Talavera, *The Green Shirts and the Others: A History of Fascism in Hungary and Rumania* (Stanford: Hoover Institution Press, 1970), 24–5. The source of statistics is usually the following two books, which are equally exaggerating and imprecise: Albert Váry, *A vörös uralom áldozatai Magyarországon* (Budapest: Légrády, 1922); and Vilmos Böhm, *Két forradalom tüzében* (Munich: Népszava, 1923).
81 Carlo Ginzburg, *History, Rhetoric and Proof* (Hanover, NH/London: University Press of New England, 1999), 5.

Epilogue

THE AGITATORS AND THE ARMOURED TRAIN

In 1969, responding to the call of the Academy of Drama and Film in Budapest in commemoration of the 50th anniversary of the First Hungarian Soviet Republic, the film *The Agitators* was shot.[1] Although the film in many ways was the outcome of the cult of 1919 in late socialist Hungary, it signalled a very important shift in the meanings of that particular event. The historical interpretations of the Soviet Republic were born to address the problems of counterrevolution during the late 1950s. In the late 1960s, however, 1919 addressed the opposite: the problems of interpreting revolution. Formally, Dezső Magyar's film is about the history of the dictatorship of the proletariat, and evokes the familiar problems of the interpretation of the Soviet Republic. Its focus is a group of Communist intellectuals formed by young revolutionaries who set off with enthusiasm and commitment to convince the masses of the cause of the proletarian revolution in the Budapest of 1919. The film takes place in the typical settings for historical representations of the Soviet Republic: in the Soviet House (the headquarters of the revolutionary government), in factories, among workers, in a baron's palace and on the front.

Nevertheless, it would be very difficult to watch *The Agitators* as a historical feature film. Although the protagonists appear in authentic contemporary costume, in scenery decorated with the posters of the Soviet Republic and creating a historical atmosphere, the uneventful structure of the film, which is full of long discussions made of recurrent philosophical reflections and regularly broken by documentary montage, would not have contributed to its broad popularity. However, deeper meanings concealed in the nonconventional structure hardly avoided the attention of more insider, intellectual and cultural policymaker visitors.

The Agitators mobilizes a peculiarly troublesome revolutionary tradition. Characters and dialogues in the film are based on Ervin Sinkó's novel on the Soviet Republic, *Optimisták* (The optimists). The novel, which meditates on radical revolt as hesitation, taking protest as a moral act, and which sprang from a particular messianic Communist position, was far from unanimously acclaimed by the authorities of Communist governments. Sinkó's work, written back in 1934, was published for the first time in Yugoslavia in 1953, while it had to wait up until 1960 for its publication in Hungary.[2] The book's interpretation of revolutionary radicalism during the First Hungarian Soviet Republic, which had enormous significance for Sinkó's Communist generation, raised different questions for

---

1 *Agitátorok*, dir.: Dezső Magyar (1969). Online: http://www.youtube.com/watch?v=vH4N_MJ2vvE (accessed 30 September 2013).
2 Benedek Balázs Vasák, 'Agitátorok. Érted, világforradalom?', *Filmvilág* 30 (November 1998): 11–13.

the creators of *The Agitators*, who were related to 1919 in an abstract theoretical way. The protagonists – appearing in poses and costumes of the Soviet Republic, members of the radical intellectual circles (Gábor Révai, Anna Szilágyi) and avant-garde art society (Tamás Szentjóby, Árpád Ajtony, Gábor Bódy, László 'Hobó' Földes) of the late 1960s – pursue heated theoretical debates on the possibilities of revolutionary action, the dilemma of violence, the criticism of new bureaucracy and the essence of working-class culture. Subsequent to the experiences of the Prague Spring and Western student movements, discussions wrapped in orthodox Marxist terms are transformed among these 1968 radicals into debates on the meaning of leftist politics, on the future and chances of revolution and social autonomy. Behind the mask of the Soviet Republic the young radical intellectuals debate 1968: for them the events of 1919 are actually the occurrences of 1968.

The authorities had radically different ideas when they issued the call for films to commemorate the Soviet Republic. The first Hungarian commune celebrated its 50th anniversary in 1969. For official interpretations of the past, 21 March 1919 had long been established as the turning point of Hungarian history and the greatest national holiday. The leadership of the HSWP planned a grandiose and spectacular celebration for the anniversary. The proposals considered the participation of numerous political and social organizations. The ceremonies, structured by a sophisticated choreography, began with a special parliamentary session of the most important party and state leaders, contemporary people's commissars still alive in 1969, persons decorated for the occasion, distinguished intellectuals and leaders of socialist brigades. The ceremonies were honoured by the presence of diplomatic bodies, and governmental and party delegations from other socialist countries.[3]

According to the proposals, anniversary commemorations would be organized in all military outposts, with the participation of veterans of 1919 if possible. A major exhibition was planned for the Buda castle as well as the issuing of anniversary stamps and reprints of contemporary political posters. Committees and organs of the Communist Youth were expected to organize memorial guards, demonstrations and the laying of wreaths. An academic conference was held at the Political School of the HSWP, the periodicals of the party – *Párttörténeti Közlemények*, *Társadalmi Szemle*, *Pártélet* – as well as the historical journal *Századok* published ceremonial issues for the occasion.[4] The commemorations arguably culminated in the unveiling at 11 am on 21 March of the central monument to the Soviet Republic, which had been planned since 1965. This is aptly illustrated by the original plans for an audience of fifty thousand, which, nonetheless, the Committee for Canvassing and Propaganda suggested reducing to four or five thousand.[5] Simultaneous to the erection of the Budapest monument several local memorials were unveiled, for instance in the small towns of Tiszafüred, Fegyvernek and Szentes.[6]

---

3 MOL M-KS 288/1969/22/1.
4 MOL M-KS 288/5/458.
5 MOL M-KS 288/1968/22/1.
6 MOL M-KS 288/41/95, MOL M-KS 288/41/47.

The Hungarian party leadership expected the evocation of the Soviet Republic to justify its own politics rather than that of the 1968 alternative leftist radicalism. The speaker, president of the Presidential Council, Pál Losonczi, who opened the parliamentary session, highlighted the following: 'The cause of socialism has really prevailed in Hungary. [...] Our people's democratic state, the Hungarian People's Republic is the rightful heir and faithful follower of the cause of the First Hungarian Soviet Republic.' Notwithstanding the relevance of historical continuity, it still remains a peculiar abstract entity in the opening speech: 'Thus the unity of past and present gives us the grounds to hope further successes come our way. We look forward with confidence to the forthcoming decades, for the further victories of socialism.'[7] The Soviet Republic became a historical event, the origins of the present, but also a chapter of the past with little tangible meaning for contemporaries. The first comprehensive historical work on the Soviet Republic – which wanted neither to draw immediate political lessons from the individual events of 1919, nor to directly reflect contemporary political conflicts in the occurrences of the Soviet Republic – was published in 1969, for the 50th anniversary. Tibor Hajdú's book considered the Hungarian dictatorship of the proletariat a historical event: a station in the road leading to the socialist present.[8]

Paradoxically, it was precisely this abstract continuity, which moved 1919 back to a perceptible temporal distance, that meant both radical intellectuals and the party leadership shared a common stake in the Soviet Republic. In June 1968, the Borsod-Abaúj-Zemplén county Communist Youth Committee, following the initiative of the Central Committee of the Communist Youth, launched an ambitious social activism program to rebuild the 1919 armoured train that participated in the battles in Northern Hungary. 'If the plan to finish the armoured train could be realized that would provide a great help to evoke the memory of the Northern Campaign', as Zoltán Nagy argued in the meeting held in the county town Miskolc on 28 June 1968.[9] The Northern Campaign raised the least problematic questions relating to 1919. During the May–June 1919 operations, the Hungarian Red Army had won considerable victories, it had succeeded in taking the centre of the Northern Hungarian industrial region, Miskolc, then it advanced towards Košice and Prešov, where it contributed to the proclamation of the Slovak Soviet Republic. The army remained undefeated, and the campaign ended in retreat subsequent to the Hungarians' negotiations with the Entente. The significant proportion of professional military officers as well as ordinary footmen regarded the northern operations as a patriotic defensive war, and it had obtained considerable social support as well. The armoured train was a legendary weapon of the Northern Campaign; it evoked images of military success during the operations and fostered social consensus. The armoured train would represent the very emotions and ideological meanings the authorities strove to associate with the Soviet Republic in a tangible way, easy to apprehend. 'Taking into account that we need to provide historical authenticity, its entire

---

7 *Magyar Hírlap*, 21 March 1969, 1.
8 Tibor Hajdú, *A Magyarországi Tanácsköztársaság* (The First Hungarian Soviet Republic) (Budapest: Kossuth, 1969).
9 PIL 289/13/1968/39.

impact should repeat what it had once realized in the events of 1919', as secretary of the county Communist Youth Committee Béla Havasi formulated.

The purpose of the initiative was the most precise reconstruction of the war gear used by the Hungarian Red Army, replicating the original in the most accurate way. To accomplish this, the Communist Youth Committee mobilized a considerable group of collaborators and experts. Dr Ferenc Csillag, employee of the Museum for Military History, described in detail the structure of the military equipment to those present in a meeting devoted to the armoured train. The armoured train used to consist of five wagons and one engine. The first carriage of the train was an open forerunning wagon, succeeded by two armoured wagons equipped with four machine guns. The train was closed by an open carriage equipped with an anti-aircraft gun and another with a cannon defending the rear.[10]

The accurate historical reconstruction, however, was hindered by several difficulties. Although the museum offered the cannon, it could not provide the machine guns. János Benedek, employee of the Railway Department of the Ministry of Transport, explained that though they would be able to obtain an appropriate locomotive, there were no wagons. In these circumstances, the construction of the armoured train seemed possible only by involving various institutions and social groups. Motivation apparently meant no obstruction: the Lenin Furnace Works in Diósgyőr (the heavy industry district of Miskolc) was willing to produce the machine guns ('We support the movement, it has a good reputation among the youth of the factory', as István Kovács, representative of the factory Communist Youth Committee, clarified); the Miskolc vehicle repair works of the Hungarian railways was prepared to transform reject wagons in voluntary unpaid shifts; the president of the county's Pioneer Association, in harmony with a representative of the waste recycling company, suggested involving children to gather and reuse waste. The Ministry of Defence was ready to provide personnel, whereas the contemporary grey uniforms were planned to be substituted by the refashioning of sixteen firefighter suits in the interest of historical faithfulness.[11] By November 1968, the vehicle repair works had obtained a few reject freight wagons, which, according to a report in a contemporary daily, seemed to promise the unexpected but fortunate opportunity of realizing historical authenticity. 'In the Miskolc yard of the vehicle repairing company, technician László Pogonyi (designer of the reconstructed armoured train) climbs under the wagons for a date. "1917", he says, "made by Ganz and Co. These wagons carrying coal, stone, sugar beet were produced then, so in 1919, when the armoured train took part in the battles of the Soviet Republic, they might transport supplies for the Red Army.' The transformation of the wagons was a serious job: the report about the process evokes to the long-gone ordinary days of the former Northern Hungarian socialist heavy industry: 'The men of Diósgyőr bring the angle iron, the metalworkers from Ózd the plates, wood is sent from the sawmill of Lád, paint is from the Tisza Chemical Works.'[12]

---

10 PIL 289/13/1968/39.
11 PIL 289/13/1968/39.
12 Cs. K., 'Jó utat, páncélvonat' (Have a nice journey, armoured train!), *Esti Hírlap*, 27 November 1968, 3.

Becoming enthusiastic over the broad social support, the Pioneer Department of the Communist Youth expanded its ideas on how to use the armoured train as part of a massive set of ceremonies. The train was planned to be prepared, as part of the pioneer movement 'The Flames of Revolution', as the mobile museum of the Soviet Republic, which would wander the country for two years with living veterans of 1919 on board. Along the way, patriotic competitions, adventure tours and rifle shooting were proposed to take place in the individual stations. The armoured train programme would end with the erection of a monument commemorating the battle of Miskolc in the neighbouring village of Felsőzsolca. For the Communist Youth leadership, the train would not only give the pioneers an enduring experience, it would also contribute to the improvement of socialist patriotism through the active participation of young people and workers, and they also hoped to disseminate the revolutionary memory of the recent past among a broad audience.[13]

The 50th anniversary of the Soviet Republic was to provide the atmosphere and experience of the revolution and revolutionary activism for broad segments of Hungarian society. The Pioneer Department and Executive Committee of the Communist Youth had already begun preparing the 'Flames of Revolution' pioneer movement in October 1967. The objectives of the programme included the desire that 'ideas of world view, morality and politics would be filled with emotional content, would relate to the life and objectives of socialist society'.[14] The real question of the programmes, dedicated to children, was how to make revolutionary action appropriate for the present by evoking revolutionary predecessors.

The initiative reflected the general difficulties of the party leadership and ideology in relation to the idea of revolutionary behaviour. How was it possible to render revolutionary fervour and enthusiasm – as appealing to the youth and as much of a principle of official political identity as it was – acceptable for the authorities and usable for the support of the government? The interpretation of revolutionary tradition, which the party leadership tried to link with the events of 1848, 1919 and 1945, remained open to independent versions, differing from the official one despite all efforts to the contrary. The organization of spring anniversaries commemorating these events – 15 March, 21 March, 4 April – regularly troubled the authorities. The proposal prepared in January 1966 by the Department of Canvassing and Propaganda of the HSWP, which issued the guidelines for the celebrations of spring 1967, stated with disapproval that 'it is in each year problematic to secure proper historical and political proportions in youth festivals'.[15]

The problems with the proportions derived, in all probability, from the significantly different public interest in the celebrations of 15 March and 21 March. The report was disappointed with the fact that, whereas 15 March was a school break, teaching still continued on 21 March. To eliminate these disproportional relations, the Department for Canvassing and Propaganda suggested organizing the Week of Revolutionary Youth

---

13 PIL 289/4/351.
14 PIL 289/3/223.
15 PIL 289/4/209.

between 15 March and 21 March 1967. To the contention of party officials, this structure would guarantee the appropriate connection of the commemorations of 1848 to the revolutionary struggles of Communists and the postwar liberation, and would create an organic unity of the legacy of 1848 and 1919 together with the present. To secure proportionality, however, 15 March was scheduled as the beginning of the celebrations that were to culminate on 21 March.[16]

In August 1966, the secretariat of the Communist Youth suggested renaming the ceremonies the Revolutionary Youth Days, after linking the two March anniversaries with 4 April. In the view of the authors who suggested in the 17 August proposal the organization of the youth days, the celebrations would serve the establishment of socialist patriotism 'by using the continuity and unity of freedom fighter and revolutionary legacy based on the revolutionary traditions' of 1848, 1919 and 1945.[17] By the 50th anniversary of the Soviet Republic, the youth days had become a spectacular nationwide series of events. That year, 1969, the opening ceremony was held in Győr on 14 March. The festive programmes of the day after were broadcast on television and a ceremonial reception was offered in the evening. Three thousand young people participated in the central laying of the wreath by the Petőfi statue on 15 March. The series of events, the 'In the Footprint of Heroes' competition, which was also broadcast in television, started on the 16th. The celebration in honour of foreign delegations (except Albania) took place on 21 March, the 50th anniversary of the proclamation of the Soviet Republic. The youth and student seminar 'Friendship' was organized for the same day. An amateur radio competition commemorating the telegraph messages of Lenin and Béla Kun occurred on the 22nd. The series of programs would end with the oath-taking ceremony of new Communist Youth members on 4 April.[18]

At the turn of the 1960s and 1970s, one of the major targets of global cultural fascination was revolution. The young generation in North America and Western Europe increasingly perceived a rigidity and conservatism in their societies and many were becoming ardently critical of the consumerism and technological alienation one was allegedly subjected to in capitalism. The cultural disappointment led many to radical politics in terms of conceiving revolutionary change and the radical transformation of capitalism. Typically, the new generation of activists and many influential intellectuals were looking for global models of revolutionary change such as Maoist China, Vietnam or the anti-imperialist struggle in Algeria. In 1968 in Paris and Berlin, for a brief period, revolution really seemed to have arrived in Europe.[19] Eastern European societies were not inimical to the global fascination with revolution. Although these countries were still largely sealed off from the other side of the Iron Curtain, it was no hermetic isolation. Information on global events and movements was transferred, not the least, because the officials of these countries sought to prove the close decline of capitalism by showing off

---

16 PIL 289/4/209.
17 PIL 289/4/250.
18 PIL 289/4/385.
19 Arthur Marwick, *The Sixties: Cultural Revolution in Britain, France, Italy, and the United States, c.1958–c.1974* (Oxford: Oxford University Press, 1998), 288–316; Norbert Frei, *1968: Jugendrevolte und globaler Protest* (Munich: Deutscher Taschenbuch Verlag, 2008), 9–187.

student unrest and anticolonial conflict. Hungary was one of the most open countries in the East. Providing society and especially the young generation with global socialist revolutionary templates was important for a Communist leadership that was deeply concerned with anti-Communist nationalist sentiment and the growing scepticism towards the future of socialism in the society that it governed.[20]

Nonetheless, the production of revolutionary models was proved to be highly problematic. During these years, one of the major theoretical and political problems facing Hungarian party leaders and ideologists was how to tackle the New Leftist criticism that perceived the elimination and abandonment of revolution itself. Radicals of 1968 both in Europe and Hungary tended to consider the reigning Communist systems as ossified bureaucrat regimes betraying the ideas of revolution and to use New Leftist radicalism to continue revolution, even against existing leftist governments. In the decade around 1968, several unofficial yet leftist critical movements still committed to the idea of socialism were born. Young persons condemned in the Budapest Maoist trial accused the Kádár regime of deserting the workers and wanted to explore unofficial forms of ideology and movement conducive to genuine workers' power. Such unofficial movements as the Orfeo group, pioneers in Hungarian experimental theatre, or the Studium Generale of the Budapest ELTE university, aimed at improving the sociocultural opportunities of marginal groups like the rural poor and workers, allegedly forgotten by the authorities. Thinkers of the Budapest New Left, recognizing the possibility of democratic socialism in the aspirations of the Prague Spring, condemned the Hungarian Communist government for repressing the attempt to correct the system.[21] The Hungarian Communist leadership tried to meet these challenges by means of concepts such as 'the revolution of the everyday' or 'everyday revolution'. According to the official position, the spectacular and violent phase of the revolution occurred at the moment of the postwar political turn and, as it followed, it had already been closed. All these did not mean for them the impossibility of revolutionary activism. The new type of revolutionary action was less spectacular, as ideologists argued, but it was still a requisite for the construction of socialism. In the new phase of 'invisible revolution', 'there is a need for thoroughly systematic, durable, long-term, patient, regular activism in economics, in culture, and also in politics.'[22]

---

20 Péter Apor and James Mark, 'Socialism Goes Global: Decolonization and the Making of a Transnational Culture in Socialist Hungary 1956–1975' (unpublished manuscript).

21 György Dalos, *Hosszú menetelés, rövid tanfolyam* (Budapest: Magvető, 1989), 28–9; Iván Zoltán Dénes, 'Diákmozgalom Budapesten 1969-ben', *2000* 20 (July–August 2008): 19–35; Orsolya Ring, 'A színjátszás harmadik útja és a hatalom. Az alternatív Orfeo Együttes kálváriája az 1970-es években', *Múltunk* 53 (3) (2008): 233–57; Simon Tormey, *Agnes Heller: Socialism, Autonomy and the Post-modern* (Manchester: Manchester University Press, 2001), 11–12.

22 Péter Rényi, 'A forradalom, mely nem falja fel gyermekeit' (The revolution that does not eat its children), *Valóság* 13 (September 1970): 19 (13–22). Literary scholar Istvan Király, one of the crucial figures in late socialist literary criticism and cultural policy, published a long treatise in the periodical *Kortárs* in 1973. In this he claimed the following: 'This revolutionary attitude means demand. Demand towards society, towards the external word as well as towards ourselves. Demand for life pertinent to ordinary days and to everyday work. One should live according to its laws every day – including very little mundane actions, too – so that one can feel the pathos of the cause, of the task, of future and the seriousness of the matter' ('A mindennapok forradalmisága' (The revolutionary mind of the everyday), in *Irodalom és társadalom* (Literature and society) (Budapest: Szepirodalmi, 1976), 622).

The Revolutionary Youth Days ensured the audience experienced the ideas and emotions of revolutionary radicalism by means of connecting it to historical events, thereby also moving them back to a safe temporal distance. The possibility of radical revolutionary action, which for the young generation of the 1960s was directed against the elite, the establishment, institutionalized and officialized forms and the generation of 'fathers', became a significant source of threat for the ruling Communist parties and governments. Contemporary revolutionary radicalism and political activism, which was shaped by the New Left, ultra-leftist, Maoist or simply antiestablishment ideas and aimed to correct socialism, had strong antiregime implications and threatened the Soviet type of ruling elite. Following the suppression of the 1968 Prague Spring and the official criticism and exclusion of New Leftist movements from mainstream institutions, developing direct political forms of activism became dangerous also for the nonconformist critical intellectuals. Paradoxically, the temporal and spatial distancing of revolution appeared safer both for critics and guardians of official socialism. As supporting revolutionary liberation movements in the Third World seemed to be the acceptable form of radicalism, revolutionary traditions and radical action in the past appeared to be an available terrain of leftist revolutionary mentality and culture.

This circumstance, however, radically changed the framing and meaning of public discussion on the First Hungarian Soviet Republic. The anniversaries of the Soviet Republic, which during the 1960s bore relatively little relevance for Hungarian society, offered exactly the temporal distance desired for addressing the issue of revolution. The abstract, barely tangible story of 1919 seemed appropriate for pursuing the abstract theoretical debates on revolution in a safe manner. The Soviet Republic, it seemed, was valuable in formulating those patterns of behaviour that realized the officially expected and desirable forms of revolutionary activism, which could also be endorsed by youth.

The main protagonist of the radio drama *The March of Fire*, which was broadcast weekly in spring 1969 to end on 21 March, was a middle-class girl named Ági, the best pupil in her grammar school class, the setting of the play. The drama, set in the school year 1918–19, contemplates the opportunities of socially committed, morally grounded action. Ági is depicted as a warm-hearted, helpful, compassionate girl whose personal history exemplifies the social transformation growing from instinctual, socially sensitive revolt into conscious Communist revolutionary behaviour. Ági's moral plan to improve the lot of the poor and marginalized is a series of failures and conflicts, and is even threatened with expulsion from school. Only the proclamation of the First Hungarian Soviet Republic is able to solve the conflict in the play: Ági, hence, avoids being expelled and begins to realize her social programme. The drama, in this way, presents Ági as a model of everyday revolutionary behaviour. Meanwhile, the girl's loved one, the young Communist worker János, sets off to the front to defend the achievements of the revolution, and Ági helps the needy and teaches proletarian children in the hinterland. The main message of the play is that for the young the everyday work of peaceful construction bears the same relevance and validity as armed struggle. At the same time, however, the drama also wants its audience to believe that the precondition for realizing socially sensitive, morally grounded leftist programs is the acceptance of the leadership of the Communist parties.[23] *The March of Fire*, set in the history of the Soviet Republic and celebrating the revolutionary activism of the young, represents what the authorities would have expected from the film *The Agitators* as well – that is to say, to demonstrate that in reality the radicalism of 1968 attacking the fundaments of Communist authoritarianism justified, albeit in a way difficult to understand, the Communist regimes. As if what happened in 1968 was the same as that which had occurred in 1919.

In terms of the genesis of 'the continuity of the counterrevolution' – the core concept of this book – the 50th anniversary of the First Hungarian Soviet Republic is part of a radically different story. This history starts in 1966, the 10th anniversary of the 1956 anti-Stalinist revolt, when the HSWP became increasingly disinterested in evoking the horrors of the 'counterrevolution', but was enormously interested in highlighting the achievements of 'revolutionary' construction. As the proposal prepared by the Committee for Canvassing and Propaganda in concert with the Department of Foreign Relations of the Central Committee on 2 July 1966 formulated:

> When preparing our plans to balance Western commemorations, we have to take care to not resurrect the Hungarian question or attribute too much significance to the anniversary with our campaign-like actions or exaggerated preparations. Our propaganda should not directly relate to the counterrevolutionary occurrences; we have to commemorate, however, the 10th anniversary of the foundation of the HSWP and the Revolutionary Worker-Peasant Government, the 10th anniversary of the December party resolution and the martyrs of the counterrevolution.[24]

The 1969 commemorations of the Soviet Republic were adjusted to these principles and to the idea of the Revolutionary Youth Days, and were inherently related to those international processes that involved revisions of the concepts of 'revolution', 'revolutionary behaviour', 'leftism' and 'socialism'. Whereas up to 1965 the Soviet Republic had been the site of discussing the 'counterrevolution', from 1966 onwards it increasingly changed into the means of interpreting 'revolution'. While until the mid-1960s it was a discourse on the counterrevolution, avoiding the direct touch of 1956, by 1969 it became the discourse of revolution replacing 1968. In 1965, the Soviet Republic was part of the history of the counterrevolution, in 1969, however, it became a chapter in a new history, the history of revolution.

The representations of 1919 remained broadly in use throughout the last two decades of Hungarian Communism, up until the late 1980s. In a period when it had become commonplace to recall the disintegration of antifascist commitments and the decline of memories of interwar authoritarianism, official political culture used the Soviet Republic as shorthand for evoking such experiences. The history of the Soviet Republic was constructed as a narrative of a heroic attempt to establish the power of workers and

---

23 The transcript of the radio drama is available in the archives of Magyar Rádió.
24 MOL M-KS 288/22/1966/1.

peasants, to fight back against the rule of the rich and the masters, and a tragic failure of the first experiment to create a just society in modern Hungary. The events and measures of 1919 were juxtaposed with the interwar period, which was painted dominantly in dark colours, highlighting privation, oppression and the final war catastrophe in 1944–45, in order to render the abstract message on the 'sufferings under fascism' a tangible experience. The memory of 1919 invaded school curricula and life in the form of competitions, patriotic sports tournaments and summer camping events. Popular 'coffee table' books were published in exceptional numbers.[25] Biographies of the leaders of the Hungarian Bolshevik regime appeared in popular illustrated style and format.[26] The history of the Hungarian commune remained also an important topic of scholarship as well. In 1979, the 60th anniversary of its proclamation was commemorated by a centrally organized academic conference.[27] In 1986, the 100th anniversary of Béla Kun's birth still generated sufficient interest to organize an international conference.[28]

Nonetheless, by the end of the decade 1919 had increasingly lost its meaning. As the marketization of economy, political pluralism and the liberalization of culture have become more and more important concerns of the elite and society, the memory of an early Bolshevik experiment in Hungary seemed more and more to be an irrelevant historical experience. Although 21 March was still an official holiday in 1989, when the first free post-Communist elections were held in 1990, the Soviet Republic abruptly lost all its possible meanings. There was only a tiny radical leftist political subculture remaining, which had grave difficulties itself coming to terms with the violence and atrocities committed by the Hungarian Communists in 1919. In the intellectual environment of the 1990s, which was interested in linking Hungary's culture strongly with some common European value system, in rediscovering some 'authentic' national history, and in finding its own ways to come to terms with capitalism, the radical, unsuccessful, leftist, anticapitalist experiment simply meant nothing. This has remained true, despite the emergence of a post-Communist anti-Communism since the early 2000s, which tries to make rather limited political sense of 1919 as possible evidence of inherent Bolshevik violence and an insidious intention to lead a vicious attack on 'authentic' Hungarian national culture.

---

25 Two such books are: Gyula Fekete, *Fortélyos félelem igazgat: Magyarország 1919–1945 között* (An insidious fear makes order: Hungary between 1919 and 1945) (Budapest: Móra, 1970) and Miklós Zalka, *Mindenkihez! A Magyar Tanácsköztársaság története* (For everyone! The history of the First Hungarian Soviet Republic) (Budapest: Móra, 1978).
26 A few examples: András Simor, *Így élt Korvin Ottó* (Budapest: Móra, 1977); Tibor Hetés, *Stromfeld Aurél* (Budapest: Zrínyi, 1978); Lajos Árokay, *Kun Béla* (Budapest: Zrínyi, 1986); Lajos Varga, *Garbai Sándor, 1879–1947: A Forradalmi Kormányzótanács elnöke* (Sándor Garbai, 1879–1947: The president of the revolutionary governing council) (Budapest: Kossuth, 1987).
27 Béla Köpeczi, ed., *A Magyar Tanácsköztársaság 60. évfordulója* (The 60th anniversary of the First Hungarian Soviet Republic) (Budapest: Akadémiai Kiadó, 1980).
28 *Kun Béla: Nemzetközi tudományos ülésszak születésének 100. évfordulójára* (Béla Kun: International conference for the 100th anniversary of this birth) (Budapest: Kossuth, 1987).

INDEX

15 March 1848 12–13, 24, 54, 76, 79, 203–4
1848–1849 revolution and War of Independence: anniversary of 76; anti-Communist reading of 24, 139, 203–4; heroes of 132–3, 145–7; myth of 29, 53–4, 152, 183, 193; representation of 12–15, 35, 37, 39, 56, 60, 149–51; tragic meaning of 195
1918 October Revolution: 40th anniversary of 139–41; events of 4, 13; heroes of 146; novels about 169–70, 172, 175; relationship to 1848 149; representation of 28, 90, 147, 206
1956 revolution: 10th anniversary of 207; anniversary of Soviet invasion in 148; changes after 15, 51, 66, 150; dead of 127–33, 143,159–60, 162–4; events of 1–2, 7, 16, 60; exhibition on 80–81; forgetting of 23, 94, 167–8; interpretation of 17–18, 61–2, 67, 142, 145, 150; relationship to 1919 82–6, 91, 93, 95–8, 123, 153, 155, 179–84; representing atrocities in 22, 65, 71–8, 87–9, 100, 136
30 October 1956 62, 64, 66, 87, 131, 136, 143, 164
39th Brigade 177

Academy of Sciences vii, 12
Aczél, György 63–5, 168
agitation: *see* propaganda
Agitators, The (Dezső Magyar) 199–200, 207
Ajtony, Árpád 200
Albert the Great 85
Alfieri, Dino 192
Algeria 96, 204
America: *see* USA
Andics, Erzsébet 12, 29, 38
anniversary: of the Hungarian Soviet Republic (30th 14, 27–30, 32–3, 40–41, 45–6, 49, 52, 146; 35th 56–8; 38th 75; 39th 94; 40th 22, 138–9, 141, 143, 149–50, 153, 155, 167, 186; 50th 8, 199–201, 203–4; 60th 208); 40th of the foundation of the Communist Party of Hungary 133 100th of 1848 13, 53; of the Polish Constitution 37; of the siege of the party headquarters 87
antifascist: antifascist myth 9, 11, 123; front 11; identity 10, 207; martyrs 6, 13, 17; powers 7; resistance 19, 20, 29, 38, 42
anti-Semitism 107, 109
Antwerp 160
apocalyptic history 89, 108
architecture 21
armoured train 7, 201–3
Arrow Cross Party: history of 6; representation of 78, 82, 100–101, 108, 111, 113; art networks 200; exhibition 79, 92–3, 151–2, 186, 192; film 177, 193; theory of 191, 197
Assmann, Jan 55
Asztalos, János 71, 131
Austria 3–4, 9, 186, 196
authenticity: criteria of 24, 103, 166, 183, 185, 188, 197; making of 201–2; manipulation of 165, 193; moral 79

Balaton, Lake 7–8
Bălcescu, Nicolae 37
Bárdossy, László 108, 111–12
Batthyány, Lajos 145
Beer, Max 38
Bélapátfalva 8
Belgrade 57–8
Benedek, János 202
Bentsur, Eytan 2
Berkesi, András 181
Berlin 3, 20, 204
Bethlen, István 6, 112
Biszku, Béla 82
body: mystical 22, 135–7, 162; physical 23, 84, 85–6, 160; political 9, 80, 111, 128, 134, 160

Bódy, Gábor 200
Bolshevik: leaders 2, 33, 170, 172, 173, 182; party 176; regime 13, 27, 60, 208; revolution 3, 4, 7, 20
Botev, Hristo 36
Bőhm, Vilmos 5, 95
Buchenwald 19, 108: shrunken head of 108
Budapest: 1919 counterrevolution in 92; ELTE University 205; 1956 fights in 16; party activists of 49; Provisional Executive Committee 76, 128–9; 1944 siege of 15
Bulgaria 6, 11, 20, 32, 36

ceremony: commemoration 41–2, 55, 76, 139, 143, 164, 204; wreath laying 148; funeral 41, 45, 128, 130, 134, 137, 147, 161–2; inauguration of the Pantheon 158–9
cinema 14, 40, 71
Clemenceau, Georges 57
Cominform 30–31
Comintern 11, 38, 51
commune, Hungarian: history of 5; leaders of 51, 159; memory of 1–3, 29, 41; representation of 52, 56, 93, 94, 100, 123, 200, 208
Communist (Bolshevik) Party of Russia 3
Communist Youth Federation: *see* KISZ
concentration camp 6, 19
continuity: artistic representation of 148; of counterrevolution 22, 81–4, 86–7, 112, 128–9, 180, 207; of medieval rulership 134; of modern Hungarian history 143,150, 153, 159–60, 186, 201; of nations 8; of revolution 23, 93–4, 134, 147, 173, 204; of the Communist Party 136–7, 155–7; of the dead 127, 130–31, 133, 135, 163–4; of the White Terror 1, 108, 117–18, 121–3; theory of 39, 43, 62, 85, 161–2; of violence 77, 82, 99–100
corpse: *see* body
corpus myticum 135, 137, 162
counterhistory 18, 122–3
Csepel 131, 132, 171
Cserny, József 136, 178
Csillag, Ferenc 202
Csorna 83
Czechoslovakia 4, 10, 17, 57, 165

Day of Soviet Intervention 16, 61, 63, 64, 142–3, 148, 164
Derkovits, Gyula 182
dictatorship of the proletariat: collapse of 120, 150; heroes of 41; historiography of 15, 39, 75, 91–2, 140–42, 168, 201; in 1956 revolution 73; in fiction 171–80, 183, 188–9; memory of 28–30, 47, 50–51, 59, 155; representation of 23, 54, 93, 138, 169; theory of 32–3, 153, 156, 199
Dimitrov, Georgi 11, 38
Diósgyőr 46–7, 202
Dózsa, György 7, 71, 88, 94, 169, 182
Donskoy 35
Dudás, József 72

Efimov, A. V. 37
Egypt 18, 195
enlightenment 181, 182, 195
Eperjes, Prešov 172
Eucharist 158, 162
evidence: historical 10, 24–5, 32, 80, 103, 165, 191; legal 8, 21, 78, 102; manipulation of 83, 118, 120–23, 166, 176, 185, 188, 192–3; material 20, 114, 158; suppression of 18, 197–8; visual 66, 67, 73, 99, 100, 184
Exclamation of the First Hungarian Soviet Republic: 30th anniversary 27, 41–2; 40th anniversary 22, 139, 143, 153, 155; 50th anniversary 200, 206; celebration of 8, 24, 75–6, 84, 94, 203–4; events of 3, 5; historiography of 90–91, 176; in 1989 208; in fiction 171
exhibition: 30th anniversary 40–41, 56; 50th anniversary 200; of national history 20; of the fascist revolution 192; of the railway workers 186; OKISZ 150–52; on the counterrevolution 79–81, 87, 129; on revolutionary art 92; theory of 21, 22, 23

fascism: Communist theory of 11, 19, 46, 75, 84, 107–10, 155, 156, 174; historiography of 9, 101–2, 119, 121–3, 208; in 1956 revolution 88–9, 96, 145, 150; Italian 192; martyrs of 129, 158, 159, 161
Fazekas, Erzsébet 38
Fegyvernek 200
Fehér, Lajos 64

Felsőzsolca 203
festival: commemorative 21, 138; historical 9–10, 12, 20, 27, 34, 55; political 23–4, 183, 203
film 14–15, 21, 40, 60, 177, 181–6, 188–9, 193–4, 199, 200, 207; documentary 21–2, 143, 183, 184–5, 188, 193, 199; feature 181, 193–4, 199; propaganda 60, 181, 186
'Flames of Revolution' 203
Földes, László 'Hobó' 200
Földes, Péter 173
Franchet d'Esperay 57
Francia Kiss, Mihály 76–7, 81–4, 86–7, 107–8, 184
Frankel, Leó 159–60
Franz Ferdinand 4
funeral: *see* ceremony

Ganz (factory) 202
Gárdos, Miklós 169–70, 172–3, 179, 192–3
German Democratic Republic (GDR) 11, 19, 36
Germany: Enlightenment in 181; historical conflicts in 21; imperial 4; in WWII 6, 23; Jews in 3; postwar West 96, 112, 159, 180
Gerő, Ernő 17, 32, 42
Giles of Rome 85
Gimes, Miklós 130
Gneisenau, August Wilhelm Antonius Graf Neidhardt von 37
Gomułka, Władysław 16
Gottwald, Klement 36, 165
Gömbös, Gyula 6, 86, 101, 184, 186
graves: of victims of Nazism 20; of Hungarian Communists 41, 125–7, 129, 162–3; of Imre Nagy 130–31; of national heroes 143, 145; of saints 134, 138; Soviet 19
Great Patriotic War 134
Grünwald 37
Gyenes, Antal 64
Gyenes, Tamás 92
Gyetvai, János 173–4, 178
Győr 204

Habsburg, Joseph 7
Hajdú, Tibor 140, 155, 201
Halbwachs, Maurice 55
Havasi, Béla 202
Hegedűs, Géza 195

Héjjas, Iván 107–8, 119
heroes' plot 125, 143, 162–4
Hetés, Tibor 179, 189, 192
Hevesi, Gyula 75
historic event 154
historical novel 44, 169, 191, 195
historical revisionism 18–19
historical typology 27, 34–5
Historical Society 12
Hitler, Adolf 6, 9; in Communist ideology 73, 84, 101, 108, 110, 121, 122, 186; image in postwar Germany 112
Holocaust 10, 18, 101, 122, 128
horthyist 72, 77–8, 86–7, 110
Horthy, Miklós 5–6, 96, 106, 114, 172; regime: Communist martyrs of 29, 132, 158, 163; connection to 1956 revolution 81, 100, 128–9; historiography of 77–8, 83–6, 88, 101–2, 112, 119–23, 150; memory of 65, 105–10, 115–17; visual representation of 97, 183, 184
Hungarian Federation of Freedom Fighters 27
Hungarian Institute for Labour History 12
Hungarian Socialist Workers' Party: *see* MSZMP
Hungarian Workers' Party: *see* MDP

Idea of Szeged 108, 116
'Illuminati' 181
Illyés, Gyula 167
imperialism: and decolonization 204; Entente 33, 142; Habsburg 54; in 1919 38, 51, 52, 57, 58, 120, 169, 176; in 1956 revolution 17, 96–7, 150; in WWI 141, 149, 184, 196; postwar 45; wartime 121
Institute of Party History 79
Ivan the Terrible 34

Jacobeans, Jacobins 145, 147, 182
Jankovich, Ferenc 195
Jasenovac 19
Jews: ancient 18, 42–3, 89, 105; and WWII 112, 122; persecution of 6, 17, 76, 82, 101, 107–8; revolutionaries 2–3
Julier, Ferenc 173

Kádár, János: after WWII 7 31, 41, 45, 126, 146; in 1956 revolution 1, 16–17, 61–6, 142, 164; role in restoring Communist power 76, 94, 133, 167–8; role in

shaping historical culture 138–9; role in the Imre Nagy trial 95
Kállai, Éva 131
Kállay, Miklós 6, 108
Kantorowicz, Ernst 136–7, 161
Kardos, György 181
Karikás, Frigyes 177
Károlyi, Mihály 4, 6, 39, 90, 140, 143, 146–7, 169–70
Kerényi, Jenő 92
Kerepesi Cemetery: and the Pantheon of the Labour Movement 143, 145, 146, 150, 160; during Stalinism 45, 50; heroes' plot in 162; in the Kádár period 125, 127
Király, Béla 86
Kiss, Károly 155
KISZ 24, 84, 131, 138, 164, 200, 201–4
Komját, Aladár 160
kopjások (András Berkesi and György Kardos) 179–81
Košice, Kassa 7, 172, 201
Kossuth, Lajos 53, 54, 94, 132, 143, 146, 151
Korvin, Ottó 4, 136, 172–3, 178
Kovács, István 65, 202
Köböl, József 64
Kraków 137
Kucs, Béla 92–3
Kun, Béla: cult of 138, 140, 176, 204, 208; death of 14, 23, 161; ideological uses of 94–5, 171–3, 179, 188–9; in 1919 1–3, 123; perception of 51, 56; statue of 8
Kundera, Milan 165
Kunfi, Zsigmond 5, 95
Kutuzov, Mikhail Illarionovich 35

Landler, Jenő 5, 40, 45, 49, 159, 184
Latorczay, Lőrinc: *see* Szim, Lőrinc
legitimacy, legitimation 1, 8, 17–18, 61, 63, 110, 165–6, 168
Leipzig 11
Lengyel, József 178
Lenin, V. I.: connection with the Hungarian Soviet Republic 51, 57, 176; cult of 33, 42, 46, 49, 182, 204; impact of 3–4; Furnace Works in Diósgyőr 202; School of the Comintern 38
Leningrad 12, 19, 134
Levski, Vasil 36
Liberation Day 24, 42, 76, 203–204
Liberty Square 143

Liptai, Ervin 174–7, 179, 188–9, 192
Losonczi, Pál 201
Losonczy, Géza 130
Ludovika Academy 78, 86, 105, 174
Lukács, György 3, 50, 95, 191
Lukács, László 163
Luther, Martin 36
Luxemburg, Rosa 3

Magyar, Dezső 199
Makk, Károly 177
Maléter, Pál 130
Manetho 18
Mao Tse-tung 49
March of Fire 206–7
Margaret Island 7–8
Marin, Louis 147
Marosán, György 49, 50, 63, 126
martyrs: antifascist 13; medieval 85; national 14, 196; of the counterrevolution 82, 143, 163–4; of the First Hungarian Soviet Republic 29–30, 41, 61, 169, 207; revolutionary 23, 125–9, 131–8, 140, 145–6, 148, 158–60
Marxism: aesthetics of 92; education of 12; historiography of 36, 44–5, 75, 183, 194; philosophy of history of 191; revisionism of 95; theory of 30, 51–2, 59, 158, 200
Mathias Corvinus 194–5
mausoleum 125, 143, 145–8, 159
MDP: second Congress of 38, 44; collapse of 60, 70, 156–7; leadership of 42, 49; politics of history of 29–30, 45, 50, 126
memorial: of mass extermination 19–20; of the counterrevolution 163–4; of the First Hungarian Soviet Republic 153, 200; of the labour movement 131, 133, 138, 145–8, 158–9; political uses of 21, 22, 125–9; Soviet 72, 143; to Jenő Landler 41, 45; to the 1918 October Revolution 139; of war 72, 135
memory: in school 208; of 1919 7–8, 29–30, 131, 140, 167–8, 179; of 1848 13, 24, 53–4, 152; of 1956 revolution 23, 164; of the Holocaust 122; of the Northern Campaign 201; of the White Terror 65, 74–5; production of 46, 59, 103–4, 125, 150, 154, 203; suppression of 14, 18, 28, 56; uses of in the French revolution 55
Mező, Imre 65, 70–71, 127, 131, 159–60

INDEX

Mezőtárkány 72
Mikus, Sándor 92
Miskolc 7–8, 72–3, 82, 88, 103, 106–7, 114, 116, 201–3
Mód, Aladár 29, 35, 38
Mohács 194–5
Molnár, Erik 44
Monor 78–9
monument 8, 15, 125–6, 128, 133–5, 138, 143, 147, 148, 203; of the First Hungarian Soviet Republic 7, 200; on Republic Square 163–4
MSZMP 8, 62, 139, 156–8, 167–8, 200, 203, 207
museum 10, 19–20, 56, 80–81, 165, 202, 203
Mussolini, Benito 6, 101, 110, 192
Münich 3
Münnich, Ferenc 50, 94, 140, 149–50, 155
Münzer, Thomas 36–7
myth: antifascist 9, 11, 123; historical 53–4, 132, 181; nationalist 3, 10, 36–8; of 'democratic socialism' 31; of the counterrevolution 17

Nagy, Imre 7, 16, 41, 60–65, 74–5, 77, 93, 95–7, 130, 142, 150; execution of 95, 130; burial of 130
Nagykanizsa 8
Nagy, Zoltán 201
Napoleon, Louis 35, 37
National Museum 56
nationalism 8, 13–14, 36, 53, 54, 168
Nazism 9
Nemes, Dezső 38, 120–21
Németh, László 167
Nevsky 35, 60
New Left 205–6
New Testament 43
Nógrádi, Sándor 64
Northern Campaign 5, 8, 176, 201
Nuremberg Trials 107
Nyisztor, György 49–50

objectivity 41, 98, 99, 184, 192
OKISZ 151–2
Old Testament 18, 42–3
Optimists (Ervin Sinkó) 199
Orfeo 205
Orgovány 74, 82, 87, 101, 119, 150, 169
Ózd 79, 202

Pantheon of the Labour Movement: inauguration of 125, 158; martyrs' sepulchre 138; representation of history in 22, 127, 132–5, 143, 147–8, 159–62
Paris 67, 85, 159, 204
partisan 27, 36, 60, 76, 130, 132
Party of Communists in Hungary 4
Peidl, Gyula 5, 65, 74–5. 96, 150
people's democracy: foundation of 14, 42; in Imre Nagy's trial 95, 96, 142; post-1956 revolution, understanding of 66, 70, 74, 77, 79, 83, 123; Stalinist concept of 46, 58; theory of 30–34, 156, 158
People's Tribunal: in Miskolc 102–3, 106–7, 109–11, 114–18; post-1956 revolution 82, 123; postwar 76, 100
Peter the Great 34–5
Petőfi, Sándor 54, 65, 132–3, 151, 204
Peyer, Károly 5, 95
photos: as historical evidence 22, 41, 66–7, 73, 97–100, 184; as museum objects 20, 79, 81, 186, 192; in propaganda 48–9, 56, 69–70, 143, 153, 165
Pieck, Wilhelm 38
Piskaryovskoye Cemetery 19, 134
Pogonyi, László 202
Poland 3, 6, 10, 17, 20, 30, 37, 195–6
Polish Workers' Party 32, 37
Prague 137, 165, 200, 205, 206
prefiguration, *praefiguratio*: as a form of Stalinist historiography 35–7; as a narrative trope 166; Hungarian Soviet Republic as 14, 23, 27, 33, 50–51; in Christian theology 42–3; in interpretations of WWII 110; the revolution of 1848 as 53, 56
Prenn Ferenc (József Lengyel) 136, 178
proof: *see* evidence
propaganda: Allied 19; antiwar 173; Committee for Canvassing and Propaganda 79, 138, 140 200, 207; counterrevolutionary 91, 190; Department for Propaganda 52; Department of Canvassing and Propaganda 202; film 14, 60, 181; for the Soviet Republic 141; history 81, 166; historians 1, 18, 22, 23, 122–3, 185–6, 197; National Propaganda Department 126; Stalinist 36–8, 44, 51, 53, 165
Püspökladány 8

Rajk, László 7, 102
Rákóczi, Ferenc 35, 60, 94, 182, 193
Rákosi, Mátyás: after WWII 7, 31, 32; as historian 39, 42; as Stalinist leader 17, 50–52, 56, 60; cult of 33, 46, 47–9; exclusion from the party 167; memory of 63, 77, 156–7
Red Army: Chief of the General Staff of 131, 179; during WWII 6, 36, 42, 109; historiography of 176, 192; Hungarian 5, 51, 57, 91–2, 105–6, 116; Hungarians in 3; in 1956 revolution 16; in fiction 172–3; in film 177, 184,193; memory of the Hungarian 7–8, 40, 45–9, 151, 201–2; memory of the Soviet 143; propaganda representation of 33, 38,153; veterans of 76, 94,149, 189
Red Terror 3, 28, 33, 50, 54, 131, 159
Republic Square: ceremonies on 143, 153, 163–4; Communist experience of 17, 73, 82; government interpretation of 64, 70–71, 127, 131; news coverage of 62; role in historical culture 87–8, 97; siege of the Party headquarters 66–7, 135, 160
resurrection 28, 77, 84–6, 158, 177
Réti, László 27, 33, 39, 42, 58–9, 74–5
Révai, Gábor 200
Révai, József 28, 31–2, 38; revolution; bourgeois 39, 147; Communist 147, 160, 206; proletarian 58, 93, 102, 129, 146, 158, 179, 199; socialist 33, 74, 141, 158–9, 169, 170, 205; of the everyday 205
Revolutionary Youth Days 23–4, 204, 206–7
Ries, István 111, 161
ritual: funeral 128, 130, 161–2; Freemason 181; medieval 137, 162; non-European 117; of historical culture 9, 20, 41, 50, 55, 145, 158; of political representation 23, 27
Romania: Communist historiography in 10, 20, 37; conflict with Hungary 21; Imre Nagy in 74; in post-WWI Eastern Europe 4, 57, 92, 171, 189; Jews in 2
Rudas, László 50
Russia: Hungarian exile in 94, 138, 158, 159, 191; impact in Eastern Europe 36, 37, 39, 57, 89, 90, 140–41; in WWII 109, 115; leftist radicalism in 3–5; politics of history in 34, 154; socialist revolution in 33, 102, 176; Tsarist Empire 196

Sachsenhausen 19
Sarajevo 4
Scharnhorst, Gerhard von 37
sepulchre 30, 41, 50, 125–7, 129, 131–5, 138, 143, 145–8
Shoah: *see* Holocaust
Sinkó, Ervin 199
Siófok 74, 87, 150, 169
social democrats: Communist criticism of 29, 36, 39, 51–2, 57–8, 123; elimination of 31, 157–8; exile in Russia 3; historiography on 89, 91, 120, 141–2, 176–7, 189–90; in fiction 170–71, 173; in government 5, 65, 74, 155; in the postwar period 28, 111, 161; legacy of 18, 132; radical 4
socialist patriotism 36, 168, 203–4
Sólyom, László 161
Soviet Union: as model 33, 58, 157; Communist exiles in 7, 29, 94, 159, 161; Communist Party of 138; during WWII 6, 42, 156; imperialism of 1, 17, 30, 37, 38, 57, 75; memory of WWII 134; nature of dictatorship in 23, 53
Spanish Civil War 94, 132, 161
Stalin, I. V. 6, 30, 31, 32, 33, 35, 37, 46, 49, 56, 59
Stalinism: among party cadres 65–6, 126; and nationalism 53; critique of 59, 60; historiography of 2; in historical culture 10–12, 14, 34, 37, 38, 102; in ideology 56; purges 7, 23, 29, 50, 51; resistance to 16–17
St Denis 137
St Paul 85
Stromfeld, Aurél 5, 179
Studium Generale 205
Szabó, István jr. 92
Szakasits, Árpád 40, 49, 50
Szálasi, Ferenc 6, 83, 85, 108–9, 111, 113
Szamuely, Tibor 3, 33, 49, 50, 159, 160
Szántó, Béla 50
Székesfehérvár 131, 137
Szentes 200
Szentjóby, Tamás 200
Szerényi, Sándor 143, 159
Sziklai, Sándor 72, 127, 131
Szilágyi, Anna 200
Szilágyi, József 130
Szim, Lőrinc 103–7, 109, 113–17
Szim-sanatorium 88, 106, 114

Táncsics, Mihály 54, 132–3, 143
tangibility: in cemeteries 19, 128, 158, 161, 164; in festivals 9, 20, 50, 55, 201, 206; in film 184; in historical theory 25 84, 86, 208; in trials 81, 103, 106, 114, 118, 196; through spectacle 23–4
Tannenberg: see Grünwald
Teleki, Pál 6
Teutoburg 36–7
textbooks 12, 20, 37–9, 48, 53, 89–3, 119
Third Reich 6
Thomas Aquinas 85
Thorez, Maurice 49
Tiszafüred 200
Tito, Josip Broz 57–8
Togliatti, Palmiro 49
tomb: see graves
Tömpe, István 139
Tóth, Ilona 73
Transylvania 2, 21, 35, 195
trial: Budapest Maoist 205; Dimitrov 11; Eichmann 122; Héjjas107–8; People's Commissar 190; post-1956 66, 72–4 (Mihály Francia Kiss 77, 81–4, 184; Imre Nagy 95–7, 130); Rákosi 47; show trials 161, 180; war crime trials (in Europe 9, 19; in Hungary 22, 100, 102–5, 110–16, 118, 119, 123, 196)
Trianon: see Versailles peace treaty

USA 30, 57, 108, 136, 204
USSR: see Soviet Union

Vántus, Károly 159
Varga, Jenő 42

Versailles 147
peace treaty 6
Vienna 91, 172, 190
Vietnam 204

Wehrmacht 6
Westminster Abbey 137
White Books 66–7, 71, 74, 78–9, 83–6, 93, 96–8, 129
White Terror: connection with 1956 revolution 1, 17–18, 66, 73, 75, 85, 87–8, 96–7, 128, 142, 150, 180; continuity of 23, 32–4, 77, 83, 100; historiography of 2, 119–23; history of 6, 76, 106–7; martyrs of 29; memory of 42, 74; relationship to WWII 101, 108, 116–7; representation in fiction 172–4, 177–8
women 44, 104, 107, 138, 171
Workers' Guard 76, 153
World War I 2–5, 107, 134, 135, 138, 141, 160, 177
World War II: forgetting of 111; interpretation of 58, 108, 109, 121, 122, 196; martyrs of 29, 133, 134, 143; persecution of Communists in 82, 84; resistance in 115

Yegorichev, N. G. 134
Young, James E. 128, 147
youth 24, 57, 80, 84, 138, 202–7
Yugoslavia 4, 19, 57, 199

Zhdanov, Andrei 31
Žižka, Jan 36
Zöld, Sándor 161